The Euro and the Battle of Ideas

The Euro and the Battle of Ideas

Markus K. Brunnermeier,
Harold James,
and Jean-Pierre Landau

PRINCETON UNIVERSITY PRESS
PRINCETON AND OXFORD

Copyright © 2016 by Princeton University Press

Published by Princeton University Press, 41 William Street,
Princeton, New Jersey 08540

In the United Kingdom: Princeton University Press, 6 Oxford Street,
Woodstock, Oxfordshire OX20 1TR

press.princeton.edu

Jacket design by Faceout Studio, Emily Weigel

Jacket images © Shutterstock and Thinkstock

Library of Congress Cataloging-in-Publication Data

Names: Brunnermeier, Markus Konrad, author. | James, Harold,
1956- author. | Landau, Jean-Pierre, author.

Title: The euro and the battle of ideas / Markus K. Brunnermeier,
Harold James, and Jean-Pierre Landau.

Description: Princeton : Princeton University Press, [2016] | Includes
bibliographical references and index.

Identifiers: LCCN 2016010112 | ISBN 9780691172927 (hardcover :
alk. paper)

Subjects: LCSH: European Union countries—Economic policy. |
Eurozone. | Monetary policy—European Union countries. | Financial
crises—European Union countries.

Classification: LCC HC240 .B77 2016 | DDC 332/.042094—dc23 LC
record available at https://lccn.loc.gov/2016010112

British Library Cataloging-in-Publication Data is available

This book has been composed in Palatino LT Std

Printed on acid-free paper. ∞

Printed in the United States of America

1 3 5 7 9 10 8 6 4 2

Contents

PART II: MONETARY AND FISCAL STABILITY: THE GHOST OF MAASTRICHT

PART III: FINANCIAL STABILITY: MAASTRICHT'S STEPCHILD

PART IV: OTHERS' PERSPECTIVES

1

Introduction

October 18, 2010, was a day that changed European politics. German chancellor Angela Merkel had traveled to the Normandy seaside town of Deauville to discuss the European crisis with France's president Nicolas Sarkozy. Press photographs show them in dark raincoats, strolling on the wet and deserted autumnal boardwalk, Sarkozy gesticulating argumentatively and Merkel apparently responding with a look of blank incomprehension. In fact, after a moment in which it looked as if contrasting German and French visions of the world were bound for a head-on collision, they reached a dramatic compromise: Germany would loosen its approach to rules and make concessions to France, if France would in return agree to "an adequate participation of private creditors." Chancellor Merkel—who enjoyed substantial public support in her country—believed that banks had been responsible for the unwise extension of credit and should bear the cost of it. An end had to be put to the bailout mentality that had followed the global financial crisis of September 2008, including the failure of Lehman and the rescue of AIG. The basic elements in the Franco-German agreement had been achieved, and kept secret, two weeks before, during an informal conversation between the two leaders at the margin of a NATO summit in Brussels.

Other European leaders were stunned when they learned of the outcome on their mobile devices. The head of the European Central Bank (ECB) immediately thought that the agreement was a mistake, and US treasury secretary Tim Geithner was enraged by the proposal, warning European policy makers that "if you're going to restructure Greece, . . . you have [to have] the ability to in effect protect or guarantee the rest of Europe from the ensuing contagion."[1] Markets shared this sentiment. Immediately after Deauville, interest rates on periphery government bonds shot up. Germans welcomed the imposition of market discipline on the periphery in Europe, while French commentators viewed the spike in rates as unjustified from a fundamentals standpoint—a pure liquidity effect.

The Deauville episode first of all made clear that differences in the German and French visions of appropriate economic policy were at the heart of the difficulty in finding a response to Europe's financial crisis. The incident also highlighted how much power in Europe had shifted away from the European Union's institutions in Brussels, the Commission and the European Council, and toward two big nation-states—countries that found it hard to talk a common language.

The euro crisis has led to the outbreak of a war of ideas in the European continent and to a seismic shift of power within Europe. Starting with fiscal problems in one of Europe's smallest economies, Greece, in late 2009, a long-simmering battle over the appropriate economic philosophy and future design of the European Union broke into the open. It is a struggle between northern, but above all German, and what are sometimes called southern, but above all French, theories. The debate is not limited to French and Germans: Finns, Austrians, and sometimes Slovaks and Poles behave as if they are more Germanic than the Germans, and France is often seen as a champion of a Mediterranean Europe. The clash played a part in the debate that pushed Britain to vote for Brexit. But in practice, the clash is often treated as if it were a war of ideas fought out across the River Rhine. Italy is divided between a north that looks intellectually and economically like Germany and a south in which there is more sympathy for French-style theories. The French and German positions outlined here should be understood as *ideal types*, a concept developed by the sociologist Max Weber to better understand problems, debates, and institutions by thinking in terms of sharply differentiated features. Weber, and every good subsequent analyst, knew well that reality was messy but thought that conceptual clarification could bring a greater realization of the roots of social peculiarities.[2]

It is this war of ideas that lies at the heart of our book. Our main aim is to provide an explanation of the long-term historical, intellectual, and cultural roots of the contrasting German and French economic philosophies. One might think that each country exclusively fights for its own material interests. Such a narrow perspective overlooks an even more important aspect: interests are interpreted through the lens of ideas, or visions. Some countries have developed their own economic traditions and schools. Given their historical paths, different countries in Europe follow different economic philosophies and derive different policy descriptions for how to respond to crisis events. Previously, these differences were always taken for granted but glossed over and never thoroughly discussed. The European integration process—arguably one of the most successful peace initiatives in history—was characterized by a tendency to be Panglossian in the face of crisis. Indeed, differences between countries were often so ingrained in national policy makers' thinking that mutual incomprehension ensued. Policy makers even used the same word for different concepts. As an example, "economic governance" for Germany meant convergence around a common stability culture, while for France it meant common initiatives to direct economic development. Similarly, Germans interpreted the euro as an improved version of the old Exchange Rate Mechanism—built around the virtues of the Deutschmark—while the French saw the euro as a new global currency and conduit for more effective Keynesian stimulus policies.[3]

Of course, there are also straightforward differences in *interests* between European countries, including between France and Germany. But interests are often seen through the lens of ideologies. The difference between European countries is often reduced by some analysts to a simple contest between creditors and debtors based on net asset positions.[4] Since the 1960s, Germany has built up a substantial net creditor position via sustained current account surpluses. France has occasionally had surpluses, but interspersed with substantial deficits. So it might be thought that Germany (and creditors in general) would focus on strict debt repayment, even if it means squeezing the pips out of debtors, and that it would prefer low inflation to increase the real value of nominal debt. By contrast, France (and debtors in general) would be amenable to debt forgiveness, or higher inflation to erode the real value of debt. But this line of argument is open to objections. The net asset position, total claims of a country's citizens toward foreigners, is the sum of net flows. However, net flows mask much larger gross flows and an accumulation of a wide variety of personal and institutional positions: there may be powerful and substantial debtors in the net creditor countries.[5] Equally important, a wise creditor will normally hope that the debtor is prosperous and dynamic so as to be able to repay debt in the future. Squeezing the pips may reduce the chances of being fully repaid. A debtor will also be aware that nonrepayment or default will damage future chances of borrowing for productive purposes. So the judgment calls on both sides depend on ideas about the other side: is debt growth enhancing (good) or a sign of profligacy (bad)? These are ideological judgments: as Weber put it in a famous analogy, "Not ideas, but material and ideal interests, directly govern men's conduct. Yet very frequently the 'world images' that have been created by 'ideas' have, like switchmen, determined the tracks along which action has been pushed by the dynamics of interest."[6]

The process of European integration is full of the same kinds of misunderstandings and misinterpretations that often characterize relationships between men and women. According to a popular American psychologist who wanted to provide a "practical guide for improving communication and getting what you want in your relationships," men and women are from different planets.[7] The book was wildly successful, with seven million copies sold. His title was adapted to international politics by Robert Kagan, who argued that Americans were from Mars and Europeans from Venus. "It is time," he said, "to stop pretending that Europeans and Americans share a common view of the world, or even that they occupy the same world."[8] Europe has now discovered that it has its own version of mutual incomprehension.

The basic elements of the contrasting philosophies can be delineated quite simply. The northern vision is about rules, rigor, and consistency, while the southern emphasis is on the need for flexibility, adaptability, and innovation. It is Kant versus Machiavelli. Economists have long been familiar with this kind of debate and refer to it as *rules versus discretion*.

Some more specific policy preferences follow from the general orientation. The rule-based approach worries a great deal about the destruction of value and insolvency and about avoiding bailouts that will set a bad example and encourage inadequate behavior among other actors (economists call this the *moral hazard* problem). The discretionary approach sees many economic issues as temporary liquidity problems that can be easily solved with an injection of new lending. Here the provision of liquidity is costless: A bailout incurs no losses; in fact, the knock-on effects make everyone better off. There are, in this vision, multiple possible states of the world—multiple equilibria—and the benign action of governments and monetary authorities can shift the whole polity from a bad situation to a good one. To this, the long-faced adherents of the moral hazard view point out that costs will pile up in the future from the bad example that has just been set.

ECB president Mario Draghi's "whatever it takes" proclamation on July 26, 2012, in London—just before the opening of the Olympic Games—was, after Deauville, the second watershed moment in the euro crisis. Draghi's promise that the ECB was willing to do "whatever it takes" to save the euro later led to the creation of the Outright Monetary Transactions (OMT) program, under which the ECB would stand ready to buy the government debt of distressed countries (under some conditionality). Proponents of the liquidity view felt vindicated that the tide had turned and that interest rates in the peripheral countries significantly declined without any outright transactions taking place. The implicit support of Angela Merkel and German finance minister Wolfgang Schäuble was crucial to the effectiveness of Mario Draghi's promise. However, conservative Germans challenged the ECB's OMT program in the German constitutional courts and the European Court of Justice. For them, interest rates had subsided only because the ECB implicitly guaranteed peripheral government debt. In the end, the credibility of the measure hinged on the interpretation of whether it was consistent with the German vision.

The rules principle emphasizes the importance of solidity—of not living beyond one's means. In the novel *David Copperfield*, Charles Dickens has Mr. Micawber tell David, "Annual income twenty pounds, annual expenditure nineteen nineteen and six, result happiness. Annual income twenty pounds, annual expenditure twenty pounds ought and six, result misery. The blossom is blighted, the leaf is withered, the God of day goes down upon the dreary scene, and—and in short you are forever floored. As I am!" The southern or French approach, by contrast, emphasizes social solidarity. Paragraph 21 of the 1793 Declaration of the Rights of Man and the Citizen—the ultimate statement of the ideals of the French Revolution—states that "Public relief is a sacred debt. Society owes maintenance to unfortunate citizens." The southern view also tried to extend the principle of solidarity across national frontiers, a move that the northerners resisted. In general, the rule-based view is concerned with price stability; the discretionary approach embraces the idea of managing the economy.

Economic Traditions Are Not Written in Stone

Almost all contemporary commentators have recognized the chasm between the two competing ideas. Many treat it as a product of plain stupidity and ignorance on one side: Paul Krugman talked about a "Dark Age of macroeconomics" in which the good lessons of the Greeks and the Romans had been countermanded by the obscurantist barbarians (from the north!) who overrun Mediterranean civilization.[9] The second interpretation is that these preferences represent deep historical traditions, cultures, and memories—so deeply rooted that they cannot be erased by the persuasive powers of superficial rationality and logic. In particular, Germans were so seared by the experience of catastrophic hyperinflation in the early twentieth century that ninety years later they repeat a meaningless mantra.

But wait a moment: Krugman's Dark Age is about the revival in the twenty-first century of the principles of Jean-Baptiste Say, a nineteenth-century economist—from France! In fact, in the nineteenth century, most French (and for that matter Italian) economists were, like Say, classical liberals who mentally inhabited a rule-based world. On the other side of the Rhine, in Germany, economists and politicians did not care much about rules—seeing them rather as a hypocritical device used by English free traders to impose their preferences on a backward continent. In other words, for a long time—basically until the middle of the twentieth century—the French were advocates of laissez-faire, and the Germans were profligates who thought that fiscal spending was the key to prosperity and success. So it cannot be true that the economic cultures are deeply and irrevocably entrenched.

As will be explained later, the German and French view of rules reversed as a result of a historical crisis of unprecedented severity: the Nazi dictatorship, World War II, and the fall of France in 1940. Germans learned that they needed rules to restrict the possibility for arbitrary government action, while the French thought that their political system under the prewar Third Republic had too little fiscal, military, and intellectual flexibility in dealing with the Nazi threat. Later, the new members of the European Union from formerly communist central Europe would learn a similar lesson as the Germans after 1945: good government and the limitation of corruption and political abuse require strict rules.

This book sets out a rather different interpretation of the persistence of clashing economic cultures. First, there are indeed different national ways of thinking about economics, but they are changeable when dramatic new circumstances arise. Second, up to now—in the context of a new crisis—rethinking has not proceeded very far. On the contrary, countries are following, on the whole, an approach of "business as usual"—digging trenches around established intellectual and theoretical propositions. The rational business of negotiation strategies developed in the course of the European crisis intensified rather than resolved the clash of cultures. As the relentless logic of events went on, the French appeared ever more French and the Germans ever more German.

The Maastricht Negotiations: Ambiguities and Master Plans

The Maastricht Treaty—the document that provides the legal framework for the euro—lies at the root of the current problems. It assumed too simply that price stability was sufficient to ensure financial stability and that fiscal policy had no role to play in the provision of price stability. It allowed French and German thinkers and politicians to operate with incompatible visions of economic governance. In short, it was about what the treaty labeled "European Union," but the Europeans looked as if they did not really intend or understand the concept of "union."

For some, Europe had now become a new sort of political entity, a postmodern, twenty-first century state in which the traditional principle of national sovereignty no longer applied. The treaty looked like a detailed and helpful itinerary to "ever-closer union." But others believed that Maastricht was simply a treaty arrangement that could be broken if conditions changed. Customary international law includes a clause known as *rebus sic stantibus*, things being as they are, that allows treaties to be broken if fundamental conditions change. There was also another ambiguity about Maastricht: all members of the European Union, with the exception of the United Kingdom and Denmark, which negotiated opt-out clauses, were committed to joining the currency union when the accession criteria were met. The result was that there was a European Union that was separate in terms of membership from the narrower euro area. That separation gave rise to a debate about multi-speed Europe. In 1994, in the immediate aftermath of Maastricht, two German Christian Democratic politicians, Karl Lamers and Wolfgang Schäuble, issued an influential paper setting out the idea of a Europe of "varying geometry" that relied on a "hard core" provided by France and Germany.[10]

For many politicians, especially for former German chancellor Helmut Kohl, economic aspects did not play a major role in the origins of the euro area. Rather, the currency union was a high-minded European political project that went way beyond economic realities. It was needed to stop the recurrence of war between France and Germany. Proponents of the "peace project theory" ignore that one does not need a currency union to improve relations with neighbors. Even worse, a malfunctioning currency union may even lead to civil war, as the American economist Martin Feldstein had warned in the late 1990s.

The debate about interests produced a much more sinister view of the origins of the euro—a conspiracy theory about a vicious, deep-seated German master plan. Because Germany typically has a lower rate of wage inflation than France and much lower rates than the Mediterranean countries, a locked currency would guarantee increased export surpluses, at the price of misery elsewhere. In this manner, a German grasp for European economic primacy would succeed at the end of the twentieth century and in the new millennium where a similar German military plan had failed one century earlier. Some of the earliest exponents of the notion that the currency was a German instrument of dominance were British, notably the former UK chancellor of the exchequer Denis Healey, but now this same notion is circulating widely, above all in Southern and peripheral Europe. In the euro crisis, Southern Europe began to talk incessantly about German hegemony. Italian prime minister Matteo Renzi complained that "Europe has to serve all 28 countries, not just one."[11] This view seems implausible, as lending and subsequently plunging one's neighbors into national bankruptcy is not a good way of building any kind of stable prosperity.

A mirror image of the idea of a German master plan is provided by the equally often-expressed claim that the euro was the price that France exacted in 1990 for its agreement to German unification. President François Mitterrand, according to this version, wanted to put an end to a Europe that was controlled monetarily by the Bundesbank. He thought that a monetary union would go hand in hand with a *"gouvernance économique"* in which France could project and extend its statist orientation to encompass the whole of Europe. Monetary union, in short, would be the Trojan horse that would carry French thinking into the heart of all of Europe. So in the euro crisis, German commentators started to talk about a dictatorship of Southern Europe or to complain that the ECB had been taken over by Southern European government officials. But this view is also implausible, as in fact Germany continues to be at the center of European policy debates.

In the end, the story of monetary union is one about dealing with imbalances and fiscal and monetary adjustments in the least politically costly way possible. As such, the monetary union reflected—and failed to resolve—many of the differences in economic philosophy between the French and the German sides. These differences came to the fore in the recent crisis.

Structure of the Book

We therefore examine in part II, "The Ghost of Maastricht," the major battlegrounds and ideological difference in economic thinking that had resurfaced again. They had already played a major part during the Maastricht negotiations in the late 1980s and early 1990s, and the global financial crisis rekindled the intra-European debate. The different visions of the economy, the clash of a preference for rules with a preference for discretion, affected the way the interests of the different countries were presented in policy debates. The creditor and debtor countries played a strategic game: both reckoned that the other side could not have an interest in letting the system collapse, and so a game of not yielding and moving closer to the brink looked plausible and attractive. In this way, the interaction of ideas and strategic reflection on interests brought Europe to the edge of the abyss. When it appeared that Germany's constitutional court—which delivered ponderous rulings on whether rescue packages were in conformity with German laws and constitutional principles—was giving the German government a reason for taking a more intransigent line, constitutional courts in Portugal and Greece started their own brand of activism by handing down rulings that austerity measures were unconstitutional.

Part III, "Maastricht's Stepchild," explores the problem of dealing with financial instability—an important omission in the Maastricht Treaty. It outlines the shift in the financial architecture and how the banking union tries to reduce financial instability in the monetary union. Prime examples of the dangerous dynamics of financial stability in the context of monetary union are Spain and Ireland—two fundamentally fiscally sound countries thrown into crisis by their own banking systems.

The third watershed moment in the euro crisis, after Deauville and Draghi's London speech, was the European debate over Cyprus in the spring of 2013. The German discussion was dominated by the perception that a great deal of the liabilities of the Cyprus banking system consisted of the assets of Russian oligarchs, which constituted a possible criminal or even security threat, and hence required no special protection by European governments. For Berlin, there was little that constituted systemic risk in the Cyprus situation, and German officials complained that "if Cyprus is systemic, then everything is systemic." By contrast, many policy makers in France, but also in Italy and Spain, feared that penalization of Cypriot depositors might lead to a bank run in other countries (including their own).

The Cyprus crisis changed Europeans' attitude toward bailouts. The new chair of the Eurogroup, the Netherlands finance minister Jeroen Dijss-elbloem, spoke of the Cyprus approach as offering a "template." Even outside Europe, it looked like an attractive solution to the problems created in the wake of the financial crisis. For instance, the influential governor of the Bank of Canada Mark Carney deduced that his country should move away from bailouts, and in May 2013, Canada launched a "bail-in regime." In Europe, the bail-in principle was integral to the proposals for banking union. Critics argue that this undermines the transaction role of money, as demand deposits should remain informationally insensitive (one shouldn't need to worry about their value), and argue instead for stricter and higher equity cushion for banks. As the proposals on a banking union were elaborated, an ever-decreasing number and type of assets were liable to the bail-in procedure. The bail-in principle suffered another hit in late 2015 and early 2016. Italian banks had sold risky subordinate bonds to Italian retail investors with little financial knowledge. As some banks ran into trouble, these investors lost large parts of their retirement savings, leading to social hardship; tragically, one pensioner even committed suicide.

While parts I to III focus on the German-French differences, part IV collects various other perspectives on the crisis. Chapter 12 examines Italy, one of the six founding members of the European Economic Community. Italy largely stood on the sidelines of the Franco-German debate and long stood as an example of the problems of inadequate economic integration in a common political area. Its historic North-South conflict was a microcosm of tensions within the currency union—and perhaps an indication that fiscal transfers alone are incapable of resolving these problems. In terms of economic philosophy, Italian economists were split between the major schools of thought outlined above as "German" and "French." Postwar Italy was initially made by such economic liberals as Luigi Einaudi, an economics professor who became the first postwar president of the Banca d'Italia and then (in 1948) president of the Italian Republic. Einaudi's emphasis on the importance of rules had a clear similarity to the thought of the German Ordoliberals. Keynesianism was at first represented by two famous Italian economists who had fled from Mussolini's Italy: Piero Sraffa at Cambridge University in the United Kingdom, who tried to combine Keynesianism and Marxism, and Franco Modigliani at the Massachusetts Institute of Technology (MIT) in the United States, one of the architects of the neoclassical synthesis.

Chapter 13 starts with an outline of Anglo-American economic thinking. Overall, Anglo-American and French philosophies have many parallels, in particular deep roots in Keynesian thinking and an emphasis on liquidity over solvency considerations. Notably, whenever US or UK politicians lectured EU officials about optimal economic policy, they almost always sided with the French liquidity interpretation—favoring big bazooka and bailout solutions. Both the French and the Anglo-American interpretations of the euro crisis stress the importance of fiscal union as a necessary stepping stone for the smooth functioning of a common currency union, although the British and the Americans primarily regarded fiscal union from an outsider's perspective. However, the Anglo-American and French philosophies also differ in important ways. First, Anglo-Americans are more skeptical about the general desirability of government intervention than the French. Both agree that the government can and should intervene in a deep crisis, but the French are more sympathetic toward a government that coordinates economic activity all the time, which includes the involvement of the government in the financial sector. Second, debt in the Anglo-American approach is a contingent construct. That means there is some flexibility in repayment that depends on particular circumstances. In times of hardship, debt is not repaid and bankruptcy laws enable a new start. The Continental European interpretation of debt and the need for repayment is, in contrast, more stringent. Third, French policy makers push for an actively managed international monetary system and see the euro as an alternative to the long-lived hegemony of the dollar. For Germany, the UK stance in favor of more trade-friendly solutions played an important role to lean against the more interventionistic French approach. The British referendum on June 23 to exit the European Union, the Brexit, can be seen as the fourth watershed moment of the crisis. It has the potential to untie the United Kingdom with Scotland (and even Northern Ireland) separating. At the same time, it also strengthens the centrifugal force within Europe. Immediately after the Brexit vote anti-European parties in the Netherlands and France called for Nexit, Frexit, and other exit referenda. Europe, and especially Germany, faces a dilemma. One has to be firm toward the UK and uphold European rules in order to avoid other countries asking for special deals—a moral hazard that could threaten to unravel the European Union. On the other hand, Germany has to avoid fueling anti-German sentiment in the current atmosphere of euro skepticism. Chapter 13 also covers the global dimension of the crisis, paying particular attention to the Chinese and Russian attitudes toward the troubles of the euro area.

The economic philosophy of the International Monetary Fund (IMF) is discussed in chapter 14. The IMF is open to debt restructuring to make debt burdens sustainable. The IMF also brought much-needed expertise and external discipline to the table. IMF conditionality and focus on structural reforms aligns with Germany's view. On the other hand, in terms of fiscal stimulus, the IMF took the French view of relaxing fiscal rules and expanding government spending. The IMF was part of the brief and apparently successful interlude of stimulus cooperation in fall 2008 and spring 2009 in the intermediate aftermath of the US subprime crisis. Complacency about government capacity to cooperate led to a resurgence of zero-sum thinking—a style of politics that had last been seen during the Great Depression.

In chapter 15, we turn to the analysis of the European Central Bank (ECB)—the only European institution whose power dramatically increased during the crisis, but an institution (like central banks all over the world) that also fundamentally changed through the adoption of nonconventional monetary policies and a new mandate on bank supervision. A game of chicken in the euro crisis occurred between the ECB and the national governments. The ECB was aware that if it were too generous, national governments would falter and stall in their reform efforts. And the national governments also knew that if they did nothing and there were a crisis, the ECB would ultimately have the responsibility of finding some way out: it would be forced to be generous. In terms of debt restructuring, the ECB's economic stance is to resist it. Their main argument is that it would undermine the role and function of money. As a consequence, the ECB also has a tendency to treat problems as temporary liquidity rather than solvency issues.

Our book highlights these differences by looking at the crisis through various lenses: the Teutonic lens and the Latin lens. The aim is to analyze differences in the hope of finding common ground, or at least a better understanding of each other's positions, and thereby possibly speeding up the crisis response.

In the following pages, the three of us discuss how this common language can be achieved. We share different national origins—German, British, French—as well as different intellectual pedigrees: economics, economic history, and public service. The following sections deal with the fundamental economic dilemmas that exist everywhere, have been magnified in the wake of the financial crisis, and are still greater in the complex situation created by a currency union; the long-standing differences in intellectual and political traditions concerning economic life; and the way that the policy discussions are reflected (and their outcomes shaped) by both constraints. When we started this collaborative enterprise, we were convinced that if we could overcome all our differences, such a reconciliation might occur on a European level. We did not want to despair, and we do not think that Europe should either.

PART I

POWER SHIFTS AND GERMAN-FRENCH DIFFERENCES

2

Power Shifts

The reason why the tensions between the contrasting economic philosophies came to the forefront during the euro crisis lies in a seismic
power shift that occurred in two stages. The first occurred in the spring of
2010, with decision-making capacity shifting from European institutions
in Brussels to the capitals of member states. Subsequently, most important
decisions were taken at an intergovernmental level. The European Council of heads of states and the Ecofin meetings of all finance ministers
became the predominant players, and the European Commission was relegated to a backseat.[1] The second power shift occurred from the national
capitals, first to Berlin and Paris and ultimately just to Berlin. That was
when differences in economic philosophy and traditions of political economy between France and Germany emerged with great clarity and when
it was obvious how profoundly contrasting the worldviews (weltanschauungen) were. In fact, small countries—such as Greece—at the height of the
crisis felt as if they had been relegated to the role of pawns in the greater
chess game between Germany and France.[2] The only European institution
that gained significantly in stature and influence during the euro crisis
was the European Central Bank, which will be examined in chapter 15,
and which served—among other tasks—as a think tank in which the
Franco-German differences could be assessed analytically rather than
fought over politically.

This chapter explains the circumstances in which the Paris-Berlin axis
came to the fore and in which the different approaches became sharply
articulated. More specifically, the questions we address in this chapter are

- Why and how did the German-French relationship become central
  to the management of the European crisis?

- What are the decisive moments and decisions that triggered a sequence of events resulting in a reallocation of power?
- What are the underlying reasons for these shifts in power?
- What role did market discipline and in particular the ongoing threat of rising interest rates play?

Lethargy of European Institutions

To start, we have to answer the question of why European institutions were so weak and ineffectual, or more generally why Europe collectively—in its supranational institutions, the Commission, the Council, and the Parliament—essentially left the business of finding solutions to just two large member states. Within the EU, the main driver for progress on integration has traditionally been the European Commission, the "Guardian of the Treaties." By extension, it often also saw itself as the "Guardian of the Union," and even the institutional embodiment of the European dream. The European treaties gave it a near monopoly on regulatory propositions and initiatives. Traditionally, the Commission and its president also felt responsible for defending and promoting the "European spirit," brokering compromises between member states and even speaking for the small (underrepresented) countries in international forums.

Traditionally, the Commission prided itself on its skillful use of setbacks and crises to push for further integration. Jean Monnet, the intellectual father of the European Union, was quite explicit about the need to take advantage of a crisis: as he put it, "Europe will be forged in crises, and will be the sum of the solutions adopted for those crises."[3] This attitude became received wisdom for the inhabitants of the world of European institutions in Brussels. It produced a certain complacency, a mental bubble, with Brussels insiders firmly believing that bad news is always good news because it demands more Europe as an answer. The Brussels view of crisis is that it provokes an institutional tweaking, an enhanced efficiency, but no fundamental change: Brussels fosters a story of incremental integration. That has worked effectively in the case of relatively small crises—say over farm subsidies, herring fishing, or mutual recognition of products—but becomes problematic in the face of existential crises.

In the current crisis, the Commission's attitude has been strikingly modest and its engagement persistently ineffective. It never took any meaningful policy initiative outside its immediate institutional fields of competence—economic governance and financial regulation. There was no big speech by Commission president José Manuel Barroso, and he was worried that the Commission might be discredited if it overstretched itself politically. The initiatives taken by the Commission were largely requested by member states (in the case of new fiscal discipline and economic governance). Initiatives that did come from Brussels—on topics such as financial transaction taxes and Eurobonds—simply fizzled out. The fact that the Commission had to share its essential competence in establishing and monitoring programs for Greece, Portugal, and Ireland with the International Monetary Fund (IMF) and the European Central Bank (ECB) in the troika (which after the Greek 2015 elections were renamed "institutions") was an obvious sign of no confidence from the member states. It is not a matter of personalities: insiders rated Barroso as the most effective Commission president since Jacques Delors.

This weakness of the Commission comes from the fact that it is fundamentally hampered by institutional constraints. One obvious such constraint was the size of the Commission. Despite the EU enlargement in 2004 and 2007 that brought it to twenty-five and then twenty-seven members, the principle of having national commissioners was retained. Each of these (now twenty-eight) figures had to have a particular policy responsibility, and the large number meant that policies were divided in often overlapping ways: thus there exists a separate directorate-general for the internal market and another one for competition. The large size of the expanded Commission means it often resembles a parliament rather than a policy-making and implementing institution: only the new Commission under Jean-Claude Juncker in 2014 brought an administrative simplification.

The particular instruments and powers available to the Commission are essentially regulatory and are not well adapted to the necessity of crisis management. Managing the aftermath of major financial crises, as opposed to trying to prevent them from developing, always involves the mobilization of substantial fiscal resources. That task inevitably remained in the hands of national governments, as the European Union had only a very small fiscal capacity of its own. Furthermore, the budget belongs to the European Union as a whole and not specific to the euro area, so budgetary measures would have faced a pushback from non-euro-area countries. In that sense, much of the popular criticism of the Commission for misman-aging the crisis is misplaced: large financial crises inevitably trigger demands for a fiscal response, which the European Union was unable to provide.

The Commission had missed three major opportunities where it might have both shaped the course of the European crisis and minimized the cost of the response. First, it was thinking about financial supervision issues in the early stages of the world financial crisis, but it failed to trans-late very general ideas about a financial framework into a concrete action program. Second, it might have considered the possibility of using the EU budget to serve as a pillar for the crisis management mechanism. Third, it might have supported Wolfgang Schäuble's short-lived initiative for a European Monetary Fund, which was briefly discussed in the Ecofin meeting on March 16, 2010. Unlike the ECB, a European Monetary Fund could have lent to sovereigns and imposed conditionality on them, that is, made structural reforms a precondition for new loans.

In addition to the European Commission, the 2009 Lisbon Treaty estab-lished the position of European Council president, with Herman Van Rompuy as the first incumbent, succeeded in 2014 by Donald Tusk, who had previously been Polish prime minister. The presidency was more vis-ible and took on important prospective tasks (the Van Rompuy reports and a variety of task forces), but it hardly managed policy initiatives. The national governments clearly did not want the EU institutions in Brussels to adopt an important role.

The First Power Shift: From Brussels to National Capitals

The initial tussle between Germany and France concerned the question of whether Europe could solve the crisis on its own or whether it needed an external enforcer such as the IMF. It was German insistence that brought in the IMF.

IMF Involvement

Since the outbreak of the global financial crisis in 2008, the first major signs of troubles in the euro area occurred in Ireland. Irish banks were badly hit by a combination of liquidity and solvency issues, and it took a blanket gov-ernment guarantee of banks' liabilities, taxpayer-funded recapitalization of major Irish banks, and later bailout programs from the ECB and IMF to stabilize the banking system.

By January 2010, it became apparent that Greece might also need external help. Were Greece to request assistance, euro-area members knew they would be confronted with a major difficulty: there was no financial instrument available. The "no bailout" clause of the Maastricht Treaty prevented euro members from directly supporting each other. The treaty also prohibited any financial help from the EU budget to a euro country. Later, in June, a way was found around this legal restriction, but at the beginning of the Greek discussions, this legal constraint was considered absolutely binding.

Euro-area governments and their leaders were thus faced with an unpleasant choice that required some sort of innovation: either they reneged on the no-bail clause; or they created new instruments; or they called for external support, which could only in practice come from the IMF. Already in 2009, the IMF had played a major role with respect to Hungary and Latvia—two EU members that were not in the euro area. The IMF program had stemmed a dangerous source of contagion that might then have affected the euro area as well as large EU cross-border banks, which owned much of the Hungarian and Latvian banking systems and also held large portfolios of government securities. In the first "Vienna initiative," all the relevant public and private sector stakeholders of active EU-based cross-border banks in emerging Europe were brought together. In 2010, the European governments ended up taking all three options. They seemingly invalidated the no-bailout provisions, created new lending vehicles, and called on the IMF to support euro-area governments.

The advantages of IMF procedures in comparison to a regional support mechanism were twofold: First, an IMF program clearly follows established procedures. It is thus less likely to produce moral hazard and the assumption that a country can, just by letting matters slip and getting into a bad situation, trigger a costly international rescue operation. Second, the attractions of an IMF deal lie in the fact that they take some of the political sting out of support operations. In the mid-1990s, for instance, a purely bilateral support operation of the United States for Mexico would have revived memories of a century-old history of US interventions. In the mid-1970s, when Italy needed international support, it could have concocted a deal with Germany, but the Germans preferred to see the IMF negotiating with Rome. Multilateralizing the deal through the IMF in both cases was a way of extracting political poison from a situation that was complicated by historical sensitivities and injustices.

On the other hand, there were many European objections. It started with the politics: French president Sarkozy was reluctant to let his political rival Dominique Strauss-Kahn, then head of the IMF and his potential opponent in the 2012 French presidential elections, gain significant influence on the European stage. But Europe's reservations went much deeper. It was a matter of European identity and European prestige. The disadvantages of the IMF approach lay in the fear that Europe might give the impression that Europeans are not capable of dealing with their own problems; that the IMF action might come too late and thus cost more than if financial crisis and contagion had been prevented at an earlier stage; and that the involvement of the IMF might give a negative signal to markets and lead to credit-rating downgrades. These were exactly the arguments that led the Japanese government to propose an Asian Monetary Fund in 1997. At the time, the plan was blocked by the US Treasury, but it might indeed have played a role in stopping contagious panic in Asia in the late 1990s.

The vision that euro-area problems should be dealt with by euro-area countries was most strongly promoted by the ECB, and it appeared to be shared, at that time, by almost all euro countries and governments.

Soon after the Ecofin meeting on March 16, 2010, the German government officially took the position that an intervention by the IMF was desirable. The decision seems to have been directly inspired by the chancellor's inner circle. Her counselors, including Jens Weidmann—a former student of Bundesbank president Axel Weber who succeeded him in 2011—did not entirely trust the EU institutions. In particular, they did not believe that they were capable of imposing sufficient adjustment on fiscally permissive countries. A telling historical example had occurred during the negotiation of the 1986 Single European Act, which laid the foundation for the subsequent process of monetary union. At that time, Greece was facing substantial fiscal and payments problems and feared being forced into a difficult negotiation with the IMF. Because the Single European Act required the unanimity of all European Community members, Greece could leverage its vote into a more or less condition-free emergency credit from the European Community. In 2010, the German government might also have thought that financial burden sharing should be extended beyond the euro area and that the IMF was well equipped and specialized in managing crisis situations. But Germany was also prepared to think of more radical measures that might be adopted, including an expulsion of Greece from the euro area.[4]

On March 27, 2010, the leaders of the sixteen euro-area countries agreed in principle on a package of instruments combining bilateral governmental loans to Greece with support from the IMF. The measures were presented as a safety net that would only be used as a last resort. For the first time in many decades, the prospect of an IMF program for a European country was becoming real. No member of the euro area has had to borrow from the IMF since the common currency officially began in 1999, and no major industrialized country in Europe has done so since Great Britain and Italy in 1976–77. This development triggered some consternation—including in Frankfurt. But Jean-Claude Trichet, then president of the ECB, realized that he needed to adjust to the new circumstances and denied having criticized the IMF, now saying only that he wanted to remind governments of their responsibilities. He qualified the result as a "workable solution," that reflected the hopes and the spirit of the time, affirming himself "confident that the mechanism decided today will normally not need to be activated and that Greece will progressively regain the confidence of the market."[5]

The German imprint on the future solution was becoming clear. First, Berlin had insisted early on bringing in the IMF. Second, German representatives, especially from the Finance Ministry, made it clear they did not want the Commission to be in charge of the rescue program. France did not object to either of those proposals, as it had its own reservations about the Commission. At this stage, crisis management turned away from Europe's supranational institutional structure and toward an intergovernmental mode, with significant consequences for the future.

Just before the European Council met on March 25–26, 2010, Germany and France worked together on a statement that proposed a European "willingness to take determined and coordinated action" to safeguard financial stability, which would involve IMF financing. Council president Van Rompuy was excluded from the talks, and the other European leaders (notably Spanish prime minister José Luis Zapatero) complained bitterly about the bilateral fix.[6] Germany at this time was under considerable pressure from domestic politics, with a fear of adverse reaction against the government parties in local elections. Finally, on April 15, Greece formally requested a bailout from Europe and the IMF, and Schäuble emphasized that a possible assistance loan should be voluntary, as Article 125 of the Maastricht Treaty prohibited states from assuming responsibility for the debts of other states.

By the end of April 2010, the main issue was to build a funding structure for the Greek program. But it was also clear that the Greek problem had morphed into something broader and that a more systemic European response was required. It was also apparent that whatever would be done would necessarily represent a fundamental innovation and that there were no traditional mechanisms in the European Union that could serve as a basis for a policy response. There could be no concrete proposal on the table at the outset. The governments were left to improvise and create a new financial structure and mechanism.

On May 2, the Eurogroup agreed on a package for Greece of €110 billion (with €30 billion coming from the IMF). They went on to decide on the principle of a general European stabilization mechanism for an amount of €500 billion with strict conditionality in the framework of a joint program with the IMF. The IMF itself under this plan would commit around €250 billion, which would allow the political leaders to announce a combined €750 billion or $1 trillion package. This was the first of such announcements, and it carried, at that time, credibility. This plan was never implemented, and history looked very different as a result.

Schäuble, initially skeptical of IMF involvement and instead a proponent of the creation of a European Monetary Fund, soon started to see the virtues of IMF involvement in the European crisis. In the end, this external involvement—and in particular the move away from centralized European power—contributed significantly toward the power shift from supranational institutions to capitals.

Intergovernmental Funding Vehicles: EFSF and ESM

The second decisive moment that marked the transition from a supranational European to intergovernmental decision mechanism occurred when European governments created a new funding vehicle—which became the temporary European Financial Stability Facility (EFSF) and later the permanent European Stability Mechanism (ESM). Both institutions are headed by Klaus Regling.

In early May 2010, it became apparent that financial support might be needed despite the fact that the treaty did not allow, and in fact prohibited, any balance of payments support from the EU budget to a euro-area member. There was a sense of urgency, and the drama of the new stage unfolded over several days. The nervousness was compounded by the "flash crash" on May 6, when high-frequency traders produced extraordinary volatility on US stock markets, with the Dow Jones index falling 300 points that day. That external event highlighted the possibility that a Greek crisis could produce a new Lehman-like meltdown. A leaders' summit of euro-area countries took place on May 7, immediately followed by an exceptional Ecofin meeting on May 9–10. On May 7, Sarkozy had proposed that the leaders should simply instruct the ECB to buy sovereign bonds, declaring that "this is the moment of truth."[7] An additional element of drama in the Ecofin meeting came from a health scare for German finance minister Wolfgang Schäuble, who had been partly paralyzed after an assassination attempt twenty years before. He had to leave the meeting and was admitted to a Brussels hospital. At the last moment, German interior minister Thomas de Maizière substituted for Schäuble, delaying the start of the meeting by several hours. At the same time, the ECB announced its Securities Market Programme, with the move immediately opposed by Bundesbank president Axel Weber (see chapter 15).

The intergovernmental design of intervention became institutionalized as the so-called troika of the Commission, IMF, and ECB. "Troika" sounded rather sinister: it is significant that in formulating descriptions of new crisis initiatives, Europe developed a proclivity to use terms that recalled Soviet-style central planning. By 2015, renaming the troika became a rhetorical part of the new Greek package; it is now simply called "the institutions."

Four important choices were made at the time of the Ecofin meeting. First, the structure created for channeling support to member states in difficulty would be private rather than public—at this stage it was called a special purpose vehicle (SPV). Second, mutualization would take place through a system of guarantees of the SPV where commitments by each country would be limited to its share in the ECB capital. Third, the European mechanism would only intervene in the framework of an IMF program with conditionality. Finally, after an intense struggle, the Commission secured the responsibility for managing conditionality on the European side (with advice and cooperation from the ECB). At that time, the legal constraints to not bailout any euro-area members were considered absolutely binding.

Later, in June, a way was found around this legal restriction. The EFSF was assigned a mandate to "safeguard financial stability in Europe by providing financial assistance" through loans to euro-area countries in financial difficulty, which they then might use for the recapitalization of banks. It was built as a private company incorporated in Luxembourg and could raise up to €440 billion on the basis of joint and mutual government guarantees, by the members of the Eurozone, allocated on the basis of shares in the ECB capital. To ensure that the EFSF had a Aaa rating, Germany and other countries with a Aaa rating subscribed more than their capital share according to the ECB capital key, and when subscribing countries were later downgraded by the rating agencies, the remaining Aaa countries needed to back more of the EFSF capital (this development helped to stoke European resentment about the rating agencies). The EFSF would borrow on the capital markets and lend the proceeds to countries that agreed on a reform program. It could also intervene in the primary and secondary bond markets, act on the basis of a precautionary program, and finance recapitalizations of financial institutions in nonprogram countries through loans to governments. The non-euro EU members were not obliged to contribute, but they provided bilateral loans for one program (with Ireland).

In addition to the intergovernmental EFSF, there was a second, much smaller, facility run by the Commission. The latter, the European Financial Stabilization Mechanism (EFSM), issued bonds worth €60 billion collateralized by the revenue of the European Commission. The volume difference between EFSF and EFSM reflects very well the power shift toward an intergovernmental arrangement. Furthermore, there was IMF support and the engagement of the ECB through an innovative program to provide liquidity to stop crisis contagion.[8]

Soon, however, the constraints brought by the design of the facility became apparent. Almost immediately, the question of the size of the EFSF, which had initially been set at €440 billion, became a major concern. As early as December 2010, the ECB was discretely pleading with governments for a doubling of the EFSF, and was trying to design a permanent successor that later materialized in June 2011. The ECB wished to make the EFSF available as a precautionary line with less stringent conditionality. The Commission supported that proposal together with a more moderate expansion of EFSF. Governments were initially not receptive. There were, in particular, some concerns that an increase in size would indirectly lead to a downgrade for some of the main guarantors.

On June 24, 2011, the European Council decided to establish a permanent crisis-resolution mechanism—the European Stability Mechanism (ESM). The function of the ESM was to perform the same activities as the amended EFSF: issue bonds or other debt instruments on the market to raise the funds needed to provide loans to countries in financial difficulties, intervene in the primary and secondary debt markets, act on the basis of a precautionary program, and finance recapitalizations of financial institutions through loans to governments, including those in nonprogram countries. While the EFSF had legally been a private agreement of the participating states, the ESM was a new international institution established through an amendment of Article 136 of the Treaty on the Functioning of the European Union.

European institutions were being created, but the impetus was coming from the large countries. Chancellor Merkel's speeches in the initial crisis debates are quite characteristic. In celebrating the Charlemagne Prize awarded to Donald Tusk on May 13, 2010, she warned, "If the euro collapses, then Europe and the idea of European union will fail."[9] A few days later, on May 19, 2010, she told the German Bundestag: "The rules must not be oriented toward the weak, but toward the strong. That is a hard message. But it is an economic necessity. That must have consequences for the European Union."[10] Such statements may have been overinterpreted as a move toward the imposition of a German Europe, especially by Merkel's critics inside as well as outside Germany. The critical German sociologist Ulrich Beck portrayed the diplomacy as a Machiavellian power grab: "The Chancellor saw the crisis as her *occasione*, 'the propitious moment.' A combination of *fortuna* and Merkiavellian *virtù* enabled her to seize the historic opportunity and to profit from it both domestically and in foreign relations."[11]

The Second Power Shift: To Berlin-Paris and Ultimately to Berlin

The intergovernmental negotiations become increasingly a clash of weltanschauungen between France and Germany. While the French initiatives focused on crisis management and enhancing liquidity provisions using

27

German fiscal solidity as a backstop to assert European confidence and stability, Germany took a long-run perspective and initially focused on updating and repairing the fiscal rule book provided by the Stability and Growth Pact. Only after these efforts failed did Germany come to rely on market discipline, reviving the no-bailout rule, and push for a debt restructuring of Greek debt.

In previous crises, Europe could count on the Franco-German couple to act as the engine of Europe. For some time, in 2010, things still looked like business as usual. Meetings between German and French leaders were taking place with high frequency. Joint positions were defined and defended in European and global summits. The Franco-German engine was running full speed, pushing Europe ahead and shaping the evolution of the Continent. Between Merkel and Sarkozy, the dialogue—sometimes direct and sometimes through backchannels—was constant and confidential. Divergences, no matter how deep they might be, were seldom aired in public, at least in official communication. It became customary, indeed almost an institutionalized feature of the European policy machine, to hold bilateral meetings to prepare and present common positions before any European summit. In effect, the basic framework was decided during those meetings.

A First Attempt: Repairing the Stability and Growth Pact (SGP)

With a lack of adherence to old rules lying at the heart of the euro-area crisis—just take the persistent misstatements about and rapid deterioration of the Greek fiscal position, directly against the requirements of the SGP—European leaders tried to develop a new, more robust rules-based framework. An important pillar of the early policy initiatives was the "six-pack"—a mechanism to identify the causes of persistent economic divergences within the European Union and correct macroeconomic imbalances (see chapter 8 for more details). The nature of the debates surrounding this and other related policy proposals illustrated again the powerlessness of the Commission. Translating ideas into concrete policy and national laws requires a push from powerful member states, in particular Germany and France.

Subsequent modifications of the functioning of European institutions showed the same pattern. To further enshrine budgetary discipline into the constitutional framework, Germany was willing to transfer some fiscal sovereignty to the European level at Brussels, but France was very reluctant to make such a step. As the French finance minister Christine Lagarde put it, "France has always been favourable to a solid and credible economic governance but not for a totally automatic mechanism, a power that would be exclusively in the hands of experts."[12] Germany had already agreed to its own law on a debt brake (*Schuldenbremse*) in 2009, in part inspired by the very successful approach that Switzerland had taken in 2001: the German law mandated progressive reductions in spending until the target was met in 2016. This principle was now extended on the European level. In the end, France reluctantly accepted the principle of a treaty revision. It would have to be limited ("surgical," as mentioned by an official spokesman): "We don't want it to open a debate on the constitution or the Union."[13] France agreed to sanction ex post those countries found in breach of fiscal rules. Their voting rights could be suspended in case of serious violations. Sarkozy was adamantly opposed, however, to any ex ante control on national budgets by European authorities, especially by the Commission.

Although there was support, especially from the French side for the crisis management via EFSF and ESM, the support for a rule-based framework to contain the future crisis was always halfhearted. The crisis response required another pillar—market discipline on peripheral member countries.

Deauville: The Power of Market Discipline

When Sarkozy and Merkel met in the old-fashioned resort town of Deauville on the French Normandy coast on October 18, 2010, they agreed on a Faustian pact. They had already extended discussions on the fringes of the Asia-Europe Summit in Brussels on October 4–5. But now the encounter had more urgency, and a remarkable deal was struck. Germany abandoned its requirement for strong ex ante control on national budgets. As a counterpart, Sarkozy accepted that the new crisis framework should provide "for an adequate participation of private creditors."[14] That new principle became known as private sector involvement (PSI) and is quite consistent with the Maastricht Treaty's no-bailout rule. It meant that holders of bonds issued by euro-area governments would be asked to take losses (in the financial jargon, "haircuts") if the issuing country needed support from other euro-area members. At least markets should provide some ex ante discipline for fiscal excesses.

Deauville was the first watershed moment of the euro crisis. It came as a total surprise, including for finance ministers, who were meeting at the same time (in Luxembourg) for an Ecofin Council. All of them discovered the Deauville communiqué—and its content—on their handheld devices. It was a total game changer, although very few government and central bank officials at the time thought through the implications for the market. One exception was ECB president Jean-Claude Trichet, who was deeply upset by the move, complaining, "You're going to destroy the euro"[15] (see chapter 15). For the first time, an official statement was casting doubt on the willingness of euro-area governments to fully service their debts, whatever the circumstances. Government debt was not *safe* anymore in the euro area. It had huge—and immediate—consequences on market dynamics. It instantly shifted the balance of power in Europe. And it opened a new and very difficult debate on the nature of the crisis and how it should be managed.

On the face of it, PSI made a lot of sense. Economists liked it because it provided a clear framework for dealing with debt sustainability. Politicians liked it because it meant "making the bankers pay" for their mistakes. Debtor countries liked it because it limited their potential contribution. Official creditors liked it because it strengthened market discipline on

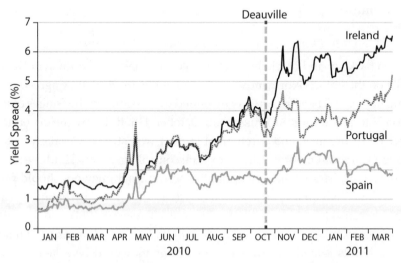

FIGURE 2.1. Difference in Interest Rates between 10-Year Sovereign Bond Yields Issued by Ireland/Portugal/Spain and the 10-Year German Government Bond Yield (Source: Datastream)

fiscally irresponsible countries. But investors hated it, because on top of taking a haircut, they had to face the new uncertainty attached to sovereign debt, which up to then had been considered perfectly safe.

Soon after PSI was decided in principle, and even before it became official policy, interest rates on peripheral countries' debt (as well as sovereign CDS) increased markedly. (See figure 2.1.) The market thought that a default of the peripheral sovereign bonds became more likely. Hence, the spreads for credit default swaps (CDS), the periodic fee a buyer of "protection" against the default has to pay, increased. The crisis also spread to Italy and Spain. Before Deauville, those two countries could have still been considered immune from the crisis, although a small deviation in interest rates had already appeared earlier. Immediately after, they started to diverge strongly from Germany, France, and other core countries. The financial pressure would later be felt by France as well. Beginning in October 2010, the crisis took a whole new turn. Markets became more sensitive to economic and political news. Funding pressures emerged both for peripheral sovereigns and banks. Some of the biggest debt markets in the world became unstable and illiquid. It was no longer a question of small, peripheral economies. The foundations of the euro area were shaken, and the repercussions were felt all over the world.

Whether consciously or not, Merkel and Sarkozy had now put Germany in a position where it could dominate the policy debate and, de facto, impose its views. Markets were now exerting direct pressure on major European economies to converge on Germany. German interest rates and German policies were the ultimate benchmarks through which all economic policies and attitudes in Europe would be judged. And the markets were the referee. Divergences and deviations from German orthodoxy would be swiftly sanctioned by deterioration in financial parameters and conditions.

This had happened before. In the 1980s and 1990s, the exchange rate was the policeman for Europe's governments. Countries with high inflation or bad economic conditions would unavoidably be confronted with exchange rate pressures inside the European Monetary System, and they would have to negotiate a realignment of their central parities under conditions agreed on by Germany. From the beginning of the euro to its tenth anniversary, there did not appear to be any equivalent police on the European fiscal street. But after 2010, interest rates on government debt suddenly appeared as a major threat to governments. Starting in October

2010, as soon as a country was seen as deviating from strict fiscal rectitude, spreads with Germany would increase. And they would also be pushed higher if growth was seen as too weak, therefore increasing the perceived risk of default. For those countries affected by the crisis, there was no winning solution in the short run, as there was no way to maintain growth while undergoing strong fiscal consolidation. Keeping the spread with Germany under control would become if not the main objective, at least the binding constraint under which all euro-area governments operated.

Mariano Rajoy, the new Spanish prime minister brought to power by parliamentary elections in November 2011, briefly thought he could free himself from the new and implicit rules of the game. He made strong statements on Spain's intentions to fully recover its fiscal sovereignty. Soon, spreads on Spanish debt started to rise, and doubts appeared about the ability of Spain to rollover its debt. As the Spanish crisis intensified in the summer of 2012, he became so irritated and afraid that he basically withdrew from politics for a few weeks and preferred to concentrate on the fortunes of the Spanish team in the European soccer championship.

France and Germany reacted very differently to this new environment. It may have taken some time for Sarkozy to measure the new balance of forces; however, by the first quarter of 2011, he had changed position. The French were forcefully trying to backpedal on the principle of PSI. In numerous encounters with their German counterparts, they tried to persuade them to give up PSI or, at least, to limit it to Greece. They never succeeded. Around those dates, leaks from the Élysée made clear that, for the first time, the French sovereign rating was becoming a concern, and the government tried to mobilize to avoid any downgrading. The dynamics triggered by Deauville were becoming increasingly clear and their implications worrisome.

By contrast, many Germans welcomed this new behavior in the markets. They were frustrated that European institutions had proved powerless in disciplining fiscal policies. They feared that even the IMF and the troika would not succeed in imposing sufficient conditionality and that moral hazard would be pervasive if financial support had to be granted to peripheral countries. The Bundesbank president, Jens Weidmann, bluntly stated, in December 2011, that he did not see any problem with Italy needing to pay interest rates as high as 7 percent on its long-term debt "for years."[16] Some German policy makers accepted the risk of contagion and increased financial instability in the euro area as a price to pay to get things right, once and for all. Although other governments often resented the new corset imposed on them, they could not resist the facts: the German economy was doing well, unemployment was low, and exports were booming. That made it difficult to challenge the German vision now that it had been adopted as the norm by investors and markets.

After the Power Shift

The decision on the Greek program in spring 2010 and the fact that fiscal power rested with national authorities led to the first power shift from the European Commission to national capitals. The Deauville decision to rely on market discipline in fall 2010 shifted power to Berlin and Paris. Politicians from other countries now complained that they could only get information about the real decisions from German or French contacts and that a game of "broken telephone" (known in the United Kingdom as "Chinese whispers" or "pass the message") was being played.[17] But there was also an immediate financial fallout. The Normandy beach agreement widened the interest rate differentials across Europe. From then onward, the crisis countries primarily became worried about their funding costs and lost influence in policy debate. France now played a double game, pushing its economic views through numerous policy initiatives but at the same time not willing to make an open break with Germany out of fear of losing the low interest rates on its debt. Any real move to policy heterodoxy would lead to a surge in debt service costs, as markets would push bond prices down and yields up. Germany was in the driver's seat, and not only because everyone wanted to extract financial support from Germany. The European institutions in Brussels did not have a good crisis. The old Monnet mechanism of using crises to integrate Europe further seemed no longer to work. States, with their own fiscal capacity, looked more and more as if they were the backstop for confidence. The logic of that process, however, would require a renationalization of the European Union, and financial markets indeed became more nationally focused than they had been before the crisis.

France and the European Commission alike have tried to reclaim some of their lost power from Germany. Take first the case of France. In 2012, French voters narrowly rejected Sarkozy's bid for a second term as president of the French Republic. The Socialist candidate, François Hollande, became president of France in May 2012, and the election initially significantly altered the dynamics of the German-French relationship. Like other newly elected leaders before him (notably the Spanish prime minister Mariano Rajoy), as well as later (Matteo Renzi in Italy and Alexis Tsipras in Greece), Hollande had placed shaking off the Germanic austerity fetters at the center of his political campaign. Hollande saw himself, and France, as the connecting link between North and South in Europe, whereas Sarkozy (despite his periodic surges of interest in a French-dominated Mediterranean) wanted to appear as coleader with Germany. In an interview, Hollande said that "France is the bridge between northern Europe and southern Europe. I refuse any division."[18] Those words infuriated German leaders who were quite aware that Hollande was hoping that the Social Democratic Party (SPD) might be in a position to form a great coalition with Merkel's Christian Democrats after the German parliamentary election of September 2013, to constrain Merkel, and to change the course of German and European policies. There was indeed a great coalition, but not much change in the tone of German politics. As a consequence, France developed a new mental map in which a new Latin bloc would form. Spain and Italy would join France in the struggle against budgetary austerity.

Once in office, Hollande literally had a bumpy start to his new relationship with the German chancellor. On the same day as his inauguration, May 15, 2012, after a rain-soaked parade down the Champs Élysées, in which he stood defiantly in an open and tiny French-made Peugeot car, Hollande traveled to Berlin for a first meeting with Merkel. Shortly after takeoff, his plane was caught in the terrible storm, hit by lightning, and was almost forced to turn back. To some observers, this was a portent of the new state of the Franco-German relationships: stormy and uncertain.

Hollande had campaigned against the treaty on fiscal discipline signed by Sarkozy and was committed to obtaining a revision. At the European Council on June 28–29, 2012, he was blocked on this issue by Merkel. Hollande had to accept the treaty as it was and got an additional growth package through, consisting essentially of a special loan program by the European Investment Bank (EIB) based in Luxembourg.

Apart from substantial divergences, there was also a major break in the style of the relationship. Contrary to the Sarkozy period, when the leaders took great pains in publicly masking their divergences and pretending they acted in a concerted way, Hollande and Merkel did not bother to conceal their differences. The tensions between the new French leader and Merkel went beyond the political—they were also emotional. During the electoral campaign in France, Merkel had, in an unusual intervention by the leader of one country in the domestic politics of another country, openly taken a position for Sarkozy. Indeed, she would have been prepared to hold joint public rallies with him—a proposition that Sarkozy nevertheless rejected as polls showed that support from the German chancellor was counterproductive. This support contrasts markedly with Merkel's stance toward Hollande, whom she refused to meet in the run-up to the election. Personal relations also did not improve much after Hollande's electoral success. For example, while Merkel invited the British prime minister David Cameron and his family at her guest residence, Schloss Meseberg, near Berlin, she did not extend the same hospitality to Hollande.

There were no systematic preparatory bilateral meetings ahead of the euro leaders' summit. Hollande publicized his differences with Merkel and seemed determined to engage in some ideological confrontation. In a wide-ranging interview for several European papers in October 2012, he acknowledged for the first time that divergences between Paris and Berlin could impede the progress toward European integration. He defended his vision of European solidarity, including Eurobonds, which he contrasted with the no-growth policies followed in Europe. At the same time, he rejected fiscal federalism and defended national sovereignty. Publicly, he would not hesitate to mention his doubts about the German course, as when he explicitly said that Merkel was essentially driven by her desire to be reelected.

The French Socialist Party went much further than the president in attempting to define a clear alternative to German policies and a "German Europe." Hollande's party produced a document for their party convention speaking of Merkel's "egoistic intransigence."[19] But eventually Hollande was obliged to distance himself from this ideological position, and the government started to discuss the desirability of a set of microeconomic and structural reforms. The turn to reform—or to making France look economically more in line with Germany—became explicit when the government was reshaped and Manuel Valls appointed as prime minister and Emanuel Macron as minister of economy. The relationship between France and Germany at the high political level also improved in response to the security crisis that followed Russia's annexation of Crimea and Russian-backed fighting in eastern Ukraine and then the escalation of the terrorist threat with the Islamist gunmen's attack on the offices of the satirical magazine *Charlie Hebdo* in January 2015. The picture of Chancellor Merkel leaning on Hollande's shoulder was widely diffused and interpreted as a symbolic reconciliation of the two European powers. France's role as a great military power made it a central player in the negotiations about containing instability in the east and brought France and Germany into a closer alignment.

A second challenge to the German dominance in Europe came through changes in the institutional structure of the European Union. In May 2014, elections to the European Parliament were intended to give a new democratic legitimacy to the Commission, as each of the European "families" of parties nominated a leading figure as their candidate for Commission president (this figure was then termed, in German terminology, the *Spitzenkandidat*). Before the elections, euro enthusiasts saw the vote as evidence that a new pattern for European democracy was emerging. Euro skeptics countered with a claim that this invention of a new political order would not work. Voters would treat the elections as they had in the past, an opportunity to sound off in protest not against Europe so much as against their own national governments. They would also vote against austerity, the fiscal orthodoxy imposed as a consequence of the need to defend the monetary union.

The most striking outcome of the election was the emergence of a new pattern. Countries voted quite differently, with two fundamentally contrasting patterns. There was no uniform Europe-wide antigovernment protest vote, no common front of the "nos." On the contrary, in many countries, including some of those most severely hit by the financial and economic crisis, voters turned out to endorse both their governments and the European project. The proincumbent effect was discernible in Southern Europe, in Spain, and most dramatically in Italy, where the new reform government of Matteo Renzi defeated expectations that Italians would deliver another big protest vote. It also occurred in the Baltic states, where the economic effects of austerity programs were most severe but where voters endorsed centrist candidates for the European Parliament. The unexpected weakness of the populist right in the Netherlands and the solid performance of the ruling Christian Democrats in Germany was a reflection of the same phenomenon: a new core Europe that is politically stable and self-confident.

Across the Rhine and across the Channel, matters looked very different. There was little stability or self-confidence. In both France and the United Kingdom, the success of insurgent populist parties shook the political landscape. In both countries, the incumbent party of government—the French Socialists and the British Conservatives—were not only beaten but came in a humiliating third place at the end of the race. The French Socialist prime minister described Marine Le Pen's National Front victory (with 24.86% of the vote) as a political earthquake. It could easily be ascribed to the massive unpopularity of France's relatively new Socialist president and his government. The parallel triumph of the UK Independence Party in Great Britain cannot be explained as just a protest vote against the coalition government, which was delivering an economic recovery. It was unambiguously a popular rejection of Europe and in particular of immigration from the European Union, foreshadowing the Brexit vote in June 2016.

Neither the optimistic nor the pessimistic forecasts about the experiment in European democracy were correct. No obvious European leader emerged by a simple operation of democratic choice. The selection of Jean-Claude Juncker, the *Spitzenkandidat* of the center-right European People's Party, as the next Commission president looked complicated and rather undemocratic. But on the other hand, there was also no uniform wave of anti-Europeanism or disillusion with the European project.

Juncker then reshaped the European Commission in two important ways. First, he introduced a new layer to the hierarchy, with seven vice presidents standing above other commissioners. Second, he appointed Pierre Moscovici, the French finance minister, a prominent critic of the arbitrariness of the 3 percent rule, as commissioner for economic and financial affairs and thus in theory in charge of the enforcement of the fiscal deficit rules. Cleverly, Juncker assigned authorities within the Commission in such a way that two commissioners—one from the left and one from the right—had to agree before passing a proposal up to his office. For example, the left-leaning Commissioner Pierre Moscovici has to find common ground with "austerian reformer" Vice President Valdis Dombroviskis first. Juncker also worked very closely with the European Parliament president, Martin Schulz, the social-democratic *Spitzenkandidat*, creating what was in effect a Great Coalition of center-right and center-left on the European level.

A third challenge, when France again seemed to try to recover the intellectual leadership in Europe, came after the election in January 2015 of a radical Greek populist government, dominated by the left-wing Syriza party, which explicitly sought to formulate an alternative to German austerity. The calculation of the new Greek government was that it could spearhead a more general movement in Europe, building a cross-national coalition, above all in Mediterranean or Latin Europe, dedicated to challenging German thinking. The head of the leftist Spanish Podemos (translated as "we can") party tweeted enthusiastically about Syriza's election victory: "2015 will be the year of change in Spain and Europe. We start in Greece. Let's go Alexis, let's go!" Anti-austerity parties in Ireland and Portugal reacted similarly.[20] In France, support for anti-austerity came even from the far right who wanted to get rid of the euro. The French National Front leader Marine Le Pen saluted "the start of the trial of euro-austerity."[21] In the crisis negotiations of June and July 2015, the smaller European countries, above all from the north and the east, took a tough line against concessions to Greece. It often appeared as if the only reliable ally of Greece was France, and France's finance minister Michel Sapin, on a number of occasions, made his support explicit. But those moral gestures did not help, and Greece was obliged to accept a radical reform packet that fundamentally expressed German priorities. Ultimately, however, neither the French shift away from Germany nor the institutional changes in the European Union have changed the balance of power in Europe much.

A fourth challenge came in the summer of 2015 with the eruption of a crisis over the stream of refugees to northern Europe. French ministers joined in the widespread attack from inside Germany and from other European countries on Merkel's alleged invitation of Syrian refugees to come to Europe. In fact, German policy was set by a prior constitutional court ruling that made migrants into recipients of welfare payments that were often higher than wages in their home countries; of a decision by the German Federal Office of Migration to suspend the elaborate Dublin rules on the treatment of refugees; as well as of Merkel's response in a television show that "Germany can do it." With complaints about the behavior of some refugees toward German women, and fears about terrorists taking advantage of the stream of migrants to plan attacks in Europe, including in Paris and Brussels, the distance between the French and the German government grew wider again.

Finally, the Brexit vote on June 23, 2016, has shaken not only the UK but also the rest of Europe. The markets were caught by surprise, and the immediate outcome was a fall in the British pound and also in stock markets across Europe. On June 24, British Prime Minister David Cameron announced that he would resign and that a new government should do the hard work of the Brexit negotiations. Both major parties fissured. Other Europeans feared that delaying tactics would cause general uncertainty, a decline in investment, and also perhaps further exits from the European Union. European leaders gathered in Berlin—another sign of the power shift. Chancellor Merkel looked again like the undisputed leader of Europe. She responded by saying that while Britain should not be treated "cruelly" and should have time to develop the exit strategy, the official Article 50 exit procedure that limits the exit negotiations to two years would not be preceded by preliminary negotiations.

Germany looked more and more dominant in Europe. The only European institution that gained slowly but significantly in influence through the euro crisis was the ECB, "the guardian of the European currency." As countries whose economic philosophy is closer to crisis management approach rather than a moral hazard long-run solidity approach hold the majority in the ECB council, Germans felt sidelined. In a sense, the ECB in Frankfurt became both a main opponent and a key partner for Berlin. Chapter 15 is devoted to the role of the ECB in the euro crisis.

The euro-crisis management saw a remarkable shift of the gravity of power from European institutions and a European process to national capitals—in particular, Berlin and Paris after the Deauville decision. Paris lost out, and the old Franco-German axis tilted in a lopsided direction largely because of the deeply entrenched French political malaise that was partly—but not entirely—a consequence of a relatively poor economic performance. The Franco-German balance affected the types of action that could be contemplated in dealing with the crisis. It is essential to not only understand the difference in economic interest but even more importantly the differences in economic philosophies. The tradition of economic thinking in Germany and other northern countries is significantly different from the more Keynesian approach prevalent in France and Southern Europe. The next two chapters highlight the differences in culture and outline the historical roots in economic thinking. Chapters 5 to 8 then sharpen the analytical difference in economic thinking and how the differences influenced the various phases of the crisis.

3

Historical Roots of German-French Differences

In the early nineteenth century, Madame de Staël, the daughter of the prerevolutionary French finance minister Jacques Necker and a leading intellectual who attempted to conduct a philosophical debate with Napoleon, wrote a tract, *De l'Allemagne*, in which she tried to explain Germany to the French. She began with the observation that "French and Germans are at two extremities of the moral chain, because the former consider external facts as the motor of all ideas, while the latter think that ideas generate all impressions. The two countries nevertheless are in basic agreement on social relations, but there is nothing more opposed than their respective literary and philosophic systems."[1] After her, a varied range of distinguished literary and intellectual figures have undertaken the same task of trying to explain Germans and French to each other, from Heinrich Heine through Heinrich Mann, François Perroux, Raymond Aron, Jean-Paul Sartre, and Joseph Rovan. On the political level, the great leaders of the mid-twentieth century who remade France and Germany after catastrophe, Charles de Gaulle and Konrad Adenauer, were both fascinated and attracted by the history of the other country. The incompatibility of thought is as striking in economics as it is in other intellectual domains, but no one has really tried to produce an intellectual reconciliation.

This chapter discusses the following questions:

- How did the very different approaches to the economy arise in France and Germany?
- How did cultural differences affect the construction of Europe's monetary and financial framework?

- What role did the difference between German federalism and a French centralized state structure play?
- Did the German Mittelstand economic structure that contrasted with the French national champions approach make formulating a common economic policy more problematic?
- How do the wage-bargaining processes in both countries differ with a cooperative German model between labor unions and employers and more confrontational labor unions in France?
- What role did the different historical inflation experiences in both countries play?
- What do these countries think of the linkages that connect them to other neighboring economies and to the global economy?

Cultural Differences

That there should be a significant divergence between Germany and France may initially be quite surprising. After all, the two countries are neighbors and have shared many political traditions and outlooks. Their legal traditions are both shaped by Roman law rather than the common law (or precedent-based) system that characterizes Great Britain and the United States. In both France and Germany, the traditions of the Enlightenment and specifically of eighteenth-century cameralism (or state sciences, *Staatswissenschaften*) laid the foundation for the involvement of the modern state in the economy. In this approach, the state and its high-minded servants were in a unique position to make judgments about the public interest and the long-term public good. What is even more surprising is that the fundamental economic orientations changed dramatically after crisis moments: in particular, the catastrophe of the Nazi dictatorship pushed Germany away from a state-centered tradition toward a rule-based liberalism. On the other side of the River Rhine, in France, traditional liberalism was discredited. France had fallen heavily in 1940, and its political, military, and economic elite had been completely discredited, not merely by the defeat but more enduringly by the subsequent cooperation or betrayal of the French elites. French thinkers became obsessed with economic planning. The reversal of economic cultures in both countries provides an extreme instance of the way that change—or progress—when it occurs in Europe, almost always takes place in the aftermath of cataclysms and catastrophes.

Cultural attitudes can combine extraordinary durability and extreme changeability. Alexis de Tocqueville, in *The Old Regime and the French Revolution*, referred in 1856 to the French as "a people so unchangeable in its leading features that it may be recognized by portraits drawn two or three thousand years ago, and yet so fickle in its daily opinions and tastes that it becomes at last a mystery to itself."[2] France was "endowed with more heroism than virtue, more genius than common sense; better adapted for the conception of grand designs than the accomplishment of great enterprises; the most brilliant and the most dangerous nation of Europe, and the one that is surest to inspire admiration, hatred, terror, or pity, but never indifference?" By the twentieth century, a similar paradox existed in Germany, a country of intense intellectuality but also of tremendous brutality and destructive power, where foreign observers felt tempted to trace the origins of twentieth-century disorders back hundreds of years, to Martin Luther, or even thousands of years, to the tribes of the ancient Teutonic forests. In Thomas Mann's iconic late-life novel, *Doctor Faustus*, in which he analyzed the condition of Germany, the main character states that the Germans are "capable of realizing antithetical principles of thinking and existence." His friend responds by saying, "A rich people." And he replies, "A confused people that confuses others."[3]

Some modern economists try to operationalize their perceptions of long-enduring national character traits into an economic model. Thus a recent attempt to understand the euro crisis tells of the incompatibility of national cultures and in particular the incompatibilities of a culture obsessed with "cheating" (Greece) and a contrary culture obsessed with "punishment" (Germany). The authors then develop a model of the interactions of choices between these two cultures and show that

> interactions between Greeks and Germans result into excessive "cheating" (by the Greeks) and excessive "punishment" (by the Germans), with a generalized loss of welfare, which is increasing in the degree of cultural heterogeneity, and which cannot vanish rapidly given the inertia of cultural norms. In such circumstances countries may reconsider participation in the union facing either the choice of breaking up and reverting to a national currency equilibrium or

otherwise considering the creation of a fiscal authority that can be endowed with any punish-forgive strategy the players agree to, hence giving a better chance of converging to a superior steady state and with lower transition costs.[4]

The intellectual exercise raises the question of how and in what circumstances a revolutionary improvement in the institutional framework can change behavior and thus also apparently deeply entrenched cultural norms. To take a famous case from another European country, Poles were held to have a lazy and cheating culture—which the Germans dismissed as *polnische Wirtschaft*—and then Poland ended communism, introduced democracy and a market economy, and within a few years occupied another stereotype, as the hardest-working Europeans. There is a powerful case that simply identifying the particularities of supposed cultural divergences allows a design of institutional mechanisms not just of accommodating but also of changing them.

Federalism versus Centralism

The Roots of French Centralism

The easiest explanation of the thought divergence of France and Germany follows simply from political structure. Cameralism, the early modern model of the bureaucratic guidance of an economy, might be an appealing philosophy for one state, but it clearly requires some sort of central direction. France, of all modern European countries, most closely resembles the ideal type of a centralized unitary state. (Italy, with great regional diversity of outlooks, social structures, and incomes, also—perhaps mistakenly— adopted the French centralized political model when it was built as a nation-state in the 1860s.) Indeed, historians have seen the centralizing urges of the French state as a long-term feature of continuity that spans deep divides between dynasties and even ideologies, from the *missi dominici* of Charlemagne and the Merovingians, to the *intendants* of the Bourbon Louis XIV, and then to the structure of departments with centrally appointed prefects after the Revolution and Napoleon, and back to the Restoration monarchy, the 1848 republic, the Second Empire, the Third Republic, and so on. According to analysts such as Alexis de Tocqueville and Albert Sorel, the historical function of the French Revolution was simply to finish or accomplish the task set by the *ancien régime*. So centralization has a history in France that goes back a thousand years or so.

From the Holy Roman Empire to the Federal Republic of Germany

By contrast, modern Germany has always been a federal system, with the catastrophic exception of the twelve years of the Nazi dictatorship that implemented a policy of unification and centralization, or *Gleichschaltung*. Before 1806, the German-speaking territories were organized in a loose association of the Holy Roman Empire, with some 350 territorial units directly subject to only a loose and cumbersome imperial judicial system and some notional limits on their foreign policy. Some of these units were quite large states—Brandenburg-Prussia, Bavaria, Saxony, and Württemberg—while the smallest were little towns or even just parts of villages. After the 1815 Vienna Settlement, some vestiges of the old order were kept with a German Confederation, composed of thirty-eight states (again, some of them were still quite small). The German Empire of 1871 was created as a result of the initiatives of Bismarck's Prussia, but it remained a league of princes, and the three large south German states, Baden, Bavaria, and Württemberg, even kept their own armies. The state structure of 1871 was retained in 1919 in the Weimar Republic, even though many critics argued that it was politically and economically dysfunctional. After 1945, the Allies—in particular the United States—rightly insisted on a revival of Germany's federal tradition. Madame de Staël made this tradition the center of her analysis when she wrote that Germans provided a contrast to Latin countries in which there was "skill in escaping from duties": by contrast, Germany lacked this *souplesse hardie* (bold suppleness) and instead was obsessed with the "honorable necessity of rules and justice."[5]

The German tradition emphasized the idea of the *Rechtsstaat*, the rule of law, or perhaps more accurately, the rule of rules. German constitutional lawyers love to quote an anecdote about a miller at the time of the eighteenth century King of Prussia, Frederick the Great. When the King wanted to seize his mill, the miller proudly replied, "Il y a des juges à Berlin." (There are judges in Berlin.) But the French playwright who popularized this anecdote, François Andrieux, also noted a certain German hypocrisy about rules: the same monarch who was forced by courts to respect the property of a humble miller had no compunction when it came to the law of other countries, and simply sent his troops to seize the province of

Silesia. "On respecte un moulin, on vole une province." (They respect a mill, they steal a province.)[6]

Federations are mechanisms for preserving differences while minimizing conflict, while central states repress conflict by overriding differences through the assertion of authority. Federations thus need rules as a way of dealing with substantial differences in outlook. In Steven Spielberg's striking 2015 movie *Bridge of Spies*, the central figure, the lawyer James B. Donovan, played by Tom Hanks, is pushed by a CIA agent to disclose his conversations with his client, a Russian spy, and then talks to the agent about the differences in their backgrounds: "I'm Irish. You're German. But what makes us both Americans? Just one thing. One, one, one. The rule book. We call it the Constitution. And we agree to the rules. And it's what makes us Americans."

In the French Third Republic (1875–1940), it was often claimed that the education minister, or the president, could look at his watch and know immediately what page every French eleven-year-old was currently studying. By contrast, in Germany, issues such as education and policing but also the promotion of economic activity remained a state affair, and the imperial government kept out of those matters. The resulting contrast is very evident from any map of the two countries' railroad systems. France looks like a gigantic spoke system emanating from Paris, the political center (and some important economic areas were not well-connected until the middle of the twentieth century: the coal-mining Nord and the ore fields of Lorraine), while Germany has multiple nodes, all connected with each other. That superior German interconnectedness doubtless also constituted an economic advantage.

The suspicion of centralizing principles in a federal state means that the Federal Republic of Germany insists more on the principle of parliamentary approval of legislation and also on checks through legal review by a supreme court (Constitutional Court, *Bundesverfassungsgericht*). A constant irritant to Germany's partners in the European Union throughout the euro crisis was the German government's worry about the need to obtain the approval of the Bundestag for each of the rescue packages. Critics also then subjected the government case to a complaint before the Constitutional Court. By contrast, controversial legislation can be implemented in France by decree law, even though critics will then denounce the failing democratic legitimacy. In 2015, a package liberalizing economic measures (the law Macron) was pushed through by decree after 111 hours of parliamentary debate and 82 hours of committee hearings demonstrated the strength of opposition within the ruling Socialist Party: the government could simply use the provisions of the Constitution (Article 49-3) on the *vote bloqué*, provisions that have been used fifty times since 1958, including twenty-eight times by the reformist center-left government of Michel Rocard, who was French prime minister from 1988–1991.[7] Germans by contrast associate decree laws of this type with the constitutional subversion that had undermined the interwar Weimar Republic and led to the Nazi dictatorship.

Banking and Finances

The federal emphasis that marks modern Germany is also evident in differences in the financial systems. The French banking system is highly concentrated. In the postwar economic upswing, the big three deposit banks were nationalized, and their investments were carefully coordinated by the French Treasury so as to accomplish the goals of economic planning.[8] A great deal of German banking remained—and remains—regional, despite the prominence of some big universal banks: between 1870 and 1945, these were called the Berlin banks, or sometimes Great Banks (*Grossbanken*), and after 1949 their successors relocated to Frankfurt (Deutsche Bank and Commerzbank). These existed alongside a well-developed system of cooperative banks and also of savings banks, which were grouped together through wholesale regional banking establishments (Landesbanken), until recently owned by the regional states.

A federation requires a stricter legal framework to balance the interests of different regions and to ensure that one does not ruthlessly triumph over the other. There need to be tighter mechanisms to control fiscal activism at the center. This is especially true of financial matters and of fiscal policy. Transfers within Germany are regulated by a complex arrangement called the *Finanzausgleich*, the terms of which are so contested that it cannot be frequently reformulated or renegotiated.

The question of federalism also affects the outlook on monetary policy. In European perceptions in the postwar world, the dollar was manipulated and instrumentalized as a tool of US policy, with "benign neglect" (in the late 1960s) or "malign neglect" (in the late 1970s) forcing other countries to carry the cost or the burden of American policies. The dollar was a "can-do" currency, in this view. The French response was to devise ways for Europe to develop its own capacity to respond by affecting the external valuation of its currency. Germans were skeptical and preferred to think of their currency as limiting rather than enhancing the room for maneuver: currency was a "cannot do that" instrument. Their view followed from the monetary character of a federation: federations need to restrict money creation because it could affect incomes in a disparate way.

Monetary instability in the past decisively helped to threaten or even to blow apart fragile political systems. The monetary authority never simply agrees to convert every outstanding obligation into money. Instead, it will decide that some industries, or some banks, or some political authorities need to be kept going for the good of the general community and that their debts should as a consequence be monetized. Those industries, banks, and political authorities that are not so privileged are inevitably resentful and see the central bank's actions as an abuse of power. In federal systems, in particular, those businesses and political authorities far removed from the center of the federation are most likely to be excluded from the monetary stimulus and hence inclined to be alienated.

Hyperinflation in early 1920s Germany fanned separatism in Bavaria, the Rhineland, and Saxony because these remote areas thought that the German central bank and the central government in Berlin were discriminating against them and privileging the capital and its interests. The separatists were radical, on the left in Saxony and on the far right in Bavaria and the Rhineland. The scar created by the memory of inflation is particularly acute in Germany, but it is by no means a purely German phenomenon. There are also more recent cases of federations eroded by inflation. In late 1980s Yugoslavia, as the socialist regime disintegrated, the monetary authorities in Belgrade were closest to Serbian politicians such as Slobodan Milosevic and to Serbian business interests. The Croats and Slovenes wanted to get away. In the Soviet Union, inflation appeared as an instrument of the central Moscow bureaucrats, and more remote areas wanted to break away. Hyperinflation thus fueled the national tensions that broke up federal systems in the Soviet Union and Yugoslavia.

The response to German hyperinflation in the 1920s was the institution of a new banking law that protected the central bank (*Reichsbank*) from government intervention. The 1957 Bundesbank Law also guaranteed the autonomy of the new central bank's monetary policy. In consequence, there were spectacular conflicts when Chancellor Konrad Adenauer in the late 1950s or Helmut Schmidt in the late 1970s attacked the Bundesbank for acting as a brake on growth (in other words, for behaving as an independent central bank is supposed to behave).

In France, until the mid-1990s, there was a general consensus that in a unitary republic an independent central bank was undesirable because it would escape from the control of the central political authority that directly reflected the will of the people. In the early 1990s, the Treasury director Christian Noyer (who later became governor of the Banque de France) stated that central bank independence was incompatible with France's republican traditions in that the Republic was "one and indivisible."[9] Centralized states such as France or Japan (which as he pointed out had an excellent record in fighting inflation) exercised political control over central banks, while independent central banks were fundamentally suited to federal states such as Germany, Switzerland, and the United States (and hence also, presumably, although he did not point this out at the time, the European Community or European Union).[10] But it was those models—largely the German and perhaps also the US one—that offered the most promising blueprint for how to construct a new European Central Bank.

Mittelstand versus National Champions

National Champions

The question of federalism has had an impact not just on the structure of the state but also on the kind of economic organization. The French economy is dominated by large, highly competitive international companies. There are more French firms among the 500 largest firms in the world than German firms: in the FT 500 list for 2014, twenty-eight French versus twenty German (*Forbes* gives a narrower difference on the basis of a slightly different methodology, thirty-one French versus twenty-eight German). The large firms have a close relationship with the government, and the government sees the promotion of their interests as a general public interest. There is a long history, from at least the nineteenth century, of French firms struggling to capture political rents, of businessmen entering politics to influence legislation, of family businessmen encouraging their daughters to marry state officials to extend their control, and of producers defining their businesses as central to national identity. Such behavior created a tradition. An infamous modern example occurred when the French government intervened to protect the large food business group Danone from a foreign takeover as a strategically vital company on the grounds that food was an expression of France's cultural identity.

Germany also has large internationally competitive firms backed by the government. There was the same sort of rent-capturing behavior in the nineteenth century: the giant electrical firms Siemens and AEG moved their headquarters and a great deal of their production to Berlin, not for resource reasons but simply because it was the new seat of the German government. But Germany also has a substantial sector of small and medium enterprises (SMEs) that are generally referred to as the *Mittelstand*. The small and medium-sized businesses have generally been the incubators in which middle-class dynamism developed and galvanized society as a whole. This is as true in the immediate past of Europe as it was in the pioneering days of the Industrial Revolution or in the European Middle Ages. In recent years, small (and often new) businesses have been the major creators of jobs. The fortunes of the small business sector have major effects on the economy as a whole. In the United States, between 1980 and 2005, all net new private sector jobs were in companies less than five years old. By contrast, most large companies have tried to rationalize or downsize employment. German statistics also show small and medium enterprises as net creators of jobs in 2000–2005 (with a million new jobs) and large enterprises as losers (a loss of 800,000 jobs).

German Mittelstand

The German Mittelstand is geographically concentrated, above all in the south of the country, in the states of Bavaria and Baden-Württemberg (as well as to some extent in the southern states of former East Germany, Saxony and Thuringia). The historical heart of the German economy in the nineteenth and early twentieth centuries, the Rhine-Ruhr basin, was just as dominated by large companies as France. There thus ensured what the sociologist Gary Herrigel calls "contrasting industrial landscapes."[11] Federalism, however, meant that the small businesses had political champions in the state as well as local governments.

As with the development of contrasting economic philosophies, the roots of the contrasting economic structures lie back a long way in time. In Europe, the key to development lay in the character of social space. In particular, it was the dynamic of urban development that produced a unique chance of mobility. Medieval and early modern Europe had two models of city. On the one side, there were the bureaucratic capitals of a large state, of which Naples was the largest sprawling example. The alternative lay in those cities dominated by mercantile activities, which were often self-governed. In these, order, justice, and harmony, coupled with education and virtue, transformed not only the city but also the surrounding lands. In the famous frescoes of Ambrogio Lorenzetti in Siena's Palazzo Pubblico depicting the "Effects of Good Government on Town and Country," there is not only dancing in city streets but the farmers outside the walls are peacefully tilling their fields. The contrasting picture shows crime, disease, and drought undermining community.

City-states in particular offered a magnet for the ambitious offspring of the land. This late medieval political form also provided a model for civic engagement that in the famous analysis of Robert Putnam still had a major impact on the effectiveness of government and of democratic politics in the twentieth century.[12] West European cities had a unique independence that produced a base for innovation. Cities acted as magnets, where people with ideas could discuss, develop, and realize them. Modern business depended on urbanity. Urban centers then connected with each other and provided a quite different basis for trade than the centrally directed efforts at procurement on the part of great authoritarian regimes.

This model of small businesses that constantly interact with each other—as suppliers, purchasers, or rivals—is still a characteristic of the business landscape of Southern Germany, Northern Italy, and Switzerland, with clusters of dynamic export-oriented niche producers. It is a model that other countries have occasionally tried to emulate with the instruments of state policy and state planning, but it is surprisingly difficult to transplant to other terrains because it depends on such a peculiar and deep historical origin.

Civic engagement, as in the Siena painting, depends on a spontaneously emerging social order. Where it is ordered from above, by a large bureaucratic state, the initiative tends to be stifled. The quest for the general good produces resources that invite the capture of rents by the politically well-connected. In that sense, the model of a dynamic middle stratum, preserved through mechanisms for self-government, is bound to be constantly vulnerable.

In continental—or more accurately in German-speaking—Europe, the productive layers are dignified with a label that seems to imply their universality: *Bürger*. The French rendition (*bourgeois*) captures the depth of meaning less adequately than the German term, although it is often used in an international discourse (many English-language indexes of historical books contain entries of this type: "middle class, see bourgeois"). *Bürger* can have a universal meaning (citizen or *citoyen*) as well as a socioeconomic one, or one that refers to educational attainment. But in each case, the central meaning is clear: a *Bürger* is someone who is capable of self-determination, who can see the fruits of his own economic, political, cultural, or social efforts. A *Bürger* is not a being that is at the blind mercy of impersonal forces; rather, the *Bürger* makes a world on the basis of a forceful and dynamic imagination. A *Bürger* is above all someone who takes responsibility for his or her own actions.

Collaborative versus Confrontational Labor Unions

Soziale Marktwirtschaft

Labor relations substantially differ across European countries. A key problem historically lay in the extent to which workers were prepared to see themselves as *Bürger*, with an interest linked to the general good and in a cooperative relationship with employers, or alternatively as *citoyens*, struggling for the general good of the republic against the particular interests—and the vices—of employers. Both sorts of identification can be seen as a kind of responsibility: but the former is to a concrete present reality, while the second is to an abstract notion of what the future might become. One of the remarkable transformations of Germany after 1945 was from a country where labor relations had been highly conflictual into one where labor was institutionalized as part of the overall social system, the *Soziale Marktwirtschaft*, through works councils and codetermination at the enterprise level. France, by contrast, continued with a basically conflictual pattern.

The extent of political and economic responsibility is directly affected by the way labor movements are organized: that helps to shape the way they see themselves. A feature of the bad political economy of Germany's interwar democracy was the existence of multiple trade unions that competed with each other and used bargaining strategies aimed at maximizing returns for their members. The case is a perfect example of the logic of collective action as explained by Mancur Olson: each collective bargaining unit looks for gains for its members at the expense of the overall community.[13] The outcome is costly for society as a whole. The best solution is to simplify the organizational structure so that there are fewer actors who are more aligned with the general interest.

That organizational simplification occurred in West Germany after World War II. There were now generally single unions that covered an entire industry, and they were not linked to a particular political party or worldview. In addition, codetermination brought worker representatives into the upper-level board (supervisory board, *Aufsichtsrat*) of German companies. In the particularly politically sensitive heavy industries—coal and steel—after the law of 1951, workers had half the seats on the supervisory board; in other industries, a law from 1952 provided for a third of the supervisory board being composed of employee representatives. In 1976, the principle of half the representatives was applied to all German businesses employing more than 2,000.

Competing French Labor Unions

By contrast, in France, the labor movement was split both before and after World War II into communist and noncommunist unions. For most of the time, by far the strongest and most organized of the union federations was the CGT, which was close to the Communist Party. The different unions competed against each other: in particular, the noncommunist unions organized in the CFDT, and the Force Ouvrière needed to demonstrate that they were not just patsies of the bosses. They generally saw their interests as fundamentally opposed to those of the factory owners, not aligned with them. In the words of the famous French workers' anthem, Eugène Pottier's "The Internationale," written in the aftermath of the Paris Commune of 1871,

No saviour from on high delivers,
No faith have we in prince or peer.
Our own right hand the chains must shiver,
Chains of hatred, greed and fear.
E'er the thieves will out with their booty,
And to all give a happier lot.

As a result, rhetoric escalated, and there is a substantially more antagonistic history of labor relations. It is filled with symbolic actions to demonstrate the principle of noncooperation: radicalized workers, for instance, liked to demolish statues of business pioneers (the result is that there are hardly any such monuments left in France).

The way the unions organized and negotiated affected economic and monetary policy. The German government, especially after the 1960s, saw the setting of guidelines for pay settlements as part of its responsibility. From 1974, when the Bundesbank moved to monetary targeting, its representatives also insisted that a major part of setting the monetary target was to give employer and worker representatives a sense of how the economy was developing and, consequently, of what would be an appropriate wage settlement. As the economist and Bundesbank president Axel Weber put it, Germany "did not deliberately opt for strict monetary targeting proposed by Milton Friedman, but rather carried out a pragmatic policy of monetary targeting."[14] Karl Klasen, the president of the Bundesbank at the time monetary targeting was introduced, explained, "On the one hand, monetary policy has in large part a psychological effect, and on the other hand the central bank needs above all to ensure that it contributes to the realization of fundamental objectives (employment, stability, etc.)."[15] As a consequence, American monetarists often treated the German practice with some contempt, thinking that it was more about talk or suasion than about creating a firm limit on the volume of money circulating. But later, when it became clear that the Friedman approach to monetary targeting had "consistently failed," in the phrase of Lars Svensson, Friedman started to cite the Bundesbank experience as "the first and most successful application of his ideas."[16]

Even in the 1970s, European officials tried to recommend the German mode of social relations as a model for the rest of Europe. For instance, Commissioner Wilhelm Haferkamp, the (social-democratic) German vice president of the Commission responsible for economics and finance in the 1970s, spoke of how "The establishment of normative projections of monetary growth as in Germany had a positive effect on the behaviour of economic actors and represented a useful concept which should be adopted on the Community level" as a means to promote "a better cooperation between the social partners and the government."[17] Monetary policy is a key part of the story of inducing an ethic of responsibility in Germany— and in prompting a renunciation of the theatrical politics of conflict and struggle.

Historical Inflation Experiences

Monetary policy can be a testing point for the principle of responsibility. How far can the interaction of powerful social actors—trade unions, employers, the government—force monetary authorities to provide an accommodative response? And does a bad memory help to shape an economic culture? The most dramatic and famous inflationary experience of the twentieth century occurred in Germany after World War I, although other Central European countries, including Austria, Hungary, and Poland, had similar experiences at that time, and the Hungarian inflation after World War II was more severe as measured by the extent of the loss of value of the currency.

The monetary disorders of the early 1920s—the Great Inflation—had a profound and long-lasting effect on Germany. But the reason why is not obvious to many modern observers, who point out (correctly) that almost no Germans alive today have experienced the Great Inflation and that there are even relatively few whose parents had a direct experience. It is often puzzling to outsiders why an event that is now so distant should have had so traumatic an impact. In addition, does the historical record not show that the economic event that immediately preceded the interwar collapse of democracy and the dictatorship of the Nazis was not the inflation but a catastrophic deflation?

It is undoubtedly true that by November 1923, the German currency, the mark, had fallen to one-trillionth ($1/10^{12}$) of its prewar value (the Hungarian forint depreciated to $1/10^{23}$). Contemporary accounts of the Great Inflation emphasize the extent to which the devaluation of money destroyed every normal expectation. In the last stages of inflation, prices changed several times a day. Shopkeepers followed the foreign exchange rates and immediately adjusted their charges. Vast amounts of paper money were needed to make even single purchases. In the longer run, inflation destroyed German savings, wiped out the capital of corporations (including banks), and made the economy of the unstable democratic Weimar Republic vulnerable to yet more shocks. It also had a dramatic effect on popular and political psychology.

The constant alteration of prices, the immiseration of large swathes of the population, and the dramatic story of fortunes made and fortunes lost as a result of speculation made ordinary Germans vulnerable and neurotic.

The rapid movement of prices made it appear that every transaction was some sort of a swindle: customers rushed to buy goods before the announcement of a new exchange rate of the dollar and blamed traders if there were no goods in the shop. Because it played along with very old, established clichés about Jewish dominance of finance, the inflationary uncertainty fueled anti-Semitism. Later on, some shrewd observers such as the scientist and writer Elias Canetti reached the surprising conclusion that it was the Great Inflation that made the Holocaust possible by creating a world in which large numbers simply seemed unreal and incomprehensible. Bureaucrats simply wrote down impossibly big sums without thinking of the human consequences.

The early 1920s were not the only German experience with inflation. In the early 1930s, it was in part fear of inflation that made the deflation and the economic crisis so severe. Then, within a few years, monetary and fiscal expansion enabled Hitler's rearmament. The effects on prices were suppressed through price controls, and the effects of the repressed inflation appeared instead in increasing shortages and in quality deteriorations (so that shoes, for instance, wore out in months rather than years). The aftermath of Hitler's inflation only became fully apparent after World War II, when part of the process of monetary reform was to cancel the "monetary overhang" and write down monetary assets by a factor of ten.

In the 1960s, such German economists as Egon Sohmen gave persistent warnings about the international inflation generated by the United States, especially through its financing of the Vietnam War. French economists were even louder on the same theme: Jacques Rueff in particular, the key adviser in de Gaulle's stabilization at the end of the 1950s, provided the clearest indictment of irresponsible dollar politics, and it was French politicians who took on the task of criticizing America's "exorbitant privilege." When, however, inflation took off internationally in the 1970s, Germany was one of the first countries to try to break inflationary expectations rather than accommodate them, while France was more accommodative and in the second half of the 1970s had rates of inflation two or three times higher than those of Germany. France no longer had the political structures that supported a sound money culture: the explosion of revolution in 1968 had the effect in France—but not on the other side of the Rhine—of unleashing a fragmentation of the left and the labor movement and a competition to take up radical stances.

4

German-French Differences
in Economic Philosophies

Economic thinking is shaped by historical experience. As this chapter details, the experience of dictatorship, World War II, and military defeat played a special role in influencing the development of economic traditions in Germany and France. The differences stretch from questions such as how to arrange competition and macroeconomic planning at home to the preferred arrangement of the global international monetary system. These differences are related to but do not clearly fall in the classic Keynesian-Austrian divide.

Overall, this chapter will try to address the following questions:

- At a high level, how do German and French economic philosophies and traditions differ?
- Are these differences written in stone or do the economic traditions evolve or even switch sides over time?
- What events shaped the economic traditions? What role did academic economists, leading newspaper writers and political figures play?
- How do French and German views differ with regard to the international monetary system? When facing the same trade-offs, do both countries choose the same outcome?

Fluid Traditions: Switch to Opposites

In the nineteenth and for the first half of the twentieth century, France could generally be characterized as dominated by economic liberalism (in the European sense) and Germany as largely statist. Then, quite abruptly, after 1945 the pattern reversed.

Nineteenth-century France had an economic philosophy largely dominated by laissez-faire, as brilliantly expounded by Frédéric Bastiat and Jean-Baptiste Say, while German thinkers elevated the state as the major economic actor. In both countries, there was always a back and forth. But the older traditions have been largely forgotten, to the extent that a recent guide on "how the French think" includes no reference to liberalism, Bastiat, or Say, but simply focuses on French étatisme and planisme.[1]

The great French classical liberals were reacting against the powerful legacy of Louis XIV's powerful finance minister Jean-Baptist Colbert as well as against abusive manipulation of money. As Louis XIV's wars produced increased economic misery, and after the death of Colbert, an alternative liberal tradition developed. Indeed, the Jansenist theologian Pierre Nicole has a strong claim to have been the first modern figure to explain that, in the world of fallen humanity, social well-being depended on mechanisms that harnessed man's self-interest and not his benevolence. His 1670 tract on *The Education of a Prince* explained that "Cupidity takes the place of charity to fill human needs, and it does this in a way that is not sufficiently admired, and that charity could not arrive at."[2] This was the worldview of Adam Smith, derived from a theological foundation. The antiliberal view powerfully reasserted itself in very destructive ways, notably, during the bubble unleashed by the Scottish adventurer John Law, who wanted to destroy competition through a new system to "combine the competing interests and make the nation wealthier."[3] By the nineteenth century, liberalism in France had clear enemies: the monetary and inflationary abuses of Law along with the paper money (*assignat*) financing of the French Revolution.

At the same time, German economists developed *Staatswissenschaft*, in which state authority solved collective-action issues and then applied that philosophy to an increasing range of economic and social problems. German liberal thinkers had in the early nineteenth century developed the idea of *rule of law* in a state formed by right (*Rechtsstaat*), and there was an alternative tradition of thinking about rules as the characteristic component of the well-ordered state. The term *Rechtsstaat* was popularized by Carl Theodor Welcker (1790–1869), a lawyer and member of the 1848 Frankfurt National Assembly, and by Robert von Mohl (1799–1875), another lawyer, in his 1844 treatise *The Science of Policy According to the Principles of the Constitutional State*. Then, however, a reaction set in, and Bismarck's political practice eroded the principles of a legally ordered constitutional state.[4] There were a few German Smithians, and Germans invented the concept of *Smithianismus*. For the most part, British thinking was dismissed as *Manchesterism*, a form of materialism devised by the cotton masters. One example is Friedrich List's famous criticism, largely unnoticed during his life, of British free-trade economics as a cynical device for ensuring that Great Britain retained preeminence while trade openness kicked the ladder away for other countries that may want to climb up to advanced industrialism. The German school had a strong interest in institutional design and in the use of institutions to tweak policy in a desirable outcome. Adolph Wagner formulated a "law of increasing state spending" (which he saw as an accompaniment of modernization), and he and his colleagues—notably Gustav Schmoller and later Werner Sombart— acquired a reputation as leftists, or *Kathedersozialisten*. In the 1930s, a brilliant French economist, François Perroux, produced an analysis of the contrast between French and German thinking, by noting that "the greatest danger lies when the two partners do not speak the same language and have different intellectual and moral values." In particular, he believed that France insisted on rules and contracts, while Germany had a feudal sense of good faith that was personalized and "mocked contracts and signatures." "The German does not have like us the sense of the permanent and absolute value of the contract."[5]

Perroux's depiction of a strict French insistence on contracts and their enforcement and a personalistic German orientation appears exactly the opposite of modern stereotypes. So it appears that German and French economic thought flipped sides from the nineteenth to the late twentieth century: the Germans moved to more economic liberalism, while the French retreated.

Both the old traditions in both countries were discredited as a consequence of the political catastrophes of the mid-twentieth century. The extent of the catastrophe, on both sides of the Rhine, indicated the necessity of a basic change of course. German writers could see how the prominent role accorded to the state in traditional economic theories might have favored Nazi etatism. By contrast, younger French thinkers blamed the do-nothing noninterventionism of the traditional liberal school for sluggish economic growth, but also specifically for fiscal austerity and consequently the failure to coordinate a viable defense economy in the 1930s. Thus, after World War II, France reacted against old-style laissez-faire and emphasized the desirability of systematic planning, and Germans recoiled from the idea of the state because its actions were arbitrary.

Of course, interest as well as ideology or institutions may have played a role in making the intellectual or ideological reversal in national thinking. But it is worth pointing out that the switch in attitudes between Germany and France cannot simply be explained by their net debtor or creditor positions. Germany, it is true, was a big debtor in the interwar period, with large current account deficits and capital inflows in the 1920s, when it was mostly in favor of debt cancellation and also ran two large inflation episodes; but it was a creditor in the nineteenth century, when the statist orientation originally evolved. France had substantial current account surpluses from 1992 to 2004.

German Economic Tradition

Hayek's Critique of a Planned Economy

The most far-ranging critic of the German or Central European model of etatism was Friedrich Hayek, an Austrian who mostly worked in the United Kingdom but toward the end of his life settled in Freiburg, in Southwestern Germany. He was largely without political influence until the 1970s. Hayek accurately identified that the interventionist approach of the Weimar Republic (which had its origins in wartime planning) created a sort of path dependency, in which the answer to failure was not an abandonment of the approach but rather a more radical version. In *The Road to Serfdom*, Friedrich Hayek asserted that Walter Rathenau, the intellectual who devised Germany's innovative planning regime of World War I, "would have shuddered had he realised the consequences of his totalitarian economics" but nevertheless "deserves a considerable place in any fuller history of the growth of Nazi ideas. Through his writings he has probably, more than any other man, determined the economic views of the generation which grew up in Germany during and immediately after the last war; and some of his closest collaborators were later to form the backbone of the staff of Goering's Five Year Plan [sic] administration."[6] Partial controls looked ineffective, so the Nazis wanted more extensive and radically enforced control. Rathenau's major collaborator, Wichard von Moellendorff, formulated his view of a new communal economy, or *Gemeinwirtschaft*, provocatively and concisely: "Up to now in Germany the principle reined: free in economic matters, constrained in intellectual and spiritual affairs. The purpose of *Gemeinwirtschaft* is to turn that upside down."[7] In practice, however, the experience of interwar Germany showed that economic constraints also contributed to the erosion of intellectual, spiritual, and political freedoms.

A widespread response to the great financial crisis of 1931 was the imposition of capital controls, which brought the state further into the micromanagement of economic activity. Economic planning, as Hayek recognized, was inherently discriminatory: "It cannot tie itself down in advance to general and formal rules which prevent arbitrariness. . . . It must constantly decide questions which cannot be answered by formal principles only, and in making these decisions it must set up distinctions of merit between the needs of different people."[8] The issue of arbitrariness applies in a particular way to the actual implementation of capital controls. They were implemented in both Austria and Germany from 1931, that is, before the onset of the political dictatorship (Hitler came to power in January 1933, and Austrian conservatives created the reactionary corporate state, or *Ständestaat*, in 1934). But the dictatorship provided more means of enforcing controls. Hayek cites the German liberal thinker Wilhelm Röpke, to the effect that "while the last resort of a competitive economy is the bailiff, the ultimate sanction of the planned economy is the hangman."[9] Hayek might actually, if he had at the time known Hitler's table talk, have cited the musings of the dictator himself: "Inflation does not arise when money enters circulation, but only when the individual demands more money for the same service. Here we must intervene. That is what I had to explain to Schacht [the president of the Nazi central bank], that the first cause of the stability of our currency is the concentration camp."[10]

The decision on who should benefit from the allocation of foreign exchange became political and arbitrary. The institution invited a political process of rent-seeking, and it was those who could develop the closest contacts with the regime who benefited most. The allocation of scarce raw materials was in fact the basis of Nazi economic planning and also an initial instrument in the application of anti-Semitism: Jews were discriminated against as far as access to imports of raw materials, and their businesses suffered as a result.

Ordoliberalism

A softer version of the Hayekian critique of the old German tradition was deeply influential in Germany and had a major political impact. Known as *Ordo-Liberalismus* (or sometimes as the Freiburg School), and chiefly expounded by Röpke and Walter Eucken, it developed the emphasis on the state that was characteristic of the old German historical school, but altered the emphasis. According to the new doctrine, rules needed to be formulated in general terms and the state's actions should be confined to the enforcement of such general laws, for instance, the laws on competition and against cartels, which had been an important part of the older German tradition of business management. Unlike Hayek, who more and more insisted on the spontaneous creation of order and rules, the Ordoliberals emphasized the need for an initial elaboration of an appropriate framework.

Their vision of order includes both a system of general rules and a mechanism by which those rules define the liability (or responsibility) of individuals, and of economic agents. The system fundamentally depends on the accountability of market participants. Any measure that limits accountability or responsibility by promising some sort of contingent rescue would create destructive incentives that would lead to the accumulation of unfulfillable expectations on behalf of the economic actors and unfulfillable liabilities on the part of the government as the ultimate insurer. As a consequence, Ordoliberals worried greatly about *moral hazard*, a term taken from insurance (a well-insured person may not take sufficient care that his house does not burn down). On these grounds, the Freiburg School and its modern successors even worry about the limited liability principle for corporations. "Unlimited liability is part of a competitive system," Walter Eucken wrote. In his eyes, the problem was that the development of the legal system and the increased complexity of laws tend to subvert the liability principle: "Its destruction by legal policy endangers the functioning of this system."[11] So too many, and too complicated, laws would breed moral hazard, and the economic agents are given incentives to game the system.

The antitrust thinking of the new German economists also meshed well with the thinking of the US military administration. General Lucius Clay, the military governor, liked to sum up American goals for the postwar German order as the four Ds: denazification, demilitarization, democratization, and decartelization. The critical document for the initial postwar occupation policy, JCS 1067 of April 26, 1945, required the prohibition of "all cartels or other private business arrangements and cartel like organizations."[12] One of the German Ordoliberals, Franz Böhm, wrote that there was "no influential and socially strong group" supporting competition "excepting the American occupation authorities."[13]

Competition law thus became a crucial part of the new German philosophy and, as advanced by Walter Hallstein, the German economist and civil servant who became the first president of the European Commission, also of European law. Ludwig Erhard, the economics minister who pushed Germany's liberalization program, made the link between competition policy and European priorities explicit. In 1952, at the launching of the European Coal and Steel Community, he stated, "We plan to create a common European market. The aim is incompatible with a system of national or international cartels. If we want to create a higher standard of living through technical progress, rationalization, and an increase in production, we have to be against cartels."[14]

The resulting vision did not completely remove the state. The Freiburg economists and also Erhard saw their ideal as a middle path between the extremes of an unregulated free market and unlimited state command, and some other economists, notably Alfred Müller-Armack, spoke of a social market economy (*soziale Marktwirtschaft*). Walter Eucken formulated the philosophy of the Freiburg School as follows: "A genuine, equitable, and smoothly functioning competitive system cannot in fact survive without a judicious moral and legal framework and without regular supervision of the conditions under which competition can take place pursuant to real efficiency principles. This presupposes mature economic discernment on the part of all responsible bodies and individuals and a strong impartial state."[15]

The German position always remained somewhat ambivalent, and the middle way could oscillate. The rejection of the past was not as extreme as it appeared in some of the Ordoliberal manifestos. Indeed, the economic historian Albrecht Ritschl has argued (controversially) that a large part of the distinctively German and rather corporatist approach to the state-business relationship was inherited from the Nazi era.[16]

ORDOLIBERALISM IN TODAY'S GERMANY

In the 1960s, the German model incorporated a good deal of Keynesianism, reaching a high point in 1967 with the Law on Stability and Growth. But even the way that German Keynesianism was formulated in terms of a foundation of stability—or a rule-based order—was very characteristic of the German tradition. In addition, in academic economics, Ordoliberalism ceased to be the prevalent tradition and was largely replaced by a US-style neoclassical synthesis. There is virtually no serious academic economist who would today describe himself as an Ordoliberal (and indeed no female academic Ordoliberal); most modern Ordoliberal academics are lawyers rather than economists. Hans-Werner Sinn, one of Germany's most publicly prominent economists, is often portrayed by outsiders as an extreme case of the German obsession with moral hazard issues, and at his retirement, the conservative Bavarian minister president Horst Seehofer celebrated him as a "Great Ordo-liberal" (which he distinguished from "narrow neo-liberals" and Milton Friedman's "Chicago boys"); but Sinn himself instead tries to present himself as simply a classical economist.

Some Ordoliberalism survived in think tanks and in the economic research institutes that are a feature of the German intellectual landscape and constitute a bridge between academia and politics. In particular, the Hamburg Weltwirtschaftsinstitut and the Cologne Institut der Deutschen Wirtschaft have been quite consistently Ordoliberal in outlook, while the Berlin German Institute for Economic Research (DIW) has long been Keynesian. The German Council of Economic Experts (*Sachverständigenrat*), which was set up by Ludwig Erhard in 1963, and which is intended to inform and educate the public rather than specifically to advise the government, often thinks of itself as emphasizing microeconomic foundations rather than macroeconomic interventionism and sees itself as embodying the legacy of Ordoliberalism.[17] But in general, Ordoliberalism has a bad reputation, especially outside Germany, with the *Financial Times* journalist Wolfgang Münchau excoriating "the wacky economics of Germany's parallel universe": "German economists," as he put it, "roughly fall into two groups: those that have not read Keynes, and those that have not understood Keynes."[18] It would indeed be peculiar if a whole country fell prey to a collective ideological imbecilism.

The traditions of the postwar era certainly exercise a substantial, almost subconscious, appeal to many Germans, and especially to German policy makers in the Bundesbank and perhaps also the Finance Ministry. It is also conspicuously represented in the economics pages of the major German newspaper the *Frankfurter Allgemeine Zeitung* (*FAZ*) and powerfully reinforced by the fundamentally even more liberal Swiss newspaper *Neue Zürcher Zeitung*. The *FAZ* is generally considered to be moderately right of center, but even the moderately left *Süddeutsche Zeitung* devotes space to the German economic tradition. In particular, since 2009, both these large German newspapers have worried about the moral hazard implications of euro rescue measures. Those traditions represent what Keynes famously called "the gradual encroachment of ideas" that rendered politicians and practical men as "slaves of some defunct economist." As the Bundesbank had a major input in the design of the European monetary union, some commentators speak of the "Ordoliberalization of Europe."[19]

But there is also something of a political pushback against the residues of Ordoliberalism. German officials in some Berlin ministries like to voice their dissent from alleged "fundamentalists" in the Bundesbank.[20] The government also started to distance itself from the Council of Economic Advisers, complaining that the economists there were too dogmatic and inflexible and were looking "too much through German spectacles" and to taking into account the weakness of demand in peripheral Europe. The Social Democratic Party (SPD) economics minister Sigmar Gabriel pointedly delayed supporting the renomination of the chairman of the economic advisers, Christoph Schmidt. The council had provoked the government by criticizing many of the policies of the coalition government and demanding a return to more Erhard-style market-friendly policies. The SPD's general secretary complained that the council was proceeding in an unscientific way.[21]

In the course of the euro debt crisis, German critics of the euro and the various rescue packages and measures liked to present themselves as the voice of the economics profession. "Economics professors" in Germany came to have a sort of ideological definition. They were the five professors who conducted a complaint against the Greek rescue package in 2009 (Wilhelm Hankel, Wilhelm Nölling, Karl Albrecht Schachtschneider, Dieter Spethmann, and Joachim Starbatty—only one of these was really an academic professor of economics, and he was retired).[22] They were the 172 professors who in July 2012 signed a letter to the *FAZ* attacking the banking union plan.[23] Or another group of five who together with other groups and with over 37,000 individual complainants organized by the Left Party in 2012 launched a constitutional complaint against ECB bond purchases.[24] The phenomenon of economics professors even eventually appeared as a new political party: Bernd Lucke (an economics professor from Hamburg) and Konrad Adam (a retired *FAZ* journalist) formed an anti-euro protest party, the Alternative für Deutschland (AfD), which polled surprisingly strongly in the European Parliament elections of 2014. These organized mobilizations of economics professors were not truly representative of the economics profession in Germany, but they wanted to give the impression that they were. Later, the economic professors were forced out of the AfD, which turned in a radical right direction.

Ordoliberalism in a European Context

The lineage from the Ordoliberals of the immediate postwar era to the modern politics of the euro does not only run in a solely German, or national, direction. Some of the background to the reversal of the German stance from etatism to an assertion of the liberal principles of economics occurred on a European level. One of the most interesting attempts to promote new economic thinking on a European level took place in Paris in August 1938. Twenty-six economists and other intellectuals, from all over Europe, had been summoned by the French philosopher Louis Rougier to discuss Walter Lippmann's 1937 book *The Good Society*. In that book, Lippmann had defended political and economic liberalism in the face of a rising worldwide tide of illiberal antiparliamentary movements based on centralized economic planning: communism, fascism, National Socialism. The meeting included two figures who would be prominent in developing the German approach to Ordoliberalism, Wilhelm Röpke and Alexander Rüstow, although interestingly (and characteristically in the light of the historical moment) none of the participants were described as German: Rüstow was described as coming from Turkey, where he lived in exile, and Röpke as "école autrichienne, Austrian school," along with Ludwig von Mises. Some of the most influential postwar French economic figures participated, Jacques Rueff, Raymond Aron, and Robert Marjolin.[25]

After 1945, the development of the European Union lends itself to the kind of analysis that the Ordoliberal school undertook immediately after World War II of the problem of the proliferation of rules and the tendency to augment or even replace general laws with particular decrees. Designed on Ordoliberal principles, as Bundesbank president Jens Weidmann recently pointed out, because of the need to observe rules in a federal setting, the European Union is vulnerable as a result of the ever more complex rules that after the financial crisis seem necessary to ensure its functioning.[26] As Eucken warned, the elaboration of such detailed rules opens the way to the assertion of particular interests and the undermining of the collective project.

The elements of the German economic intellectual tradition can be summed up as follows:

1. A focus on the legal, moral, and political foundation of free markets in agreed rules, which may be treaties or laws or also common or shared understandings.[27]

2. A strong emphasis on responsibility and accountability. Participants in the market and those in the political process both have a responsibility. For market participants, the responsibility is a financial one—they need to pay the price of failure; politicians are accountable to voters. In short, as a Bundesbank official recently put it, those who have control and take risks also need to face the consequences of their actions.[28]

3. A concern with the potential for moral hazard arising out of lender of last resort activities. The IMF package for Mexico in 1994–5 was heavily criticized by German officials as encouraging reckless behavior on financial markets by increasing the likelihood of future rescue operations.

4. A concern that lender of last resort (LLR) action may corrupt or pollute monetary policy, because a central bank that has an LLR obligation might be force to give financial sector stability priority over price stability.

5. A belief that firm or binding rules are needed to shield monetary policy from fiscal dominance, namely, the view that government, by raising the permanent level of expenditures without at the same time raising taxes, can affect the current and future flows of the monetary base and, hence, of the money stock and of the inflation rate.[29]

6. A strict approach to government debt and to debt ceilings. Germany pioneered an approach that it now proposes to Europeanize, with a 2009 law mandating a deficit limit at the federal level

of 0.35 percent of GDP by 2016 and an elimination of deficits for states by 2020. German think tanks like the idea of a Europeanization of fiscal rules enforced by some sort of fiscal or debt council.[30]

7. Growth is not achieved by the provision of additional money or resources but by structural reforms.[31] Additional money is a sort of trickery, doomed to failure, and analogous to trying to pull yourself out of a swamp by pulling on your bootstraps.

8. A belief that present virtue—or austerity—is rewarded by future benefits.

French Economic Tradition

France too began the postwar era by rejecting the economic orthodoxies of its past and by seeking to Europeanize its new priorities. The economist and economic historian Alfred Sauvy characterized the old economics, which emphasized the limitations on government action, as contributing to "Malthusianism," low growth and stagnation. Low growth and stagnation had weakened France politically, socially, and also militarily. The obsession with balanced budgets had led to a cutting of defense expenditures that made France more vulnerable. The architect of the "super-deflation" of the 1930s, Pierre Laval, was also the man who after 1940 went furthest in the political compromise with Hitler. Malthusianism thus was held to bear the ultimate responsibility for the military collapse of 1940 and the end of the French Republic.

Part of the Malthusian picture had been French unwillingness to take John Maynard Keynes seriously. Keynes was not a popular figure in France, doubtless because of his well-known criticism of the 1919 Versailles Treaty, and in pre-1940 French debates, the role of the state was not seen primarily in terms of macroeconomic stimulus. The new postwar French alternative to Malthusianism particularly emphasized the need for the state to coordinate and plan investment. An unplanned or spontaneous market order was likely to lead to underinvestment and low growth. There was thus a need for *planisme*.

The new concern always sat uneasily with many of the views of the most prominent French economists. Jacques Rueff had gone to London with General de Gaulle but remained an advocate of an enlightened liberalism as well as of monetary orthodoxy: he pleaded continually for a version of the gold standard. The later Nobel Prize laureate Maurice Allais made his reputation with a 1943 book, *A la Recherche d'une Discipline Economique. L'Economie Pure*, in which he sought to find a solution to "the fundamental problem of any economy": how to promote the greatest feasible economic efficiency while ensuring a distribution of income that would be generally acceptable. Though it is sometimes claimed that Allais's approach to capital and time preference laid the foundations for subsequent planning, he always considered himself an economic liberal. He attended the first meeting of the Mont Pélerin Society in 1947, and though he refused to sign the Statement of Aims, he wrote to Hayek that he wished to express his "profound agreement with economic and political liberty." His dissent was based on the view that land should be held as national property: in every other respect, he was a classical liberal.[32]

The Influence of Engineering

The new French tradition had its roots not so much in high thought, in the works of France's most prominent economists, but rather in the work of practical economists who were trained in institutions that had been conceived as oriented toward the service of the state. Allais in fact had begun as an engineer trained at the École Polytechnique. The strength of that engineering tradition is the basis of the conclusion of the sociologist Marion Fourcade that "French economists hold more favorable attitudes toward state intervention than practitioners in other advanced industrialized countries." Among French economic practitioners occurred a confluence of "a 'sociological' tradition, which affirmed the need for economists to look for the human act behind any economic phenomenon," with "a financial technocracy in the form of the Inspection des Finances, as well as various specialized elite corps (Mines, Ponts) in the interests of orchestrating the development of key industries."[33]

That tradition went back a long way. The Corps des ponts et chaussées (Corps of Bridges and Roads) had been set up in 1716 and organized as a school in 1775. The original intention was to provide an accurate mapping system so as to allow the construction of a national road network for the whole of France. In 1794, a parallel École Polytechnique was established to train "national engineers." A third mining school (École des Mines) had been founded in 1783. The products of these schools pushed for elaborate and unified transportation, communications, and eventually also energy transmission systems. They made roads in the eighteenth century, canals and railroads in the nineteenth century, and electricity grids and high-speed train networks in the twentieth century. They habitually disdained economic calculation in realizing their technical vision.

Critics observed that the schools were proud of their complete ignorance of the economic principles of diminishing marginal utility and the time value of capital.[34] The French planning tradition achieved a new momentum in wars: in World War I, when Etienne Clémentel and Ernest Mercier tried to imitate the German war planning approach of Rathenau, and again in World War II. Some historians have consequently argued that the planning approach that dominated the post-1945 Republic was already evolved under the collaborationist wartime Vichy regime of Marshall Philippe Pétain.

Even the brief narrative of the evolution of the French planning tradition makes it clear how much interaction there was with Germany. Frederick the Great in Prussia admired French economic planning methods and tried to promote similar developments. He imported technicians and engineers from France and England. So did other German states, with a famous mining school founded in Freiberg (Saxony) in 1765. The École Polytechnique found many imitators in Germany, from the Technische Hochschule in Karlsruhe (1825) onward. Indeed, Germany came to be more widely regarded as the best practice model of technical education.

Past Liberal Tradition: Say and Bastiat

The practical economists or technicians who were produced by the corps and polytechnics were not major economic theoreticians. The theoreticians on the other hand were classical economic liberals. The nineteenth century in France was intellectually dominated by a passionately articulated economic liberalism, with Jean-Baptiste Say (1767–1832) arguing immediately after the French Revolution in his *Treatise on Political Economy* (1803) that it was a "gross fallacy" and "productive of infinite mischief" that "what government and its agents receive, is refunded again by their expenditure." He went on to establish Say's Law: "Supply creates its own demand."[35] The journalist Frédéric Bastiat (1801–1850) became probably the most brilliant expositor of the principles of laissez-faire and the denouncer of the fallacies of protectionism. He radiated an indelible optimism about the beneficence of economic processes. In his last pamphlet, in the aftermath of the 1848 revolution, he concluded that "legislators and do-gooders [should] reject all systems, and try liberty."[36] Later, those principles of liberal economics were magisterially expounded by Paul Leroy-Beaulieu at the new School of Political Science (Sciences Po) and then at the Collège de France. The liberal tradition of economics had in part evolved—and Sciences Po founded—as an explicit counterweight to the engineering or technocratic vision presented by the graduates of the professional schools.

Planning

The first "Monnet plan" was already formulated in 1946. Heavy industry and especially steel figured prominently in the national investment plans, and individual businessmen were frightened of appearing as laggards or saboteurs. The result was massive investment and quick expansion. The government was obsessed with targets of production: growing more quickly than German steel and warding off the new and threatening Italian challenge to its industrial strategy. The political scientist Jack Hayward terms the French steel complex one of "industrial patriotism."[37] The French political class saw big steel mills as modern cathedrals that gave expression to a national revival, "redressement national." The chief architect of France's postwar plan, the banker and visionary of European unity Jean Monnet, in Gaullist language, called for "*une politique de grandeur pour l'acier*," and indeed he saw some mechanism for extending French control over the continental European steel industry as key to postwar political stability.[38]

Technological specialists would bring France out of stagnation.[39] In the immediate aftermath of the war, there was an intense discussion of nationalization as a way of raising production. The old Colbertist tradition of a state-guided economy was augmented by admiration for the achievements of Soviet planning. French policy makers believed the Soviet Union had both avoided the Great Depression of the 1930s and won the war because of planning. There was an additional moral aspect of this question, a biblical conversion of swords into plowshares: as the left-wing Force Ouvrière argued, "What had made war should now serve peace."[40] Gigantism itself was sometimes also presented as a response to the new German challenge: *Le Figaro*, for instance, in 1956, in a gloriously mixed metaphor referred to a "steel fever on the other side of the Rhine in which France should not let herself be outpaced."[41] Rueff compared the idea of planning to the author Edmond Rostand's depiction of the famous cockerel, Chantecler, who believed that the sun rose each morning because he crowed.

Such initiatives at the European Recovery Program (or Marshall Plan) helped to establish a general idea that planning might transform the whole European business structure. What the historian Charles Maier termed the "politics of productivity" demanded a new relationship with labor, which would be mediated through the state.[42] For steel and coal, planning was given a European context by the Schuman plan and the establishment of the European Coal and Steel Community (ECSC). France also Europeanized its preference structure, and many political figures saw the primary desideratum as the establishment of a mechanism for economic governance that allowed Europe to undertake the same coordination as French policy makers had managed to apply on a national level.

The highest achievements of the French tradition were seen in the coordinated nuclear power network built up by Electricité de France and also in some spectacular examples of ingenious but ultimately failed technology. In civilian aerospace, France built the first short- and medium-range passenger jet aircraft, the Caravelle, in the mid-1950s, and then in the 1960s, the supersonic aircraft project that resulted in the beautiful and fast but not commercially viable Concorde. In 1978, Frances's telephone company launched Minitel, a sort of predecessor of the Internet, with online videotext linked to commercial applications. France's high-speed train system, the TGV, launched in 1981, was unique in Europe and only emulated much later by Italy, Spain, and Germany—with the United Kingdom still contemplating such a move.

The aura around France's attachment to the plan as an instrument of national revival lasted a long time. France's planning institution, the Commissariat Général au Plan, existed until 2006, when it was renamed the Center for Strategic Analysis, which in 2013 was renamed the Commissariat général à la stratégie et à la prospective (CGSP). There had already been an attempt to transform the institution in the mid-1980s, but it had been vigorously resisted. At that time, Pierre Massé, an engineer from the École des Ponts et Chaussées and the principal architect of planning in the 1960s, who was also a disciple of the public pricing principles elaborated by Maurice Allais, had complained that "suppressing the plan in the name of an impulsive liberalism would be giving up the major weapon in the struggle against the dictatorship of the short term."[43]

Aspects of the older tradition remained in one area: the argument that currency stability was an important objective of policy and that something like the gold standard was a desirable international discipline had a powerful appeal. This case had been brilliantly and persuasively made by Jacques Rueff, who emerged as the economic guru for General de Gaulle; but it was also taken up by the left quite enthusiastically, above all because it could be mounted as a critique of the United States and the manipulation of the dollar in the Bretton Woods era in the interests of American foreign policy. We deal with the international economic aspects of French thinking in the last part of this chapter.

Contemporanous Economic Thinking in France

As in Germany, most modern French economists have largely moved away from the traditional concerns of both nineteenth-century liberal economists and postwar French politics with planning growth and with dirigisme. Indeed, French academics have made a decisive contribution to the literature on time consistency and the consequent significance of the correct formulation of rules. In that sense, they have done more than the German Ordoliberals to present a version of a system of rules that is really applicable to the complexities of a modern economy, in which competition is not an obvious result of economic activity. Jean Tirole and Jean-Jacques Laffont in particular have been instrumental in developing a new approach to the provision of incentives by regulators, in which the dangers of creating moral hazard play a key role.[44]

The visions of the past influence the way that economics is seen. Most French economists complain—as did the recent best-selling author Thomas Piketty of *Capital*, a dramatic manifesto on how capitalism does not provide a self-sustaining and politically acceptable model of growth—that "economists are not highly respected in the academic and intellectual world or by political and financial elites."[45] In fact, a popular and intellectual culture exists that sees economists as narrow-minded and soulless technocrats who force a dehumanized concept of rationality on their fellow citizens. Raymond Barre, a European commissioner who then became prime minister from 1976 to 1981, was lauded by the president at the time, Valéry Giscard d'Estaing, as "the best economist of France."[46] But "economist" was a dirty word. As the late 1970s were a time of increased inflation and unemployment, the end of the postwar euphoria of *les trentes glorieuses*, and a period of general disenchantment with the political elites that had until then managed the Third Republic, the concept of economist as ruler looked sinister rather than beneficent. In the 1990s, another economist finance minister, Dominique Strauss-Kahn, also attracted more criticism than praise. A dissident economist who saw himself in the left-wing, critical, and above all political tradition, Jacques Sapir, complained that economists were undermining democracy.[47] Bernard Maris, the journalist and economist who was tragically killed in the terrorist attack on the satirical magazine *Charlie Hebdo*, concluded, "What were economists for, one will ask a hundred years from now? To make people laugh."[48]

That kind of critique sat well with a country that was increasingly obsessed with the parallel stories of national decline and triumphant globalization. The approach of modern mainstream French economists does not translate well into the policy debate, which is still dominated by the older and rather eclectic visions of how an economy functions. In general, The French press—notably *Le Monde*—is committed to the attractions of interventionism. French politicians from every part of the spectrum denounce neoliberalism (though this term was born in Paris in 1938 in the Rougier-Lippmann seminar). Jacques Chirac denounced "Anglo-Saxon ultraliberalism." Sarkozy criticized "Anglo-Saxon Europe, that of the big market"[49] and repeatedly said that it was his mission to assert the values of French and European humanism as an alternative to the international economic system. A powerful statement of the world of French thought—which was presented as a revolution against traditional Anglo-Saxon economics—was the report of a commission called by Sarkozy and cochaired by Jean-Paul Fitoussi (along with two distinguished but left-leaning non-French Nobel Prize winners, Joseph Stiglitz and Amartya Sen), in which the central role of government in the economy was emphasized and a plea made for a more extensive assessment of the role of "well-being."[50]

Even economists like to participate in the backlash against modern economics. Distinguished (and numerate) figures such as Edmond Malinvaud and Thomas Piketty complain about the overmathematization of economics. The same sort of public mobilization of economists for a political cause that took place in Germany against rescue packages occurred in

France against the German doctrines and against austerity politics. In September 2010, over 700 French economists signed a widely publicized manifesto for "an alternative economic and social strategy" for Europe, attacking the "false economic platitudes" of "neoliberal dogma."[51] The manifesto was drawn up by four economists, three of whom worked at governmental research institutes, and the fourth was an adviser to the antiglobalization organization Attac.

The modern French consensus that presidents and economics professors alike shared may be summarized as follows:

1. Rules should be subject to the political process and may be renegotiated.
2. Crisis management requires a flexible response.
3. Constraining the freedom of government to act—and to borrow— would be undemocratic.
4. Monetary policy needs to be used to serve more general goals than simply price stability, such as being concerned with economic growth.
5. The lessons of the Great Depression include the principle that adjustment to international imbalances should be undertaken symmetrically, with surplus countries doing their part.
6. As multiple equilibria are possible, choosing an unpleasant trajectory for the present is likely to perpetuate rather than remove constraints on growth.
7. Present virtue is self-contradictory and self-defeating.

International Economics

Another important dimension of economic thinking along which the German and French philosophies differ markedly is international economic relations, in particular as regards cross-border capital flows. These disagreements also flared up during the negotiations preceding the ratification of the Maastricht Treaty in 1992. The German philosophy calls for free trade, fair (or undistorted) competition, and open international capital markets. Capital controls were considered as arbitrary, favoring certain industries, and inviting political lobbying. Thus, a world in which exchange rates are free to move, in which no coordinated multilateral interventions are necessary to deal with macroeconomic shocks, and in which capital can flow freely is very much in keeping with the German tradition. The French philosophy, in contrast, is much closer to the original Keynesian position (evolved as a response to the Great Depression) of fixing exchange rates, controlling capital flows, and fostering multilateral adjustment via inflationary policies in surplus countries.

Trilemma

A useful organizing principle for a discussion of these philosophical differences is the trilemma of international macroeconomics. Basically, this trilemma states that an economy cannot simultaneously have a fixed exchange rate, an independent monetary policy, and allow capital to flow freely; it must pick two out of three (figure 4.1). What kind of arrangement a country ultimately chooses has profound implications for its ability to deal with and adjust to adverse macroeconomic shocks. The German and French philosophies differ notably in their attitudes toward the desirability of capital flows—is one of the apparently desirable goals at the heart of the trilemma actually a desideratum?—and in how different economies, especially those linked together via some kind of exchange rate mechanism, should respond to asymmetric shocks.

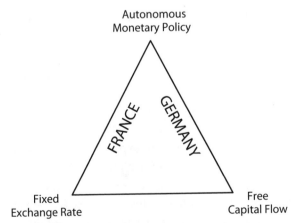

FIGURE 4.1. Trilemma Depicted as a Triangle

Theoretically, the trilemma tells us that we have to pick one side of the triangle. Practically, Germans picked the capital flow side, while the French had a preference for fixed exchange rates. Along many dimensions, this trilemma is of course a simplification. In practice, as scholars investigating the exchange rate trilemma demonstrated, it is empirically hard to determine a pure policy stance in the trilemma: there are varying degrees of commitment to a fixed exchange rate regime, varying degrees of openness to international capital, and varying extents of monetary autonomy.[52] In practice, there are thus almost no cases where policy is positioned so as to fully abandon one corner of the trilemma, and practical policy stances fall somewhat in between the corner positions. The corners simply represent the boundaries of the possible. The discussion of the trilemma thus serves as a Weberian ideal type rather than an exposition of the world as it actually is.[53] But France and Germany tugged to be in different parts of the triangle.

Economists and policy makers alike have paid special attention to countries with debt issued in a foreign currency, and this was an issue that became a central component of the euro crisis. The fact that debt has to be serviced in a foreign currency puts a substantial constraint on monetary policy freedom, even in a world with floating exchange rates and freely flowing capital. Still, the trilemma is useful as a first-pass organizing device, and history provides us with numerous useful examples of how the underlying trade-offs were resolved in the past.

Gold Standard

The gold standard was the dominant international exchange rate system between the mid-nineteenth century and the early to mid-twentieth century, and many modern commentators make analogies between the gold standard and the European currency union, in that both suppressed the autonomy of monetary policy. Under the gold standard arrangement, the central bank of every participating country must stand ready to exchange its currency for gold at some fixed ratio. How do economies in this system deal with asymmetric shocks, say an expansionary demand shock for one country and a contractionary one for another? The answer is the famous price-specie flow mechanism. In a system with gold backing, trade naturally leads to a flow of gold into surplus countries. As long as central banks in the surplus countries do not sterilize the gold inflows, prices will be pushed up. The opposite happens in deficit countries, and so imbalances tend to auto-correct. In a world where trade deficits can be financed via credit extended from surplus to deficit countries, however, this mechanism does not work anymore as there is no compulsion to adjust. Explicit policy interventions are thus needed to move the price levels in the desired directions. This important caveat illustrates well the importance of capital flow considerations in the analysis of international monetary arrangements.

Bretton Woods

After World War II, the gold standard was succeeded by the Bretton Woods system, a system of fixed exchange rates (with occasional realignments) and constraints on capital flows that was explicitly designed to give more monetary policy autonomy. At the heart of this system was the US dollar as its leading currency. All currencies were fixed against the dollar, and the dollar itself traded at a fixed rate against gold. This system was clearly closer to the French than to the German ideal. But France did not like the extent to which it relied on the US dollar, and General de Gaulle famously tried to revive gold as an alternative. Greatly influenced by the economist Jacques Rueff, de Gaulle had repeatedly insisted that a genuine gold standard would work better than the mixed gold-dollar system of the Bretton Woods regime.

The Bretton Woods regime allowed for occasional realignments, but still—as in any fixed exchange rate system—the adjustment problem always loomed large. Tensions particularly rose in the later stages of the Bretton Woods system, especially in the later 1960s, as Germany increasingly built up trade surpluses that reflected a favorable development of productivity gains as well as the containment of wage costs through a collaborative and collective approach to wage setting. (Trade surpluses would become the hallmark of late twentieth-century German-style capitalism.) By contrast, deficits in Germany's trade partners reflected either lower innovation or (especially in late 1960s France and Italy) a less disciplined approach to wages in an era of full employment and increased social and political radicalism (reflected in large numbers of days lost in strikes).

At the beginning, in the era of fixed exchange rates and controlled capital markets, even relatively small deficits could not be financed, and they produced immediate pressure on the exchange markets. The deficit countries then had to apply fiscal brakes in a stop-go cycle. Germany's partners, notably France, were faced with the prospect of austerity and deflation to correct deficits. This alternative was unattractive to the French political elite because it constrained growth and guaranteed electoral unpopularity. Their preferred policy alternative was thus German expansion, but this course was unpopular with a German public worried about the legacy of inflation and was opposed by the powerful and independent central bank, the Deutsche Bundesbank. Solving the question of the German current accounts in the European setting at first appeared to require some sophisticated political mechanism, and also public debate, that would force French politicians to undertake more austerity than they would have liked and Germans less price orthodoxy than they thought they needed.

By the early 1970s, capital flows had become so large, and the system so unstable, that an answer needed to be found. Again, the German view was that capital flows simply could not be contained and controlled effectively (and, furthermore, any sort of control would invite lobbying and lead to favoritism toward certain sectors). The logical conclusion was that capital should flow freely and exchange rates should be left free to adjust, restoring the balance between countries. The French view was diametrically opposed, calling instead for even more active management of capital flows (through tighter capital controls) as well as inflationary policies in surplus countries. This is the spirit of Keynes, who back in the early 1940s called for the entire international monetary system to be structured so that countries running excessive surpluses would be penalized, while those in deficit were to be supported. The tightening of capital controls was related to the deep-seated French belief that exchange rates, if left to float freely, are excessively volatile, and similarly so are capital flows. Exchange rate overshooting and sizable international capital flows are then argued to actually be destabilizing. French policy makers often expressed a longing for stable rates, and exchange rate stability required more policy coordination. In particular, the inflationary policies in surplus countries were supposed to restore a balance in competitiveness and so restore equilibrium for the wider global economy.

The flipside of such stabilization policies are the destabilizing effects of divergences in inflation between high-inflation debtor countries (under Bretton Woods, Italy, for example) and low-inflation credit countries (for example, Germany). Cross-border capital flows into debtor countries often financed investment in nontradables (in particular in the housing sector) and consumption (both public and private), thus pushing up domestic wages without improving international competitiveness. Given fixed exchange rates, such divergent trends in wage inflation go hand in hand with a relative loss in competitiveness for the debtor countries; that is, unit labor costs in debtor countries rise markedly vis-à-vis the creditor countries.

Persistent inflation divergences in a system of fixed exchange rates *with free capital flows* have yet another destabilizing effect, as highlighted by Alan Walters (the economic advisor to Margaret Thatcher) in his well-known "Walters' critique." The basic argument goes as follows: Consider two countries in the system, say Italy and Germany, with Italy experiencing an expansionary aggregate demand shock and Germany hit by a contractionary shock. Following the shocks, inflation rises in Italy and falls in Germany. As capital flows freely, and assuming that the fixed exchange rate system is credible, nominal interest rates in Italy and Germany must be the same, so the inflation divergence means that the real interest rate in Italy is lower than in Germany. This low relative real interest rate provides an incentive for Italians to borrow, while the high rates in Germany induce Germans to save. Walters' original argument then was that this would spur a further economic divergence; output would rise even further in Italy and drop even further in Germany. Taking a more international perspective, we also see that the divergence in real interest rates means that credit flows from Germany to Italy will occur. Interestingly, these patterns very much resemble the buildup of imbalances within the euro area prior to the eruption of the euro-area crisis (with the role of Italy being taken by many periphery economies).

In the end, the Bretton Woods system collapsed; it simply did not incorporate a sustainable and credible way of dealing with the adjustment problem. Afterward, the global exchange rate system started to move very close to the German ideal: free capital flows and floating exchange rates. Later (in the 1980s), this became part of the Washington Consensus (which, interestingly, was also pushed by various French politicians, for example, Jacques Delors), as we discuss in chapter 14.

European Exchange Rate Mechanism

In Europe, however, matters continued to look different. European governments felt that volatile intra-European exchange rates would be detrimental to the European project, and so, in 1978, they launched the European Exchange Rate Mechanism (ERM for short), an attempt to recreate the Bretton Woods system in a European context. The philosophical differences between the German and French sides as regards the adjustment question of course continued. Indeed, the German Bundesbank had always been hesitant about the ERM and so had insisted at the outset on an opt-out should the exchange rate system impose too heavy a cost (i.e., too much expansion) on German monetary policy. In a further nod toward German interests, this rather loose form of exchange rate management still allowed for quite flexible rebalancing. Otmar Emminger, who became Bundesbank president in the 1970s but was a central intellectual presence of the German Bundesbank already before then, had advocated flexible exchange rates in the late 1950s.

In the European Monetary System, the Bundesbank consistently pressed for more regular realignments. In the eyes of the Frankfurt bankers, it was France's reluctance to devalue in line with changes in labor competitiveness that was placing strain on the system. Abolishing the exchange rate (through the institution of the monetary union) and committing to a notion of price stability provided the only way of resolving this long-standing debate. A case in point is Italy: Every once in a while, Italy would have its target parity vis-à-vis the other currencies in the system adjusted downward. But precisely because such realignments are allowed for, the arrangement cannot be fully credible, and so it remains very much prone to attacks.

With the availability of capital, current account imbalances were sustainable for much longer periods (though, of course, not forever). The effects of movements in capital in allowing current account imbalances to build up to a much greater extent and ensuring that corrections, when they occurred, would be much more dramatic was already noticeable in the 1980s, before the move to monetary union. These forces were, of course, not limited to Europe but also played out on a global scale. As the dollar was soaring in the mid-1980s, American manufacturing came under threat, and so a protectionist backslash appeared possible. In response, the finance ministers of the major industrial countries pushed for exchange rate agreement. At the G7 meeting at the Louvre in 1987, the finance ministers agreed to lock their exchange rates into a system of target zones. In practice, nothing came of that global plan, but then Edouard Balladur, the

French finance minister who had largely been responsible for the Louvre proposal, came up with a tighter European scheme—a first step toward European monetary union. When German foreign minister Hans-Dietrich Genscher appeared sympathetic, Europe's central bankers were asked by the president of the European Commission, Jacques Delors, to prepare a timetable and a plan for currency union. The Delors committee met between September 1988 and April 1989 and produced its report, long before anyone had German unification in mind.

Large buildups in imbalances convinced Europe's policy makers that a monetary union was the only way of avoiding the risk of periodic crises with currency realignments whose trade policy consequences threatened the survival of an integrated internal European market. Also, a reorientation of French policy—the adoption of the policy of the *franc fort* after 1983, a strong French currency with lower inflation—laid the basis for the appearance of convergence after an episode of political and monetary instability in the early 1980s due to a brief experiment in socialist economics by the French president François Mitterrand.

With the 1986 Single European Act, the single common market was also established. Importantly, it included the liberalization of capital flows. Germany pushed hard for a quick implementation, whereas France, unsurprisingly in light of its historical attachment to exchange rate controls, initially wanted to delay freedom of capital as much as possible. In the end, France agreed to implement the capital flow liberalization in 1990, but many blamed the liberalization for the crisis that soon engulfed Europe.

The combination of fixed—but not irrevocably so—exchange rates and free capital flows set the system up for crisis, and indeed in 1992 and 1993, there were two big exchange crises that nearly killed the European Monetary System. The background for these crises was the fiscal stimulus associated with German reunification, which brought with it substantial inflationary pressure in Germany and a tightening of Bundesbank policy. To defend the ERM currency parities, other central banks then naturally also had to tighten but, fearing the associated recession, were generally unwilling to do so.

Speculators realized this fundamental dilemma and bet on it. In September 1992, the British pound was attacked. George Soros, a wealthy Hungarian-born hedge fund manager, sold short more than $10 billion in pounds. Ultimately, on Black Wednesday, September 16, 1992, the United Kingdom was forced to withdraw from the ERM. A day later, Italy withdrew as well. In July 1993 the speculators also started attacking the French franc. The French and German central banks (under pressure from the German government) spent large sums to defend the French franc, and German interest rates were lowered. Ultimately, on August 1, 1993, the band within which the exchange rate was to stay was widened from 4.5 percent to 30 percent.[54]

Germans persistently believed that such a union could only occur on the basis of a prior policy convergence. A term that was frequently used, especially by the Bundesbank, was that monetary union could only come as a *coronation*—the final symbolic act—of an integration that had been prepared by solid policy work. That position was contrasted with the French one, which held that adopting new institutions could quickly force convergence (an approach that was sometimes derided as "rushing fences").

In sum, one should add the following two international points to our list for the German economic philosophy above:

9. Net exports are considered a gauge of competiveness and a signal of economic health and strength.
10. Germans prefer flexible exchange rates in an international setting with open capital markets.

In contrast, for the French economic tradition, the following two points are more appropriate:

8. Exports that are too high are not a sign of strength but an indication of the application of a beggar-thy-neighbor mercantilist principle.
9. The international monetary system should be multipolar, and effective policy coordination should include the active management of capital flows to stabilize exchange rate movements. Fixed exchange rates are a desirable reflection of states' ability to impose discipline on disorderly markets.

PART II

MONETARY AND FISCAL STABILITY: THE GHOST OF MAASTRICHT

5

Rules, Flexibility, Credibility, and Commitment

As the previous chapters highlighted, there is no single, coherent economic philosophy within Europe. Rather, different nations have retained their own distinct economic philosophies and view European-level institutions—and ways to improve them—in this light. Before 2007, these differences in interpretation and outlook merely lurked in the background. But with the advent of the European crisis, deep fissures have come to the fore. Many of the differences that were hotly debated in the lead-up to Maastricht arose from different economic traditions on each side of the Rhine River. These differences reemerged during the euro crisis. It is characteristic of the European integration process that many fundamental differences were brushed aside, with each side going away after a successful negotiation, believing in their idiosyncratic favorite interpretation of the international agreement. André Szász, a Dutch central banker, once formulated the characteristic outcome in these terms: "a compromise not in the sense that member states resolved their differences by meeting each other on intermediate positions, but rather they agreed on documents which they felt left them free to continue to push for their own preference."[1]

The second part of the book, consisting of chapters 5 to 8, will analyze the differences in economic thinking that were already part of the Maastricht negotiations and resurfaced again during the euro crisis. This chapter focuses on rules versus flexibility and commitment.

Germany insisted throughout the Maastricht negotiations that future rules for the European Union should be enshrined in strong institutional design. The main German concern was that large fiscal debt burdens would lead to monetary financing and ultimately to a quasi-default through price inflation, as occurred in the 1970s, most prominently in Italy and in the United Kingdom. The independence of the European Central Bank would provide another important safeguard against the monetization of public debt. Combining this with the no-bailout rule in the Maastricht Treaty, "outright default"—rather than default via inflation—was the only remaining safety valve in the system. Sovereign debt interest rates were to reflect this default risk and so provide individual governments in the monetary union an incentive to keep their debt at a sustainable level. The agreed Stability and Growth Pact should provide an additional safeguard that government debt does not exceed certain levels. These institutional pillars were key to the German vision of the euro area. The French endorsement of these principles, in contrast, was more lukewarm; the French view stresses the costs associated with the loss of flexibility that comes with a rules-based framework and praises the virtues of ex post intervention. French policy makers focus on managing the current crisis. They are willing to interpret rules flexibly, but they are also willing to enter extreme commitments if it helps to overcome the current crisis. In contrast, Germans see rules as a way to avoid the build-up of future risks and are worried that a flexible crisis response sows the seed for the next crisis.

In particular, this chapter tries to answer the following questions:

- What advantages do rules and autonomous safety valves have in avoiding and managing crises, and what are their costs?
- How do rules help to overcome time-inconsistency problems—that countries find it advantageous to first create the impression that they would do one thing but ex post do another?
- Historically, how were the gold standard, currency pegs, and other external commitment devices used to find the right balance between containing time-inconsistency problems and maintaining flexibility?
- How can reputation replace external commitment devices?
- How can delegation to an independent central bank help to overcome time-inconsistency problems? In particular, can an institutional environment in which an independent central bank and a government are engaged in a "game of chicken" help to find the right balance?

Time-Inconsistency: Ex Ante versus Ex Post

Flexibility, but Favoritism

At the heart of the "French" philosophy lies the possibility for flexible policy responses for crisis management purposes. This central authority approach reflects an underlying trust in the corrective powers of government. In France, a highly centralized country, crisis management was fully delegated by the people to the presidency—since Charles de Gaulle had drawn up a new and more effective constitution for the Fifth Republic with a "domaine réservée" (de Gaulle was thinking mostly of foreign policy, though). In times of crisis, the French see redistribution as an effective crisis management tool. For example, after the Lehman bankruptcy in September 2008, the French president Sarkozy was perceived as an effective and decisive leader in times of financial troubles.

Germans fear such centralized redistributive powers may lead to favoritism and excessive lobbying efforts, especially by influential and well-connected parts of the society. The "German" philosophy, in contrast, emphasizes the virtues of a rules-driven framework. The state establishes an ex ante system of rules and autonomous safety valves. Individuals, regions, and the state itself act within the confines of this system. Rules also guide people's expectations. In the words of Jürgen Stark, a German former member of the ECB executive board, rules act as guardrails and so provide long-run stability. Experimentation in crisis times is, in contrast, frowned upon as ad hocery. Most importantly, from the German perspective, the knowledge that ex post in a crisis situation the government will provide some help to some groups in society leads to huge distortions in behavior ex ante, which sows the seeds for the next crisis. Moral hazard problems are thus a major concern for Germans. In short, the French focus on managing the current crisis; Germans focus on avoiding future crises.

Time-Inconsistency since Odysseus

Ideally, a government would like the public and market participants to believe that they will to a large extent refrain from accommodating various interest groups in times of crisis. However, when crisis occurs, without binding rules they would surely change their minds out of expedience. Forward-looking market participants anticipate that words are cheap and earlier promises will not be followed through in the absence of binding rules. In the economic literature, this tension is known as a *time-inconsistency problem*. What's optimal ex ante is not optimal ex post. For example, a government might want to convince the public and investors that it will not default on its debt or dilute it through inflation. If investors believe the government, they will charge a much lower (risk-free) interest rate. However, the government's temptation to default or monetize debt is high after an adverse shock, say a small recession, when in principle it is able to repay its debts. A potential default would free up funds to stabilize the economy, and this is naturally more attractive than increasing tax revenue or slashing expenditure to satisfy government debt obligations. Default, however, comes with some cost. As the country is temporarily excluded from international financial markets, it cannot have a primary deficit and has to balance its budget. But, financial markets forget and forgive relatively quickly, and so governments regain access to funding relatively soon after restructuring has taken place.

In short, governments would like to bind their hands ex ante to a pre-specified response, but deviate from it ex post. Even the Greeks of antiquity were aware of these time-inconsistency problems. Odysseus anticipated that he might be tempted and distracted by the irresistible sound of the Sirens so that he might deviate from his planned course and navigate his ships into the rocks and sink—but he nevertheless wanted to hear their sound! He therefore ordered the oarsmen in his ship to put beeswax in their ears and to tie him to the mast of the ship. He also instructed his men not to heed his cries while they passed the Sirens, anticipating that he would need the commitment device (the mast) not to change his planned behavior. This raises the question whether there are analogous commitment devices for honoring public debt.

Self-Committing Sovereigns, an Oxymoron?

How can a sovereign nation-state credibly commit to anything when the definition of the sovereign is that it makes (and can change) the rules?

The earliest answer to this conundrum was given by the English in the aftermath of the Glorious Revolution—the overthrow of King James II by a union of English parliamentarians and Dutch stadtholder William III—in the late seventeenth century.[2] Prior to the revolution, the increasing fiscal needs of the Crown led to expropriation of wealth through the redefinition of property rights in favor of the sovereign and periodic defaults (such as the "exchequer stop"). All of this was possible because the sovereign could readily alter the rules of the game—it was not credibly bound by them in any shape or form. The institutional changes brought along by the revolution were designed to address this. In particular, after 1688, the (new)

Crown had to obtain parliamentary assent to all its changes to existing arrangements. Because the Parliament represented wealth holders, this substantially limited the ability of the Crown to renege on its debt. In this setup, the newly created Bank of England (as the main holder of government debt) played a key role. It held sovereign debt, and its equity was by and large provided by the class represented in Parliament, who could control the budget; thus, sovereign defaults became politically unacceptable.

In today's economies, governments credibly commit to repaying their debt in a similar fashion. Debt is widely held by domestic citizens—that is, voters—which makes it politically extremely costly to default. This mechanism is important even if most claims were held by foreigners: in times of crisis, foreigners know that they can sell their debt to domestic investors, and these investors will be willing to buy the bonds precisely because their holding of the debt makes default less likely. Similarly, selling newly issued debt to institutions that are at the heart of a country's economy can serve as another powerful commitment device. For example, a government will think twice about whether to default on systemic (undercapitalized) banks, as at the end of the day it simply has to bailout these banks and so has achieved little from the restructuring of its debt.

External Commitments: Currency Pegs, Unions, and the Gold Standard

Historically, government often looked for other external commitment devices that make it difficult to inflate away the public debt. The basic idea underlying the use of external commitment devices is rather simple. A country pegs the value of its own currency to some anchor—either foreign currency or a commodity (gold)—over whose value it has little control. If the value of the anchor does not change too quickly, and if the peg is credible, then the domestic currency will also remain stable.

From Currency Pegs to Currency Unions

Many countries around the world tie or have tied the real value of their currency to a foreign currency (or a basket of currencies). The strength of such a commitment depends on the cost of escaping it. A target zone setup or a *currency peg*, like the European Exchange Rate Mechanism (Snake), which was introduced before the euro in March 1979, is a relatively weak form of fixing. The exchange rate can fluctuate within a certain band, which is subject to occasional realignments. A stronger form of commitment is a *currency board*. For example, Hong Kong has a currency board with the US dollar. In such a system, the domestic money supply is backed entirely by foreign currency. In other words, the central bank will be willing to freely exchange (at par) local currency for foreign currency. The strongest commitment is to join a *currency union*, as exiting the union typically destroys the banking system and makes the payment system dysfunctional. In a sense, then, a currency union is the tightest imaginable straitjacket. Such external commitment devices do, however, come with a costly loss of flexibility. When bad states of the world arise, countries with a strong monetary reputation can use up reputational capital, while countries bound by an external commitment device have to pay the breakup costs exactly when it hurts the most.

Golden Fetters: Ex Post Costs and Lessons for Today

During the era of the gold standard in the late nineteenth and early twentieth century, most advanced economies had pegged the values of their currencies to the price of gold, keeping the value of their currency practically fixed. To ease the pressure of these golden fetters, countries quite routinely went on and off gold, in particular during the turbulent 1920s and 1930s.[3] The tradition of a peg to gold was continued after 1945 with the Bretton Woods quasi gold exchange standard. At the heart of this system was the US dollar, fixed to gold at a price of $35 per ounce. All other currencies then had fixed exchange rates against the dollar. To give the system some flexibility, occasional realignments of foreign exchange rates vis-à-vis the dollar were allowed. Alternatively, exchange rates may be fixed against each other, not against an underlying commodity.

A brief look back into history illustrates the ex post costs that monetary straitjackets can impose on an economy. In the aftermath of World War I, the United Kingdom returned to the gold standard in 1925, and did so at the old parity. Its export industry never quite recovered from the associated loss of competitiveness in international markets. Soon after, in 1926, France returned to the gold standard at a substantially devalued parity and enjoyed a rapid recovery in the later 1920s. The mirror image of this took place in the early 1930s: the United Kingdom abandoned the gold standard early in 1931 and recovered quite quickly after the Great

Depression, while France fought at all costs to defend the parity and was mired in a long recession until it was forced off gold in 1936, five years after the British devaluation.

Many commentators—in particular on the political left—see these experiences as a cautionary tale for the current Greek predicament. Hard money and austerity, the strategy followed by the United Kingdom in the immediate aftermath of World War I, and by Greece currently, is self-defeating, for deflation increases the real debt burden faster than any feasible amount of fiscal prudence can reduce it. The British experience after the Great Depression, or even more starkly in the aftermath of World War II, offers an alternative path: sharp devaluations and financial repression are believed to have facilitated a fast recovery—applied to Greece, of course, this would mean that the euro itself is the straitjacket holding up recovery. But if there are fundamental rigidities that limit adjustment, a devaluation would only provide a temporary stimulus. Leaving the euro would in that case carry with it costs that far outweigh the benefits of depreciation.[4]

Internal Commitments: Reputation and Institutional Design

Reputation

As an alternative to credible external commitment, a government may try to build a *reputation* for not defaulting either outright or through inflation. So far, we viewed the interaction between government and financial markets in a static light—the government may or may not default today, then borrow again in the future, and our analysis ended. In reality, however, governments and financial markets interact on a repeated basis. It may be worthwhile for a government to swallow today the bitter pill of not defaulting (and raising tax revenue instead), thus signaling credibly that it will restructure its debt only in extreme circumstances. As a consequence, investors will charge a lower risk compensation, and so the borrowing rates are lower.

REGAINING REPUTATION AFTER THE 1970S:
UNITED KINGDOM VERSUS ITALY
Acquiring a reputation to honor the debt and not to inflate takes a long time of sustained effort. But reputation can easily be lost. In the 1970s, high

inflation in both Italy and the United Kingdom lowered the government debt burden. A surprise inflation with annual rates exceeding 20 percent brought with it a massive redistribution from households to the highly indebted state. In the 1980s and 1990s, Italian households had learned their lesson and were no longer willing to buy long-term, fixed-rate securities issued by the government. Italy was punished for its earlier sins by having to pay high real interest rates for over a decade. The United Kingdom escaped this trap only by adopting, under Margaret Thatcher, a program of fiscal stabilization that was unpopular and controversial (having been denounced at the time by 364 leading economists). No Italian government contemplated anything along the Thatcher lines.

CREDIBILITY AND CLEAN SLATE

A reputation is only credible if the promise is not too extreme. That is, ruling out debt default even in extreme circumstances and hardship is never credible. Indeed, the concept of reputation building is also closely linked to the idea of a default designed to create a clean slate. Naturally, countries with a low overall debt burden have more room to maneuver, as investors believe—even in the case of reasonably large adverse shocks— that a rebalancing is possible without debt restructuring. Hence, a rule that limits ex ante the debt buildup, like the Stability and Growth Pact, helps to maintain a good reputation. In addition, maintaining credibility might require a government, under certain circumstances, to first renege on its existing debt, thereby getting rid of its legacy debt and improving resilience to future shocks. This is, for example, the case if a country suffers from debt-overhang problems.

Delegation to Independent Institutions and a Game of Chicken

Another way to mitigate the time-inconsistency problem to which elected policy makers, especially before elections, succumb is via a clever institutional design. The above mentioned Glorious Revolution in 1688 England is one example of such an (self-committing) institutional arrangement. *Delegating* authority to a credible independent institution is one answer to this problem. For example, an independent and conservative central banker, who is not bound by electoral considerations, could be put in charge. A conservative central banker can credibly stick to a specific inflation target, as he would not be tempted to engineer an inflation surprise to temporarily boost the economy.[5] An institutional separation of authority was seen as a commitment tool to overcome the time-inconsistency problem.

CENTRAL BANK INDEPENDENCE AND GERMANY'S EXPERIENCE IN THE 1970S

In countries with independent central banks, inflation was less of a problem during the 1970s stagflation decade. The German Bundesbank acquired a reputation for achieving monetary stability at a time when the economy had to overcome two oil price shocks. The idea of the fathers of the EMU was to transfer the stellar reputation of the independent Bundesbank to the new European Central Bank so that all euro-member countries could enjoy the same low-interest rate environment. Legally, the ECB became one of the most independent central banks in the world. Its president and the executive board are elected for eight years, without the possibility of renewal. Chapter 15 describes the institutional features of the ECB in detail.

MONETARY AND FISCAL DOMINANCE

Central bank independence should shield the ECB from undue fiscal influence. Splitting up the euro-area authorities into a single monetary and multiple (currently nineteen) fiscal authorities was considered a safeguard against high inflation. If the fiscal debt burden started to mount, an independent central bank would refrain from inflating the debt away and force the fiscal authorities to cut expenditures or raise taxes. Under such a regime, the monetary authority is in the driver's seat. The academic literature on the fiscal theory of the price level refers to it as *monetary dominance*. The contrasting regime—in which the fiscal authorities through the issuance of large amounts of debt determine the outcome—is referred to as *fiscal dominance*. In that regime, the central bank is forced to use the printing press to guarantee government debt sustainability.

A GAME OF CHICKEN

In reality, a game of chicken between the central bank and the fiscal authority arises in times of crisis. Figuratively speaking, one can imagine two drivers, each heading for a single-lane bridge from opposite directions. Each driver knows that if he veers first, he will concede the bridge to his opponent. However, if neither swerves, the ultimate outcome will be a collision. Each side hopes to intimidate the other by refusing to swerve. What makes all of this an *escalating* game of chicken (or war of attrition) is that losses do not have to be realized now but can be pushed into the future—at the cost of getting larger and larger over time. Individually, each party hopes that the other one will blink first and assume the losses, and so resolution of the crisis is pushed back further. An escalating game of chicken in which neither party can be forced to submit and in which neither party has strong commitment power could well lead to delays magnifying initially small losses into unbearable ones.

The founding fathers of the EMU wanted to ensure that the ECB, with its rigid focus on inflation and strong form of independence, is able to play the game of chicken without being pressured into submission by the national fiscal authorities. This grim game of chicken scenario was thus supposed to provide the required checks and balances on fiscal policy. Except for some brief and mostly rhetorical interventions by French policy makers, the independence of the ECB was never under question during the euro crisis.

A good example of the constraining role of the ECB in relation to government actions came with the two letters addressed to the Italian and Spanish governments in August 2011, with the signatures of both the president of the ECB, Jean-Claude Trichet, and the national central bank governors, Mario Draghi (who would be Trichet's successor) and Miguel Ángel Fernández Ordóñez. (See chapter 15 for details.) The letters included not only fiscal demands but precise conditions on pension reform, the liberalization of services, a loosening of collective bargaining, and the implementation of an unemployment insurance scheme. Italy started to implement the reforms, but most were left to Silvio Berlusconi's successors as prime minister, Mario Monti, Enrique Letta, and Matteo Renzi. Similarly, in Spain, Prime Minister Zapatero did not act, but the letter provided a basis for the policy agenda of the government of Mariano Rajoy.

Managing Current versus Avoiding Future Crisis

Germans like to emphasize that rules guide the expectations of all market participants and in particular that a commitment to a rules-based framework can yield long-term benefits, for example, in the form of stable government debt and low inflation. Imbalances are less likely to build up and future crises can be avoided altogether. French policy makers are focused on managing the ongoing crisis. Their approach is two-pronged: They don't mind breaking rules if the additional flexibility helps to resolve the current crisis; and they don't mind entering straitjacket commitments in order to lower current funding costs even when it potentially exposes them to a much more severe crisis in the future. They are convinced that any hint of sovereign default is likely to set off a crisis of confidence. It would be like making a small hole in the dam that would not be a safety valve but rather produce a torrent and tear the dam. In contrast, Germans always liked the idea of a systematic availability of escape valves. Many historical examples teach us that straitjacket commitments, such as a strict adherence to the gold standard, can have detrimental consequences. Rules have to be sufficiently fine-tuned and adjust to circumstances. However, as no rule can include unforeseen contingencies, it is important to maintain some degree of flexibility.

Monetary Policy Rule with Time-Varying Flexibility

Central banks are always oscillating between rules and discretion, and are reluctant to think that they could simply be replaced by a machine that would mechanically apply a policy rule. Particularly in moments of distress, they are used to being called to deliver extraordinary actions. The US Federal Reserve was permitted under Section 13(3) (as amended in 1932) to supply extraordinary lending in "unusual and exigent circumstances." It did not use that power very much in the Great Depression, but did a great deal in response to the crisis of 2008. The power was then subjected to political control in the Dodd-Frank Act.

A key feature of an adequate rules-based environment is monetary independence. However, as illustrated well by the crisis of the euro area as well as by the American experience, this independence should and will be weakened in times of crisis, as fiscal and monetary authorities necessarily work together. A prominent example of the new importance of politics was Berlin's implicit backing of Draghi's London "whatever it takes" speech; without this backing, Draghi's words could never have the impact that they in fact had. (See chapters 7 and 15 for more details.) But the prominence of politics also raises new problems. As ties between monetary and fiscal authorities increase, a game of chicken commences. How this game of chicken is resolved will then set the stage for the future institutional environment.

Straitjacket Commitment versus Debt Restructuring as Insurance

Similarly, it is difficult to ex ante specify the exact circumstances when a government could default. Note that (government) debt has a dual role. First, it allows the government—just as ordinary debt instruments do for individuals—to smooth its expenditure. This also means that government debt can potentially be used to stabilize the macroeconomy. Second, government debt is also an insurance vehicle—if default occurs only in extreme circumstances and hardship is shared with bond holders.

A historical illustration of this is the default history of King Philip II, who ruled Spain from 1556 to 1598. For him, both income and expenditure were highly volatile, and so default was always in the cards. On the revenue side, he had a relatively stable domestic tax base from Spain, but he also received considerable income from the New World. The latter revenue was highly volatile and mainly depended on whether ships filled with silver (and other treasures) managed to make their way safely back to Spain or were sunk in storms or captured by English privateers or pirate vessels. On the expenditure side, the constant threat of war (including defending the silver fleets and the silver mines) loomed large. His creditor banks—the German Fuggers and various Genoese banking families—understood the precariousness of the sovereign very well, and so default (meaning a conversion of high-interest, short-term securities into longer-term bonds) was always part of the implicit government debt deal. Government debt thus clearly had the insurance aspect described above.[6]

Overall, European policy makers and the public should agree on the extreme circumstances under which they will find default as a last option—essentially acting as a safety valve. The events around Deauville in October 2010—when the restructuring of private Greek debt was first announced, which ultimately occurred in February 2012—revealed that various euro-area member states disagreed about the circumstances under which a debt restructuring should occur. While the IMF and Germany lobbied for restructuring of privately held debt, France and especially the ECB were strictly opposed to it.

6

Liability versus Solidarity:
No-Bailout Clause and Fiscal Union

To further safeguard against the monetization of government debt, particularly in the case of outright insolvency, Article 125 of the Maastricht Treaty provides for a *no-bailout clause*. The German economic tradition puts a strong emphasis on liability for one's own actions rather than ex post transfers to shift the costs onto another party. The German philosophy, which derives from a long history of decentralized power and a federal nation structure, is naturally inclined to give freedom to individual economic agents and regions and is correspondingly wary of the moral hazard problems that excessive insurance brings with it. German policy makers often reiterate that every member country has to do its own homework and that relying on bailouts from others distorts incentives. They often refer to Goethe's aphorism: "Let everyone sweep in front of his door and every city quarter will be clean."[1] The liability principle (*Haftungsprinzip*)—that entities with the freedom to act are also liable for its consequences—is sacrosanct in Germany. German policy makers see two ways forward: (1) a decentralized fiscal order in which each country is liable for its own debt or (2) a fully integrated fiscal union in which spending powers are transferred to a European authority. Only the second arrangement would permit Eurobonds with joint liability.

French policy makers never attached the same importance to the no-bailout clause in the Maastricht Treaty. France's philosophy, which reflects its centralist tradition, is by contrast more willing to facilitate ex post transfers. The solidarity motto "fraternity" is after all part of the slogan of the French Revolution. This willingness to insure, even at the cost of moral hazard problems, resonates with the tradition that within France the central government in Paris essentially controls all important areas of policy.

Interestingly, while French policy makers were more receptive to the idea of fiscal transfers to peripheral countries, they were very reluctant to cede fiscal control to a European authority in Brussels. Having joint liability without joint control can only be rationalized if one believes that all transfers and bailouts are solely needed to overcome market inefficiencies and temporary liquidity problems, as we will discuss in the next chapter.

This chapter addresses the following questions:

- Why did the no-bailout clause fail to provide adequate incentives for prudent fiscal behavior? Also, why do financial markets fail to provide the right incentives in good times and then overreact with sharp interest rate increases in bad times?
- Is a fiscal union the answer to the euro area's current ailments, and, in particular, will it be effective in reducing mounting debt repayment burdens? Can fiscal union insure individual countries against asymmetric shocks or will it necessarily end up as a transfer union?
- Do fiscal unions without a transfer of control to Brussels provide the right incentives for governments?
- How should we interpret the historical experience of Italy's lagging South, the Mezzogiorno? Is it a warning example that fiscal unions might not lead to convergence in living standards but rather to a productive European core and subsidy-dependent periphery?
- Do Eurobonds with joint liability help to solve the current crisis while at the same time laying the groundwork for the next crisis? Are there alternative solutions that are not subject to the problems associated with joint liability?

The No-Bailout Clause

A Rule and Its Consequences

Legally speaking, the German view clearly prevailed in the Maastricht Treaty negotiations. Both a monetary bailout through monetization of debt and a fiscal bailout were made illegal, and the restriction was enshrined in an international treaty. The ECB was prohibited from directly buying government debt. In addition, a fiscal bailout provided by the European Union or any national government was made illegal by the no-bailout clause.

Hence, outright debt default was the only remaining safety valve for a country to absorb national shocks possibly resulting from the previous excessive buildup of imbalances. The possible contagion and spillover effects that such a default may impose on others were underestimated when the Maastricht Treaty was signed in the early 1990s. The effects that might occur from contagion and spillovers only became apparent later in that decade during the Southeast Asian crisis and Russian crisis.

In the German view, the no-bailout clause of the Maastricht Treaty was seen as a key part of the overall institutional rules of the game. Making it part of an international treaty, rather than simply domestic law, was seen as a particularly strong rope with which to tie countries to the mast of fiscal orthodoxy. This, coupled with rigid fiscal rules, could keep the incentive structure for all member states as before. From the French perspective, by contrast, the no-bailout clause in particular was seen as an unimportant add-on. As was the case so often in the history of the European project, these differences were papered over for a long period of time.

Market Discipline

The no-bailout rule through market discipline ideally provides incentives for the fiscal authority to behave prudently in good times and avoids a possible run-up of government debt. Countries with higher debt levels are more likely to (outright) default on their debt and hence pay a higher interest rate to creditors ex ante. Market discipline relies on informationally efficient markets, the existence of which some observers questioned even then. This was the reason why Germany pushed for a second pillar to the treaty, the Stability and Growth Pact (SGP), with its 3 percent deficit rule.

The problem before the euro crisis was that market participants and financial institutions never took the no-bailout rule seriously, adopting the French nonchalance vis-à-vis the no-bailout clause. That approach made sense in that the French view was reflected in bank regulation. The Basel rules require banks to hold an equity cushion against their risky positions, but all euro-area government debt was treated as free of default risk, carrying a zero-risk weight. In other words, despite the fact that outright default was seen as the only safety valve, banks were not required to fund holdings of government debt with any equity. Moreover, the ECB treated all euro-area government debt equally: all government bonds could be used as collateral without any differential haircut or safety margin. Both rules were in direct contradiction to and undermined the principle of the no-bailout clause. Not surprisingly, the interest rate differential across various government bonds virtually vanished with the introduction of the euro.

When the euro crisis broke out, Germany believed that the no-bailout clause embedded in the treaty would be strictly enforced. It was, therefore, keen on preserving strong conditionality, even if that meant bringing outsiders, that is, the IMF, to enforce multilateral discipline inside the euro area.

That position was shared by a large number of Northern countries that were determined to stick to a strict interpretation of the no-bailout clause of the Maastricht Treaty. They viewed any support to problem economies, even temporary, as setting a dangerous precedent. The European Economic and Monetary Union (EMU) was a monetary union with clear and strong safeguards against fiscal irresponsibility.

Fiscal Unions

Fiscal Union as Insurance against Asymmetric Shocks

From a German perspective, the no-bailout provision was essential to provide the incentive for everyone to keep their own houses in order. Others saw fiscal bailouts as a stabilizing insurance mechanism that insures countries against adverse asymmetric shocks. Princeton's Peter Kenen was one of the most prominent academics arguing that a fiscal redistribution scheme has to substitute for the missing safety valve that a flexible exchange rate adjustment would otherwise provide.[2] The key assumption in the Keynesian literature is that prices and wages are sticky and do not freely adjust to shocks. A currency union fixes exchange rates and hence also makes foreign prices and wages rigid. Redistributional fiscal measures and bailout schemes are needed as alternative shock absorbers.

Such a fiscal insurance mechanism could work between states or across individuals. In the United States, substantial redistribution occurs between individuals living in different parts of the country. For example, residents of Florida received transfers totaling 4 percentage points of their GDP after the bursting of the housing bubble, which hit Florida especially hard.[3] In contrast, Spaniards who suffered a similar housing bubble bust did not benefit from such a European-wide individual insurance scheme.[4]

The Maastricht Treaty never supposed that the European Monetary Union should include such an insurance scheme. Europe was not intended as an instrument for fiscal solidarity. From a German perspective, such schemes are plagued with moral hazard. If individuals or individual member countries of a currency union will be bailed out through a generous insurance scheme, they have an ex ante incentive to misallocate resources, overinvest, and take on excessive risk. If things turn out badly, others bail them out. If they turn out well, its benefits predominantly accrue to the member country. Allowing one's banking system to grow excessively is one prominent example. Cyprus, Malta, Luxembourg, and Ireland were attracted to such a business model. It yields significant extra benefits and tax revenues in good times. However, when the model goes bust, other Europeans are expected to share the burden.

To contain moral hazard problems, it is necessary that common fiscal rules are strictly enforced or that key budgetary decisions are centralized in Brussels. While France itself is a very centrally organized state, French policy makers have a strong aversion to any form of multilateral control of national budgets. They could not condone anything that would cede budgetary powers to Brussels and initially also resisted German efforts to strengthen supranational surveillance and enshrine it in a new treaty.

EURO-WIDE INDIVIDUAL MINIMUM UNEMPLOYMENT INSURANCE
Transfers between governments in Europe are seen as problematic. The better way of discussing transfers within a large and diverse political order is to think of them as individualized or personalized. In particular, a European-wide social security system would be a logical completion of the free movement of labor in the single European market. It would also indicate that the insurance principle is not just appropriate for financial institutions. It would provide an important buffer in that booming areas would pay in more, and shrinking areas would draw out more, without these payments going through government bodies and appearing as transfers from north to south, whether within a country such as Italy or in the whole of the European area. It would also not require any treaty change, unlike many other reform suggestions that involved building fiscal capacity.

There is a historical precedent for such a development from the history of the United States, which really only became an example of effective fiscal federalism in the Great Depression. Franklin Delano Roosevelt's New Deal effectively built the elements of a more effective response to severe shocks. The 1935 Social Security Act contained two elements that were critical. There was a retirement system, with individual benefits that depended on the total amount of the individual's contributions (total cumulative wages), funded by a payroll tax. A contributor could seamlessly make contributions while working in different states and retire anywhere they liked. There was also unemployment insurance, an obvious desirability at a time of mass unemployment (with 12 million Americans out of work). But the benefits were limited (initially to just 13 weeks), and the levels of payout and the assessment of contributions were set by the individual states, although the trust fund was administered at the federal level. The modern European equivalent would be either to add a European element to existing national schemes or to build a fund that would provide reinsurance in the event of catastrophic events or developments.

Both the French and the Italian governments have cautiously endorsed a Europeanized unemployment insurance scheme with many safeguards in the transition phase. Italy in particular found it hard to introduce a national scheme in light of its large north-south wage differentials. Thus, the Italian document emphasizes the gradualism of long-term implementation: "If properly designed, [the scheme for European unemployment insurance] could trigger gradual approximation of national institutions, smoothing the main differences and causes of segmentation. The scheme should include an appropriate incentive structure in order to limit moral hazard and avoid permanent transfers from some countries to others."[5] But the Italian proposal suggests that funds would be sent from Brussels to member countries in the case of undesirable labor market dynamics. "It would provide temporary relief to those countries that are hit with a shock that generates more unemployment than is tolerable—and then it would be taken away."[6] There is, however, in this kind of mechanism a risk that the transfers are seen as political payments from one state to another—a situation that the US scheme of the 1930s carefully avoided.

Unemployment insurance schemes have been endorsed by the Commission and have also been set out by some German academics.[7] But to convince a broader segment of the German population and the policy community, a really effective measure to limit moral hazard would be needed.[8] Like the problem of designing better bank insurance, there is a danger that any new mechanism might be overwhelmed by demands and appear to be regionally imbalanced, that one area is systematically drawing out all of the resources of the insurance pool. Consequently, the viability of such a scheme fundamentally depends on making labor markets more adaptable so that the threat of large-scale unemployment swamping and destroying the insurance system is reduced. There is a case for linking unemployment insurance through explicit conditionality to the adoption of effective labor market reforms. There would always be the possibility of reversibility, and citizens of countries that might undo labor market openness would then lose access to the European insurance. Such conditionality would make clear the intended effect of insurance as a contribution to making Europe's labor market dynamic. The approach would also include a standardized administrative framework to ensure that similar standards are applied across European countries to the classifying of workers as unemployed.

Optimal Currency Area without Fiscal Union

While Peter Kenen stressed the importance of a fiscal union, other academic contributors to the optimal currency area literature worked out conditions under which asymmetric shocks can be dealt with, even absent floating exchange rates and a fiscal redistribution scheme. Others questioned the usefulness of exchange rate movements altogether; for these economists, giving up exchange rate flexibility is no big sacrifice.

What asymmetric shock absorbers are available—other than exchange rate flexibility and fiscal redistributions? Robert Mundell argued that the free movement of labor and capital renders an economic region an optimal currency area, as this mobility can mitigate asymmetric shocks and hence make exchange rate adjustments largely expendable.[9] In 1999, he received the Nobel Prize in Economics for this insight and other contributions.

Labor Mobility

When a country in a currency union is hit by, say, an adverse productivity shock, high labor mobility allows otherwise unemployed workers to relocate to other parts of the currency union. Greater labor mobility makes it easier for a currency union to absorb asymmetric shocks. During the Maastricht negotiations in the 1990s, many US economists argued that the United States constitutes an optimal currency area because workers move relatively freely across state boundaries, in contrast to Europe, where linguistic, cultural, and other barriers hinder labor mobility. In the United States, differences in employment rates are ironed out through the migration of workers from high-unemployment to low-unemployment regions. A vivid example of this would be workers moving from Michigan—a state mired in industrial decline—to North Dakota, which until recently benefited from a shale gas boom. Interestingly, however, in recent years, labor mobility in the United States has declined markedly.[10] While the US labor market is still more fluid than the European labor market, the gap has narrowed.

The basic labor mobility argument overlooks the fact that young, productive people leaving their highly indebted country comes at a large cost. When productive and innovative (young) people abandon their country, the debt has to be paid off by a smaller, less productive, aging population. In a sense, individual citizens have an option to walk away from their government debt obligation by leaving the country. Emigration can be seen as an individual's private default option on government debt.

Free Capital Movement

Like free labor movement, free capital flows help to absorb asymmetric shocks. A negative productivity shock is not so detrimental if capital can be easily reallocated to more productive regions in the currency union. Hence, in a world with perfect and complete capital markets, exchange rate flexibility is less essential.

However, in reality, financial markets are beset by frictions. Frictions prevent households and firms from perfect risk sharing and consumption smoothing over time. Financial market imperfections can lead to a buildup of imbalances and bubbles. Before the euro crisis, capital flowed to the peripheral countries—to a large extent intermediated through the banking system. This led to financial instability and endogenous asymmetric shocks. Chapters 9 and 10 discuss how excessive capital flows, especially if they are in the form of short-term debt, can reverse abruptly and plunge whole economies into difficulties. An economy is most prone to the hidden buildup of imbalances when measured volatility is low; a phenomenon known as the *volatility paradox*.[11] Counterintuitively, financial deepening via a partial removal of financial frictions may actually increase financial instability by facilitating excessive capital flows. This calls for a carefully thought through macroprudential regulation of financial markets.

A fiscal union with fine-tuned shock-contingent bailouts, à la Kenen, has to overcome the challenge that private trading activism might partially undo the bailout insurance scheme. This calls for additional distortionary taxes and possibly even for extreme measures such as the prohibition of certain financial markets.[12] Going down this route shows the complexity that such a scheme would involve. Political lobbying pressures might interfere with and pervert regulation such that it would protect certain interest groups rather than serving the common good.

Openness

Ronald McKinnon argued that openness—the free flow of goods and services as well as free factor mobility across industries—is the crucial criterion for an optimal currency area. Small countries with more open trade flows should find it more beneficial to join a currency union.[13] Later research questioned McKinnon's hypothesis, arguing that reduced trade barriers lead to more specialization across countries. Countries that are highly specialized and less diversified across industries face more asymmetric shocks, as they are exposed to specific industry shocks.

"Original Sin" Undermines Benefits of Flexible Exchange Rates

While German Ordoliberals see exchange rate fluctuations as a stabilizing mechanism, many modern Keynesians question the usefulness of flexible exchange rates as a safety valve altogether. The reason is what economists refer to as the "original sin." When the domestic interest rate is high, banks, firms, and even households have a tendency to take on debt in foreign currency. They try to take advantage of the lower foreign interest rate but underestimate the risk that the exchange rate might move against them. For example, many mortgages in Hungary and Poland before the crisis were written in euros and Swiss francs, allowing borrowers to benefit from lower interest rates but also subjecting them to the subsequent depreciations of the forint and zloty.

If firms and households are indebted in foreign denominated debt, devaluing a currency comes with a catch. On one hand, a devaluation increases the country's competitiveness as real wages in the international context fall. On the other hand, the value of the debt in terms of domestic currency rises, making it harder to service the debt. The real debt burden rises. That is, the country faces an external "Devaluation Dilemma."

Economists who stress the original sin problem argue that fiscal shock absorbers are needed even with flexible exchange rates. Consequently, they assign a lower cost to joining a currency union.

Fiscal Union as Transfer Union

TRANSFER UNION VERSUS INSURANCE

If bailouts benefit different regions at different times, a fiscal union can be seen as an insurance mechanism. German policy makers worry not only about the moral hazard implications of such an insurance arrangement but also about the prospect that the fiscal union could evolve into a permanent transfer union. Fiscal transfers could turn out to become a one-way street. The theme of "no transfer union" resonated with great amplitude with the publics in Germany, Austria, the Netherlands, Finland, and other Northern countries. The perceived fiscal irresponsibility of countries such as Greece contributed to this popular rejection of a transfer union.

INFLATION THREAT OR PERMANENT FISCAL TRANSFERS
DUE TO THE DEVALUATION DILEMMA

In the 2000s, the euro area got caught in a trap. First, peripheral countries ran up excessive (private and public) debt. Second, average increases in prices and wages exceeded those in Germany. For example, Greece's per capita nominal unit labor costs grew by 9.9 percent in 2002, while in Germany unit labor costs only rose by 0.8 percent in the same year.[14] This growth differential persisted until 2010, as figure 6.1 shows. As a consequence, peripheral countries lost their competiveness relative to Germany.

Excessive past wage growth typically requires a real wage cut. Prior to the euro, countries that lost their competiveness could always devalue their currency. In the 1980s and 90s, the European Exchange Rate Mechanism, the "currency snake," allowed peripheral countries to occasionally realign their currency. Such external devaluations enabled countries to maintain their competiveness.

Within a currency union, an external devaluation is not possible. Instead, adjustment must take place via internal devaluation, that is, via lower wage growth. Over the course of the euro crisis, nominal wages in peripheral countries such as Spain and Portugal fell significantly. These reductions hit younger workers in particular, whose jobs were far less secure than older workers, as figure 6.2 shows.

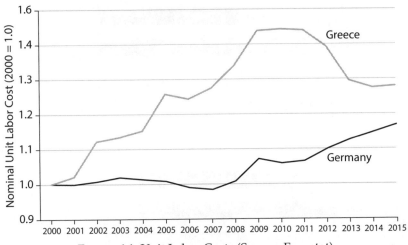

FIGURE 6.1. Unit Labor Costs (Source: Eurostat)

However, a nominal wage reduction comes with the internal "Devalu-ation Dilemma" similar to the external "Devaluation Dilemma" that arises with foreign denominated debt. Lower wages make it more difficult for workers to service their debt and mortgage obligations. Some of them will find it so burdensome that their payments will become delinquent; they might ultimately default on their debt. This dynamic is likely to create additional financial stability problems.

Instead of cutting nominal wages in the periphery, the alternative is to increase wages in the core of the euro area. This increases price inflation in the core and hence dilutes the value of nominal claims of the savers in the core. Of course, one main lesson from Japan is that it is not easy to gener-ate inflation. This is especially the case when one wants to stipulate infla-tion for specific regions of the currency union.

In such a situation, policy makers are caught between a rock and a hard place—or, to borrow a German phrase, policy makers have a choice between plague and cholera. To avoid default, the choice seems to be between higher inflation in the core or fiscal transfers to compen-sate for the loss of competitiveness and associated high unemployment in the peripheral countries. Higher inflation at the core has the advan-tage that the relative wage adjustment restores peripheral countries' competiveness. In contrast, transfers delay relative price adjustment, lead to allocative inefficiencies, and might therefore turn out to be permanent.

FIGURE 6.2. Changes in Average Wage for Different Age Cohorts,
2010–2013 (Source: Eurostat)

TRANSFER UNION CEMENTING THE PRODUCTIVITY GAP:
THE MEZZOGIORNO FEAR

The policy option of using (permanent) fiscal transfers to contain delinquency and default rates on existing debt ignores the lack of competitiveness and associated high-unemployment rates in peripheral countries. Such an arrangement has severe long-run costs. The high-unemployment rate in the periphery invites proactive young people to emigrate to the productive core of the euro area. Their emigration makes the periphery rely even more on transfers. Instead of facilitating economic convergence, a productivity gap will be cemented.

Fiscal transfers also distort economic activity. People in the periphery might find it more worthwhile to pursue rent-seeking activities and hunt for subsidies instead of doing something productive. Government payments, for instance, for civil servants, that might be appropriate for high-productivity parts of the country, may be too high in low-productivity areas, making government employment look more attractive than private sector work.

This is how Italy's South, the Mezzogiorno, became progressively more dependent on Northern Italy. On average, (private sector) workers in Italy's South earn around half as much as those in the North ($16,000 vs. $37,000) and are twice as likely to be unemployed (20% vs. 10%).[15] As a result, government employment looks more attractive in Sicily or Naples than in Milan. This might be one explanation as to why regional convergence in Italy faltered after the 1970s and why Italy's subsequent economic performance was so weak. Analogously, if Europe's policy makers were to adopt permanent fiscal transfers without addressing the underlying productivity gap, a similar divide may well take root within Europe.

The United States provides another example of the unintended consequences of using permanent fiscal transfers in an attempt to address an underlying productivity gap. From the 1970s, Puerto Rico's economic convergence with the US mainland began to reverse—as in Italy's Mezzogiorno. The Commonwealth of Puerto Rico became more dependent on fiscal transfers, with transfers from the US federal budget amounting to some 7.5 percent of GDP. By 2015, when a long-standing fiscal crisis led to debt defaults, many observers concluded that Puerto Rico was the Greece of the United States. It had a high poverty rate, even higher than that of Greece (45% relative to 36%), higher debt relative to government revenue, and higher interest rate payments.[16] Federal transfer payments had created, rather than solved, a poverty trap.

FAMILY TRANSFER UNION ANALOGY

The divide between the old and young provides another analogy to the transfer union besides the north-south divide. Wealth is disproportionately held by the older generation, particularly in peripheral European countries. In addition, older workers hold insider jobs that enjoy substantial privileges and protection. Restrictive labor regulations prevent the young from entering the labor market, robbing them of the opportunity to accumulate their own human capital. In response, many parents pay "family transfers" to their children—for example, by letting their adult children live in their homes. Indeed, Italians often speak of an institutionalized "Hotel Mama" arrangement.

Transition Phase to a Fiscal Union

While the Maastricht Treaty did not include any provisions for a fiscal union, recent events called for (at least some limited form of) fiscal union or coordination. As a fiscal union is plagued with moral hazard and other problems, some transition of power to the center is unavoidable. However, the traditional French central state solution seems politically infeasible. Even France is reluctant to transfer some budgetary power to Brussels. The alternative is a traditional Swiss/German rule-driven solution. Member states should strictly adhere to a set of prespecified rules. The Stability and Growth Pact (SGP) put in place in the 1990s followed this approach. However, the SGP was both insufficient and only halfheartedly implemented.

There are historical examples where the transition of budgetary power to the center was made attractive by offering member countries a better debt-financing instrument. Thomas Sargent in his Nobel Prize lecture in 2011 popularized Alexander Hamilton's successful 1790 negotiation of a federal assumption of the high levels of state debt in the aftermath of the War of Independence. The background to the 1790 assumption was a no-blame principle. The thirteen states had not been responsible for poor fiscal performance: that was a consequence of the external circumstances of the war. It might plausibly be argued that at least some European debt problems (especially for countries such as Spain and Ireland, with a strong precrisis fiscal performance) are also not the consequence of bad fiscal policies but of the global financial crisis and the institutional design of the currency union.

However, the transition of power to the center was apparently not sufficient. The United States' federal assumption of state debt in 1790 did not produce a responsible system of state finance, and within the subsequent half century, there were numerous state-level defaults and a debate about new assumptions of state debt and new ways of attenuating state indebtedness. States' fiscal irresponsibility also gravely damaged the reputation of the federal government and made external borrowing prohibitively expensive. The revenue stream assigned to service the new federal debt was also a cause of dissent and in the end contributed to the civil war. The immediate consequence of Hamilton's excise duty was a revolt in Pennsylvania (the Whiskey Rebellion of 1794). States were in the longer run divided over the shape of tariffs, which the nonmanufacturing Southern states saw as disadvantageous to them because they relied on cotton exports and the import of British manufactures.

Eurobonds

During the euro crisis, a debate about Eurobonds emerged. However, the introduction of Eurobonds was not linked with a budgetary transition of power to Brussels. Eurobonds without the transition of budgetary power would have undermined the two-pillar strategy of the Maastricht Treaty and Stability and Growth Pact: first, market discipline through credible enforcement of the no-bailout rule should (1) through interest rate responses provide member states the right incentives to contain public debt levels and (2) further rules to limit budget deficit and debt levels.

The Eurobond debate mirrors an earlier debate between Germany and France about the sequencing of the European integration process. Prior to the Maastricht Treaty, Germany resisted the European Monetary Union for a long time because it viewed a common currency as the final coronation of a political union with fiscal union. This was a strongly held view, despite the fact that historically the (first) unification of Germany in 1871 was partially preceded by a currency simplification (the actual creation of a new German currency, the mark, came only after the unification in 1873). Interestingly, Bismarck had similar problems with certain fiscally irresponsible states (Fürstentümer) within a loose confederation (North German Bund) prior to the foundation of German Empire in 1871.[17]

The French and Italian approach was to push ahead with the monetary union and hope that the missing elements would fall into place in due time. Crises might erupt, but they might be useful to follow through with the next steps at a time when "there is no alternative" (TINA principle). Such a fait accompli strategy was part of the European integration process from the beginning, but it also estranged the project from the general public. In a similar spirit, the introduction of joint liability through Eurobonds might resolve the current crisis, but the moral hazard implication would lead to further crises in the future—which would hopefully enforce through the TINA principle further integration rather than mutual resentment.

Blue and Red Eurobonds

Among the prominent Eurobond proposals was the blue and red bonds proposal by the think tank Bruegel.[18] Blue suggests safety following from debt mutualization, and red suggests risk. Blue bonds would cover public debt up to 60 percent of a country's GDP and importantly would enjoy joint and several liability. That is, if a country defaults, the other countries have to bail it out and cover the shortfall. The red bond wouldn't enjoy such a joint liability. Blue bonds would be guaranteed by all euro-area countries, and, hence, their interest rate would be very low—a big saving for the peripheral countries. One might think that this proposal also gives the right incentives not to get into excessive fiscal debt, as any extra euro of debt (once the blue bond debt limit of 60% of GDP is exhausted) has to pay the high red bond interest rate. However, although the incentives go in the right direction, their magnitude is limited. To see this, consider a country that decides to raise its public debt level from 60 percent to 61 percent. Without blue and red Eurobonds, the country would have to pay a higher interest rate for all of its 61 percent of debt. With blue and red Eurobonds, the country has to pay a higher interest rate only for the extra 1 percent of debt. The marginal incentive not to increase the debt exists but is much weaker than in the absence of blue and red Eurobonds.

Redemption Fund

The German Council of Economic Experts, an independent body often referred to as the "five wise men," proposed an alternative Eurobond construction, the redemption pact.[19] Instead of introducing a joint and several liability for the first 60 percent of public debt, in their proposal all debt beyond 60 percent would enjoy debt mutualization. That is, countries that run up large public debt levels would be the biggest beneficiaries of this scheme, while crisis countries with low debt level would not benefit as much. An integral part of the debt redemption pact was that countries would have to commit themselves to reduce their current level of public debt to 60 percent of GDP within twenty-five years. Debt mutualization would lower the interest rate burden and help to reduce the debt level over time.

Nevertheless, this scheme would have implied a severe twenty-five-year austerity program for most countries in the euro area. A main challenge of the redemption fund scheme is to determine what to do with a country that violates the rules during such a sustained period of debt reduction. Would European authorities be tough enough to expel such a country knowing that this will make things worse, or is it more likely that a new compromise would be found? Knowing this, countries' efforts to follow the agreed rules would be limited. The proposal thus faces a severe time-inconsistency problem.

Eurobills

Christian Hellwig and Thomas Philippon proposed Eurobills. Eurobills are classic Eurobonds with joint and several liability, but they are limited to only short-term debt, say up to one year.[20] Many Eurobond proponents saw Eurobills as an entry point to get a foot in the door for classic Eurobonds a few years down the road.

European Commission's Stability Bonds

In November 2011, the European Commission launched its stability Eurobond proposal involving joint liability.[21] European Commission president José Manuel Barroso had picked up on the substantial academic discussion and argued forcefully that "Stability Bonds could potentially quickly alleviate the current sovereign debt crisis, as the high-yield Member States could benefit from the stronger creditworthiness of the low-yield Member States."[22] The low-yield member states inevitably worried that the proposal would make their borrowing more expensive. Germany, the Netherlands, and Finland immediately objected. Angela Merkel quickly stated that the Commission proposals were "extraordinarily inappropriate" and "troubling" and that they would not "allow us to overcome the currency union's structural flaws." Barroso rather casually rejected the German response as a worry about timing. He also opined that it was the task of the Commission to lead the way out of the mess: "The point is if the Commission couldn't do this, who could?"[23]

ESBies

Earlier on, the Euronomics group put forward a fundamentally different proposal that did not involve any form of joint liability.[24] The idea of

113

European safe bonds (ESBies) is that a private institution or public agency would buy a portfolio of European government debt (up to 60% of GDP) and issue senior and junior European bonds. When a euro-area member state defaults on its public debt, the junior bond takes the hit. That is, junior bondholders assume the risk, while the senior bondholders are protected by the junior bondholders. The primary objective of this proposal is to explicitly address market inefficiencies. The flight-to-safety phenomenon led to rate spikes in the periphery as the crisis became more severe and simultaneously depressed interest rates in the core. The ESBies proposal would redirect cross-border flight to safety to flights from the European junior bond to the European safe bond. More details of this proposal are presented in chapter 11.

Hollande's Revival Attempts

After François Hollande became president of France in May 2012, he also made the creation of Eurobonds a priority. At his first summit as president on June 27, 2012, as he set out his "vision of growth," he was firmly blocked by Merkel, who had said a few days earlier that Eurobonds would never be created "in my lifetime."[25] As she told the German Parliament, "Apart from the fact that instruments like Eurobonds, Eurobills, debt redemption schemes and much more are not compatible with the constitution in Germany, I consider them wrong and counterproductive."[26] Several times during the following year, Hollande kept mentioning Eurobonds, knowing that he was confronting Merkel on an issue on which she could and would never yield.

ESM and QE: Eurobond through the Backdoor

In a sense, the bonds issued by the European Stability Mechanism (ESM) can be seen as Eurobonds of all euro-member states. Likewise, when the ECB started its quantitative easing (QE) measure in January 2015, several German observers complained prior to the ECB QE announcement that such an intervention would be an introduction of Eurobonds through the backdoor. The ECB did not want to undertake fiscal decisions and hence initially limited joint loss sharing to 20 percent. As described in detail in chapter 15, the lion's share of possible losses has to be absorbed by the relevant national central bank.

Policy Recommendations

As was highlighted throughout, the main benefit of individual liability is that it avoids moral hazard. However, for extreme adverse events, excessive emphasis on individual liability is counterproductive; in such circumstances, the solidarity principle should dominate. The European community thus needs a discussion of the extent to which it is willing to assume tail risk for its members. A commonly acceptable cutoff needs to be identified, agreed upon, clearly communicated, and enforced in future crises. Common liability for extreme crisis events must then go hand in hand with some kind of common control, as is to some extent reflected in nascent moves toward a more credible imposition of budget discipline in the euro area. This linkage also applied in the case of the discussion of unemployment insurance, where conditionality and uniform administration would be a key to credibility.

The discussion of European liability for the tail risk of states, however, is implicitly limited to the case where governments refinance through debt: either they repay or they default. In principle, it is possible to go beyond the limitations inherent to debt instruments and move to something more akin to government equity: GDP bonds. The basic idea is simple: GDP-linked bonds pay nothing if GDP is sufficiently depressed relative to some benchmark and pay high returns when the economy is booming. This makes payments procyclical and ensures that borrower and lender incentives are aligned. The real problem of such arrangements is a statistical one: Why should creditors trust the national accounts? In an environment such as the euro area, external auditing—via some euro-area-level authorities, like Eurostat—could be an answer to this problem.

The ability to restructure government debt in an orderly way and repay only part of the debt can be seen as an insurance mechanism. After a country suffers an adverse asymmetric shock, it can reduce its public debt burden by defaulting on it. Of course, debt restructuring should only occur in extreme tail events. Importantly, even in these extreme situations, restructuring needs to follow clear rules in order to limit economic disruption. In a multicountry currency union, it also requires a safe asset, like ESBies and firewalls that should only be used in case of insolvency to avoid spillovers to other countries. This requires us to distinguish between insolvency and illiquidity, which naturally leads to the next chapter.

7

Solvency versus Liquidity

In the early phase of the euro crisis, the no-bailout clause of the Maastricht Treaty was taken literally, and, hence, countries could not receive any bailout funds. France and other peripheral countries interpreted funding shortages of countries as a pure liquidity problem and dismissed any concerns about solvency. Germans, on the other hand, saw the funding shortages as signs of insolvency due to earlier fiscal excesses or problems caused in the banking sector.

The German economic philosophy and the French tradition may in principle agree that one should only intervene to solve liquidity problems and that, in the case of insolvency, bailouts should be ruled out. In practice, however, there remains a big divide between the German and French views. If in doubt—which is virtually always the case—the Germans view any problem as a solvency problem, while French view it as a liquidity problem. From a French perspective, liquidity provision is not a bailout; they see intervention as not violating the no-bailout clause.

While French policy makers see high interest rates as an unnecessary drain of resources by which a temporary liquidity problem morphs into a permanent solvency problem, for many Germany policy makers, they are a necessary evil to convince politicians to undertake growth-enhancing but unpopular structural reforms. Absent any enforceable rules, market discipline enforced through higher interest rates is the only force that sharpens policy makers' minds to push through reforms. Silvio Berlusconi, the Italian prime minister until November 2011, was an exemplar of such behavior. Only the constant threat of high interest rates ensured a concerted effort to implement structural reforms. When an intervention by the ECB abruptly lowered interest rates after August 5, 2011, Berlusconi promptly reneged on former promises, undid structural reforms, and went back to business as usual.

This difference between German and French views also translates into differences about whether and how aggressively the ECB should intervene. As long as pure liquidity problems are addressed and no fiscal resources are needed, the ECB as the monetary authority should supply the necessary funding. In contrast, in the case of insolvency, losses have occurred, and these losses have to be distributed. Any bailout involves fiscal resources and should have budgetary implications. Hence, it is outside the realm of the central bank. Mario Draghi, the president of the ECB, stretched the limits and by doing so saved the euro.

More specifically, this chapter attempts to answer the following questions:

- At a conceptual level, what are the differences between insolvency and illiquidity? What role do financial imperfections play?
- Why did Mario Draghi's "whatever it takes" speech make such a big difference?
- Do high interest rates morph a liquidity problem into a solvency problem, or are they needed to provide the right incentives for policy makers to implement necessary fiscal reforms?
- What are the costs of delaying a debt restructuring of insolvent countries? What should be done if one is unclear whether one faces a solvency or liquidity problem?
- What kind of policy tools should governments use in dealing with liquidity and solvency problems? Are fiscal measures needed, or is monetary policy preferable? In particular, what should be done if it is not certain whether the underlying problem is one of solvency or liquidity?

Buildup of Imbalances and the Naked Swimmer

In the first decade of the new millennium, several countries in the periphery of the euro area enjoyed strong growth—significantly above the euro-area average. The preferred explanation for this above-average growth was the convergence theory. Peripheral countries with a lower GDP per capita were catching up with the core countries in which the GDP per capita was higher.

An alternative explanation is that GDP growth was simply driven by cheap credit, and the growth path was unsustainable. For example, excessively high public expenditures in Greece before the crisis artificially boosted Greek GDP numbers. In 2010, Greece's annual public deficit reached a level of 15.7 percent of GDP, adding to a stock of public debt of 129.7 percent of GDP. In Spain, cheap credit led to an expansion of low-productivity sectors, particularly construction, providing a temporary boost to GDP but masking stagnant productivity. Cheap funding allowed inefficiencies to build up, reform efforts to falter, and capital and labor to be misallocated to low-productivity sectors.

The euro crisis uncovered many of these problems. The Spanish blog www.nadaesgratis.es adopted Warren Buffett's metaphor of a "naked swimmer." Only when the tide goes out and the water level recedes does it become apparent whether the swimmer is naked. Similarly, the GDP numbers prior to the crisis were artificially inflated with cheap financing, creating a negative output gap. That is, measured GDP exceeded potential sustainable output. The crisis then reveals that these numbers were not sustainable.

Independently of whether one believes in the convergence theory or the unsustainable credit boom theory, an adverse shock leads to a deviation from the projected path. Two questions arise: (1) does there exist a smooth transition path to the new sustainable growth path without debt restructuring, and, if so, (2) do financial markets allow the government to take this path or will financial markets freeze abruptly and suddenly cut off the supply of funding? Crucially, the first question is about solvency, while the latter is about liquidity.

Solvency

A country is insolvent if providing an extra euro of (bailout) funds yields less than the euro put in. When the present value of future tax revenues falls short of expenditures, the extra euro will be (partially) used up for paying off existing creditors rather than bridging a temporary funding gap. Without a default on existing debt, only tax increases, expenditure cuts, or growth-enhancing structural reforms can make the country solvent again. Defaulting on debt can free a country from its payment obligations and in so doing return it to solvency. Excessive debt levels cause a debt overhang problem. New investors are reluctant to provide additional funds, even if

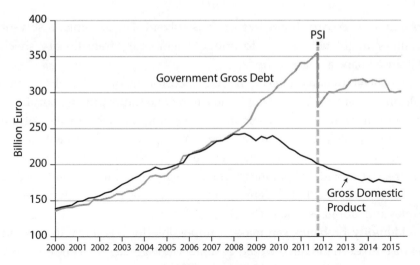

FIGURE 7.1. Greek Nominal Government Debt and GDP Level
(Source: Eurostat)

investments are profitable, because they know that, in case of success, a large fraction of the returns will accrue to existing legacy bondholders.

Many German observers saw Greek public finances early on as a solvency problem and demanded debt restructuring already in the summer of 2010. They accused European policy makers of carrying out what in domestic law would be a *"Konkursverschleppung"*—an illegal late filing of a bankruptcy petition. Recall that the actual debt restructuring was only agreed upon by Merkel and Sarkozy in Deauville in October 2010, and it finally occurred in February 2012 (see figure 7.1).

German "solventists" are skeptical that flooding the economy with liquidity and replacing dried-up excessive funding with public funding will ultimately solve the underlying structural supply-side problems that built up during the credit boom. They are calling for structural reforms and possibly an early debt restructuring, despite knowing that default might hurt a government's reputation and increase its future funding costs.

Liquidity

A country's finances are liquid if it can obtain enough funds to serve all its current funding obligations. A country can suffer from liquidity problems even when it is solvent. Financial frictions might prevent a country from obtaining necessary funds even if it is solvent. For example, a solvent country might not be able to bridge a temporary transitionary shock because financial markets froze.

Financial friction can be on the side of borrowers or lenders. For example, the government might not be able to pledge future primary surpluses because it cannot credibly commit to repaying the debt because of the time-inconsistency problem described in chapter 5. Governments face a maturity mismatch because their tax revenue stream is long term, while their short-term debt liabilities become due in short intervals and need to be rolled over regularly.[1] Debt borrowing involves leverage that concentrates and amplifies risk.

Liquidity problems can make it impossible for a country to raise an extra euro even though it would generate value greater than one euro. For example, a small shock might get amplified into a big loss through an adverse feedback loop, and it would have been worthwhile to counteract the amplification early on. In other words, multiplier effects magnify a potentially small trigger event.

If the "bailout multiplier" is positive and larger than one, it is worthwhile chipping in the extra funds, that is, the country faces a liquidity problem. In contrast, when extra funds are mostly used to pay off existing creditors instead of boosting future cash flows, the multiplier is smaller than one, and the country faces a solvency problem. The bailout multiplier can even be negative, as a bailout can distort the future behavior of market participants and politicians in a bad way—a phenomenon that economists refer to as moral hazard.

Multiple equilibria—self-fulfilling prophecies—can be seen as an extreme form of amplification. While an amplification mechanism translates a small trigger into a large dislocation, multiple equilibria can lead to large dislocations, even in the absence of a fundamental trigger. Simply, the fear itself can trigger a worse outcome. To be more precise, given the same economic fundamentals, there could be two possible outcomes (equilibria): a good and a bad one.[2] If investors believe that the government is going to repay its debt, they will offer attractive refinancing terms. Given these low rates, the government will then find it optimal not to default. But in the other equilibrium, investors expect the government to default and hence will charge high interest rates, and, given these rates, default may well become optimal. This, in turn, justifies ex post the high ex ante interest rates, and so we have a second equilibrium. A "run" on government debt can occur in the second equilibrium, especially when government debt is very short-term. A multiple equilibria conundrum is the most classic, pure liquidity problem. In this case our multiplier is infinitely large, as one may not need to invest a single euro to avoid the bad outcome. All that one needs is to switch people's beliefs.

Importantly, such liquidity-run risk can be ruled out if a country's central bank can print its own currency. Market participants know that if such a run were ever to occur, the country's central bank could simply print money and pay off the short-term debt, and hence investors would never run in the first place. After the shock has passed, the central bank has to make sure to scale back its liquidity operations to avoid any inflationary impact. But fundamentally, the central bank effectively ensures coordination on the "good equilibrium" without any accompanying inflation.

However, if the government debt is in a foreign currency, the country does not have the option to fend off such run threats. Government debt is then subject to liquidity risk, and the interest rate includes a liquidity-risk premium. Countries with debt in euros act as if their debt was in a foreign currency. That is, euro-area countries, like subsovereign units elsewhere such as Puerto Rico or US states, are subject to liquidity-run risk. Economics professor Charles Goodhart referred to the debt of governments in the euro area as "subsidiary sovereign debt."[3] The comparison between Spanish and British ten-year government bond interest rates underscored this important aspect. According to observers, both countries were in a similar situation in terms of solvency, but with the major difference that the British government could credibly overcome temporary liquidity shortfalls and hence did not pay a liquidity-risk premium, while Spain did not have that option. (See figure 7.2.)

Not only is each member state of the euro area exposed to liquidity risk, but contagion risk makes it likely that such runs spread across countries. A run that is a jump to the bad equilibrium in one country might serve as a coordinating signal to market participants to run on the debt of other countries as well. This can lead to a domino effect and hence to a rise in interest rates in several peripheral countries at the same time. As mentioned in the introduction, the Deauville agreement between Merkel and Sarkozy to restructure Greek debt held in private hands led to an increase in the interest rates on government debt not only in Greece but also in other peripheral countries.

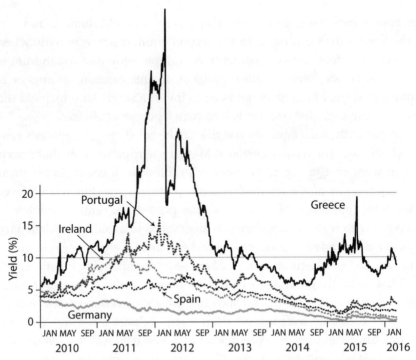

FIGURE 7.2. Sovereign 10-year Bond Yields (Source: Bloomberg)

Draghi's "Whatever It takes" London Speech

Emboldened by the outcome of the Brussels summit of June 2012 (which established a European banking union and so showed to the markets that "Europe can still act"), Mario Draghi gave a decisive speech in London on July 26, 2012. Prior to that in a private meeting, Draghi had told European Council president Herman Van Rompuy that the Brussels summit clearly demonstrated that Europe could still act when needed, and, more importantly, that Germany would not let the euro fall. At the same time, Draghi had learned from his past experience in the financial world and general market intelligence that banks were building up larger and larger hedging positions with respect to the collapse of the euro. He thus sensed that there was a strategic opportunity: if the speculative momentum were to turn, the banks would be forced to unwind these positions to cap their losses, and the euro would be secure.

It is against this background that, on July 26, 2012, he gave the subsequently celebrated London speech with this dramatic line: "Within our mandate, the ECB is ready to do whatever it takes to preserve the euro. And believe me, it will be enough."[4] This speech led to a subsequent decline in interest rates across all of peripheral Europe. The actual program, Outright Monetary Transaction (OMT), was only made public in September. Many French and Anglo-Saxon observers interpreted this decline in interest rate spreads without the central bank spending a single euro as clear evidence in favor of the multiple equilibrium interpretation. German economists countered that the decline in interest rates is no surprise because the ECB essentially extended a free contingent guarantee to government bondholders. If interest rates were to go up, the ECB would intervene and buy government bonds. With interest rates only allowed to go down, market participants, believing that they could count on the ECB, repositioned themselves and drove the rate down.

Reasons Why Draghi's Speech Made a Difference

The conviction of markets that the tide had been turned may look curious. Why did this one speech make such a difference? Earlier speeches by Angela Merkel and others, declaring that everything possible was being done and that Europe would stand or fall with the euro, had not fundamentally impressed the market.

At least three reasons can be outlined. First and foremost, the markets realized that there was backing from Berlin. Both Merkel and Schäuble implicitly supported the ECB approach, to the extent that some officials at the Bundesbank were disappointed and found themselves on the defensive. Draghi showed a Machiavellian mastery of the art of politics. With his London speech, he was leaning out the window as far as he could, but not so far as to fall out of the window. Figuratively speaking, Merkel and Schäuble were holding him, stabilizing him without pulling him back. The June summit in Brussels had given him the signal that Europe was capable of acting.

Second, Draghi's market intelligence helped him to get a good sense of how financial market participants would react. In the spring of 2012, many financial institutions started to take on hedges against risk that some countries were to leave the euro area. These hedges became increasingly expensive, as buying protection makes the underlying break-up event even more likely. Indeed Draghi had been disturbed by questions from market participants asking how they should rewrite credit default swaps for the case of a collapse of the euro. He also knew that once the momentum began to reverse, institutions that had bought this protection would make losses and reverse their action. As president of the ECB, Draghi was powerful enough to at least temporarily stabilize the situation and by doing so cause large temporary losses on these hedging positions. As hoped, the momentum reversed.

Third, the vagueness of the speech made it difficult for opponents, especially for skepticists in Germany, to attack. Ambiguity is often a critical tool of policy, especially for central banks. Draghi did not specify how he would achieve the goal of preserving the euro or which instruments and measures he would use. As soon as the ECB announced specificities, the measures were subject to legal challenges.

OUTRIGHT MONETARY TRANSACTIONS (OMT) AND THE GERMAN CONSTITUTIONAL COURT

Thus, it was only in early September 2012 that the official program, termed Outright Monetary Transactions (OMT), was announced. The promise of OMT involves the purchase of government debt in the secondary market if that country is in a program. There would be strict and effective conditionality attached to an appropriate European Financial Stability Facility/European Stability Mechanism (EFSF/ESM) program: either a full macroeconomic adjustment program or a precautionary program (Enhanced Conditions Credit Line), analogous to the IMF's conditional credit line. The September statement also made it clear that such programs would be worked out in coordination with the IMF, if possible. Critics joked that it was analogous to Voltaire's observation that the Holy Roman Empire was neither holy, nor Roman, nor an empire.[5] The OMT transactions were not outright, in that they were indirect through the EFSF/ESM programs; not monetary, because they were basically fiscal; and not transactions, because they weren't taking place.

Illiquidity Morphing to Insolvency

The Draghi speech was so important because, even in an economy with perfectly sound fundamentals, an illiquidity problem can easily morph into an insolvency problem. As soon as a government has to start paying higher interest rates, the cost of debt service drains resources, and interest rates for the private sector in form of higher mortgage rates and loan interest rates will also rise. As a result, the worries of investors leads to a deterioration of economic performance; with it, tax revenue also declines.

The intellectual argument, that even fiscally solvent countries could be victims of a run on their debt, mirrored concerns expressed in public by numerous policy makers. Non-euro countries (and above all the United States) were afraid that contagion could develop and affect major peripheral economies: Spain and Italy. Using the G7 and G20 forums, they provided open and increasingly vocal policy advice on the necessity for the euro area to present a "big bazooka." The pure existence of the big bazooka would reassure investors.

Crossing the Rubicon via Default

Determining whether the underlying problem is a liquidity or solvency problem is challenging. If one ignores a liquidity problem and does not provide extra funding, it can morph into a solvency problem. If one delays fixing a solvency problem, debt-overhang problems become more costly, and taxpayers will be worse off. Even worse, delay changes expectations about future behavior and might sow the seeds for the next crisis.

There are also differences about how various remedies work. For example, outright default and quasi-default via inflation work out differently. Outright default is to some extent like crossing the Rubicon: the government passes a point of no return. This is particularly costly if it later turns out that the underlying shock was only a temporary liquidity shock. In contrast, default through inflation can be fine-tuned ex post. As monetary easing begins, inflationary pressure builds up gradually. If, however, the shock turns out to be a pure funding liquidity shock, then inflation may never actually materialize.

These two forms of default differ in two more dimensions. First, an outright default has a sharp cutoff date. In particular, this means that debt maturing just before the restructuring is paid back in full, while debt with a longer residual maturity suffers a haircut. In contrast, inflation rises gradually, hurting all bondholders across various bond maturities. Second, the differences in the redistributive consequences of inflation and outright default go beyond the treatment of current bondholders. When a government defaults outright, the owners of government bonds take the biggest hit. Additionally, if a large fraction of bonds is held by (undercapitalized) banks, there may be further second-order effects, so the impact of the default may well stretch beyond the immediate circle of debt holders. Partial default through inflation, in contrast, leads to losses for *all* nominal debt holders, while those who are indebted or hold large real claims are the big winners. In a world with financial frictions, this wealth redistribution matters.

Sovereign-Debt Restructuring and Insolvency Mechanism

An outright default due to a debt-restructuring process triggers several costs. Of particular importance is the hold-up problem, where a small group of investors delays the restructuring process. Countries can issue their debt under domestic law, London law, or New York law. London law and in particular New York law are stricter than domestic law. In international courts, creditors have better access to effective legal recourse than in domestic ones. The main benefit of issuing debt under international law is that it acts as an ex ante commitment device to not default (because default becomes more costly) and hence lowers interest rates. On the other hand, when default occurs, these extra costs can be quite harmful. A recent example is the case of Argentina. Here, a small number of investors ("vulture funds") rejected the proposed debt restructuring and effectively blocked Argentina from using the US payment system. The vulture funds thus created a severe hold-up problem, thereby jeopardizing the entire process and inflicting more pain on the Argentinian economy. A second important ex post cost is contagion effects. Debt restructuring in one country leads to negative spill-over effects to other countries as their refinancing costs also rise.

These costs are bad ex post as they limit flexible policy response in times of crisis. However, from an ex ante perspective, ex post restructuring costs enhance the credibility of long-term commitment as they allow the country to commit to not default and hence reduce the ex ante interest rate. This leads us back to the time-inconsistency problem discussed in chapter 5. Interestingly, the ex post hold-up costs can be so large that they even hurt ex ante. For example, the introduction of collective action clauses (CAC) that require a super majority among bond holders to block a debt restructuring lowered not only ex post hold-up costs but also the ex ante interest rate governments have to pay for their debt.[6]

A common remedy for these problems is a sound, orderly, and credible restructuring mechanism. This mechanism should impose large costs for restructuring if a default is not necessitated by fundamentals but, at the same time, only entail small costs when debt is truly unsustainable. In particular, such a mechanism would effectively deal with the run problem: If the mechanism is credible, then purely liquidity-based runs are unlikely. And, finally, such an optimal mechanism, when combined with effective firewalls, should also deal with contagion problems.

Fiscal Push: Increasing Scale and Scope of EFSF and ESM

In the case of an intervention, the additional issue arises as to whether fiscal or monetary authorities, that is, governments or the ECB, should intervene. This debate was an important part of the euro crisis. If one faces a pure temporary liquidity problem, a central bank can handle it. However, if the action involves some credit risk, the intervention becomes a fiscal issue and should be handled fiscally by the governments. From a German perspective, any credit risk that the ECB might assume endangers its independence and ultimately its price-stability mandate. In addition, mistaken bailout leads to moral hazard problems. In contrast to German policy makers, French policy makers did not attach such an importance to the distinction between fiscal and monetary bailout schemes.

France and peripheral countries employed a dual approach. Some initiatives involved liquidity support provided by fiscal means using the newly established European fiscal-funding vehicles, the temporary EFSF and its successor, the permanent ESM. Other, and often very creative, initiatives involved monetary financing.

The German solvency view versus French liquidity view continuously conflicted, especially when interest rates started to rise on Italian and Spanish debt in the fall of 2010 after Deauville. For some, the high level of sovereign spreads in Spain and in Italy was a sign of insufficient fiscal adjustment (or of an excessive public exposure to bank liabilities), creating a credit (solvency) risk for the state. Others attributed these high spreads to the fact that those countries had no national currency anymore, and, as a consequence, there was essentially a liquidity problem: investors in government bonds were not protected against rollover risk.

As the situation in debt markets continued to deteriorate, in 2011, a debate progressively emerged as to whether governments in peripheral countries were facing a solvency or a liquidity crisis. This was also the moment when German-French differences in approaches explicitly crystallized. France, followed by other euro members, and encouraged by non-euro countries, started pushing for a broader use of the EFSF/ESM as a liquidity support for countries under stress. They were—and still are—highly conditional and could only be activated together with an EU-IMF program. Their amounts were limited. Loans were initially priced with a high (penalty) interest rate and decisions had to be taken unanimously by all euro-area member countries.

But the EFSF and its successor, the European Stability Mechanism (ESM) were not instruments adapted for liquidity support. They were too limited in magnitude to compensate for a major shock in a big country such as Spain. They could not be activated quickly. Unanimity in the decision process also prevented a full and speedy utilization of the EFSF as a crisis management tool. The question of the size of the EFSF became a major concern. As early as December 2010, the ECB was pushing governments to expand the EFSF. Among nonperipheral countries, France was the most anxious to expand the size and scope of the EFSF. In March 2011, Finland stood alone in opposing an increase in EFSF lending capacity because it had parliamentary elections coming. Special collateral arrangements had to be made for Finland.

EFSF as Liquidity Instrument

The European Council meeting in Brussels on July 21, 2011, marked the shift toward reshaping the EFSF as a liquidity instrument. As usual, the summit meeting was prepared during a bilateral German-French meeting that took place in Berlin on July 20, 2011.[7]

The EFSF could be used as a precautionary instrument. It was also agreed that the EFSF may buy debt on the secondary market on the basis of analyses by the ECB and decisions by mutual agreement of participating members. Its proceeds may be allocated by the beneficiary government to the recapitalization of its banks. President Sarkozy spoke of the "beginnings of a European monetary fund."[8] But this was clearly not a fund with the capacity of the Marshall Plan to spur European investment, the kind of large-scale intervention that many critics in the United States and Europe were hoping for as a solution to Europe's problems. In the subsequent months, Brussels tried to wrestle with the problem of enhancing the muscle of the facility.

The impact of the summit on markets was very short lived, despite the major changes introduced in the crisis management framework. The technical issues related to the quality and extent of the guarantee hurt its impact. First, the market realized that the seniority provision—that EFSF bond holdings were senior to publicly held bonds—meant that a possible bond purchase by the EFSF would make the remaining publicly held bonds more junior. Very soon, interest rates on peripheral debt started to increase again; the Franco-German spread widened significantly; and sentiment on some euro-area banks deteriorated markedly.

Second, and more importantly, as a private entity issuing bonds, the EFSF had to be rated. And, by nature, the mutualization of risk and the limited responsibility of each country created a potential vicious circle: when a member needed EFSF support, its guarantee was not available anymore. (The IMF suffers from a similar problem of construction: the reserves are deposits from member countries in their own currencies, so in a crisis, the supply of useable funds contracts.) To protect the creditworthiness of the EFSF and to ensure an Aaa credit rating, rating agencies asked for precautions and cushions to be built into the system, which limited the EFSF lending capacity to €220–€330 billion. The positive impact of a big bazooka—that had originally been billed as the "one trillion" announcement—soon dissipated. The necessity for a stronger, more permanent mechanism was therefore becoming apparent. The debate over its shape created increasing tensions between Germany and France.

At the summit of October 26, 2011, it seemed that an ingenious scheme had been adopted to maximize the financial power of the rescue fund while minimizing the amount of capital that the European governments would need to put up. The solution was to build on the principle of cofinancing with external (private or public) investors, with the EFSF taking the first-loss tranche. In effect, the Europeans were borrowing from the principles on which the private securitization market had been established: the EFSF would provide a first-loss tranche insurance for government bonds, up to an agreed percentage.

ESM: A Permanent Facility

The EFSF was set up as a temporary funding facility because of the less-lenient initial no-bailout interpretation of the Maastricht Treaty. It was planned to end in 2013. In contrast, the European Stability Mechanism (ESM) would be permanent. It was to take over the tasks previously undertaken by the EFSF and the EFSM. For a while, they would run in parallel to maximize firepower. In particular, the EFSF would continue to fund the existing facility agreements for Portugal, Ireland, and Greece. The combined lending capacity of EFSF/ESM stood at €700 billion. Learning from past mistakes, the ESM came with a new emergency decision-making procedure under which financial assistance may be granted if supported by a qualified majority of at least 85 percent of the votes cast. In fact, the ESM is something akin to a European Monetary Fund; it uses a guarantee from member states to help other member states in distress. The difference is that the conditionality for help is imposed by the European Commission (or troika), rather than the ESM itself, and that the IMF does not borrow on private capital markets.

The ratification of the ESM treaty was full of stumbling blocks. Most notably, in October 2011, the Slovakian center-right government of Iveta Radicova fell when, after the parliamentary vote on ratification of the ESM treaty, the Slovakian Parliament decided not to contribute to the Greek package. A small party in the four-party coalition opposed the package as a "road to socialism."[9] It was easy to claim that the whole exercise was unfair, in that the beneficiaries, the Greeks, were far richer in terms of GDP per capita than Slovakians.

Despite these troubles, the final version of the ESM treaty was signed by euro-area member states on February 2, 2012.[10] The ESM itself was scheduled to start operating in September 2012. Unlike the EFSF, the ESM bond holdings did not enjoy seniority over publicly held bonds. (Policy makers had learned that without this pari passu provision, the more the ESM intervens, the more junior private sector creditors would become, and the action might thus have no effect on credit spreads.) In addition, if the ESM's capital were to be reduced in the aftermath of a borrower default, the prescribed leverage ratio would be maintained and automatically limit the lending capacity: there would be no new loans.[11] These provisions made the ESM quite secure for the creditor governments and for the rating agencies, but rather ineffective as a potential crisis lender. The

German Constitutional Court accepted the ESM in a verdict that largely rejected the complaints of some conservative German economists and politicians.[12]

However, despite all these fiscal efforts, the impact on sovereign interest rates in peripheral countries was limited.

Monetary Push

"Lender of Last Resort" for Governments

France, increasingly frustrated by the inability to implement and significantly expand the EFSF/ESM, started to lean toward using the ECB as a liquidity backstop (encouraged by positions taken by non-euro governments). French officials were very much aware of German opposition. They may have thought it was mainly of a legal and formal nature and could therefore be circumvented by a properly designed scheme. After all, Germany had accepted the financing of governments by banks, themselves funded by an unlimited liquidity provision by the Eurosystem. In terms of money creation and monetary impact, there was no big difference. Furthermore, other central banks around the world were purchasing public debt on a large scale.

Once the liquidity approach to the crisis gained credence, it was only a matter of time before calls were formulated for the ECB to take more decisive action and stabilize public-debt markets. The idea of the central bank as a lender of last resort to governments was floated. It extended the traditional lender of last resort rule to illiquid but solvent banks recommended in Walter Bagehot's famous book *Lombard Street* of 1873. Market analysts and some government officials jumped onto this bandwagon, but most kept their recommendations private, with the sole exception of the United Kingdom, whose ministers called openly for ECB interventions.

Not surprisingly, those ideas were rejected by German authorities (the government and the Bundesbank) as being in contradiction with the prohibition of monetary financing. French officials tried to build schemes through which ECB financing would come without limits, but indirectly. The first idea was to give the EFSF/ESM a banking license, hence allowing it to refinance its loans with the Eurosystem, technically giving it infinite firepower; this was not accepted by Germany. A second possibility was to use IMF resources to be combined with the EFSF/ESM. That would necessitate, however, an increase in resources that took a long time to materialize and was politically sensitive in an IMF context: in particular, it needed the assent of the US Congress.

French SDR Push

In the second half of 2011, France put an additional proposal on the table: using SDRs to finance the guarantee part of the expanded EFSF. At this stage, the German-French debate became closely intertwined with the G20 French presidency.

The focus point for the French initiative was the IMF's special drawing right (SDR), an instrument originally devised in the context of the global fixed exchange rate regime of the 1960s to provide more liquidity for the international monetary system. SDRs had never in practice played a significant role in the international monetary system. Sarkozy and his advisers believed that an SDR initiative would appeal to the Chinese leadership, as they were unsatisfied by the position of the US dollar in the international monetary system.

One consequence of this strange twist in the debate was to bring the Bundesbank to the core of the policy dialogue. The Bundesbank president together with the German Finance Ministry were de facto the deciding German voices on those issues. The Bundesbank was historically very hostile to any increased role for the SDR and was certainly incensed at the idea that it could be used to ease financing constraints of euro-area governments. Back in 1994, the then Bundesbank president, Hans Tietmeyer, had plunged the IMF annual meeting in Madrid into a crisis when he blocked plans agreed on by all the G7 finance ministers to issue SDRs for use in enhancing the IMF's power to support indebted developing countries. Jens Weidmann, Tietmeyer's successor, also totally opposed the idea of using the SDR to rescue European governments, and his lead was followed by the German government.

The Cannes G20 Summit was supposed to be a crowning achievement for the French G20 presidency. Instead, it ended in disarray, when Europe proved incapable in sorting out its own divergences and difficulties. Barack Obama, under pressure from his own Congress, was deeply reluctant to contribute to an expansion of IMF funds without clearer signs that the euro area was sorting out its problems. Admitting he had been given "a crash course in European politics," the US president urged the Greek and Italian Parliaments to take decisive action to control their deficits and so combat what he described as some of the psychological origins of the crisis.[13] He also urged the euro area to start putting some resources into its European Financial Stability Facility (EFSF). There was a moment of great tension when, under joint pressure from the United States and others, Merkel resisted and said that, after the war, the Allies had given monetary policy autonomy to the Bundesbank and they had to live with it now.

Quantitative Easing

The differences between German and French attitudes again became very apparent in the fall of 2014 when inflation expectations dropped across Europe, including in Germany. The ECB was considering large-scale purchases of government debt from all member states of the euro area. It had strong support from the French side, while Germans mostly opposed quantitative easing. Further details of this program, which was announced in January 2015, are discussed in chapter 15.

Policy Recommendations

Solvency and liquidity are difficult to distinguish in practice. Should debt prove to be unsustainable, debt restructuring should be possible with as little disruption as possible. This calls for an effective debt-restructuring and insolvency procedure for government debt.

Importantly, any debt restructuring needs to be preceded by the creation of strong firewalls to avoid contagion and spillover effects. The experience after Deauville and during the first Grexit (Greek exit) rumblings in the summer of 2012 illustrate what happens if no such firewalls are in place: spillovers threaten the cohesion of the currency union. In contrast, during the Graccident (Greek accidental exit) discussion of 2015, firewalls—in particular, the ECB QE program—were in place, and contagion effects were accordingly contained.

When it is not clear whether a country is insolvent or simply illiquid, restructuring might take the form of reprofiling: the maturity of all debt is simply extended. This buys extra time for all parties involved and eliminates illiquidity runs.

Another important issue concerns the question of who should have the trigger rights for a government default. Finding an optimal sovereign debt-restructuring mechanism, especially in the case of the euro area, is not easy. The ESM could in theory, like the IMF, insist on a debt restructuring as a precondition to provide liquidity support. Recall that the ESM can only lend if the public debt level is sustainable. Such intervention is, of course, immensely contentious.

8

Austerity versus Stimulus

Even during the Maastricht negotiations, policy makers had doubts that the no-bailout rule would impose enough market discipline in good times. It was realized that market discipline (through the credible threat of higher interest rates after imprudent behavior) cannot be exclusively relied upon to ensure government debt sustainability. German policy makers in particular have always understood and internalized the necessity of fiscal rules to limit the overall public debt level. Without such a framework, government debt might eventually reach an unsustainable path, thus forcing the central bank to adopt an inflationary policy.

Accordingly, it is not surprising that the Stability and Growth Pact (SGP) was basically invented by the German Ministry of Finance. "Drei Komma Null," the deficit convergence criterion, had become the endlessly repeated mantra (and, in France, nickname) of the then German finance minister Theo Waigel.[1] Jürgen Stark, who was then in the German Finance Ministry and later became vice president of the Bundesbank before he became the ECB's chief economist, was one of the strongest defenders of fiscal rectitude and the SGP. Interestingly, the exact number, 3.0 percent, was derived by a Frenchman, Jacques Delors, when he as French finance minister pushed for the strong franc, the *franc fort*, in the early 1980s. Still, French adhesion to the SGP had from the beginning only been half-hearted. Only at the last moment, under strong pressure from Germany and the Bundesbank, was the SGP at last accepted during the final preparations for the launch of the euro. At the time, the new socialist prime minister Lionel Jospin—a former Trotskyite—had insisted on a change in the name of the pact, bringing "Growth" into the title on the same footing as "Stability."

Starting from the negotiations for the Maastricht Treaty and the SGP, fiscal policy rules following the traditional German rigorist approach clashed with deeply ingrained Keynesian instincts in France. The main controversy was whether the 3.0 percent deficit rule should also be applied in times of recessions.

The importance of the German tradition may have been blurred in the first decade of economic and monetary union (EMU) as Germany itself seemed to agree to a weakening of some rules. France and Germany both first ignored the SGP and then had it temporarily suspended in November 2003 as a counterbalance to the threat of recession. In 2005, the disciplinary mechanism was again softened; many processes became merely discretionary, and new procedural provisions made it harder to take action against noncompliant states. By the end of the 2000s, however, Germany was moving back to a more conservative stance. In particular, the Bundestag, in 2009, enacted a debt brake (*Schuldenbremse*), with the intention of limiting over the course of a business cycle the volume of new public debt issued, both at the federal level and at that of the Länder (German states), and in effect imposing a balanced budget from 2016. The 2009 decision was treated as a major German success, and Germany wanted to see other European countries adopt similar legislation.

In particular, Germans thought that government debt to GDP ratios in most European countries were already excessive and that the underlying problems were structural. A fiscal stimulus would only distract and delay necessary structural reform that could restore Europe's competitiveness in an increasingly global world economy. In Germany, fiscal stimulus is viewed as a *"Strohfeuer"* (literally, a straw fire, which would loosely translate to a "flash in the pan"). Fiscal stimulus delivers some short-term boost, but this boost is not sustainable, only serves to temporarily cover up underlying structural issues, and in the long run might do more harm than good.

Overall, the debate is not about the desirability of consolidating and reducing the sovereign debt burden; the large run-ups in debt levels of the past few years probably make this a necessity. Rather, the debate is about how this reduction is best achieved. Now, the first important thing to realize is that society ultimately cares about debt *ratios*, that is, debt over GDP, not debt levels per se. Policy makers can push down this ratio either by decreasing the numerator (debt) or increasing the denominator (GDP). Alas, measures that push down debt (austerity) also have a tendency to push down GDP, and, conversely, measures that might increase GDP (stimulus programs) at the same time increase debt. The question, thus, is the following: to minimize fiscal debt burdens, should governments try to push austerity efforts as soon as possible or might such front-loaded austerity actually be self-defeating?

In this chapter, we will first review debates among academics, professional economists, and policy makers about the need for stimulus measures in downturns. We will then review recent developments in the European crisis through the lenses of these analytical reflections, highlighting the differences in approaches between France and Germany.

In particular, this chapter will address the following questions:

- How does government spending work to stimulate an economy, and what is the Keynesian multiplier? In particular, when is government spending particularly effective, and, conversely, when is austerity particularly harmful?
- Should contractions always be interpreted as harmful deviations from the economy's potential? Or can GDP growth be excessive and unsustainable and recessions be seen as a correction?
- Has the public debate on creditor conditions in bailouts unfairly lumped austerity measures and structural reforms together?
- What general lessons about the optimal conduct of fiscal policy in times of crisis can we draw?

We start this chapter with three sections of academic reasoning before outlining how the political austerity versus stimulus debate played out during the euro crisis.

The Fiscal Multiplier Debate

In this debate, the French philosophy aligns itself naturally with those cautioning against the self-defeating nature of excessive austerity, while the German philosophy is wary of delays in necessary fiscal adjustment and structural reforms. Both views are deeply rooted in a long-standing debate about the economics of fiscal policy interventions. These concerns, in turn, reflect the demand-side versus supply-side perspectives.

The first thing to realize is that a macroeconomy is fundamentally different from the individual economic agents populating it. For the economy as a whole, the spending of someone is always the income of someone else. The gut feeling of many politicians—that a state should be run like an individual household or firm, a feeling that Keynes called the "fallacy of composition"—fails to grasp this fundamental distinction. For concreteness, suppose, following the analysis of Keynes in the 1930s, that all households save, say, 10 percent of their income (so the *marginal propensity to consume* out of current income is 90%). A €1 increase in fiscal expenditure increases the income of some household by €1, and so this household spends an additional 90 cents. These 90 cents in turn are extra income for another household, which then spends 90 percent of that income (i.e., 81 cents), and so on. All in all, GDP will have risen by €10, so there is a government spending multiplier of 10.

We can draw three important lessons from this classical Keynesian analysis. First, expenditure increases should be more effective than tax cuts. In our simple model, a tax cut of €1 would increase GDP by only €9, not €10. Second, in this Keynesian world, a decrease in the share of income dedicated to spending—that is, a conscious, economy-wide effort to increase savings—may well be counterproductive. The *share* of income saved will of course rise, but overall income may fall so much that aggregate savings also go down. This is the so-called paradox of thrift. And, third, in a world of heterogeneous agents (with different marginal propensities to consume), fiscal measures should target those individuals who tend to spend a large share of their income. If, for example, the measures were targeted at individuals who only spend 50 percent of their income, the multiplier would only be 5.

The GDP impact of these demand effects depends very much on the behavior of the supply side of the economy. If supply does not react, demand shocks will simply translate into higher prices and not move output much. That is, instead of quantities, prices react. If, instead, prices are sluggish to respond (they are "sticky"), then quantities—like GDP and employment—also respond. In that case, an increase in prices is accompanied by a decrease in unemployment. This negative relationship between inflation and unemployment is known among economists as the *Phillips curve*. The more flexible the prices, the more a given boost to demand is reflected in higher prices rather than higher employment. Thus, in a world with quite flexible prices, government spending multipliers are likely to be quite small, and vice versa.

The Classical Rebuttal

The original Keynesian analysis was, however, soon challenged on various grounds. As Milton Friedman stressed in the early 1950s, the old Keynesian multiplier story relies on the implicit assumption that the marginal propensity to consume is invariably fixed and, in particular, does not depend on expectations of future income. But individuals should take their future income into account; in the words of Friedman, their consumption should be based on their "permanent," or lifetime average, income.[2] Applied to our Keynesian multiplier analysis, this simple realization has a profound implication: Households are fully aware that today's government spending must be financed by higher taxes now or in the future, so their lifetime income has not changed at all. And so, under some auxiliary assumptions (such as a lack of borrowing constraints), their private saving will rise in anticipation of future tax increases. This idea— basically a reminder that even for a government that can borrow there is no free lunch—is the famous Ricardian equivalence result. In flexible price models that explicitly incorporate this mechanism, government spending multipliers usually hover around zero.[3]

The empirical evidence is, however, not favorable to this pure form of the Ricardian equivalence result. As it turns out, the consumption-savings trade-off is not primarily driven by permanent income; for example, even temporary tax rebates are found to have had profound impacts on consumer spending behavior.[4] Credit constraints are a widely cited explanation for this: households that cannot borrow as much as they would like will consume out of a temporary increase in income, even if their permanent income is unchanged. Overall, these findings suggest that the simple Keynesian consumption model may, despite its shaky theoretical foundations, still be a useful approximation of reality.

Limited Crowding-Out Effects with the Interest Rate Close to Zero

Before we can laud the virtues of government stimulus, however, we need to take interest rates into account. In the original Keynesian model reviewed above, interest rates in the wider economy were assumed fixed. But in practice, any stimulus-providing government must somehow finance its spending, and usually this is done through extra borrowing. In normal circumstances, this borrowing will push up the risk-free interest rate; hence, consumption and, in particular, investment will fall. These contractionary effects tend to make the multiplier much smaller. Notice, however, the qualifier "in normal circumstances": in times of deep economic crisis, the interest rate required to put spending back up to normal levels may be far below zero. But as people always have the option of just hoarding cash (which pays zero interest), the nominal interest rate simply cannot fall much below zero—the dreaded zero lower bound (ZLB). The ECB's decision to set a slightly negative rate shows that the bound is not strictly zero. In deep recessions, when without the ZLB the interest rate would be deeply negative, a fiscal stimulus would only lift this hypothetical shadow interest rate. However, this hypothetical increase is irrelevant, since the actual interest rate is stuck around zero. Hence, as the actual interest rate does not move, there is no crowding-out effect.

This, in a nutshell, is why the economic theory literature differentiates between multipliers in normal times and multipliers in deep recessions. The fact that excessive Greek government spending prior to the crisis boosted Greek GDP indicates that even in normal times the fiscal multiplier is not zero. Of course, the fiscal multiplier in times of crisis seems larger. The Greek post-2010 spending cuts leading to contraction larger than predicted lends credence to this claim.

And there are yet more reasons to increase government expenditure if aggregate output is depressed. Low output and austerity may well leave lasting scars if unemployment is already very high, possibly due to the continued erosion of human capital, a hypothesis that some have called the "hysteresis" effect.[5] A sudden fiscal contraction can hence give an economy growing at stall speed the final push into recession. Finally, in an environment of extremely low interest rates, government investment projects become more profitable as they can be funded more cheaply.

All of these arguments were among the key motivations underlying the initial calls for government stimulus back in 2008.

Interest Rate Credit Spreads

There is yet an important dimension to the interest rate debate when a country borrows in a foreign or common currency: borrowing interest rates on government debt are not necessarily risk-free rates. With excessive government borrowing, sovereign debt may actually be viewed as risky, and so yields on government debt could spike even in a ZLB environment—something the Keynesian analysis presented above simply does not consider—and potentially even flip the sign of the multiplier. In light of this, talk about confidence effects gained traction within policy circles after 2010. It was widely argued that decisive fiscal austerity would create confidence in the sustainability of public finances and coordinate the economy on a low spread, low default risk equilibrium. In contrast, delaying the required consolidation may well erode confidence and could push the economy toward a bad equilibrium. The higher the outstanding stock of debt, the more likely such an adverse scenario becomes. Paul Krugman, arguably the most prominent modern Keynesian economist along with Joseph Stiglitz, repeatedly ridiculed this view by terming this concern the "confidence fairy."[6]

There is yet another layer to the confidence story. Historically, we can observe a reasonably tight link between sovereign risk and borrowing conditions in the wider economy. For example, rating agencies regularly take a country's debt rating as the ceiling for all corporate debt residing in that country. Given this link, a decline in confidence would worsen funding conditions not only for the government but for everyone in the country. Hence it should have further negative second-round effects on overall economic activity. Phrased in the simple language of multipliers, this reasoning implied that, against the background of excessive government debt, extra spending and a delay of the necessary consolidation would produce very little in terms of output benefits, and output may even *fall*, implying a negative multiplier.

The Multiplier in International Context

Much of the discussion was implicitly framed in the context of a single country. However, fiscal stimulus by a country that is very open to trade might spill over to other countries rather than help the country itself. In other words, the government fiscal spending multiplier with respect to its own domestic economy output falls as an economy's propensity to import rises. This dimension is also important for understanding the debate surrounding German stimulus. Germany as a very open economy would benefit less from a domestic demand stimulus, not only because its output gap is close to zero but also because a fiscal stimulus would spill over to its neighbors. The German reluctance to start a stimulus program—and the periphery's interest in such a demand boost—is thus immediately understandable from simple self-interest. This provides a revealing example of how deeper underlying philosophical motivations align with short-term self-interest.

The Empirical Dimension

Empirically, the multiplier is difficult to measure because it depends on the (unobservable) counterfactual—how the economy would have fared without a stimulus or austerity measure. To derive the counterfactual scenario, theoretical models are employed. The first thing to say is that there is not a consensus multiplier that has emerged from the recent wave of research. For example, in her 2011 survey article, Valerie Ramey finds that "reasonable people can argue that the data do not reject 0.5 or 2."[7] Of course, the way GDP is measured in the national accounts, any extra euro spent by governments automatically increases GDP by definition by one euro. Whether the multiplier is larger or smaller than one depends on whether it stimulates extra output or crowds out private consumption or investment due to a higher real interest rate.

If a consensus emerged, it is that the government spending multipliers in recessions exceed those in expansions and that the multiplier depends on the stance of economic policy.[8] For example, Robert Hall finds a multiplier between 0.5 and 1.0 when monetary policy makers can lower the interest rate but argues that the multiplier may be as high as 1.7 if monetary policy is constrained because the interest rate cannot be reduced below zero percent.[9] Calibrations of a New Keynesian model at the ZLB give a multiplier as high as 3–4. In an influential study, IMF economists concluded that government spending multipliers at the trough of the European recession were much larger than originally believed.[10] Instead of calibrating theoretical models to obtain a counterfactual scenario, other researchers exploit regional differences in government spending within a country. For example, Nakamura and Steinsson find multipliers consistent with these high numbers.[11] Stimulus skeptics point out that in countries with high levels of corruption, there is a high probability that stimulus funds would be diverted.[12]

Researchers that stress the virtues of austerity highlight that fiscal prudence could indeed be short-term *and* long-term beneficial.[13] They also stress that expenditure cuts are more effective than tax hikes. Proponents of austerity measures like to point to the case of Canada in the mid-1990s. Canada was able to consolidate the budget and at the same time experience positive growth. Pro-stimulus commentators are also quick to reject the positive Canadian experience and argue that this was only possible because fiscal prudence was accompanied by expansionary monetary policy (and so an exchange rate depreciation), which, coupled with strong economic performance in the United States, led to an export boom.

The Output Gap versus Unsustainable Booms Debate

New Keynesians tend to argue that the economy has a natural state, but the economy deviates from it because of price and wage rigidities, financial frictions, and other imperfections. Following Milton Friedman's influential 1968 presidential address, new Keynesians focus on the notion of the output gap, the difference between the natural level of output and the actual level of output. The natural level of output is the output level that would be obtained if the economy could flexibly and instantaneously adjust at all times to all shocks hitting it. Actual economies fail to attain this frictionless benchmark, and the economy fluctuates around it, sometimes above, sometimes below, with accelerating inflation or disinflation taken as a signal of what the sign of the output gap is.

THE RULER OR PLUCKING MODEL

An older Keynesian tradition has experienced a revival since the crisis, through authors like Paul Krugman.[14] It argues that there is a potential amount of output that economies almost always fail to achieve. This makes business-cycle peaks the natural measure of productive capacity and suggests extrapolation from past business-cycle peaks to measure current output gaps, an approach that has been called the *ruler model*. In other words, recessions are only temporary phenomena.[15] In Milton Friedman's 1964 *plucking model*, recessions temporarily pull the economy down. The deeper the recession, like the harder one pulls down on the string of a guitar, the larger the bounce back to where the old (from peak-to-peak) trend line should be.

While the US economy typically returned to its prerecession trend potential (and hence recessions were temporary) for most of the postwar era, this was not the case for many other countries, as recessions permanently decreased output. In a recent paper, Olivier Blanchard, Eugenio Cerutti, and Lawrence Summers show empirically that not only the level but also the growth rate permanently decreases in many countries.[16] The U.S. data since 2010 suggest that this is may also be the new reality for the United States: the guitar string does not pluck back.

Keynesians favorite explanation for this empirical finding is the hysteresis hypothesis: long-lasting recessions destroy human capital and workers' skills, depressing the economy further in the long run. This provides an additional reason for undertaking aggressive stimulus interventions in order to counteract hysteresis effects. Elsewhere Larry Summers went further, suggesting that the output gap was not temporary but permanent, and that industrial countries were in "secular stagnation," requiring large scale investment, even at the cost of inducing bubbles, in order to escape from the predicament.[17]

"Boom-and-Bust" Theory of Unsustainable Booms

According to the Austrian "boom-and-bust" theory, booms can be excessive and unsustainable especially when they are fueled by credit expansions and accompanied by malinvestment. Imbalances and bubbles can emerge. In these cases subsequent recessions are simply corrections of earlier excesses.[18]

In Greece, government expenditures artificially boosted the economy. Before 2007, capital flows within Europe led to an appearance of a convergence in GDP, but fundamental misallocation of resources and production capacity in fact exacerbated the gap. Imbalances and bubbles built up, whose bursting culminated in the euro crisis. The GDP growth rates were artificially inflated and did not reflect underlying economic strength. For example, Greece's GDP grew by 69.1 percent from 2000 to 2008, considerably larger than the 35.6 percent growth for the other twenty-seven EU countries.[19] In 2010, its annual deficit level ultimately turned out to be 15.7 percent of an inflated level of GDP. From a German perspective, it is difficult to imagine that a further increase in government spending would improve the situation. The decline of the Greek economy is thus seen as a correction of earlier excesses, even though there might be some overshooting.

In other parts of Europe, such as Spain, capital inflows mostly ended up in the less-productive sectors, like housing. Total productivity did not increase; most of the GDP growth was due to increased usage of capital. Credit booms could hurt growth by inducing labor reallocations toward low-productivity growth sectors such as the construction sector.[20] In sum, increased government spending and international capital flows were for many years simply a palliative that covered up structural shortcomings. Such a cover up can only work for so long. German skepticism toward euro-area countries spending their way out of the crisis was deep rooted.

To get the economy growing again, what is needed are not extra spending measures but rather fundamental reforms dealing with structural problems in the public and private sectors (clientelism, cronyism, vested interests, entrenched elites).

Politics Connects Structural Reforms and Austerity

Theoretically, one can consider the debate between austerity and stimulus as independent from the debate over whether to push through structural supply-side reforms or not. Both debates are however linked when one takes political economy considerations into account. US economists have the strong view that reforms are best done in good times because economic growth provides extra revenue to pay off people who lose from the reforms. Also, in New Keynesian models, structural reforms can be counterproductive when monetary accommodation is ruled out because the interest rate cannot be set far below zero.

In contrast, Germans are convinced that serious structural reforms in Europe are almost impossible to achieve in good times for political reasons. This attitude possibly reflects the federal structure in which many entities can block political initiatives. The fact that structural reforms are disruptive in the short run and only boost the economy in the long-run—possibly after the next election cycle—is another factor making politicians myopic, overly cautious, and reluctant to undertake structural reforms. Jean-Claude Juncker colorfully summarized European politicians' dilemma as: "We all know what to do, but we don't know how to get re-elected after we've done it."[21] Only when uncertainty about current status quo is great and the situation bleak, can politicians clearly credibly communicate to the public that changes are needed.[22] The famous TINA (There Is No Alternative) principle enunciated by Great Britain's Margaret Thatcher also applies to structural reforms. Unpleasant choices can only be made when the situation is really desperate. Easy money and stimulus spending are excuses that allow governments to avoid tough choices; and avoiding tough choices erodes the administrative quality of institutions. Another reason why politicians are less reluctant to conduct reforms in times of crisis is that the short-run pain inflicted by reforms can less clearly be blamed on the politicians' actions rather than on the general business environment.

Germany's Experience with Painful Structural Reforms

In arriving at these conclusions, Germany drew from its past experience, with two episodes being of particular importance. First, right at the beginning of the history of the modern Federal Republic, in the late autumn of 1950, with Germany mired in a deep balance of payments crisis, the German government—against the recommendations of some foreign commentators—stuck with its economic liberalization program and tightened fiscal and, in particular, monetary policy, with some very unpopular interest rate hikes. The apparent success of this operation—and so a fundamental trust in the virtues of fiscal prudence—became ingrained in the German psyche. Later, especially in 1978 and in 1987, Germany resisted foreign and especially American pressure to engage in fiscal expansion, and the result made Germany stronger in the face of unexpected challenges that could not have been anticipated: the second oil price hike in 1979 and the move to German unification in 1989–1990.

A second decisive learning experience, in the mid-2000s, was Chancellor Gerhard Schröder's implementation of reforms to increase labor flexibility and competitiveness. In part, this measure was a response to competition from emerging Asian and Latin American producers, and the response also included the outsourcing of many elements of the production chain to low-wage neighboring countries to the east. The reforms were implemented because politicians saw no other easy way out. The view within German ministries is that politicians will always try to avoid politically costly structural reforms even if they boost growth in the long run. In the mid-2000s, Germany implemented reforms only because it had no alternative. These reforms were fiercely opposed by trade unions and many voters and by many in the then ruling party, the Social Democrats. A politically savvy politician would stay away from unpopular reforms that only pay off in the long run.

Many of Gerhard Schröder's political advisers worked hard to find an easier way out, such as an interest rate cut by the ECB or a fiscal stimulus. However, these options were denied at that time: the ECB was not able to cut the interest rates as a lower interest rate would have been suboptimal for the euro area as a whole. This was also the reason why the German media and economists did not criticize the ECB. Second, at the European Commission—with Klaus Regling as general manager—pressure was exerted to abide by the rules of the SGP. Schröder had forged an alliance with the then French president Jacques Chirac to weaken the SGP. Klaus Regling resisted, and he submitted a court case against the European Council's decision to weaken the excessive deficit procedure for Germany and France. Only losses in German regional elections and strong arguments by German economists made Schröder concede and opt for reforms. Labor market and pension reforms were implemented. At that time, the *Economist* famously called Germany "the sick man of Europe."[23] After a few years, Germany benefited from the reforms and presented itself as a model for the rest of Europe.

OTHER STRUCTURAL REFORMS IN EUROPE

The roots of the concerns that drove the Germans lay further back, in the perception that under the Nazi dictatorship the expansion of state expenditure had been a way of increasing state control and the possibilities for arbitrary and corrupt actions. The experience of communist-planning regimes also drove many in former communist countries to view government deficits and debt through a similar lens. Leszek Balcerowicz, in Poland, the major architect of the country's post-1989 reforms, warned insistently about the dangers of a government debt buildup and installed a clock that vividly showed the rapidity of modern Poland's debt accumulation. The Bulgarian finance minister and Deputy Prime Minister Simeon Djankov liked to stress that the hawkish approach to government finance in the East was a valuable lesson for Europe as a whole and that there was a virtuous grouping of European countries with the pleasant-sounding acronym BELLs (Bulgaria, Estonia, Latvia, and Lithuania) that stood in contrast to the horrible sounding Mediterranean PIGS (Portugal, Italy, Greece, and Spain).[24]

The Latvian reform program in particular was an international casus belli for the contrasting economic schools, with Paul Krugman insisting that the stabilization program was impossibly harsh and could not succeed. The Latvian prime minister, years later, liked to point out how Latvia had shown that tough medicine worked, saying, "Krugman famously said back in December 2008 that Latvia is the new Argentina, it will inevitably go bankrupt, and now he has difficulty apparently admitting he was wrong."[25]

The perspective among Keynesians, especially in the United States, is quite different. They would argue that it is easier to push through structural reforms in good times because it is less painful. This difference in views became apparent during a panel discussion between Larry

Summers and Wolfgang Schäuble during the IMF and World Bank annual meetings in fall 2014. Both were outspoken. Summers said, for example, that "What's happening in Europe is not working" and "The monolithic focus on the financial deficit to the exclusion of the investment deficit, which causes growth deficit, has been a very substantial error."[26] Schäuble replied, "You have to know the specificities of Europe—on average (Europeans') expenditure for social purposes in relation to GDP is double compared to the US, Canada and Australia."[27] He also repeated that structural reforms can only be agreed upon and implemented in crisis times.

The European Policy Debate on Austerity versus Stimulus

The European policy debate was characterized by an initial coordinated attempt to overcome the contagion that spread from the demise of Lehman in 2008. Afterward, Germany tried to consolidate public finances while France and other countries called for more stimulus packages. The term *austerity* is a misnomer, as all the various EU packages to peripheral countries were in fact *still relaxing austerity*. Without all these packages, the adjustments required to bail out countries, particularly in Greece, would have been more savage than anything observed in practice. Of course, it may be argued that the fiscal adjustment should have been even more gradual, but domestic political considerations in creditor countries proved to be a hard constraint.

Coordinated Global Stimulus after the Lehman Crisis

The crisis years were accompanied by a constant back and forth between calls for fiscal rectitude and the need for government stimulus. By the time the global financial crisis broke out in 2007, Germany had a strong budget position, having absorbed the consequences of reunification in less than two decades. The same principles were to be applied to the rest of Europe. However, at the height of the financial crisis in late 2008, after the Lehman collapse, policy makers everywhere, including Germany, acted in unison to prevent a repetition of the Great Depression: radical fiscal expansions were called for, and worries about future deficit corrections were pushed aside. Precisely this happened, for example, in Italy and Spain, where large stimulus measures were unveiled at the peak of the crisis. The London G20 summit in April 2009 had explicitly called for coordinated fiscal expansion.

German Attempts to Repair the Stability and Growth Pact

This thinking had changed, however, by early 2010: in February, the G7 finance ministers agreed that the world economy appeared to be healing and turned their focus to fiscal consolidation. Indeed, in the aftermath of the crisis, fiscal coordination and fiscal discipline came to be a calling card of the Brussels authorities. Germany was especially eager to work with the European Commission to repair and update the SGP through the EU institutions, so that it should not seem that this concern was a particularly German obsession.

Strengthening national fiscal rules meant, in the view of the Commission, a consistent approach to accounting (ESA95 accounting required for EU level fiscal surveillance), sufficient capacity in national statistical offices to comply with EU data and reporting requirements, and forecasting systems that provide reliable and unbiased growth and budget projections. But the new initiative also meant "national fiscal rules that reflect Treaty obligations and respect Treaty reference values on deficit and debt, and are consistent with the medium-term budgetary objective."[28] How could that be achieved?

On September 29, 2010, the European Commission announced a "six-pack" as a mechanism to identify the causes of persistent economic divergences within the European Union and correct macroeconomic imbalances. The directives were implemented by the European Council in November 2011.[29] The Fiscal Compact is an intergovernmental agreement (based on the Vienna protocol), which ultimately was signed in March 2012 by EU members, with the exception of the Czech Republic and the United Kingdom. The European Commission has some oversight powers, but, legally speaking, it is outside the EU treaty framework.

Interestingly, the Germans and the French (and in particular other Southern countries) differed quite strongly in their interpretation of these measures. According to the German perspective, the imbalance monitoring and correction procedure is simply a new, more sophisticated check on the fiscal excesses of governments. In contrast, many Southern member states emphasize less the government debt dimension of the imbalance procedure and instead focus more on current account imbalances, with the persistent German surpluses seen as one of the biggest threats to euro-area stability. Indeed, in the macroeconomic imbalance analyses of 2014 and 2015, Germany was identified as one of the member countries with a substantial imbalance.

The German focus on more stringent debt-level controls is also reflected in a simultaneous push toward the introduction of debt brakes everywhere in Europe. On December 5, 2011, Merkel and Sarkozy recommended this path as a general European way to better fiscal discipline. The *Economist* speculated that *Schuldenbremse* (debt brake) would "enter the French or Italian languages the way 'kindergarten' has become part of English."[30] The design certainly looked more like Berlin than Paris or Brussels. The French press started to compare Sarkozy to the pro-appeasement Third Republic prime minister at the time of the infamous 1938 Munich Agreement, Edouard Daladier, who had yielded to Hitler. The British prime minister, David Cameron, made his opposition clear, perhaps because Great Britain at this time was struggling with a large deficit (with public borrowing at almost 10% of GDP in 2010 and 7.8% in 2011).

France reluctantly accepted the principle of a treaty revision. It would have to be limited ("surgical," as mentioned by an official spokesman): "We don't want it to open a debate on the constitution or the Union."[31] France agreed to sanction ex post those countries found in breach of fiscal rules. Their voting rights could be suspended in case of serious violations. Sarkozy was adamantly opposed, however, to any ex ante control on national budgets by European authorities, especially by the European Commission.

The French view reflected a broader stance in the Southern periphery of Europe: The appetite for a European fiscal rule book that limits deficit spending was not there. In particular, as austerity measures were enacted, growth began to stall, and calls for a slowdown in the pace of consolidation—or even for renewed stimulus—grew louder. This constant back and forth between consolidation and stimulus continued throughout the crisis and its aftermath.

Hollande's Push for More Stimulus in Europe

In the euro area, the debate about austerity gained even more impetus in the run-up to the French presidential elections in 2012, when François Hollande made relaxation of austerity one of his main campaign issues. Interestingly, in the lead-up to the elections, Hollande sent some of his closest advisers to talk with the Southern governments about a change of course in Europe; they reported back, perhaps correctly but also perhaps exaggerating what they heard, that Madrid and Rome were now hoping that France would take a lead and stand up against Merkel, Germany, and austerity. Later, at his inauguration, Hollande promised that he would "propose to my European partners a pact that ties the necessary reduction of deficit to the indispensable stimulation of economy."[32]

Hollande's election caught the mood of a Europe that seemed to be turning against the austerity policies associated with Germany and Merkel. According to this critique, Europe needed growth to be able to pay off large volumes of public and private sector debt. The emphasis on fiscal consolidation as a way of reducing the burden of debt was in consequence counterproductive. The critique, powerfully deployed in the *Financial Times* by Martin Wolf and by former US treasury secretary Larry Summers, marked a dramatic revival of the traditional Keynesian approach to the management of crises.[33] This position seemed to be supported by research from the IMF, which calculated much larger fiscal multipliers than had previously been assumed. Hollande drew on this substantial Anglo-American critique when denouncing "ruthless austerity," stating in the course of his presidential campaign that "It's not Germany that decides for the whole of Europe."[34] It also looked as if the new Spanish and Italian prime ministers, Mariano Rajoy and Mario Monti, both of whom had undertaken a considerable amount of reform, were backing the Hollande claim; even in the Netherlands, a clearly Northern country, the government collapsed because it was unable to push through spending cuts.

Another interesting reflection of the ongoing austerity versus stimulus debate can be found in the design of the European budget. Unsurprisingly, Hollande was pushing for an ambitious budget, supporting the significant increase in expenditures proposed by the European Commission despite the fact that France was, after Germany, the second-largest net contributor. In contrast, Merkel aligned herself broadly with the very rigorous position defended by Cameron (the UK traditionally opts for smaller European budgets) and, in the process, ended up isolating Hollande. The French leader was heavily criticized at home for what was seen as a defeat. The symbolism was hard to miss. Hollande deliberately skipped a conciliatory meeting convened during the night by European Council president Herman Van Rompuy (which Merkel and Cameron attended). Instead, he stayed in bilateral encounters with Southern countries, including a long meeting with Prime Minister Rajoy. In these circumstances Germany saw Britain as a vital ally against a southern bloc.

Hollande also opened up the attack on Germany on another front. On February 5, 2013, in a speech in the European Parliament, Hollande passionately advocated a proactive policy of depreciating the euro exchange rate. He was immediately and officially contradicted by the German government, which published a statement according to which the exchange rate is not an appropriate tool with which to improve competitiveness, as exchange rate movements only produce short-term stimulus effects.[35]

Syriza's Push for More Stimulus in All of Europe

The poster child for the failures of the euro area's institutional backdrop, for the dangers of fiscal imprudence, and for the harsh costs imposed through constant back and forth between proponents and opponents of austerity, is Greece. The austerity debate was present throughout the entire Greek ordeal, but it resurfaced especially powerfully after the formation of the Syriza government in Greece in January 2015. The party had campaigned on a platform of undoing most of the austerity measures imposed by the troika in the previous years. Syriza's objective was to move to stimulus policy across all of Europe, and it was willing to subject the Greek population to a standoff with European authorities and national governments lasting several months.[36] At this point, however, even other peripheral countries were opposed to granting Greece extra leeway, primarily because it would boost left-leaning opposition parties in their countries. Perhaps the most visible achievement of the new Greek government was to replace the name "troika" with "institutions."

Once in office, Syriza's leaders tried to find wider support for their vision of more classically Keynesian policies everywhere in Europe, going as far as gambling financial and social stability in their own country to shift the debate toward their position. Ultimately, Syriza's unwillingness to negotiate led to a referendum about the conditions of Greece's bailout, which the Greek population rejected with a 61 percent majority. But with the other finance ministers of the euro area continuing to sideline Greece and the risk of a Grexit looming, the Greek government was forced to change course and accept the conditions of the creditors. Meanwhile, Grexit fears, political uncertainty, and bank closures pushed the Greek economy into a tailspin. This sparked the austerity debate even more.

Even though a better program would have produced a smaller contraction, it would also have been the subject of politicized debates in the creditor countries. At some point, the creditor publics and parliaments might well have determined that they had had enough, the program would have collapsed, and the Greek economic disaster would have been even worse. In a world shaped by the slogan of "no taxation without representation," the extent to which a program was needed meant that democratic processes gave creditor parliaments a say over the future of debtors. The debate about debt and program design thus set the stage for a conflict between democracies: debtor democracies expressing a preference for less adjustment and creditor democracies for less financing.

Lessons and Policy Recommendations

Putting everything together, one must conclude that there exists no simple "one size fits all" policy recommendation. This is also the reason why the European deficit mechanism went beyond a simple 3.0 percent rule and was significantly fine-tuned. Arguably, the rule book became too complex. Overall, one can distill three general lessons about optimal fiscal policy in the context of the challenging environment of the euro area over 2011–2016.

First, there is probably a good case to be made for delaying fiscal consolidation if credibility is already strong. Intuitively, the confidence arguments at the heart of the austerity case do not really apply to countries with a strong reputation on international financial markets. Highly indebted countries, in contrast, are faced with a dilemma. Immediate fiscal retrenchment may well prove to be counterproductive, but similarly fiscal lenience now will undermine the credibility of promises for future prudence. Without credible commitment devices for future consolidation, highly indebted countries are, as far as austerity is now concerned, "damned if they do, and damned if they don't." Institutional arrangements and credible ex ante rules might help to overcome this dilemma— and this is the idea underlying some of the more recent institutional innovations of the euro area. Consider, for example, the Fiscal Compact (a set of stricter fiscal requirements) and the "six-pack" (a set of regulations strengthening deficit procedures and increasing macroeconomic surveillance with a particular focus toward macroeconomic imbalances). Very much in keeping with the German tradition, these new institutional structures reflect a firm belief in the power of rules-based frameworks to create credibility. These rules are based on an additional treaty outside the regular EU framework and with different voting rules on enforcement. If only the overall credibility of the regulatory framework were greater, so the underlying argument runs, individual countries with low credibility could readily reach an optimal adjustment path with a low interest rate. For the highly indebted countries of the euro area periphery, in contrast, many of these new institutional provisions are simply an unnecessary straitjacket, sacrificing growth at the altar of credibility.

The second lesson relates to the optimal design of any given austerity or stimulus measure. The simple Keynesian story told at the beginning of this chapter suggests that fiscal retrenchments based on spending cuts would be more costly than those based on tax hikes. The credibility story, however, runs directly counter to this: spending cuts are more credible than tax increases (as they are less easily reversed), and so a decisive spending cut may actually result in smaller losses in output than a comparable tax increase. This argument was put forward in a string of very recent, well-discussed academic papers.[37] Another (and somewhat related) point about the optimal design of a stimulus package is the following: stimulus measures should, particularly in an environment of high-debt burdens, always be designed so that they can be reversed rather easily. Otherwise, the credibility of long-term consolidation plans would be undermined. One key difference between Europe and the United States is that in Europe temporary stimulus measures are politically more difficult to reverse.

Third, it may be a good idea to combine much-needed structural reform with some extra government spending or growth-stimulating tax cuts. Naturally, fundamental structural change begets uncertainty, and uncertainty weighs down on investment and consumer spending (as precautionary savings rise). In the language of our simple Keynesian multiplier analysis, the marginal propensity to consume falls, and so output slumps even further. In such an environment, government spending can pick up some of the slack, push up demand, and so stabilize output. And if the underlying structural reforms are wide-ranging enough, in these particular circumstances, credibility issues should not loom as large.

PART III

FINANCIAL STABILITY: MAASTRICHT'S STEPCHILD

9

The Role of the Financial Sector

The design of the Maastricht Treaty was, as we discussed in previous chapters, explicitly motivated by monetary and fiscal stability concerns. Financial stability, in contrast, hardly played a role; it was simply taken for granted. But the German and French economic philosophies also differed on how to manage the financial sector.

In the late 1980s and early 1990s, when the Maastricht Treaty was negotiated, the financial system was much smaller in size, less concentrated, less complex, and less risky. The world had not yet experienced the financial contagion that occurred during the Southeast Asia crisis in the late 1990s. Even so, the original plan would have given overall supervisory and regulatory powers to a European central bank. The Bank of England pushed strongly for this despite strong resistance, above all from the German Bundesbank. The German economic tradition favors a clear delineation in the assignment of responsibility, while the centralized approach of Great Britain (and also France) favors an all-encompassing perspective. In addition, there was bureaucratic resistance from existing national supervisors to a transfer of powers to a central authority. The compromise at Maastricht resulted in rather limited coordination of national supervisors; thus, the ECB was ultimately not given any substantive supervisory and regulatory powers. Until the outbreak of the financial crisis in 2007–2008, almost no one thought that this was a problem.[1] The euro crisis ultimately led to the creation—in stages—of a banking union in Europe, with the ECB at the helm of the single supervisory mechanism.

From the 1980s, the financial system and the potential threat that it posed changed for several reasons. First, euro-area banks' lending activity increased markedly after the introduction of the euro. At the time, this was seen as part of a desirable integration process. Regulators overlooked the fact that a substantial fraction of this new lending was short term (especially interbank funding) and devoted to propping up a property bubble rather than to the promotion of new investment opportunities. Ireland and Spain in particular were the recipients of substantial bank-intermediated capital flows, which served primarily to fund the construction and acquisition of property.

Second, European banks significantly expanded their global activities, raising dollar-denominated funding from US money market funds (MMFs). Moreover, large universal banks became increasingly important market makers on global capital and derivatives markets. This heightened activity engendered a substantial increase in the riskiness of the European banking system. Because the ECB cannot—at least, not without a backup swap line from the US Federal Reserve—provide dollar liquidity to its banks, European banks' reliance on MMF dollar funding added another dimension of systemic risk.

Third, the number of transactions within the banking system increased significantly. In standard economic models of banking, a single bank channels funds from savers (depositors) to borrowers (investing firms or households). From the 1980s, however, intermediation chains became much longer, and, hence, the system turned into something more akin to a complicated web of funding arrangements. Another important, albeit German-specific, trend began in 2001, when it was agreed that the German Landesbanken—a group of state-owned banks—would lose their state guarantees, in line with European competition law. The German government successfully bargained for a transition period, so the Landesbanken had until 2005 to issue state-guaranteed bonds. They duly rushed to increase their bond issuance and invested a large fraction of the new funds into US mortgage securities, many of which went sour after 2007.

Most sources of financial instability were overlooked in the Maastricht Treaty. Underlying this neglect was a misguided belief: as long as the central bank can guarantee price stability, ran the argument, microprudential regulation would be sufficient to ensure stability of the financial system. The story we just told lays bare the shortcomings of this view. To understand better where precisely the fathers of the Maastricht Treaty failed to take account of systemic risk, we need to look more closely at the economics of the financial sector.

As has been a recurring theme in this book, the associated policy responses will be interpreted in the context of the battle of economic ideas. Again, we make the point that interests must be viewed through the lenses of underlying economic philosophies.

In light of these developments, this chapter answers the following questions:

- How did banking change in the run-up to the crisis? What were the extra risks that came with the shift from traditional funding from retail depositors to interbank wholesale funding?
- What special role did the international cross-border dimension play in short-term interbank funding?

Traditional Banking

Universal Banking

The role of traditional banking is to channel savings to borrowers and productive sectors. Its main purpose is to mitigate financial frictions that hinder direct-funding arrangements between borrowers and lenders. From the nineteenth century, France and Belgium evolved a holistic model of banking in which banks performed multiple functions: as deposit takers, sources of short-term finance, issuers of securities, and long-term investors. The Belgian and French model of the "Société Générale" was then adopted in Germany, where the result was known as the universal bank. The large joint stock banks founded between 1850 and the 1870s—Disconto-Gesellschaft and Darmstädter Bank and later Deutsche Bank and Dresdner Bank—had close relations with the major German manufacturing companies and were therefore decisive in the early history of German industrialization.

In Germany and France, and indeed in continental Europe in general, banks play a predominant role in the provision of funding for business investment. In the United States, by contrast, the capital market is a more readily available source of financing for larger corporations. In 2008, the ECB estimated that banks provide 70 percent of financing for corporations in the euro area but only 20 percent in the United States.[2]

Publicly owned banks have also played an extensive part in French and German economic life. In France, economic planning consisted for a long time in national-level schemes for credit allocation (*encadrement du credit*). Although federal Germany's approach is less focused on national plans for business development, publicly owned banks are similarly important: the savings banks (*Sparkassen*) are locally owned, with state-level Landesbanken acting as regional clearinghouse. The savings banks have a high degree of public trust and are widely seen as offering superior banking services to ordinary customers, but they are also the major source of credit for the small and medium-sized—often family-owned—business sector (*Mittelstand*) that constitutes one of the key features of the German model for industrial success.

The Process of Money Creation

Banks lend to borrowers and create credit and money simultaneously. As a concrete example, suppose that a borrower goes to a bank and asks for, say, a mortgage of €1 million. If the bank is willing to grant the mortgage, it will credit the borrower €1 million in the form of deposits. Assets and liabilities of the bank have thus expanded simultaneously, and the bank has in essence created its own funding through the very process of lending. Because the new entries on both sides of the bank's balance sheet are in the name of our soon-to-be homeowner, there is no intermediation of loanable funds between savers and borrowers at the time the loan was made. Only if the seller of the house accepts the buyer's deposit at the bank as valid payment does intermediation indirectly take place, as the seller then essentially lends funds to the borrower through the bank.

For this process to work, it is necessary that third parties accept deposits—the newly created purchasing power—in exchange for goods and services. Third parties will accept deposits as a medium of exchange as long as they are confident that they could safely withdraw their funds. To instill confidence, the bank needs to have sufficient liquidity, for example, in the form of loanable funds deposited by savers. Overall, then, the key outputs of the bank's production function are its standardized, ideally risk-free (and therefore extremely liquid) deposits (IOUs). Precisely because they are standardized, these IOUs can easily be netted; positive and negative holdings simply cancel each other out. The bank's IOUs are thus a veritable means of payment—in short, a money. In contrast to the money provided by the government (which comes from *outside* the economic system), this form of money created by the financial sector is called *inside* money. In a modern economy, more than 90 percent of the total money supply consists of inside money.

Liquidity and Maturity Mismatch

Banks' peculiar business model brings with it some serious problems that can be best understood by examining balance sheets. On the asset side of a typical balance sheet are the loans that a bank extends to its clients; on the liability side sit the deposits. This confronts banks with two challenges. First, loans are risky, while deposits are intended to be safe. This mismatch subjects the bank to default risk, also known as credit risk. Second, loans are typically long term, while deposits can be withdrawn from the bank at any time and without notice. Banks are subject to maturity mismatch. Finally, banks provide *liquidity transformation*. Their liabilities are extremely liquid, whereas their assets are mostly illiquid.

It is important to distinguish three notions of liquidity. First, *market liquidity* refers to the ease with which assets can be sold without any substantial price impact. Second, *technological liquidity* refers to the ease with which investment projects can be reversed (liquidated) part way through their lifespan. Third, *funding liquidity* refers to maturity and stability of the funding arrangement. Along all three dimensions, bank deposits are highly liquid. By contrast, long-term projects financed by bank loans are likely to have low market and technological liquidity. The bank thus faces funding liquidity risk: if all savers attempt to withdraw their deposits at the same time (because they are deemed liquid), the bank may not be able to repay them, even if it is fundamentally solvent (because the loans that it holds are illiquid). This highlights the distinction between illiquidity and insolvency and is analogous to the discussion on sovereign debt in chapter 7.

How can the bank reduce these risks? First, note that banks typically lend to many borrowers. If credit risk is imperfectly correlated—such that not all borrowers default at the same time—then individual borrowers' risks partially offset each other. The bank can then diversify its idiosyncratic risks (by granting loans to different borrowers that are unlikely to default at the same time). Additionally, the bank can reduce its funding liquidity risk on the liability side (by increasing its stable funding, such as equity or long-term debt) and on the asset side (by holding safe assets, such as cash or central bank reserves, with negligible credit risk and high

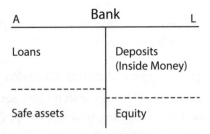

FIGURE 9.1. A Typical Traditional Bank's Balance Sheet

market and technological liquidity). Our typical bank now has equity and deposits on the liability side and safe assets, in form of cash and reserves, as well as loans on its asset side (see figure 9.1).

Banks can reduce credit and liquidity risks but not eliminate them entirely. In light of the risks at the heart of banks' business model, we may ask why savers do not cut out the middle man by lending directly to borrowers rather than depositing their funds into a bank. The answer is that banks are in general better at lending than individual savers for a number of reasons. First, banks identify more easily projects that are worth funding and pursuing. Underlying these arguments is what economists refer to as asymmetric information: Borrowers know more about their projects than any individual lender, but dedicated lenders, such as banks, can at least mitigate information asymmetries. Second, owing to their expertise, banks can more easily enforce repayment than an individual lender. Third, banks can lend to many different borrowers, making it easier to diversify idiosyncratic risks.

Modern Banking and Capital Markets

The Initial Blaming of Anglo-American Banking

Modern banks have moved beyond this traditional model of banking. What continental Europeans described as "Anglo-Saxon financial capitalism" expanded dramatically from the 1990s, with banks no longer funding themselves exclusively through deposits on the liability side and holding complex structured financial products as well as plain-vanilla loans on the asset side. Initially, many European politicians viewed the financial crisis as a uniquely American phenomenon and even as a verdict of history on Anglo-American finance. German and French policy makers and the public at large see a difference between their banking systems, which aim to serve the general economy, as distinct from short-term, speculative, Anglo-Saxon banking.

The political discussion about financial capitalism was already well under way before the financial crisis. In the currency crises of the early 1990s, there was widespread outrage over the activities of such speculators as George Soros, whose enormous bet supposedly forced the United Kingdom out of the European exchange rate mechanism. French finance minister Michel Sapin compared modern currency speculators to the *agioteurs* who had been guillotined during the French Revolution and, in January 1993, warned that they would "pay for their mistakes" if they persisted. In 2005, Franz Müntefering, then chairman of the German Social Democratic Party (the SPD), referred to financial investors—private equity and hedge fund managers—as "locusts" (*Heuschrecken*) that stripped healthy businesses bare. The term set off a big debate; even the German Council of Economic Advisers discussed the "social coldness" of modern investors. Immediately after the Lehman collapse in September 2008, Peer Steinbrück, then German finance minister, put this diagnosis as a challenge not just to the United States but also other countries, notably the United Kingdom, which seemed to have Americanized their financial system. The problem, according to Steinbrück, lay in overreliance on highly complex financial instruments propagated by globalized American institutions. Steinbrück commented at that time, "The financial crisis is above all an American problem. The other G7 financial ministers in continental Europe share this opinion."[3]

As we shall see, these critics of so-called Anglo-Saxon banking overlooked the fact that it was European, more than American, banks that had become the largest global players, investing in complex securities and relying on short-term wholesale debt to fund their operations.

Mark-to-Market Assets and Wholesale Funding

Modern banks differ from traditional banking in important ways.[4] On the asset side of their balance sheets, a larger share of their assets is marked-to-market. Banks hold a larger share of securitized assets than simply loans. Securitization combines many loans (often mortgages) in a large pool in an attempt to remove idiosyncratic risks via diversification and then splits future revenues arising from repayments on the underlying loans in various claims. These claims are then sold to other financial institutions. Overall, the share of assets that are constantly marked-to-market is much larger than in a traditional bank that retains all of the loans that it originates. The modern bank can thus realize losses very quickly and is also dependent on the willingness of other financial institutions to buy its securities, if necessary.

On the liability side, modern banks have found a new source of funding beyond deposits or shareholder equity: the wholesale funding market. Rather than borrowing from households, banks nowadays obtain much of their funding from other financial institutions, mostly through two vehicles. The first is short-term borrowing in unsecured interbank markets. Unlike normal depositors, other financial institutions are well informed (or at least think that they are) and for this reason will be quick to withdraw funding if they suspect difficulties, long before regular retail depositors would contemplate doing so. The second source of wholesale funding are repos, the sale and repurchase agreements, where the bank agrees to temporarily sell some of its securities to other financial institutions and later repurchase them at a pre-agreed price. The difference between the current market price and repurchase price reflects the interest rate on the agreement, also known as the *repo rate*. Importantly, repos are safe for the lender and hence "money-like." Indeed, they are included in the conventional broad money measure, known as M3.[5]

Connected to this "moneyness" of repos are three of their most important characteristics. First, securities are sold in repos for a price below their market value, the difference being a so-called haircut or margin (which the lender retains as a safety cushion). Repos are a collateralized lending arrangement, where the loan amount is the value of the collateral asset minus the haircut/margin. As a (wholesale funding) lender can suddenly raise margins, the borrowing bank is exposed to a funding risk. Second, repos have rather short duration and thus have to be rolled over frequently. As a result, they can quickly disappear as a source of funding. Third, repos enjoy seniority over demand deposits and unsecured interbank loans. Hence traditional unsecured funding providers become also less stable.

The bottom line is that, unlike deposit funding, wholesale funding is fickle. Funding risks for modern banks are thus much larger than for their traditional counterparts.

A final important consequence of the modern banking system is that it can amplify asset-price cycles. Suppose the price of some particular asset increases. Because modern banks' assets are largely marked-to-market, they can immediately realize the associated gains. This increase in the value of potential collateral makes it easier for the banks to obtain wholesale funding in the repo market. Banks can then lend more freely, the cost of loans falls, the demand for the asset rises, and its price increases yet further. For some time, this process may appear as if it is capable of generating endless prosperity. But, like a rubber band being gradually stretched, the tension builds until the rubber band—and the repo market—finally snaps.

German Landesbanken and French Banks

The public in Germany and France was outraged when American-style financial problems appeared in their banks. French banks became very dependent on dollar funding from US money market funds. In Germany, some of the most costly problems appeared in the Landesbanken.[6] Public sector banks, such as the Landesbanken in Germany, became active players in the modern banking landscape. Such banks have special principal-agent problems: with their downside risk limited by extensive public guarantees, bank managers have an incentive to take on excessive risks to generate short-term profits. In the Asia crisis of 1997–1998, it was the Landesbanken rather than the larger private banks in Germany that had exposure to Korean *chaebols*. The fallout generated a push to privatize the public sector banks and subject them to market discipline, but this did not remove the implicit guarantee.

In the 2000s, Landesbanken had engaged heavily via offshore vehicles (mostly in Ireland) in the US subprime market. The Sachsen LB and the LB Rheinland-Pfalz needed to be rescued with public money and were then consolidated with the more solid LB Baden-Württemberg (where the traditional *Mittelstand* orientation was much greater). Another Landesbank, West LB, required €8 billion of assistance. IKB bank, a German institution that had its roots in the public sector encouragement of *Mittelstand* finance, was bailed out in 2007 and then sold to a private equity firm. One of the few bankers worldwide to be jailed as a consequence of the crisis was Gerhard Gribkowsky, head of risk management at Bayern LB. An estimated 70 percent of the losses borne by the German state resulted from public sector banks and another 20 percent from the Munich Hypo Real Estate Holding AG. Hypo Real Estate was founded in 2004 as a "bad bank" by HVB, which itself was the result of a 1997/8 shotgun merger between Bayerische

Hypotheken- und Wechselbank and Bayerische Vereinsbank, designed to hide the losses of Bayern Hypo in Saxony. The merger was arranged under the influence of the state of Bavaria, which owned 10 percent of the shares.[7]

Bank collapses and bailouts, and the revelation of large speculative losses in January 2008 as a result of a rogue trader at the Société Générale, were politically traumatic moments for Europeans. They led to a demand that banks should be brought back to their traditional function and that the "Americanization" of finance that had taken place over the previous twenty years should be reversed. Governments had been forced by the magnitude and impact of the financial crisis to adopt a role that was at odds with the emphasis on responsibility (*Haftungsprinzip*) that the German tradition in particular emphasized.

Oddly, however, the focus of attention was less on public banks than on the private sector, as public ownership and control was widely regarded as an appropriate response to the crisis. An indication of this new political climate was given by the change in the relationship between Chancellor Merkel and Joseph ("Joe") Ackermann, head of Deutsche Bank, who was the public face of the drive for high returns and a move toward investment banking. Ackermann was a key adviser to the chancellor in the early phases of the financial crisis. On April 22, 2008, Merkel arranged an elaborate (and taxpayer-funded) dinner party in the Berlin Chancellery for him as a birthday party. By 2009, the relationship was more strained, as Deutsche Bank made it a point of honor to resist the government's attempt to recapitalize all banks according to the US model (whereby Treasury Secretary Paulson had simply compelled the largest banks to participate). It was not just the chancellor who felt this way: in public discussion, Ackermann and Deutsche Bank became the principal villains of the German story, even though Deutsche Bank did not directly cost the taxpayer money; its size simply meant that any problem, if it did materialize, would be prohibitively expensive for the taxpayer.

Cross-Border Capital Flows and the Interbank Market

Initial Capital Flows and the Convergence of Interest Rates

The completion of monetary union in 1999 removed exchange rate risk. Afterward, lending to sovereigns and banks in periphery countries in the euro area (including Spain, Portugal, Ireland, and Greece) was viewed as

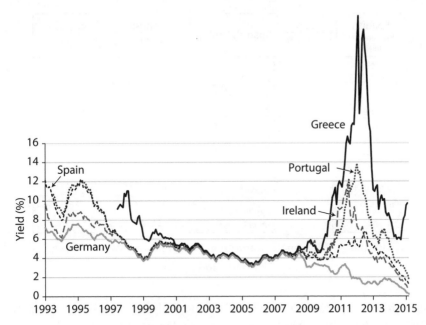

FIGURE 9.2. Yield of 10-Year Government Bonds (Source: Bloomberg)

no more risky as lending to core countries. The convergence of long-term interest rates within the euro area, which had already started in the early to mid-1990s, thus accelerated. Figure 9.2, which shows yields on ten-year government bonds over the past two decades, illustrates this development.

Substantial capital flows from core to periphery countries accelerated from the early 2000s. Interestingly, this occurred not just in the euro area: the West Balkan countries, Albania, Bosnia and Herzegovina, Croatia, the former Yugoslav Republic, Macedonia, Montenegro, and Serbia, most of which were not even in the European Union, experienced similar inflows, with large current account deficits and strong economic growth up to 2008, and a massive problem afterward.[8]

A large fraction of the capital flows were short-term credit flows involving cross-border wholesale funding—lending from bank to bank in the interbank market. To picture more clearly the main thrust of these flows, consider the following stylized example featuring Germany and Spain as our representative core and periphery countries. Spanish banks drew parts of their fund from their domestic deposit base. In the years leading up to the crisis, German financial institutions (banks or money market funds) provided their Spanish counterparts with additional cheap,

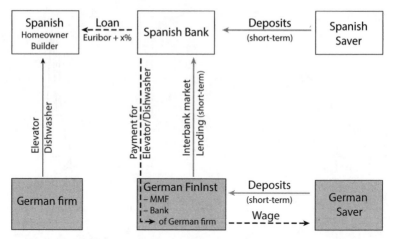

FIGURE 9.3. Schematic Representation of Fund Flows between Germany and Spain

short-term wholesale funding mostly through the interbank market. Spanish banks then duly extended more loans to domestic borrowers (in particular homeowners), usually at flexible rates (typically at the floating LIBOR/Euribor rate plus some fixed surcharge). The borrowed funds were in part used to pay for German products: suppose the Spanish borrowers purchased, for example, German appliances such as elevators or dishwashers. The payments then went back from Spanish banks into the German financial system, ultimately helping to pay the wages of German workers. Figure 9.3 depicts this stylized process.

This stylized example can help us understand the emergence of property bubbles in Ireland and Spain. Ireland enjoyed strong export growth from the late 1980s, accelerating in the mid-1990s, when the Irish economy earned its "Celtic Tiger" moniker. This export growth translated into strong economic activity and a general sense of economic security among Irish households. This, together with low nominal and real interest rates as a result of monetary union, resulted in a dramatic expansion of housing demand and, with a slight lag, an expansion of housing supply. Expectations of ever-increasing home prices then led to speculative house purchases, which boosted prices and drove the construction boom even further. Soon prices diverged far from anything resembling fundamental values. The credit expansion was financed through large-scale foreign borrowing by Irish banks. In summer 2008, the Irish banking system was thus in a very vulnerable state, overexposed on its asset side to the domestic housing market and on its liability side to international interbank borrowing.

The Spanish story looks eerily similar: a generally booming economy, policy initiatives promoting home ownership, favorable demographic environments, and low borrowing costs due to interest rate convergence all gave a boost to domestic housing demand. As in Ireland, these favorable fundamentals created expectations that prices could only continue to go upward; speculative house purchases started, and house prices soon departed from plausible equilibrium valuations. In fact, annual house price increases until 2006 regularly outstripped 10 percent and overall between 1997 and 2008 almost tripled. As in Ireland, investments were by and large financed through credit provided by the domestic banking sector. An important player in the Spanish banking sector are *cajas*, small-scale savings banks whose market share increased from around 20 percent of total assets in 1980 to around 40 percent in 2010. Two things about the *cajas* are important to know: First, cajas' credit expansion was very much geared toward the booming real estate sector (much more than for other Spanish banks). Second, cajas had over time become increasingly reliant on interbank markets to obtain their funding. We thus see the same vulnerability (on the asset and liquidity side) as in the Irish banking sector.

Sudden Stop of Short-Term Funding

With the onset of the global financial crisis in 2007, cross-border capital flows toward the periphery (and thus in particular those going to the Irish and Spanish housing sectors) suddenly stopped. Returning to our example of figure 9.3, when German banks refused to roll over short-term debt of Spanish banks, the interbank market froze. As Spanish banks had extended long-term loans to their customers, they suddenly faced a huge liquidity shortage. The interbank market interest rate (LIBOR for dollars or Euribor for euros) skyrocketed as lending to Spanish banks was now very risky. German banks were concerned about Spanish banks' solvency and preferred to park their excess funds with the ECB. Spanish banks, cut off from funding from the interbank market, tried to obtain funding from the ECB instead using their loans and other assets as collateral. In other words, the ECB stepped in as intermediary providing loans to (risky) Spanish banks and offering German banks a safe spot to park funds. This activity showed up as TARGET2 imbalances within the Eurosystem.

Many commentators in fact argue that the current predicament of the euro area should be interpreted as a classic balance of payments crisis, with capital rushing out of the weak periphery and into the strong core. But if this is so, why is there no such balance of payments crisis in the United States? After all, the United States also had states hit hard by the bursting of the property bubble (for example, Florida and Arizona), while other states were much less affected. In fact, there are no current and capital accounts tracking trade and capital flows within the United States, so why should such flows in the euro area matter?

Cross-Border versus Domestic Credit Flows

Former ECB president Jean-Claude Trichet always insisted that the euro area should be treated and considered as a single entity, for example, within institutions such as the G7 and G20. This would imply that cross-border credit flows within the euro area are similar to domestic credit flows. Indeed, within a single currency area, erratic exchange rate fluctuations—which impair balance sheets and throw economies into crisis—are switched off. This eliminates the main reason for instability. However, it also raises this question: why did cross-border credit flows *within a currency union* contribute to financial instability?

Was it the fact that cross-border capital flows in the euro area were largely short term, making the entire arrangement susceptible to sudden reversal? Yet within-country funding is also often short term, so this is not a peculiarity of cross-border capital flows. A second important facet of cross-country flows in the euro area is that much of the funding came in the form of wholesale, interbank funding. Because of this funding structure, capital flows into the periphery could dry up and reverse quickly. Still, this is not a feature unique to international capital flows, as much within-country funding is also interbank and wholesale. Just consider, for example, Northern Rock, a UK bank that suffered a bank run in 2007. It was reliant on wholesale funding, and it was precisely this reliance that made Northern Rock so vulnerable to a run. Other UK banks also relied on wholesale funding, but the larger banks had European subsidiaries that had access to ECB liquidity at a time when the Bank of England was reluctant to provide liquidity out of moral hazard concerns.

Do cross-border capital flows within a currency union deserve special attention because they can lead to inefficient investment and misallocation?

Capital flows into the periphery financed extra consumption (as in Greece and Portugal) or investment in low-productivity sectors that produce non-tradable goods (such as the construction sectors in Spain and Ireland). Extra financing thus fueled growth only temporarily and perhaps with lasting detriment to productivity. This dim conclusion contrasts sharply with the benevolent convergence view that was, up until the beginning of the euro crisis, widely presented as a rationale for capital flows from core to periphery. According to this convergence view, capital rushed into the periphery simply because investment opportunities were more attractive; capital flows just accelerated the economic catch-up of the periphery. Observed productivity trends reveal this benevolent story to have been fatally flawed.

Still, misallocation also happens within countries, as the aftermath of the German reunification illustrates. In the early 1990s, capital poured from Western into Eastern Germany, triggering a postreunification construction and housing boom. Later, many of these loans turned sour. The Bayerische Hypotheken- und Wechsel-Bank, for example, was very active in financing this boom. By the late 1990s, it had been forced to merge with the Bayerische Vereinsbank, and many of its old bad loans would, a couple of years later, be spun off into a sort of bad bank, called Hypo Real Estate (HRE). The HRE then also got itself in trouble, and, in 2008, the German taxpayer had to bail it out.

So far, we have not been able to come up with a truly convincing argument as to why special attention should be devoted to international capital flows, at least not above and beyond that afforded to national flows. The American approach of not tracking capital and trade balance flows within the currency union could thus be applicable to the euro area as well. This conclusion, however, would be premature. Instead, it is useful to approach the discussion from another angle: what, in an economic sense, distinguishes a country within a currency union from geographical units within a country?

In traditional Keynesian models, countries are characterized as an area of *common* price and wage rigidities. And, indeed, the years in the run-up to the euro crisis saw substantial divergences in country-level inflation rates and wage increases, with those in the periphery far outstripping the price increases in the core, in particular in Germany. Cross-border capital flows into the periphery typically financed investment in nontradables (in particular in the housing sector) and consumption (both public and private), thus pushing up domestic wages without improving international competitiveness. Given fixed exchange rates within the euro area, such divergent trends in wage inflation go hand in hand with a relative loss in competitiveness for the periphery; that is, unit labor costs in the periphery rose markedly vis-à-vis the core. The divergence in competitiveness was covered up by the temporary convergence in GDP levels. This demand push—which can be related to the Walters' critique discussed in chapter 4—boosted the misallocation of investment to low-productivity sectors in the European periphery.

Importantly, there are two more differences between cross-border and domestic credit flows. First, within a country, the allocation of the fiscal costs that may follow from resource misallocation and malinvestment is clear; in a currency union, it is not. Credit flows in the 2000s had, to an extent unanticipated at the time of Maastricht, provided (through low interest rates) an effective subsidy to borrowers in the periphery countries, including government borrowers, but with risks building up for Europe as a whole. When the risks materialized, the painful question inevitably arose of who should bear the cost of those past subsidies. Second, national governments' policy response typically put national interest over the interest of the currency union. Chapter 11 explains how uncoordinated national policy initiatives may simply push losses onto foreigners and rather than alleviating may in fact worsen the crisis. Before that, chapter 10 outlines amplification mechanisms and the various national crisis management tools.

10

Financial Crises: Mechanisms and Management

As we have seen in the previous chapter, the transformation of a traditional into a modern banking system—a web of financial claims, long
intermediation chains, and asset holdings that are marked-to-market and
funded with international wholesale money market funds—exposed the
European banking system to additional risks. These risks are endoge-
nously amplified by various adverse feedback loops and spirals. Against
the background of this marked increase in riskiness and interconnectedness, it is unsurprising that European financial systems were not well
equipped to deal with the fallout from the global financial crisis in 2007–
2008. Banks across the continent, particularly in Germany (the Landesbanken) and France, were hit through their direct exposure to US subprime
lending. Even more important than this direct exposure was a secondary
indirect channel, operating through the overexposure of European banks
to interbank wholesale funding markets. As these markets froze, banks
could not roll over their short-term wholesale funding and so were forced
to reduce lending. In Ireland and Spain, this sudden reduction in credit
provision popped the inflated housing bubble; financial distress consequently shot up, and economic activity plummeted. A more stringent regulatory framework prior to the crisis and supervisory forbearance in the
early phase of the crisis meant that the Spanish *cajas* (the Spanish savings
and loans) were able to delay this day of reckoning somewhat longer than
their Irish counterparts.

With financial systems across Europe increasingly fragile, policy makers
tried to prevent spillovers into the real economy by bailing out their own
national banks. Notable examples of bailouts are the Irish recapitalizations
of AIB and the Bank of Ireland; the German bailouts of IKB Bank, Hypo

Real Estate Holding, WestLB, HSH Nordbank, and Commerzbank; the Franco-Belgian involvement in Dexia; and the forced merger of several Spanish cajas. Government debt duly skyrocketed in many member states, and the sustainability of government finances was soon called into question. But without credible fiscal backing, the health of domestic banking sectors was again in question, and so a diabolic loop between banks and sovereigns emerged.

In this toxic environment, financial institutions tried to reduce the riskiness of their positions through investments in suitable safe assets. To make matters even worse, German government debt—not a European-wide asset—was identified by investors as the desired safe asset, setting in motion huge intra-area capital flows that would further destabilize the situation in the periphery. With individual sovereigns unable to continue to safeguard their own financial systems, area-wide bailouts became necessary. The debates surrounding these bailouts took place against the backdrop of the classic liquidity-solvency tension between the German and French economic philosophies. No individual crisis reflects these tensions better than the Cypriot experience: exasperated with a seemingly never-ending stream of bailouts justified through fears of contagion, German policy makers declared that "if Cyprus is systemic, then everything is systemic," and forced private bank creditors (depositors) to bear part of the burden in bank recapitalization. Instead of bailing them out, they were bailed in.

The decline of banking activity lowered credit and money growth, contributing to a low-inflation environment. Part of the policy response involved aggressive, unconventional monetary policy measures, including, from early 2015 onward, outright quantitative easing, that is, central bank purchases of sovereign bonds. Reactions to this policy initiative again well illustrate the differences in the German and French views, as we will see.

Specifically, this chapter addresses the following questions:

- How does the distinction between solvency and liquidity of sovereign governments translate to banks? Do the German and French differences in identifying a problem as a solvency or liquidity problem also extend to the banking sector?
- What amplification mechanisms and adverse feedback loops translate small shocks into large dislocations?

- How do risks become systemic? How do risks spill over to other banks, sectors, and countries? How did the German and French views differ regarding the severity of various contagion risks?
- How do problems in the financial sector spill over to its sovereign government, and vice versa?
- How did these feedback loops and spirals impact banks' money creation? Did they lower inflation and thereby challenge debtors further?
- What monetary and regulatory policy measures can mitigate the amplification and spillover effects? What are the long-run moral hazard costs of these measures?
- What fiscal and bail-in (haircut) measures are part of the right policy mix during the crisis? What other ex ante policy measures can help to prevent future crises?
- Did the battle about whether governments or the central bank should recapitalize the banking sector lead to a second game of chicken?

Financial Crisis Mechanisms

It is in dealing with the aftermath of the financial crisis that the big divides in European policy making appeared. France continuously pushed the idea that Europe should follow similar steps as the United States and aggressively use taxpayer funds to support the banks, concentrating on dealing with the immediate problem at hand. Germany, meanwhile, adopted an insolvency perspective, which in retrospect considered the precrisis cross-border capital flows to the periphery excessive and focused on avoiding future crises. France focused mostly on the present, while Germany concentrated on the past and the future; the French observed that not fixing a bad present would make the future worse, while Germans worried that focusing on fixing the present would make for a worse future. To understand these differences in philosophy more clearly, we need to review the actual financial crisis mechanisms in some detail.

Banking can help to channel funds to productive sectors and create safe assets for investors. However, banking is inherently fragile and subject to runs, as discussed in the previous chapter. The recent trends toward securitization and wholesale funding combined with cross-border flows only increased these underlying weaknesses. In this section, we outline the mechanisms that explain how small shocks (1) amplify via spirals into large shocks, (2) spill over to the whole banking system and (3) lead to a diabolic loop between banking and sovereign risk.

Liquidity and Disinflationary Spirals

Even a small shock to the ability of end borrowers to pay back their debt can significantly impair the financial system in the absence of any central bank or government intervention.[1] This can most easily be seen by dissecting the impact of a shock in four steps. The first step is simply the immediate impact of the adverse shock on end borrowers' ability to repay their loans. As a direct result of the shock, the value of banks' assets falls. This drop is more visible if a bigger share of banks' balance sheets is marked-to-market. As a matter of simple accounting, any given drop in the value of banks' assets must—given fixed liabilities—go hand in hand with a drop in equity of precisely the same size, measured in euros. But as a bank's assets usually far outstrip its equity, the decline in the value of the assets will, in percentage terms, be dwarfed by the percentage decline in the equity buffer. As a result, the bank's leverage ratio will shoot up.

This leads us to the second step: the banks' response. For their IOUs to still be considered safe and qualify as inside money, the banks need to bring their leverage ratio back down to acceptable levels. How far they want to push down leverage is very much a function of the severity of the liquidity mismatch between assets and liabilities. In practice, bringing down leverage almost always means shrinking the balance sheet (rather than raising new equity). Banks will thus do two things: they will (1) extend less new credit and (2) try to sell existing loans. As far as new credit, the reduction in fresh credit supply hurts all existing and potential borrowers, from hopeful homeowners to the corporate sector. In short, we have a veritable crunch in credit supply. During the euro crisis, the credit growth rate was extremely weak (see figure 10.1).

The reduction in credit supply will, due to supply-chain interlinkages, translate seamlessly into dropping credit demand: if one firm in a supply chain has a credit supply problem and cuts its production, all firms in the chain will produce less and consequently demand less credit. The

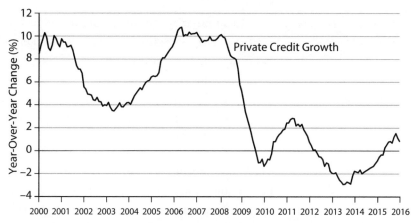

FIGURE 10.1. Credit Growth in the Euro Area (Source: ECB)

reduction in fresh credit supply also reduces credit demand by others. Overall, then, it directly reduces overall economic growth and so undermines the ability of borrowers to service their debt even more. Let us now turn to sales of existing loans. Such sales are problematic because no other bank is willing to buy (they are all overleveraged, after all), and thus at best the only potential buyers left are the savers. As they can neither diversify across as many borrowers nor enforce payment as well as banks, the savers will not be willing to pay much for these assets. Thus asset prices will drop.

The third and fourth steps describe the amplification due to spirals that are caused by banks' responses. The basic logic underlying these two steps is something game theorists call *strategic complementarity*: For example, the more other banks shrink their balance sheets, the more an individual bank will want to shrink its balance sheet too. This in turn increases other banks' incentive to shrink their balance sheets even further, and so on. As a group, all banks can ultimately be worse off. Crucially, if the strategic complementarity effects are strong enough, a multiple equilibria setting can arise. Then, even without any adverse underlying shock, the mere fear that banks may become insolvent could prompt substantial deposit withdrawals and so push the economy into a "bad equilibrium." This dynamic, at play during the Great Depression, was intuitively understood by Franklin D. Roosevelt, who in his inaugural presidential address in 1933 stated, "The only thing we have to fear is fear itself." To summarize, strategic complementarities create adverse feedback loops and propagate through the system. Let us now investigate the third and fourth steps in more detail.

Liquidity Spiral

The third step is the *liquidity spiral*. This liquidity spiral actually comes in two variants, with the first known as the *loss spiral*. As banks fire sell some of their old loans, their assets fall in value, and so equity declines further, setting in motion yet more fire sales. The severity of this spiral is again very much a function of the share of assets marked-to-market. Indeed, if the adverse feedback loop is strong enough, these fire sales can lead to a decline in equity greater than the decline in assets, so the leverage ratio may not come down after all and a self-defeating deleveraging paradox can emerge. In modern banking systems, there is a second distinct dimension to the liquidity spiral known as the *margin* (or "haircut") *spiral*. The first thing to note is that during a crisis, funding liquidity worsens. Borrowers are afraid that they will not be able to roll over existing short-term unsecured debt or, if they can, only with worse terms. For collateralized funding, like repo funding, haircuts rise, so a collateral asset worth, say, €100 can now be used to raise only €80 instead of €95, as before. As a result, financial institutions have to deleverage even more. Again, if banks are unwilling to issue new equity, the only way to do so is to sell off assets. But again, as all are selling, this leads to a further fall in prices and an increase in volatility and uncertainty, which serves to justify the high haircut requirements.

Disinflationary Spiral

Finally, the fourth step is a disinflationary spiral: as banks shrink their balance sheets by selling loans and extending less new credit, they also shrink the liability side, that is, the amount of (inside) money they create. Because outside money is by assumption fixed (absent any central bank intervention), this fall in the supply of inside money means that total money supply declines. In addition, the demand for money rises as banks intermediate less funds and hence diversify less risk. Firms and households have to hold more idiosyncratic risk and demand more money for precautionary reasons. The decline in money supply and increase in money demand causes disinflationary pressure. That is, inflation falls below expected inflation and below the inflation target. Relative to expectations, the value of money rises and so does the real (inflation-corrected) value of the banks' liabilities; after all, the banks owe the savers money. This increase in the real value of money hurts the banks' equity even further, necessitating yet more fire sales. In short, the liquidity and disinflationary spirals feed into each other, creating a vicious circle.

Even the inflation rate in Germany was subdued and missed the ECB's inflation target. Ireland's banks were hit early on after the demise of Lehman Brothers, and the Irish inflation rate declined and even turned negative in 2009. The Greek crisis was initially primarily a fiscal (government debt) crisis. Inflation only tanked in late 2012, when the banking sector became increasingly impaired. The Spanish inflation rate declined from 3.1 percent in 2011, to 2.4 percent in 2012, and then to 1.5 percent in 2013. In 2014, it turned negative to –0.2 percent and in 2015 it was –0.6 percent.

The Paradox of Prudence

To summarize, an adverse shock hits banks on both sides of their balance sheets and sets in motion a behavioral response by banks that result in two dangerous spirals. As each individual bank tries to deleverage in order to be micro-prudent, paradoxically the overall (endogenous) risk in the economy rises. The "Paradox of Prudence," that micro-prudent behavior leads to macro-imprudent outcomes, is analogous to Keynes' Paradox of Thrift.[2] The old paradox of thrift is about the level of consumption and savings—as discussed in chapter 8, each individual's attempt to save more leads ultimately to less savings in the macroeconomy, while the new paradox of thrift is about risk. Each individual bank's attempt to reduce risk leads to overall more macro risk.

Spirals in the Nonfinancial Sector

But it is not only banks that suffer from impaired balance sheets; end borrowers, who were only mentioned in passing in the analysis above, generally have similar problems. They are often highly leveraged, and so they also have to fire sell assets after a reduction in credit supply. Firms with high operational leverage—that is, with a high ratio of fixed to variable costs—will be hit particularly hard. In times of crisis, there are, just as with banks, no remaining natural buyers for the borrowers' capital goods, and so prices may fall substantially. The more specialized a sector in the economy is—that is, the more specific capital goods are to particular production purposes—the more dangerous the adverse feedback loop. To give a concrete example, airplanes and specially tailored machines can only be sold to other industries at large discounts, while more generic fabric buildings are more fungible and therefore easier to sell.

Yet another brake on growth is the following: because end borrowers are so desperate to repay their debt, they will forgo more attractive projects, even if the funding is available. In short, a borrower's hurdle rate—the return required to undertake a particular investment project or consumption decision—rises in the crisis. The disinflationary spiral, which increases the real value of debt and erodes the borrower's wealth, amplifies all of these effects. Of course, the real sector that is most indebted and so suffers the most from these spirals differs from crisis to crisis. For example, in the Japanese lost decade, the nonfinancial corporate sector struggled the most, while more recently, in the United States, overstretched homeowners were subject to many of the adverse feedback mechanisms just discussed. Spain and Ireland largely replicated the US experience; in Italy, the family businesses that constituted the historic core of the Italian economy were badly hit.

Systemic Risk: Spillover Risk to Others

Overall, all these adverse amplification mechanisms mean that a small shock can translate into a large economic downturn. But the amplification of small shocks is not the only problem with our financial economy. There is also substantial contagion risk: interconnectedness and spillovers capture the cross-sectional dimension of systemic risk at a given point in time; measuring and containing these spillovers is part of a new macroprudential policy effort. Because of interlinkages between the financial industry and the real economy and between the financial industry and the state, a crisis can soon spread through the entire system. Economic linkages between member states in a currency union have a similar effect.

This potential for negative contagion within and across sectors lies at the heart of the current macroprudential policy discussion about institutions that are too big to fail, too interconnected to fail, or too big to save. The French and German views, of course, come down on different sides of this debate. The French philosophy takes the adverse loops just described very seriously and so calls for aggressive intervention in times of crisis to stop amplification and contagion and to ensure coordination on the "good equilibrium." The French view pushed this as a strong argument in favor of bailouts, even when the underlying problem might be an insolvency problem. The German philosophy, on the other hand, is as always very much concerned about moral hazard problems and fears that intervention now may sow the seeds for a future crisis.

Contagion fears were also the reason for a change of IMF policy. To participate in a Greek 2010 bailout program with debt sustainability far from certain, the IMF actually had to bend its own rules. As will be discussed further in chapter 14, the IMF introduced a "systemic exemption" in its rulebook, allowing for the usual safeguards on sustainability to be relaxed if there is a concern about spillovers to other countries. These considerations very much reflected the French perspective. It is sometimes argued that there was a substantial element of hypocrisy in the German position and that, in effect, the May 2010 program amounted to a bailout of German and also French banks. Germany could not directly bail out its banks because the German government had previously conducted a large and politically unpopular bank rescue of €480 billion in the immediate aftermath of the 2008 crisis. What is striking is that both German and French banking systems had a similar degree of exposure, but by 2010, their governments saw the issue in very different ways. The German emphasis on moral hazard was intellectually appropriate, but it might also have reflected the deep discomfort with the legacy of the 2008 German domestic bank rescue.

The German-French disagreement yet again flashed up during bailout versus bail-in discussions in Cyprus in March 2013 as well as the Grexit discussion in the summer of 2015. (See pages 197–199 for details.) The German frustration with what they perceive as an excessive focus on contagion, or "bad equilibrium," considerations is well reflected in the complaint that "if Cyprus is systemic, then everything is systemic," stressing the fact that the adverse contagion effects would fall mostly on Russian oligarchs.

Again during the Grexit discussion in summer 2015, France openly went against Germany, fearing contagion risk. French prime minister Manuel Valls stated, "We can't take the risk of Greece leaving the euro area."[3] This is despite the fact that in the 2015 "Graccident" (Greek accidental exit) episode, contagion risk was effectively contained via the ECB's large-scale asset purchase program. Markets trusted this firewall, and so the bond market's reaction to increased fears of a Greek exit from the euro was very much muted.

The moral hazard concerns point us in another important direction: systemic risk is not only cross-sectional but also has a time series dimension. During times of relative economic and financial calm, banks gradually take on more risk and so the system becomes increasingly vulnerable to adverse shocks. This building up of risks in the background during tranquil periods is also known as the *volatility paradox*.[4] Expectations of ex post bailouts of course only serve to make matters worse.

The Banking-Sovereign Diabolic Loop and Safe Assets

SAFE ASSETS TAUTOLOGY AND THE GOOD FRIEND ANALOGY

The final important layer of our crisis analysis is the interaction between the banking system and the state. The first thing to note here is that banks in particular (and the wider financial sector more generally) hold reserves and government debt as "safe assets" on the asset side of their balance sheets. But what actually is a safe asset? How does it differ from a risk-free asset?[5] While a risk-free asset pays a certain amount at a certain horizon (say in three months or thirty years), a safe asset pays off when you need it—in times of crisis. In a sense, a safe asset is like a good friend: you can count on it when needed. Another characteristic of safe assets is the safe asset tautology: an asset is safe if it is perceived to be safe. If everyone believes that a certain asset is safe, everyone will buy this asset in times of crisis, so its value spikes during distress. And so it is indeed a "good friend." Thus, yet again, we see an example of familiar multiple equilibrium logic. The classic example of this is gold. A commonality of these safe assets is that their values spike in times of crisis, not because their fundamentals have improved in any sense but rather because there is a common belief that their values will rise. Thus, safe assets have a bubble component to them.

We can apply these lessons to government debt. If government debt is indeed perfectly safe, investors may rush to purchase more of it, thus pushing up prices. Becaue, as we discussed above, banks generally hold substantial amounts of government debt, these price gains will help stabilize the financial system in times of crisis. This is, however, fundamentally different if government debt is suddenly viewed as unsafe. Government debt loses its default-free status if the government refuses to cut expenditures or raises taxes (fiscal dominance) and the central bank refuses or is unable to inflate debt away (monetary dominance). In this case government bonds suffer losses after an adverse shock.

Diabolic Loop

Banks that hold government bonds incur losses and two forms of diabolic loops occur.[6] (See figure 10.2.)

First, banks cut back on their loan supply, and so with less credit going to the economy, growth slumps. This lowers tax revenues, and at the same time, raises government expenditures (e.g., due to increased unemployment insurance payments), threatening the sustainability of government finances and lowering government bond prices further. Second, with weaker banks, the probability that the government has to bail out the bank rises. This further strains government finances, lowers bond values, and hurts banks again. Prime examples of this diabolic loop in action are the experiences of Ireland and Spain, where ailing financial systems and overindebted sovereigns threatened to bring each other down. Of course, the same logic can also be reversed to a "virtuous loop."

This tight nexus between solvency fears for governments and solvency fears for banks is empirically most clearly documented in figure 10.3. Countries for which it is more expensive to insure their default risk, that

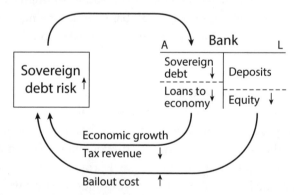

Figure 10.2. The Banking-Sovereign Diabolic Loops: Bailout and Credit Crunch

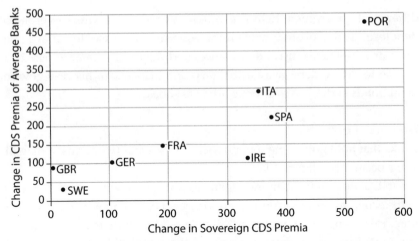

FIGURE 10.3. Change of CDS Spreads of Sovereign and Average Banks between January 2010 and July 2012 (Source: Bloomberg)

is, for which the CDS spread on their debt is higher, also exhibit higher average CDS spreads in their banking sector.[7]

The diabolic loop also lies at the heart of the controversy about bail-in versus bailout. The French tradition, very much aware of the feedback loops we just discussed, calls for bank bailouts to stabilize the economy and so ultimately the sovereign. The German tradition, in contrast, realizes that the very expectation of such bailouts is among the most important reasons for why sovereigns and banks are so closely tied together in the first place. Ex ante, banks should be made sound through higher equity requirements, preventing, in particular, banks from paying out high dividends just before a crisis. We will return to this point in our later discussion of financial dominance.

Exposure Limits or Taking Banks as "Hostage"

In 2015 the German Bundesbank and some of the northern countries pushed to impose exposure limits on banks' holding of domestic sovereign debt in the hope of breaking the diabolic loop. This initiative met fierce resistance from France and south European central banks, who argued that at the height of the crisis only domestic banks were "willing" to buy government debt from vulnerable countries. In their view, domestic banks acted as a stabilizer for government bond markets. Forcing domestic banks to hold domestic government debt also serves as a commitment device for the government not to default on its debt since any subsequent default would trigger a widespread banking crisis and send the economy into a tailspin. Taking the domestic banks "hostage" however constitutes a "straitjacket commitment" that it is too strong as it rules out any debt restructuring even in extreme circumstances and might stifle growth in the long run.

Crisis Management: Monetary Policy

As we have seen, a financial economy is, by its very nature, not robust to adverse economic shocks. Balancing the various forces is challenging. It has been a recurring theme in this chapter that financial crises carry with them substantial disinflationary pressures, and the current state of the euro area is a good example of this. Credit growth is subdued everywhere, and even in (comparatively) vigorously growing Germany, inflation in 2009 and then again after 2013 began to undershoot the target of 2 percent inflation. We have, however, also seen that most financial crises stir up sovereign debt problems, and the crisis of the euro area is no exception to this. If fiscal authorities refuse to cut budget deficits (in a fiscal dominance regime), the central bank will sooner or later be forced to monetize the deficit and print more money, creating strong inflationary pressures. In that case, there would be two forces—a disinflationary and an inflationary one—pulling the economy in opposite directions. In a crisis, it is very difficult to balance these opposing forces, and the system is very unforgiving to small mistakes. In a sense, this is like riding a bike: it is easy to ride a bike if it goes at a reasonable speed, but keeping the balance once the bike slows down is rather difficult. And just as it is hard to predict whether the biker will fall down on one side or another, it is hard to know whether the economy in a crisis will drift into deflation or inflation. This, in a nutshell, is why there was so little agreement about the medium-term outlook for inflation during the crisis years.

In general, governments and central banks can change this either via ex post intervention in times of crisis or by fundamentally altering the design of the financial system (ex ante policies). We start with a discussion of ex post emergency stabilization measures. Essentially, any kind of ex post stabilization involves some kind of redistribution toward the ailing financial sector and other overly indebted sectors.

Monetary policy can induce portfolio rebalancing effects, which lead to changes in risk-taking behavior and risk premia, causing further asset price changes and so further redistributional wealth shifts. Overall, the inflationary pressures brought by expansionary monetary policies tend to erode the real value of debt contracts. Aggressive monetary policy easing thus induces redistribution toward borrowers, and so the debt overhang and recapitalization problems discussed above are alleviated. Another positive second-round effect common to all these expansionary measures is related to risk-taking behavior. In times of crisis, uncertainty increases, and so consumers accumulate precautionary savings while banks lend less and firms invest less. Expansionary monetary intervention stimulates output through the various channels and thus reduces uncertainty and so stimulates spending further.

Fiscal policy measures undertaken by the governments are the focus of subsequent subsections. At the end of this chapter, we link all of this together via the notion of *financial dominance*.[8] In a financial dominance regime, a strategically weak financial sector pays out high dividends at the onset of a crisis and then, through its systemic importance, forces either the central bank or fiscal authorities to assume losses during the crisis. This recapitalization occurs through one of the channels mentioned above, which we now will outline in detail.

Interest Rate Policy

Banks can borrow and deposit reserves at the central bank at a certain interest rate. Varying this interest rate is the key monetary policy tool. From this short-term rate, the central bank indirectly, through expectations of future rate cuts or hikes, affects long-term yields and bond prices as well as risk premia. The literature distinguishes between the interest rate, exchange rate, and the risk-taking channels.

Various Transmission Mechanisms

In (New) Keynesian models, the nominal interest rate matters because of price and wage rigidities. As prices and wages only adjust slowly, quantities have to adjust. That is, price rigidities allow demand shocks to depress output and lead to underemployment. In contrast, in a world in which prices always flexibly adjust, the interest rate is constantly at its natural—or "Wicksellian"—level, and the economy is always at full employment.

The same rigidities that depress output also give monetary policy its traction and allow central banks to stabilize the economy. The underlying mechanism is the following: because prices only adjust slowly, a reduction in the nominal interest rate automatically brings with it a decline of the real (inflation-corrected) interest rate, at least in the short run. This lowers the real costs of capital for firms and induces consumers to bring consumption forward. Demand is stimulated, and so output and inflation tend to pick up. At the same time, given rigid wages in the short run, positive price inflation means that real wages fall, and so firms are willing to hire more workers and satisfy the increased demand. This part of the monetary policy transmission mechanism is referred to as the *interest rate channel*.

Rate cuts also act on the real economy through their effect on the exchange rate, the *exchange rate channel*: a lower policy rate goes hand in hand with an exchange rate depreciation, thus making exporters more competitive and at the same time making imports more costly. This, at least, is the standard story (borne out in the euro case by the experience of QE and its effects on the exchange rate in 2014–2015).

An important implicit assumption underlying conventional analyses of this sort is that money and credit markets function perfectly all the time. Among other things, this assumption ensures that risk premia at best change gradually. Matters clearly look a bit differently in our financial economy. Here, ubiquitous debt-financing frictions mean that a reduction in the effective risk-bearing capacity of the financial sector, brought about by some adverse shock, goes hand in hand with an increase in various excess risk premia. In this environment, monetary policy works through redistribution and an adjustment of risk premia. The intent of central banks to push financial institutions toward more risk-taking is known as the *risk-taking channel* of monetary policy. This could lead to lower financing costs, stimulating further investments and pushing the economy to a higher growth path—the positive take. Or, alternatively, it may simply mean higher leverage and a boost to insolvent zombie banks, thus sacrificing financial stability—the critical take.

Money versus Credit View

To understand precisely the links between monetary policy and financial frictions, it is a good idea to go back to the old money and credit views of monetary policy. The money view, which can be traced back to Friedman and Schwartz's monetarism and even to the work of Irving Fisher on the Great Depression, is focused on the disinflationary spiral that we analyzed above. Note that in our analysis of amplification mechanisms, we assumed that outside money stayed fixed, while the behavior of banks caused a fall in inside money. At the same time, the demand for money rises. If, instead, the central bank expands the outside money supply—something Milton Friedman pictured as a helicopter drop of cash—then disinflationary pressure is reduced, and so the disinflationary spiral can be switched off. As the amount of inside money declines, as banks shrink their balance sheets—or, even worse, as some banks go bankrupt (as was the case during the Great Depression)—an increase in outside money helps replace the missing inside money (and meet the increased money demand). The money view, emphasized very much by those in the monetarists' camp, focuses primarily on the liabilities side of banks' balance sheets.

In contrast, the credit view, pushed primarily by Yale economics professor James Tobin, stresses the importance of restoring bank lending and so is more concerned with the asset side of banks' balance sheets. Not all forms of credit, however, are equally desirable. "Healthy" credit should, so the argument goes, be expanded, while credit from zombie banks (undercapitalized banks with negative equity) or vampire banks (insolvent banks that offer high interest rates on deposits to attract new funding) is to be curtailed.

To understand better this distinction between "healthy" and "unhealthy" credit, we need to look more closely into the behavior of zombie and vampire banks. Zombie banks, undercapitalized and artificially kept alive, gamble for resurrection. Rather than granting new loans to profitable projects, they opt for risky loans that turn out well if the economy recovers soon but can cause large losses otherwise. If everything turns out well, the bank generates profits and is resurrected, allowing it to function normally again. But if—as is more likely—the loans turn sour, the bank remains insolvent but is even deeper in the red than before. Shareholders, who are protected by limited liability, will not be concerned about this. The same cannot be said about the government, which may in the end be forced to bail out the bank to minimize contagion risk, or about demand-deposit insurance funds. Zombie banks also tend to roll over loans they have extended to insolvent zombie firms. By giving the zombie firms new loans, the zombie bank ensures that it can declare the loans on its books as non-delinquent and meanwhile gamble that the zombie firms resume repayments. Again, savings are diverted away from new productive projects to old, unproductive ones. So-called vampire banks—zombie banks that are short on funding—act in the same way, but in addition also try to attract demand deposits from competing banks. By offering extremely high interest rates on their checking accounts, these vampire banks (metaphorically speaking) suck out funds from their healthy competitors.

Japan in the 1990s provides a troubling illustration of the damage zombie and vampire banks can do to an economy and suggests that policy makers should try to identify and wind down such institutions as soon as possible. In the recent euro-area crisis, various Spanish financial institutions were arguably in danger of becoming zombie banks. It had become clear early on in the crisis that some of the Spanish cajas were insolvent, but Spanish policy makers for a long time clung to the hope that they could stabilize these savings banks by merging them into a new conglomerate, labeled Bankia. This bank, however, was declared insolvent by its auditors (and not by the supervisors, who had continued to apply regulatory forbearance) and hence required a further government bailout in 2012.[9]

Fundamentally solvent, but undercapitalized banks, on the other hand, would lend to the right projects but—because their leverage ratios are uncomfortably high—instead decide to scale back their operations. That is how Italian banks largely responded to the debt crisis, pushing for higher levels of collateral as a way of restricting their lending. As already discussed above, their timid behavior in extending new loans leads to a credit crunch among the productive sectors in the real economy.

One (politically infeasible) way to undo their undercapitalization and so encourage new lending is through a direct "gift" of outside money. With such a gift, banks now suddenly have more assets, and so—because liabilities are unchanged—equity will rise. If the entire capital shortfall stemming from the crisis is compensated for in this manner, banks have no reason to hand out less credit than they did before the shock. Overall, we have seen that, at least in theory, central banks can, through the expansion of outside money, switch off the liquidity and disinflationary spirals. The economy thus recovers through a redistribution of wealth.

STEALTH RECAPITALIZATION THROUGH INTEREST RATE CUT

In reality, of course, redistribution via monetary policy occurs in subtle ways, and this brings us back to our discussion of interest rate policies. Rate cuts can also have strong effects on bond and equity valuations. For example, a long-lasting cut in the short-term policy rate increases the relative value of long-term bonds, and so holders of such instruments—of which banks are a large group—benefit. A perfect illustration of all this is Alan Greenspan's decision, back in 1990, to turn monetary policy around to avoid a major crisis of US commercial banks.[10] Of course, these valuation impacts are not uniform across the financial sector, as different banks hold assets and liabilities of different maturity. In Europe, banks held large positions in government bonds. For example, Mario Draghi's London speech led to large capital gains on these positions, which stabilized the banking sector.

However, lower interest rates can also diminish banks' long-run profitability. As interest rates decline, banks' interest rate net (profit) margin, the difference between their lending rate and borrowing rate, also declines. Whether the positive re-evaluation effect or the negative net interest profit margin effect dominates depends on banks' asset holding and the maturity of these assets. An interest rate cut beyond a certain rate, the "reversal rate," reverses its impact. Instead of being accommodative, the rate cut beyond the reversal rate becomes contractionary as it can destabilize the financial system. Hence, the reversal rate forms the effective lower bound on interest rate monetary policy.

Large-Scale Asset Purchase Programs: Quantitative Easing (QE)

Such pure interest rate policies, however, will not work if the interest rate required to rebalance the economy toward its full-employment equilibrium level is significantly below zero. Because nominal interest rates cannot go very far below zero, central banks that only have the interest rate tool at their disposal cannot in such an environment induce the extra required spending, as it can neither stimulate spending directly nor recapitalize the financial sector through fiscal redistribution. But as the recent crisis has shown, central banks are not completely powerless, even when the interest rate is its effective lower bound, the reversal rate. First of all, they can target specific asset prices and so achieve redistribution through large-scale asset purchase programs: quantitative easing (QE). Through the portfolio rebalancing effect, the central bank's asset purchases will drive investors into other (possibly riskier) assets and so push up the prices of these riskier assets.

One vivid example of this mechanism is the Federal Reserve's purchases of mortgage-backed securities. These purchases led to direct capital gains for many banks and so achieved the desired redistribution. Remember, balance-sheet impairments need not be limited to the banking sector. In the subprime crisis, homeowners suffered as well, depressing overall demand in the economy. The Federal Reserve's purchases of mortgage-backed securities also lowered mortgage rates, and so indirectly boosted house prices. This, in turn, helped many homeowners who were previously underwater and provided extra stimulus to a distressed sector of the economy.

Large-scale asset purchase programs can also work through the signaling channel. As the central bank purchases assets, such as long-dated bonds, it exposes itself to losses when it raises rates in the future. Hence, the central bank becomes more reluctant to raise rates early on. In other words, QE signals that the central bank will keep the short-term interest rate low for a long time.

In Europe, various asset purchase programs were proposed. Under the outright monetary transactions (OMT) (and more generally Draghi's pledge to do "whatever it takes" to save the euro), the ECB would purchase the government debt of distressed countries—countries in an official ESM program. Hence, this asset purchase program is tied to strict conditionality and so controls dangerous game-of-chicken dynamics. Interestingly, the mere announcement of this program led to a large increase of prices, therefore a decrease in interest rate, of government debt for periphery countries, illustrating the power of a credible central bank commitment. Overall, the Draghi speech that presaged the OMT program proposal amounted to a stealth recapitalization of peripheral banks. Without the speech, it is not clear whether these banks would have been able to survive any subsequent stress tests.

In January 2015, the ECB started with an outright QE program. This and other ECB programs are discussed thoroughly in chapter 15.

Collateral Policy

Instead of purchasing assets outright, central banks also lend to banks that provide assets as collateral. In general, if a financial institution wants to borrow funds directly from the central bank, it has to deposit certain assets as collateral. Central banks have two degrees of freedom in their collateral policy: First, they can decide which kind of assets they accept as collateral. And, second, they can set the haircuts they apply to the different assets that they do accept. The ECB, for example, throughout the crisis, decided to lend against a wide range of collateral and reduce haircuts for particular asset classes. The list of specific changes is too long to elaborate here, but to gain a rough understanding of the ECB's actions, it suffices to note that the credit threshold for most assets to qualify as collateral was over time reduced from A– to BBB–. In particular, the policy changes were designed to make it easier for banks to use asset-backed securities as collateral for borrowing. These measures drew harsh criticism in the German media, where one story in particular received a lot of attention: the use of professional soccer players as collateral. As reported by *El País* (and quoted in the German newspaper *Handelsblatt*), the transfer rights to Cristiano Ronaldo and Kaka, two soccer players for Real Madrid, were part of the collateral underlying credit extended to the Spanish banking conglomerate Bankia.[11] In the case of default, the rights to Ronaldo and Kaka would in principle have been claimed by the ECB, leading to jokes about whether the ECB intended to create its own soccer team.

Banks of course benefited from this relaxation of collateral rules, as they could borrow money more cheaply from the ECB, and at the same time saw the value of any asset eligible as collateral boosted. A common thread running through all these interventions is that they also spill over to other asset classes. Assets differ in their risk profiles, and so, if the central bank's actions make a particular asset less attractive to hold, investors will partially substitute it with other assets.

Lender of Last Resort Policy

As argued famously by Walter Bagehot in *Lombard Street*, part of a central bank's responsibility should be to accommodate banks' demand for funds in times of crisis (at a penalty rate). By making the required funds available, the central bank can break the threat of self-fulfilling fears about bank solvency, and prevent pure liquidity shocks from morphing into solvency crises. The lender of last resort function of a central bank is thus all about illiquidity and does not concern itself (at least in theory) with insolvency problems. In practice, however, it is difficult to distinguish between insolvency and pure illiquidity crises. It is for this reason that agreement among economists does not stretch beyond the fact that modern financial systems need a lender of last resort of some sort.

The conflicting schools of thought particularly differ in their suggestions about the terms at which emergency funding should be made available. Predictably, the German view is very much in favor of stiff penalty rates, while adherents to the French philosophy fear that, if the terms of the lender of last resort window are too taxing, financial crises will spread before the central bank's help is ever even called upon. Note also that Bagehot was very explicit in limiting his analysis to banks: the central bank should not help out the state and act as a market maker of last resort. Some modern commentators do not agree with this rigid stance and instead, in line with our earlier analysis of self-fulfilling government debt crises, would prefer the central bank to stand ready to buy sovereign debt to allow coordination on good equilibria.

Ex Post Monetary Policy: Bottleneck Approach

Armed with this knowledge of the monetary policy transmission mechanism, we can now ask what the optimal ex post monetary policy precisely looks like. The first step toward an ideal policy reaction is to identify the sector that is undercapitalized. It could be the corporate sector accumulating too much debt (as was the case in Japan in the 1980s) or it could be households that saw an unhealthy run-up in debt levels (as happened in the United States in the years leading up to the crisis). Having identified the sectors that need the most help, the next step is to avoid the amplification mechanisms and adverse spirals described above. By limiting the redistributional effects associated with these spirals, the required risk premia fall, hurdle rates are reduced, and the economy recovers. To achieve the desired redistribution, the central bank can pick among the different instruments discussed above.

Because debt financing typically runs through the financial system, the travails of any single overly indebted sector are often intimately connected with troubles for the intermediaries. Redistribution in times of crisis thus often means redistribution in favor of the financial system so as to strengthen again its intermediation capabilities. If central banks indeed take the dismal situation of the financial system as given and adapt their policies accordingly, we are in a world of financial dominance. Given the generally close ties between financial systems and governments, such financial dominance may in fact be a form of hidden fiscal dominance: banks are weak because they were pressured into providing cheap finance to domestic governments, and so the central bank saving them is tantamount to the central bank indirectly granting the government access to the printing press. This is just one example of the dangers associated with the provision of ex post insurance to the financial sector and will be discussed in greater detail later on.

Crisis Management: Fiscal Policy and Regulatory Measures

Fiscal policy measures strain the government's fiscal budget: (1) Government guarantees only do so when called upon, (2) direct bank recapitalization schemes, for example through equity injections, do so for sure, (3) bail-ins force other investors to share the burden, while (4) recapitalization through other means have no direct, but might have indirect, costs.

Government Guarantees

Governments may decide to issue blanket guarantees for domestic bank assets. If this guarantee is credible, then any liquidity-related problems will immediately dissipate. Government guarantees of this sort are generally not viewed as a crisis measure; basic kinds of deposit insurance are in place in many advanced economies, motivated as a means of staving off bank-run dynamics and so ensuring coordination on the good equilibrium.

The Irish crisis experience, however, shows that extended government guarantees may also function as a crisis response tool that goes beyond fixing a liquidity problem and the taxpayer eventually may have to foot the bill. At the height of the financial crisis in 2008, the Irish government extended existing deposit insurance schemes to a two-year blanket guarantee for the liabilities of all Irish banks, including all sorts of deposits, senior unsecured debt, subordinated debt, and asset-covered securities. The problem with this policy measure was that some Irish banks were fundamentally insolvent. As we saw above, Irish banks were overexposed to the domestic housing sector and extremely reliant on wholesale funding on the euro-area interbank market. As this market dried up, credit extension collapsed, and the Irish property bubble popped. Existing loans thus turned sour, and liabilities started to exceed assets: Irish banks had become insolvent. Given this insolvency, it is not surprising that the Irish government's controversial blanket guarantee ended up settling Irish taxpayers with billions of debt. In the words of Patrick Honohan, governor of the Central Bank of Ireland, the crisis was "one of the most expensive banking crises in world history."[12] In sum, what was fundamentally a solvency problem was erroneously treated as an illiquidity problem.

Direct Recapitalization

The most direct way of recapitalizing the domestic banking system is through direct equity injections. Through a direct injection of equity, domestic governments can help to alleviate any solvency problem, usually in return for sufficient control over the business practices of the bank in question. Given the substantial cost of operations of this sort, and the likely financing of bank recapitalization through increased public debt, the link between bank and state solvency is clear. In short, diabolic loop considerations (as discussed above) loom large.

The direct recapitalization path was followed by, among other countries, Germany, Ireland, and Spain. In Germany, various Landesbanken with significant exposure to the US subprime market were bailed out in the immediate aftermath of the 2008 financial crisis. In Ireland, continued problems even after the blanket guarantees forced the government to directly recapitalize the country's three main banks (Allied Irish Bank, Bank of Ireland, and Anglo-Irish Bank), with the fiscal authorities taking €2 billion in preference shares in Bank of Ireland and Allied Irish Bank and €1.5 billion in preference shares in Anglo Irish Bank.

In Spain, crisis dynamics of a very similar sort to that in Ireland forced large-scale recapitalizations. Cajas were overexposed to the bubbly domestic housing market and overreliant on wholesale funding, so the global financial crisis sent the Spanish housing market crashing, and with it the balance sheets of cajas. Compared to the Irish experience, relatively prudent bank regulation (high capital buffers, low exposure to complex derivatives markets), forbearance accounting (delaying foreclosure), and the creative reclassification, refinancing, and extension of existing loans all helped to delay the inevitable.[13] However, by 2010, it had become clear that intervention was necessary. The Spanish government directly recapitalized its banks through the Fund for the Orderly Restructuring of the Banking Sector (FROB). After the capital injections, the authorities pursued the strategy of systematically restructuring (in the case of cajas consolidating), with a view to later selling off the resulting entities.

The Irish and Spanish recapitalizations, however, proved insufficient, and so, as the diabolic loop started to emerge in full force, international bailouts became inevitable. For Ireland, the international bailout totaled €85 billion, with €67.5 billion of external support (EFSF, EFSM, and IMF) and €17.5 billion from the Irish Treasury and the National Pension Reserve Fund. This had become necessary, as by October 2010 Irish sovereign bond yields were above 7 percent and the budget deficit had reached €16.7 billion, together threatening the financing position of the Irish government. The direct bailout was supplemented by ECB-provided liquidity supply for Irish banks (which had also been effectively locked out from markets). The bailout program would prove to be a success, with Ireland successfully exiting on December 15, 2013. Market bond rates on Irish debt by that time had reached a historic low.

The Spanish bailout program followed somewhat later, as the Spanish government officially requested assistance in the summer of 2012. This bailout, coming as part of a financial sector adjustment program rather than the more general economic adjustment program for other member countries, was especially geared toward the financial sector and as such was much less politically charged. The total bailout package amounted to €100 billion, an amount that was supposed to cover the estimated capital requirements for the restructuring and recapitalization of Spanish banks and, beyond that, provide an additional safety margin. There was a bail-in of junior bonds: one of the features of bank rescue that later became standard.

As a large economy, Spain of course had more bargaining power than previous bailout recipients, and so it is unsurprising (also in light of the earlier reforms enacted by the conservative Rajoy government) that the austerity requirements of the Spanish adjustment program were comparatively less stringent. This also connects with the idea that the Spanish financial sector adjustment program was viewed as less intrusive than conventional economic adjustment programs. Still, with the recapitalization of banks channeled through the Spanish government, the diabolic loop was not truly broken, prompting calls that the ESM should be able to directly recapitalize ailing financial institutions. These proposals will be discussed later in the context of banking union.

Bail-Ins: Cyprus

Yet another way to recapitalize an ailing banking system is to "bail-in" bank creditors. That is, the bank's creditors (in particular deposit holders) have to share in the costs of bank insolvency or restructuring by having a certain fraction of the debt they are owed written off or converted into equity claims. On the face of it, bail-ins impose much lighter burdens (if any) on the fiscal side and so can help break the diabolic loop between state and sovereign. At the same time, however, bail-ins ex ante can weaken financial intermediaries by removing any implicit expectations of government bailouts and ex post can substantially weaken the economy in question by expropriating bank creditors (and in particular ordinary depositors).

CYPRUS: THE BACKGROUND

It is instructive to review these issues through the lens of a particular example: Cyprus. Cyprus had joined the European Union only in 2004 and signed up to the currency union in 2008, when the global financial crisis was already having an impact. Cyprus as a country pursued a business model of fostering a large banking sector through low taxes and weak regulation. A large fraction of bank funding came from Russia and other post-Soviet states, including untaxed "black" money from rich oligarchs; but it also attracted a considerable amount of deposits from Greeks, especially once uncertainty emerged about Greece's position within the currency union. Cypriot banks offered high deposit rates and invested the proceeds in risky high-yield instruments, including Greek government papers (a strategy that had often been justified by the principle of matching the nationality of liabilities, the deposits, and assets, the Greek government bonds). The selective default of Greece on its debt thus significantly hurt the Cypriot banks, but, with emergency liquidity provided to Cypriot banks, there was not much panic before mid-2012. Direct aid from Russia (amounting to €2.5 billion) as part of "a friendly agreement with no strings attached" also helped.[14]

THE CYPRUS BAIL-IN SOLUTION

In the summer of 2012, the rating agency Fitch downgraded Cypriot sovereign bonds, making them ineligible to serve as collateral accepted by the ECB. The Cypriot government then formally requested a bailout. The European Commission, the ECB, and France were inclined to follow this request with the provision of a straightforward bailout, as already applied to several other periphery countries. They emphasized the possible contagion effect that bail-in might have on the rest of Europe. By contrast, the IMF and also Germany pushed for a bail-in solution in which some of the losses would be imposed on bondholders and even the depositors of the Cypriot banks.

Ultimately, the German view prevailed. German policy makers liked to make the argument that this was the line against financial irresponsibility that could be held: if Cyprus is systemic, then everything is systemic, and the no-bailout rule is totally undermined. The decision appeared especially easy given that a bailout would help the rich Russian oligarchs who had parked black money in Cyprus: it would be a transfer of wealth from poor German taxpayers to corrupt billionaires. That was obviously a difficult proposition to sell in German politics. From this perspective, the Cyprus banks had offered high deposit rates and speculated on holding Greek debt, hoping that there would be no default. The disagreements around the Cypriot bailout/bail-in negotiations thus highlighted the divergence between the "German" moral hazard–driven insolvency approach and the French liquidity/multiple equilibrium explanation of the problem.

On March 16, 2013, representatives from the Eurogroup, European Commission, ECB, the ESM, and IMF met in Brussels. The ECB was represented not by Draghi but by Jörg Asmussen. The agreement provided a bailout of €10 billion, making Cyprus the fifth country, after Greece, Ireland, Portugal, and Spain, to receive money from the European Union and the IMF. But the €10 billion was not enough to meet the financing needs of the banking system, and the remaining shortfall would be filled by imposing losses on creditors, including depositors.

Because Cyprus banks' liabilities were almost exclusively in the form of demand deposits, they had to be touched. The initial suggestion presented an apparently sophisticated way of avoiding the appearance of default: a confiscatory tax on deposits. The Cyprus government refused to impose a tax on large deposit holders of two digits. That is, deposits of more than €100,000 should not be taxed more than 9.9 percent. The tax-haven banking business model shouldn't be jeopardized. This translated into a tax levy for small deposit holders of 6.7 percent. Adopting this package required that no funds could be withdrawn from banks, and the flow of international capital was shut down. In effect, there was now a Cyprus euro deposit that was not worth the same as euro deposits elsewhere.

The Brussels deal had to be approved by the Cypriot Parliament, and its announcement led to riots in Cyprus. For one week, Parliament tried to come up with a different solution. Many proposals were discussed by local politicians, including robbing the local population of its pension funds. Russian president Vladimir Putin called the tax on bank deposits "unfair, unprofessional and dangerous."[15] Mostly, local unrest focused on the German government as the source of the confiscatory package. Merkel intervened, and the next weekend a new European solution was proposed. One weekend later, a final agreement was found. The Laiki Bank was shut down, all insured depositors preserved their first €100,000, and large depositors, mostly wealthy Russians, received some claims on the remaining bad assets. The largest bank, Bank of Cyprus, survived, but it appeared that depositors over €100,000 would lose some two-fifths of their claims.

A TEMPLATE FOR THE REST OF EUROPE?
The eruption of the crisis in Cyprus brought the Eurogroup of Finance Ministers (Ecofin) into the unexpected limelight. Its head, the Dutch finance minister Jeroen Dijsselbloem, would later, in an influential interview, go on to expand on the logic that motivated the decision to bail-in bank depositors. There should no longer be any automatic assumption that all deposits in all banks were guaranteed; that was a quite recent doctrine that had emerged accidentally in 2008 after Ireland had unilaterally extended a guarantee (that it could not really afford) to all its bank depositors. Instead, depositors in failed banks would be required to take a loss, and the result would be a reduction in the cost of bank rescues and a breaking of the diabolical loop of banks and sovereigns. According to press reports, the Cyprus operation would be a "template" for subsequent bank rescues. Within minutes, bank stocks significantly lost value in peripheral Europe, while sovereign bond yields stabilized. Other governments were

immediately scared by the possibility of bank-run contagion, as nervous large depositors might shift their funds, and the word "template" was withdrawn. Even Wolfgang Schäuble made an announcement that it was not meant this way.

Despite this backtracking, euro-area officials were quick to point out that the principle of bail-in would remain. For example, the Irish finance minister later commented, "Bail-in is now the rule."[16] The credibility of these claims, however, is very much open to debate. First of all, the extent of future bail-ins was quite imprecise, as the official bail-in provisions explicitly excluded a long list of creditors: covered deposits; secured liabilities, including covered bonds; liabilities to employees of failing institutions, such as fixed salary and pension benefits; commercial claims relating to goods and services critical for the daily functioning of the institution; liabilities arising from a participation in payment systems with remaining maturity of less than seven days; and interbank liabilities with an original maturity of less than seven days were all excluded. The intent was to protect the interbank market, but it was also clear that the measure would protect the ECB and national central banks from losses.

In addition, the bail-in provisions allowed national authorities to, at their discretion, exempt even larger groups of creditors as long as one of the following conditions was satisfied: (1) if bondholders cannot be bailed in within a reasonable time, (2) if the provision of critical functions was threatened by bail-in, (3) if bail-in would lead to contagion, and (4) if bail-in would lead to value destruction that would raise losses borne by other creditors.[17] This extraordinary list made it appear quite unlikely that there would be a large bail-in—or a large rescue of the national budgets of countries with failed financial institutions. And in fact even subordinated debt (which was widely viewed as a prime candidate for bail-in) might be problematic. The bail-in discussion raised the fear that imposing too much of the cost on the private sector would generate another round of financial instability, or a repeat of the market response to Deauville.

The ECB in particular pushed back against the idea of bail-ins that might lead to a "flight of investors out of the European banking market, which would further hamper banks' funding going forward. All in all, an improperly strict interpretation of the State aid rules may well destroy the very confidence in euro area banks which we all intend to restore."[18] Overall, then, the peculiarities of the Cypriot situation seem to have provided most of the impetus to the bail-in decision, and it is rather dubious that the same principles would be applied to other countries. The new rules on banking resolution and bail-in would come into effect at the beginning of 2015, but in advance doubts arose about the extent to which they would really be applied.

BANK FAILURES, PORTUGAL, AND THE ECB's ASSET QUALITY REVIEW

A first test of the new rules came in August 2014. The Portuguese family-controlled Banco Espirito Sancto was involved in a fraudulent funding scheme. The curious name ("Holy Spirit Bank") originates in the story that the bank's founder, José Maria do Espírito Santo e Silva, descended from an abandoned child, who had been discovered in a Lisbon church and raised by nuns. The bank held many loans on its books that had been extended to other businesses of the same family, to some extent in the former Portuguese colonies, notably Angola.[19] With the new resolution rules due to take effect in two steps in January 2015 and 2016, shareholders and junior bondholders were left holding only the worst assets. The bank was split into a "bad bank" with the toxic assets and a new bank Novo Banco, funded with €4.9 billion from the Portuguese government. The investment banking part of the new bank was eventually sold off to a Chinese investor, Haitong Securities, for €379 million.[20] Senior bondholders in Novo Banco obtained, in effect, a guarantee through a €4.5 billion loan—an operation that provided a signal to the rest of the European banking sector. That loan may have limited possible spillover and contagion effects on the rest of the European banking sector, and fears that a new banking crisis would undermine the stabilization of the euro area receded.[21] The fact that senior bondholders were still partially bailed out showed that the application of the not yet implemented rules would become very difficult.

The next test of the new arrangements, which gave the ECB a great deal of power through its new supervisory powers, came with the announcement of the results of the comprehensive assessment consisting of an asset quality review (AQR) conducted by the ECB and the third EU-wide stress test, conducted by the EBA, on October 26, 2014 (a Sunday, when the markets were closed). The ECB examined 130 large European banks, with only 13 facing a total capital shortfall of €9.5 billion. The most problematic was the oldest European bank, Monte dei Paschi di Siena, with a €2.1 billion shortfall. The Italian banks had suffered from two decades of slow Italian growth, but also from governance problems: many of the banks, including Monte dei Paschi, were run by foundations that were intricately interconnected with local politics and demanded dividend payouts even when profits were dwindling.

BAIL-INS AND FINANCIAL ILLITERACY

Bail-ins also raise an additional problem if retail investors with little detailed experience of financial markets bought securities that were in reality some form of subordinated bond that would require to be bailed in, in the case of a bank's failure. This problem became particularly acute in Italy at the end of 2015, but this issue was also widely debated in Germany in the wake of the September 2008 Lehman crash, with some lawsuits filed by retail investors against banks and court verdicts in favor of the investor. Sometimes bank representatives reacted unwisely and blamed the "greed" of clients who wanted returns of over 6 percent; comments like this inevitably triggered a discussion about bank mis-selling of investments to the financially illiterate.[22] A similar debate occurred after the Italian government had to rescue and restructure four regional banks in 2015 and an elderly holder of subordinated bonds of the Banca Popolare dell'Etruria e del Lazio killed himself. The Italian finance minister commented, "It cannot be ruled out that the four banks sold subordinated bonds to people with a risk profile which isn't compatible with the nature of these securities."[23] The EU commissioner for financial services, Jonathan Hill, echoed this critique with the by now familiar accusation that banks were "selling unsuitable products to people who maybe didn't know what they were buying."[24] The Italian response was to set up a special fund to assist on a case-by-case basis those who lost large amounts in the course of the bank resolution. A long-term solution would be to treat this issue as a consumer protection issue to be handled by more effective regulation of bank customer practices.

The bank rescue issue also raised questions about differences in national approaches, with Italians claiming that the move to the banking union that limited state support for banks was unfair in the light of the post-2008 story of European banking support. A website by the Italian Economy and Finance Ministry, with the English heading "Pride and Prejudice," pointed out that Italy had devoted the lowest amount to bank rescue: while Germany had paid €247 billion, the United Kingdom €164 billion, Spain €56 billion, and France €51 billion, Italy had only spent €4 billion.[25]

In January 2016, as the new resolution rule came into force that at least 8 percent of assets have to bailed in, the European Commission created a loophole for Italian authorities. They were allowed to extend guarantees at market prices for packages of nonperforming loans that burden banks' balance sheets. These guarantees should help banks sell their troubled loans to hedge funds and outside investors. The fact that Italian state guarantees are only granted at market prices ensures that the guarantees do not constitute a subsidy or a violation of the bail-in principle. Some commentators question whether this action does not distort market prices and fear that it undermines the newly found bail-in regime.[26] It is therefore still open how much the bail-in regime will be watered down.

Recapitalization through Other Means

TEMPORARY MONOPOLY RENTS

Finally, we turn to various less conventional ways of recapitalizing domestic banking systems. A first potential strategy is to grant the firms in question, generally banks, temporary monopoly rents. If a whole sector is inadequately capitalized, firms in this sector retreat and compete less fiercely with each other. This boosts their profit margins and future earnings, so current stock prices and the underlying franchise value increase. As a result, funding constraints are relaxed. This strategy of course only works for sectors that are critical for the functioning of the economy and so not easily substitutable. The classic example of this is the financial sector. Here, the regulator can protect incumbents by restricting the issuance of bank licenses. From an ex ante perspective, the possibility to grant this monopoly power can be seen as an insurance scheme that the real economy extends to the financial sector.

This ex ante insurance, however, comes with at least two significant drawbacks. First, preventing others from entering the market also limits the number of potential buyers of legacy assets. To avoid the fire-sale liquidity spirals described above, recapitalization through temporary monopoly power is typically accompanied by very generous forbearance arrangements. Losses are hidden, and banks are allowed to continue rolling over zombie loans. Second, reduced competition in one sector—in particular, a crucial one such as banking—can hurt other industries more than it benefits the distressed sector. For example, a temporary monopoly strategy for the financial sector would result in a reduction in new lending, putting downward pressure on aggregate output and so making other outstanding loans more risky. Ultimately, if these feedback effects are sufficiently strong, the indirect costs of the recapitalization could outweigh the benefits. Overall, then, the monopoly strategy crucially hinges on all other sectors of the economy not being balance sheet impaired. If they are, the economy will suffer from a serious credit crunch and dive into a long-lasting recession. This is precisely what happened in Japan's lost decade.

INVITE NEW RISK-BEARING CAPITAL

An alternative strategy, or, better said, the opposite strategy, is to invite new risk-bearing capital and open up new funding channels. Taking again the example of the financial sector, the inflow of additional risk-bearing capital enhances competition and restores credit. There are, of course, different ways to attract new capital. For example, the regulator could allow foreign firms with similar expertise to enter the market. Another simple form of attracting new capital is to force banks to issue new equity. On their own, individual firms would be reluctant to do so because of the associated stigma, but centrally enforced, coordinated actions are of course free of such considerations. Thorough and publically communicated asset quality reviews could have a similar effect: they would reduce asymmetric information, reduce the stigma, and encourage the issuance of additional equity. The issuance of "contingent convertible bond," so called CoCos, was pushed as a "cheaper" alternative. Cocos is a hybrid fixed-income security that counts toward capital requirements as it can be converted into equity in case a pre-specified trigger is reached. CoCos have come under increased criticism lately and remain untested as an effective crisis management tool. A third way to attract new funding is to increase the efficiency of direct-lending arrangements, for example, via the corporate bond market or private debt, a theme that also the capital markets union puts forward. This opens up a new funding source for large corporations. A final possibility is to revitalize the shadow banking system, as was done in the United States in 2009 through various programs by the Federal Reserve and the US Treasury.

Independent of how precisely extra risk-bearing capital is attracted, it will enhance competition and so put pressure on—rather than boost—the profit margins of incumbents. Individually, then, each bank will oppose a forced recapitalization. Viewed in aggregate, however, banks profit from new capital, as legacy assets can be sold at higher prices and expanding credit supply ensures that existing loans are less likely to become delinquent. Overall, trying to attract new risk-bearing capital is likely to be a lot more disruptive than propping up existing banks, and, in particular, "too interconnected to fail" considerations loom large. At the same time, such a disruptive way of dealing with the crisis is of course very effective in solving the long-term problems posed by zombie and vampire banks.

In this spectrum of recapitalization policies, the French philosophy is very much in favor of the temporary granting of monopoly rents. This preference is in keeping with the French view's underlying distrust of unregulated market forces and its belief in the power of centralized, coordinated intervention. The German view comes down on the other side. Recapitalization through new capital may be disruptive, but at least it avoids serious moral hazard problems. Such considerations naturally lead us to our next topic: optimal ex ante policy.

REGULATION, FINANCIAL DOMINANCE, AND A SECOND GAME OF CHICKEN

The interpretation of the crisis as fundamentally a problem of inadequately regulated financial markets produced new regulatory initiatives. The German 2008 risk limitation law (*Riskobegrenzungsgesetz*) forced disclosure of investors taking over a 10 percent stake in publicly quoted companies. Temporary short-selling bans were used to stabilize financial markets, although they may have contributed to a longer-term and deeper loss of confidence. In 2012, France and Germany introduced—after a long debate in which the measure was extensively supported by politicians, churches, and intellectuals—a financial transactions tax.

As the demands to tighten banking regulation, limit the scope for Anglo-Saxon financial activity, and make banks pay some price were the major areas of agreement across the Rhine, it is hardly surprising that they became the major fields for policy initiatives in dealing with the aftermath of financial crisis.

Underlying all these different approaches to stabilization and particularly financial sector recapitalization is a common theme: the threat of financial dominance. Recall that, as we discussed in chapter 5, the fiscal-monetary interactions can be characterized either by monetary or by fiscal dominance. If the central bank is weak, debt is inflated away. And if the central bank is strong, fiscal authorities need to make sure that debt is on a sustainable path. What regime we end up in is the result of a dynamic game of chicken.

The presence of a nontrivial financial sector adds a further dimension to these considerations. A financial dominance regime is one in which, through strategic weakness, the financial sector has succeeded in forcing the costs of recapitalization onto either the central bank or fiscal authorities. In good times, the financial sector earns a risk premium; in bad times, it manages to avoid bearing losses. This is achieved through dividend payouts in the early phases of crisis coupled with a refusal (or inability) to issue equity at the trough of the crisis. To safeguard the rest of the economy, either the central bank (through direct redistributive monetary policy or expansionary interest rate policy) or the fiscal authority (through direct recapitalizations) has to intervene. Which authority in the end bears the costs—and whether financial stability ends up jeopardizing price stability (with central bank intervention) or debt sustainability (with fiscal intervention)—is the result of a second game of chicken.

Ex Ante Policy: Preventing a Crisis

We have surveyed the vast array of different crisis response policies. Better than ex post crisis management, however, is ex ante crisis prevention. That is, a fundamental question for regulators is, how can we prevent crises or at least reduce their severity should they happen? This focus on ex ante rules-based environments is very much in keeping with the German tradition. Redistribution toward sectors with impaired balance sheets—either via monetary policy intervention, the granting of monopoly rights, or outright bailout—can be useful immediate ex post crisis management tools, but they also engender a host of immediate and long-run problems. The provision of insurance will, as time and again pointed out by adherents of the German philosophy, give rise to standard moral hazard problems. Banks know that the monetary and fiscal authorities will do everything in their power to redistribute income toward the banking sector in times of crisis, and so banks behave imprudently ex ante. The construction of an adequate ex ante policy framework explicitly builds upon these considerations.

An optimal policy has to take insolvency and illiquidity considerations into account. To avoid liquidity and disinflationary spirals, an optimal ex ante monetary policy rule cuts interest rates after a negative shock and raises interest rates after a positive shock. Crucially, this recapitalization should offset the redistribution induced by the amplification mechanisms but not fully bailout a sector that, in anticipation of crisis redistribution, has taken on excessive amounts of risk. Alas, drawing this line is fraught with time-inconsistency problems. Just as central banks have an incentive to inflate economies ex post given inflation expectations (see chapter 5), they also have an incentive to stabilize the economy through redistribution more than was expected beforehand. Overall, then, both the provision of insurance itself and the tendency of central banks to provide excessive amounts of insurance raises thorny moral hazard problems.

There are, however, some actions that the central bank can take to limit the fallout from these moral hazard issues.

The first thing to note is that redistribution through interest rate cuts is a very blunt tool and may fuel bubbles. Within any given distressed sector, the benefits of the policy intervention should ideally accrue mostly to those firms who behaved (in comparative terms) the least imprudently. In other words, the insurance has embedded in it an extra reward for good behavior, and this can give rise to a beneficial race to the top.

Second, just as with the ordinary inflation bias discussed in chapter 5, the central bank can reduce its redistribution bias through a rigid ex ante commitment to a policy rule. Alas, the economy is too complicated for a rigid, fully specified ex ante rule to be optimal. History does not repeat itself; it only rhymes, and for this reason some discretion will always be needed to manage a financial crisis. We have also seen in chapter 5 that it is impossible to design rules for all possible contingencies, so in extreme tail events, a departure from the rules-based framework may be optimal.

Third, in line with our discussion in chapter 5, the central bank can try to build up a reputation for the prudent use of its stabilization tools in times of crisis. If such a reputation is built up credibly, then households, the corporate sector, and above all banks will think twice before accumulating excessive amounts of debt and risk, and the central bank may never actually be forced to use its stabilization tools. Even more so than in the case of the classical inflation bias, however, it is hard to build up a reputation for such monetary restraint in times of crisis.

Fourth, and most importantly, the central bank can combine its insurance policies with strict rules that limit aggregate risk-taking. For example, strict limits on loan-to-value ratios or stringent haircut rules can quite effectively put the brakes on banks' risk-taking behavior. The macroprudential toolkit thus allows the monetary authority to provide more tail insurance without the associated moral hazard complications. In short, macroprudential tools are a perfect complement to and closely interwoven with conventional monetary policy. This distinguishes macroprudential regulation from microprudential policy measures, which are often seen as quite divorced from the rest of the financial sector. Macroprudential regulation of this sort is an effective response to the time-series dimension of systemic risk. Systemic risks typically build up below the surface in times of tranquility and then materialize during the crisis. Effective macroprudential regulation captures this buildup and acts against it.

Nevertheless, macroprudential policy measures are no panacea: by their nature, they are very targeted and invite regulatory arbitrage. Macroprudential measures may thus turn out to be powerless or, worse yet, induce undesirable side effects. A case in point is the procyclicality of the precrisis Basel II regulations, which required a tightening of lending standards at times when economies would rather benefit from a marked expansion of lending. Another potential problem concerns the risk weighting of assets according to the Basel standards. Assigning zero-risk weights to government bonds may counteract the fiscal-bank diabolic loop in times of crisis, but ex ante could well contribute to the buildup of systemic risk.

Irrespective of the specifics of the ultimately agreed-upon optimal policy rule, society will in the end provide some tail insurance to its leveraged sectors. How much tail risk society or, conversely, nominal claim holders should assume is a political question and depends very much on the underlying economic philosophy of the country. One of the main points of this book is that Europe has, up until now, avoided giving a single clear answer to this question. There clearly is no agreement among member states, with followers of the German tradition very aware of the moral hazard problems, while those influenced by French thinking call for more insurance and aggressive intervention in times of crisis. And these calls for crisis interventionism are yet another source of conflict: in the French tradition, emergency measures are part of the standard crisis-fighting toolkit, but German philosophy interprets every intervention as setting a precedent and so creating a new, permanent rules-based environment for the euro area.

Banking Union, European Safe Bonds, and Exit Risk

U p to this point, our discussion of banking crisis mechanisms and crisis management could just as well apply to individual countries rather than entire currency blocs. We now instead turn to considerations that are special to currency unions, in particular, to one in which a deeply integrated political and fiscal union is, at least in the short and intermediate perspective, more utopia than a political feasibility. The heterogeneity of the economic philosophies and politics of the different members of the union together with a large and nationally fragmented financial sector created significant economic and financial stability challenges, not all of which were foreseen by the policy makers who wrote the Maastricht Treaty.

Given this reality, the recipe policy makers pursued was that of a minimal currency union: a search for the minimal requirement for a functioning and stable common currency, without necessitating deep political integration, that keeps loss sharing to a minimum. Of course, views among the major European actors clashed about these minimum requirements.

Important economic distortions arise in a currency union in which national governments can undertake actions at the expense of others, often resulting in delayed appropriate policy responses. Yet, perhaps as Monnet ingeniously predicted, problems and crises created by these distortions call for new instruments and institutional structures to deal with them, eventually leading to more integration. For this "Monnet process" to work, however, it is essential that all parties understand each other and agree on the necessary institutional structure.

Yet, there is much discordance. Brussels—home to the European Commission—is usually the voice pushing most forcefully for a centralization of powers, including a fiscal union. French policy makers are open to fiscal transfers to secure financial stability, but they are reluctant to pass additional national power to Brussels. Germans already view themselves as the paymasters of Europe and fear that bank bailouts lead to a transfer union through the backdoor. Where France ultimately saw costless liquidity problems, Germany saw solvency problems that ultimately require transfers. The result was a search for a stable minimum currency union: no transfer except in hidden ways; active macroprudential policy, primarily at national levels; and limited Europeanization of liquidity instruments.

After laying out a variety of economic distortions that arise in an incomplete currency union, we proceed in this chapter to survey the steps undertaken during the euro crisis. We pay particular attention to the proposal of a euro-area-wide banking union. Subsequently, we study the important role of safe assets for a stable financial system in a currency union and the instability that can arise when investors fear that a country may exit the currency union. Finally, we draw some policy conclusions from this analysis.

This chapter addresses the following questions:

- What incentives do national policy makers have to push losses onto foreigners? Why is it said that banks are global in good times and national in crisis?
- How do concerns about redistributional issues across member states of the currency union undermine the central bank's lender of last resort activity?
- What kind of institutional design is necessary to dissuade individual countries from rushing toward a ring-fencing of their own banks' assets?
- Would a European banking charter that makes all aspects of finance, including the tax revenue in good times and costs in crisis times, be the solution?
- What is the importance of euro-area-wide safe assets to contain flight-to-safety cross-border capital flows in times of crisis?
- How does the redenomination risk of exit from a currency union affect interest rates and undermine cohesion of the currency union?

Banking in a Currency Union

At the height of the crisis, the crisis countries together with France made a strong push toward the creation of a banking union. The origins of the idea of banking union, however, can be traced back to initial debates about the monetary union in the late 1980s. According to the initial plans, the central bank would have overall supervisory and regulatory powers. Yet, that proposal met resistance from the German Bundesbank in the early 1990s. Hans Tietmeyer, then president of the Bundesbank, was concerned that supervision by the central bank would implicitly signal a bailout guarantee and hence lead to moral hazard problems. The political debates (discussed in detail in chapter 15) eventually led to an article (Article 25) in the ECB statute allowing the latter to "offer advice" (but not really act) and another one in the Maastricht Treaty (Article 105, now Article 127 of the Lisbon Treaty) that contained enough hurdles to make euro-area-wide banking supervision de facto impossible.

The understanding that consequently emerged after Maastricht was that potential solvency problems in a financial institution should be dealt with by the treasury of the country in which the institution is headquartered; that liquidity problems of an individual institution are dealt with by the national central bank; and that liquidity problems that threaten the monetary system as a whole are dealt with by the ECB.[1]

Yet, the recent financial and debt crises made clear that the lack of a clear European institutional regulatory framework resulted in economic distortions with detrimental outcomes. Importantly, redistributional issues across the member states of a currency union emerged—a phenomenon that is politically less relevant within a country than across countries. This subsection discusses these distortions and the policy response that was provided, namely, the creation of a banking union. The latter amounted to a change in the institutional framework of the euro area built on three pillars:

- First, a single rather than a merely coordinated European approach to banking supervision.
- Second, a single resolution mechanism to wind down failed banks.
- Third, a fiscal backstop so that banks that are insolvent may be recapitalized, and possibly joint deposit insurance so that the retail depositors of banks that are illiquid need not fear a run.

Finally, the last part of this subsection covers the recent discussions about a capital markets union at the euro-area level.

Economic Externalities and Distortions

A currency union between potentially very different countries can face, in theory at least, a host of problems. We highlight in this section a multitude of such problems: a rush to ring-fence assets at a time of crisis at the expense of others; a desire to push losses onto foreigners; a tendency to treat all problems as a liquidity problem that should be addressed by the ECB; and ways to undermine the ban of monetary financing. We will consider each in turn.

RUSH TO RING-FENCE AND THE DIABOLIC LOOP IN INTERNATIONAL CONTEXT

As soon as an internationally operating bank runs into trouble, national regulators tend to ring-fence and grab its assets. Financial stability questions, and especially resolutions, bail-ins, and bankruptcy procedures, are dealt with at the national level. In Mervyn King's often quoted phrase, banks are "global in life but national in death" well summarizes the situation.[2] If, out of national interest, all regulators in times of crisis decide to simultaneously ring-fence assets, the solvency even of an otherwise healthy bank can be undermined. Regulatory responses thus must be coordinated. If market participants start to doubt the ability of national regulators to coordinate as required, their willingness to provide the bank with sufficient funding is undermined. This by itself puts financial institutions under pressure, leading to their potential demise—which would then ultimately justify the ring-fencing.

In other words, coordination problems and insolvency dynamics can be self-fulfilling. The United Kingdom's use of antiterrorism laws to seize Icelandic bank assets illustrates the extent to which countries can go in their attempts to seize assets, and also the damage that a lack of coordination can bring. Overall, this suggests that, at times of crisis, uncoordinated national resolution of banks can have very disruptive effects for international capital flows.

The tendency of banks to be global in life and national in death brings with it yet another problem: it introduces substantial procyclicality into the system. In good times, global banks manage their liquidity globally, with temporary liquidity shortfalls in one part of the world easily offset by liquidity surpluses in other parts. In times of crisis, however, these diversification benefits evaporate and they have to manage liquidity locally.

The underlying reason why ultimate regulation, and particularly resolution powers, for financial institutions lies in national hands is that these tasks typically require fiscal funds. And, crucially, the fiscal capacities to backstop the financial system differ across countries. In countries with large fiscal capacity and well-capitalized domestic banks, the state can credibly backstop its financial system while the domestic banks insure the sovereign against refinancing risk. Matters look different in a country with inadequate fiscal capacity and a weak financial system: here, the diabolic loop between sovereign and banks discussed in the previous chapter will emerge in times of crisis. Different countries in a currency union thus differ both in their ability to stabilize international capital flows and in their susceptibility to sudden reversals of these flows.

Pushing Losses onto Foreigners—Reluctant International Support

Recall from our earlier discussion of financial dominance that if banks are well capitalized, they are concerned that in times of crisis losses will be pushed onto banks. For example, a change of private insolvency laws, making foreclosures impossible or easing default on private loans and mortgages transfers losses from households to banks. Now, if banks are owned by foreigners (nonvoters), the incentive to pass these laws is much higher. As a result, banks become more "national" in times of crisis by withdrawing from foreign markets and are unwilling to transfer free liquidity from their home country. This, of course, is just an extension of an argument that we saw earlier. For similar reasons, governments are more willing to default on their debt if it is mostly held by foreigners. Hence, foreigners may be reluctant to hold sovereign debt as a crisis emerges.[3]

This economic distortion is probably also the reason why there are so few genuinely pan-European banks. Indeed, banks under such a system favor indirect financing through a chain of intermediation, whereby final lending to households is primarily conducted by local banks. Europe looks as if it has many cross-border banks, with giant institutions such as Deutsche Bank (based in Germany), or Santander (Spain), or Unicredit (Italy). But in legal reality, these are groups in which separate banking companies exist in different countries that are treated as separate by national regulators. The complexity can especially be seen in the case of

Unicredit, whose subsidiaries include the German HypoVereinsbank, which in turn owns Bank Austria, which in turn has subsidiaries in many Central and Eastern European countries, both inside and outside the euro area. When it comes to profits, the groups report an overall figure; when it comes to regulation—and the potential absorption of losses—they are national entities: Bank Austria is not the same as Unicredit SPA (in Italy) or Unicredit AG (in Germany: HypoVereinsbank is a brand, not a legal entity).

The inability of a government to commit not to subsequently expropriate foreigners is also a reason why bank recapitalization and stabilization measures by European authorities proved to be so difficult. If a European agency were to provide funds to recapitalize a country's banks, local politicians can simply push losses from the household sector onto the banking system by allowing mortgage debtors more easily to default on their payment.

The Tendency to Treat Problems as Liquidity Problems Requiring Central Bank Liquidity Provision

The desire to push losses onto foreigners is linked to solvency versus liquidity considerations. A central bank can stabilize an economy in times of crisis by providing emergency liquidity support to troubled financial institutions. However, as has been a theme throughout this book, it is often difficult to separate solvency and liquidity issues. Naturally, national regulators will be reluctant to resolve insolvency issues if domestic banks rely on foreign liquidity funding (or funding by the euro-area-wide lender of last resort). Indeed, whenever in doubt, domestic regulators have an incentive to call any problem a liquidity problem and request help from the ECB, as possible default losses by the latter would be shared instead of being solely imposed on the national authorities.[4]

Treating funding problems, if in doubt, as liquidity problems rather than solvency problems is in line with the French philosophy: no actual losses will ever occur if only the ECB's liquidity support is wide-ranging enough. The German view, in contrast, rests on the belief that there are solvency, and not only liquidity, problems, and so in the end substantial losses are likely to materialize. The question of which nation should bear these losses gives our earlier financial dominance discussion an international dimension. If the ECB intervenes, it might end up bearing the losses.

If the national authority deals directly with a solvency issue, the national member state could then suffer the losses. Thus, the structure of the euro area gives rise to an additional complicating layer in the form of a second game of chicken between fiscal authorities and the central bank. In this game, no one wants to absorb the losses; so the can is kicked down the road, and losses keep on growing. In the end, the situation is much worse than it would have been if the losses had been realized collectively and structural reforms had been implemented right at the beginning.

Clearly, if supervision is national and information is not shared at the European level, there is no way to settle illiquidity versus insolvency disputes, and so mistrust spreads. This simple insight means that liquidity support in a currency union is politically difficult, as it may involve redistributional fears—and may explain why central bank interventions are more controversial in cross-border currency unions.

Using Banks to Get around Monetary Finance
The Maastricht Treaty explicitly bans any form of monetary financing of government expenditures (Article 122). But the restriction on central bank action is less watertight than it appears. A country can circumvent this ban by convincing banks through regulatory pressure to buy risky government debt. The local banks can then refinance their purchase via the ECB using government debt as collateral. Should the government debt need to be restructured, the ECB will make losses—a case of government-debt monetization. The associated costs would have to be borne by all member states. Again, within a currency union, some losses can be pushed onto foreigners.

Banking Union as a Solution
As the crises spurred, these different economic distortions emerged to haunt countries of the euro area, in particular creating clashes between Northern creditors and Southern debtors. A natural response to these distortions and the sovereign-bank diabolic loop presented in the previous chapter is the creation of an area-wide banking union.

The Global Financial Crisis as a Catalyst
In 2009, in the early stages of the global financial crisis, when it appeared to be a largely American crisis but one that was having bad consequences

above all for French and German banks, the issue of coordinated European banking supervision reemerged. An expert group, chaired by a former IMF managing director and governor of the Banque de France, Jacques de Larosière, was formed. The group proposed the establishment of a European System of Financial Supervision (ESFS), including the European Systemic Risk Board (ESRB) for macroprudential oversight, and the European Banking Authority (EBA) to improve the coordination of national banking regulation and supervision throughout the European Union. Along with the EBA, the European Securities and Markets Authority (ESMA) and the European Insurance and Occupational Pensions Authority (EIOPA) became collectively known as the three European Supervisory Authorities (ESAs).

One task of the EBA was to conduct stress tests for euro-area banks, with the first such exercise having been conducted by EBA's predecessor, the Committee of European Banking Supervisors (CEBS), in 2010. The weakness of the stress test gravely undermined the effectiveness and credibility of Europe's response to the banking crisis. Most market participants correctly deduced that the tests were, in sharp contrast with the more stringent US tests in March 2009, a whitewash. The EU-wide stress test exercise was repeated in summer 2011, as the debt crisis really began to take hold, and the aftermath undermined the credibility of the newly established EBA. Eight banks (five of them in Spain and two in Greece) failed the stress test, but all German and French banks were declared to be safe. A large Belgian-French bank, Dexia, passed the tests with a core tier one capital ratio of 10.3 percent (well above the 6% threshold), but had €3.4 billion of exposure to Greek bonds that were in default and derivatives positions that lost value as German government bond yields declined. As a consequence, Dexia was bailed out by the Belgian, French, and Luxembourg governments in October 2011. It was also around this time that the diabolic loop between sovereign and banks started to emerge in full force, undermining further the results of earlier stress tests and suggesting that new solutions would be needed.

THE BIG PUSH: BRUSSELS 2012

In the summer of 2012, several countries, including France and the peripheral member states, made a big push to extend the ESM mandate to include the recapitalization of banks. The idea was to use the European Stability Mechanism (ESM) to directly support domestic banking systems, through recapitalization, without the national sovereign itself having to borrow and apply for a full-fledged EU-IMF program (which would come with strong conditionality attached). Germany, of course, was strongly opposed to direct recapitalization through the ESM. German politicians saw the danger that legacy losses from previously excessive borrowing would be transferred to European taxpayers and were reluctant to use German deposit insurance funds to bail out troubled banks in Spain. Equally important, Germans were concerned that recapitalization through the ESM would set a bad example for the future and lead to moral hazard down the road. And finally, any departure from the conditionality of external support was viewed as undesirable.

It is against this background that, in June 2012, a remarkable compromise was reached. Going into the Brussels summit, Merkel was determined to hold up the German position and resist an extension of the ESM mandate. In the end, however, she accepted a clever compromise, closely linking the extension of the ESM to the implementation of the banking union. Direct recapitalization of banks by the ESM, particularly in Spain, could only occur once the new European single supervisory mechanism was in place. The logic was impeccable: it made little sense to pour European money into banking systems when balance-sheet quality could not be independently verified by European authorities. Tactically, she had conceded nothing. Germany could oppose and delay the implementation of a banking union as long as necessary; and so she kept control over the extension of the ESM. Nevertheless, Merkel was immediately criticized at home for accepting a compromise. Parliament rebelled against the whole idea of the banking union, which was seen as a potential channel to put fiscal transfers into effect.

The entire agreement occurred on the same evening as a soccer match in Warsaw—the semifinal of the European Championship, which pitted Italy against Germany, with Italy winning, thanks to two spectacular goals by Mario Balotelli. The government leaders apparently followed the game closely in the initial part of their deliberations, and the results seemed to boost the confidence of the Spanish and Italian prime ministers. The council lasted until five in the morning, and Mario Monti, thinking he had worn down the Germans, scored a similar victory to that on the soccer pitch. It looked as if Chancellor Merkel was agreeing to easier access to ESM funds and to a role of the ESM in recapitalizing banks after the establishment of the European Single Supervisory Mechanism (SSM). Monti was not really a football fan, but he allowed himself to be carried along in a fervor of patriotic sentiment; in Italy, he was celebrated as another "super Mario."

Divergences became apparent as soon as the meeting ended. Whereas the communiqué stated, "We ask the Council to *consider* these proposals as a matter of urgency by the end of 2012," council president Van Rompuy declared, in his own press statement immediately after the summit, that the leaders had "asked the Council to work in a very speedy way so that we *can have results* by the end of the year."[5] There was more than a nuance, but rather a true difference in perspective. This reflected on the schedule for implementation. Germany tried to deflect any pressure on the schedule by emphasizing publicly that the quality of the new arrangement was more important than any time limit. Reticence to move and the desire to bid for time was obvious in many countries. In fact, a subsequent September summit failed to confirm agreement on the timetable. Only with considerable pressure and persuasion, in particular from the ECB president, were leaders able to come to an agreement at their last council meeting of the year, on December 13, 2012. An agreement on direct recapitalization of banks by the ESM was reached, but only in 2014. Merkel had again scored a remarkable tactical victory.

Moving Toward Single Supervision

Most early progress toward a banking union was made on the supervision pillar. The main question, of course, was whether the ECB should act as the euro-area-wide financial supervisor. Putting financial supervision and monetary policy into the same institution has obvious appeals, but also drawbacks. The key advantage is that information flow between financial supervisors and monetary policy makers is quick, allowing in particular a quick monetary response to financial distress. Furthermore, as we have seen above, single supervision can deal with the problem of national regulators declaring everything a liquidity problem necessitating ECB intervention.

Some German commentators, however, feared that errors in financial supervision may impinge on the central bank's reputation and so undermine price stability. In particular, it was feared that policy makers may try to use the monetary tools at their disposal to paper over any mistakes made in bank supervision. These doubts notwithstanding, the ECB was ultimately given "ultimate responsibility for all specific supervisory tasks related to the financial stability of all Euro area banks," while national supervisors would "continue to play an important role in day-to-day supervision and in preparing and implementing ECB decisions."[6] At the same time, the Commission proposed that the EBA should develop a single supervisory handbook "to preserve the integrity of the single market and ensure coherence in banking supervision for all 27 EU countries."[7] Overall, gaining the power of single supervision was a major victory for Mario Draghi and the European Central Bank (see chapter 15).[8]

A Single Resolution Mechanism

The second important step toward completion of banking union was the creation of the Single Resolution Mechanism. In July 2013, the Commission laid out a proposed procedure for the resolution of failed banks through a Single Resolution Mechanism backed by a Single Bank Resolution Fund. This was intended to bring substantial advantages over a complex network of national procedures and funds: strong central decision making was supposed to ensure rapid and effective decision making, avoid uncoordinated action, minimize negative impacts on financial stability, and limit the need for financial support. Its legal basis lay in Article 114 of the Treaty on the Functioning of the European Union concerning "the establishment and functioning of the internal market." The associated regulation was put forward by the European Commission in July 2013 and entered into force on August 19, 2014.

Parallel to this, negotiations continued over the direct bank recapitalization through the ESM—as usual a contentious issue in Germany. Under the proposal, the initial recapitalization required to reach a Common Equity Tier 1 ratio of 4.5 percent would come from the member country in which the bank is headquartered; beyond that, the ESM would contribute in tandem with the member country. The country would provide the equivalent of 20 percent of the total amount of public contribution in the first two years of direct bank recapitalization. Deposits were secured up to €100,000, an amount justified by the "transaction role of money."[9] After that amount, at least 8 percent (of total assets) was to be bailed in. (As mentioned in chapter 10, this rule went into effect in January 2016.) It is important to note the incentive effect: the new regulation gave banks an incentive to hold more capital to provide more protection to bondholders. The resolution funding would be provided in the first instance by national resolution authorities and after the transition period by the Single Resolution Fund ("backstop regulation") with a target size of €55 billion. This is a modest amount set against overall euro-area GDP in 2013 of €9,600 billion, total assets of euro-area banks of €23,126 billion, and equity of €1,340 billion. These bail-in provisions—and the compromise that they ultimately reflect—were clearly motivated by the precedent set in Cyprus and the associated bail-in (German view) versus bailout (French view) discussion.

COMPLETING THE BANKING UNION: DEPOSIT INSURANCE

As expected, the third pillar of the banking union—the creation of a deposit insurance as proposed by the European Commission—has proved the most contentious. Wolfgang Schäuble, the German finance minister, clearly marked his opposition against such insurance.[10] Many other member states of the euro area also take the position that national deposit insurance systems first need to be set up before an EU-wide mechanism could be considered. Many national, including German, banks are strictly opposed to the Europeanization of deposit insurance. It is thus unsurprising that progress on this third pillar of the banking union is lingering, to say the least.

Going beyond Banks: A Capital Markets Union

Beyond the banking union, discussions about the creation of a capital markets union started to emerge among European policy makers in mid-2014. Importantly, this union would take place at the European Union level (instead of just for members of the euro area), as it is primarily the European Commission that is pushing for its existence.

The objectives of a European capital markets union are twofold. First, the union would reduce reliance on banks: traditionally, banks in Europe control about 80 percent of the funding to firms, in particular to small and medium-sized ones (SMEs). It is hoped that a further integration of capital markets will bring this figure closer to its American counterpart, where firm financing goes mainly through capital markets. As Juncker himself put it, "This would cut the cost of raising capital, notably for SMEs, and help reduce our very high dependence on bank funding."[11] Moreover, equity financing is less prone to financial instability, as it is not subject to runs and does not need to be rolled over. A second objective of the capital markets union is to harmonize rules: currently, investments require local knowledge due to cross-country heterogeneity in regulations. Harmonizing the rules would hence help to create smoother capital transfers.

Safe Assets: Flight-to-Safety Cross-Border Capital Flows

Safe assets are essential for a well-functioning financial economy. They provide a store of value for many institutions whose other holdings are risky. These institutions want to park part of their wealth in assets that they can fall back on should they get hit by a large shock. A safe asset is different from a risk-free asset. A risk-free asset carries no risk over a given horizon. In contrast, an asset is regarded as safe if it has high value whenever the holder wishes to redeem it; in short, it is like a good friend (recall our definition in chapter 10), and not necessarily one-to-one connected with fundamental cash flow payoff. For example, the German government debt at the height of the crisis appreciated even though Germany's risk—measured, for example, via CDS spreads—heightened.

Archetypal safe assets are central bank reserves (if risk of inflation is low) and gold, but also government debt. Government debt has a dual role. Not only does it help the government to fund the provision of public goods and services, but it also serves as a notionally safe and liquid store of wealth, an interest-bearing asset that institutions can rely on should their funding dry up. In fact, the European banking regulation treats all euro-area government debt as risk free and assigns a zero-risk weight to it—something that became problematic. The reason is twofold. First, government debt is free of liquidity risk if a country's central bank can provide temporary liquidity support. Hence, government debt is not subject to temporary runs. Yet this condition is harder to fulfill in the euro area in which individual countries do not have an autonomous central bank. Second, European banking regulations assumed sound fiscal policy across all euro-area countries and consequently assumed away default risk. However, this presumption is in violation with the agreed-upon no-bailout clause in the Maastricht Treaty. And during the euro crisis, it became apparent that the market doubted the "safe asset status" of the government debt of many peripheral countries.

In this section, we focus on the problem that emerges if the safe asset is not symmetrically distributed across the member state countries. If the safe asset in a currency area is associated with a particular member state rather than being a euro-area-wide asset, international capital flows can reverse very suddenly once an adverse shock hits. When market participants fly to safety, they cause large distortions. In the euro crisis, for example, capital rushed out of the periphery and into the core (in particular into Germany) every time the crisis intensified.

Flight-to-Safety Cross-Border Capital Flows

In the euro area, the German ten-year bund currently serves as the predominant safe asset. Its value increased whenever the euro crisis intensified, even though at the same time its fundamental value declined (as reflected in an increase of the German CDS spread—a measure of the riskiness of German debt). Figure 11.1 shows this for the ten-year interest rate and ten-year CDS spread for the period from April to October 2011.

Hence, whenever the risk increases, the yield of the German government bond goes down, that is, its value increases. This seems counterintuitive, but it is the defining feature of a safe asset. It gains value not because fundamentals move in the right direction, but because others also perceive that it is safe—almost a tautology. This hints to the fact that a safe asset has some features of a "bubble." This is easily illustrated with gold: as crises

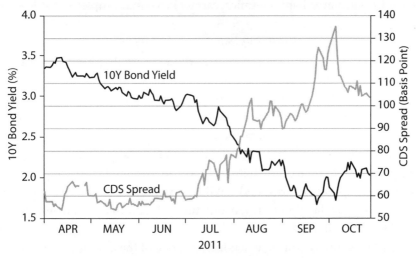

FIGURE 11.1. German CDS Spread and 10-Year Bond Yield

become more severe, its price typically rises, even though its fundamental usefulness for, say, jewelers remains unchanged. This is simply because in times of crisis people want gold as a safe store of value. Note that safe asset status can also be lost. Spanish sovereign debt was probably a good safe asset before the crisis, especially for Spanish banks. But suddenly investors stopped believing in this asset: its safe label was lost, and interest rates moved by more than fundamentals would suggest. Losing safe asset status is like a bubble bursting.

It is often argued that the German government debt enjoys a liquidity premium because its market is deep. While it is true that the German bunds' trading volume is high, it is however the feature that the bunds' value appreciates exactly in times of crisis that makes it a safe asset. Another example of a safe asset is the US Treasury bond. Paradoxically, the price of the US Treasury bond jumped up when the United States was at risk of defaulting on its debt payment obligations due to the standoff between the US Congress and the Obama administration in the summer of 2011. Again, this highlights the distinction between fundamental value and the price of safe assets.

Yet, the key difference between Europe and the United States is that US Treasury bonds serve as a single safe asset for an entire currency area, while in the euro area, the safe asset is not issued by all member states: it is German, not European. Arguably, without a currency-area-wide safe asset, the euro-area banking union cannot be called complete.

European Safe Bonds (ESBies)

As we discussed in chapter 6, during the most acute phase of the euro crisis, various proposals for (some sort of) Eurobonds were introduced. Almost all of them involved some debt mutualization. The primary objective of most of these proposals was to lower governments' funding costs and, in doing so, bring down the cost of private borrowing. In light of continual violations of euro-area fiscal rules, together with the incompatibility of common liability with the "German" liability principle (that refuses to separate control and liability), it is unsurprising that German chancellor Angela Merkel ruled out full debt mutualization with joint liability in her lifetime.[12]

The Euronomics group, which includes one of the authors of this book, proposed an alternative without any joint liability: European safe bonds

(ESBies).[13] The objective of these bonds is to create a European safe bond, thereby limiting cross-border flight-to-safety distortions during crises. Moreover, banks could hold ESBies as a safe asset, thereby breaking the link between bank risk and sovereign risk described in chapter 10.

To this end, ESBies work as follows. First, an entity—which could be public (e.g., a European debt agency) or private (e.g., a large bank or asset manager)—would purchase a portfolio of government bonds. This portfolio would be balanced in proportion to the size of governments' debt up to a certain ceiling (such as 60% of GDP). Against this portfolio of euro-area government debt, the entity would issue a European safe bond (ESBies) and a European junior bond (EJBies). The entity would then have the following balance sheet structure:

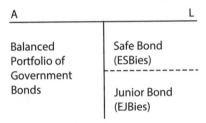

FIGURE 11.2. Balance Sheet of European Debt Agency or Private Institution That Creates ESBies and EJBies

The ESBies proposal involves pooling of national bonds and tranching the pool into a senior and junior bond. If a national government were to default on its debt, the asset side of the issuing entity's balance sheet would shrink, and its liability side would therefore shrink accordingly. Importantly, these losses would first be borne by holders of the junior bond. The junior bond therefore protects the senior bond. The senior bond (ESBies) would be a European-wide safe asset. Any flight to safety would no longer occur across borders, but from the European junior bond (EJBies) to the European safe bond (ESBies).

The second advantage of ESBies is that it can eliminate the diabolic loop between sovereign and banking risk, if banks were to hold the European safe bond (ESBies) instead of national government bonds. The senior bond (ESBies) then serves as safe asset for the financial sector, while the junior bonds would be widely held by many market participants, firms, and households (as is the case with municipal bonds in the United

States). Placing the junior bond should not be hard in an environment in which everyone searches for higher yields and many institutional investors want to hold bonds with long maturity. Insurance companies and pension funds especially have an incentive to counterbalance their long-term liabilities with long-term (junior) bonds to hedge their interest rate risk. To ensure that banks switch to the senior bond as their safe asset, regulation should favor such a shift by assigning lower exposure limits or capital charges (risk weights) on ESBies compared to an equivalent pool of national government bonds. Interestingly, by eliminating the diabolic loop, national defaults become less likely and correlated, which also makes the junior bond less risky.[14]

As ESBies would be essentially free of default risk, the ECB could use them to conduct open-market operations without taking on any default risk, as the Fed does with US Treasury bonds. With ESBies of different maturities, one would get a whole risk-free yield curve that could serve as a European benchmark that the ECB could influence.

Redenomination and Exit Risks

Redenomination risk refers to the risk that, say, Greek households become concerned about the prospect that capital controls make it impossible to bring "Greek euros" outside of Greece or that they are involuntarily converted into a new Greek drachma. As such redenomination risk does not exist for "German euros," a Greek euro will necessarily be worth less than a German euro.[15] As long as the Greek euros can be converted one-to-one into German euros, Greeks may thus decide to withdraw their deposits from their Greek banks and try to buy German bunds or even deposit their funds at German banks. The resulting lack of funding for Greek banks will thus become an even more urgent problem, while German banks have yet more excess savings that they possibly park with the ECB. The ECB will thus be forced to intermediate even more and channel funds back.

TARGET2 imbalances become important in case of an exit from the currency union. As such, they measure the exposure of the rest of the system to a particular national central bank should this country exit the euro. Greek citizens who transfer bank deposits from a Greek bank to a German bank account run up TARGET2 claims. By transferring funds to a German account, Greek citizens avoid devaluation losses as they hold "German euros." However, in case of an exit, these devaluation losses would show up as losses for the other national central banks in the form of lost TARGET2 claims if there is no hope that the Greek central bank would repay its TARGET2 liabilities after an exit.[16]

Importantly, even the possibility of an exit opens up the possibility of a speculative attack. Investors and speculators alike might run and push the country toward exit from the currency union. In other words, the threat of an exit can be self-fulfilling. There is one equilibrium in which investors believe no exit will occur and a Greek euro has the same value as a German euro. But there is also another equilibrium in which doubts about the homogeneity of the euro area induces speculators to bet on an exit. When the exit risk starts to materialize, prudent investors hedge this redenomination/exit risk, leading them to short sell Greek euros and buy German ones, thereby contributing to the likelihood of the exit. As long as both euros trade one-for-one, the cost of such a trade is only the interest rate differential—earning the low German interest rate and forgoing the higher Greek interest rate. Ultimately, however, the exit equilibrium might prevail.

Philosophical Stands

The fathers of the Maastricht Treaty were fully aware of this destructive mechanism and hence intentionally did not include any provisions for euro-area member countries to leave the common currency union. This corresponded very much to the French view, which saw the creation of European money as providing effective barriers against speculators. By not specifying any exit rules, chaos would arise in case of exit, and that fact would provide ex ante commitment to defend the common currency area without limitations. Such an "ostrich policy" of ignoring any exit threat, while ex post naïve, provides strong ex ante commitment and deters speculators from attacking a particular country in a currency union.

Moreover, the French philosophy also stresses the signaling power of a potential exit: if a country leaves the euro area, this is proof of the reversibility of the euro and so of the wider European integration process. Once one country leaves, markets will start to attack other weak member states. This will translate into a higher interest rate burden for these countries. Their government debt thus carries an extra price tag due to redenomination risk.

Ultimately, speculative attacks can lead to disintegration of the currency union. The redenomination risk is one of the rationales that the ECB, as the guardian of the currency, put forward to justify its interventions.

By contrast, an exit might not be simply due to a temporary speculative attack but necessary for a country to regain lost competitiveness. An exit and associated devaluation of its new currency might be unavoidable, especially when an internal devaluation is not feasible because of nominal rigidities or political pressures. In other words, a country might not simply face a temporary liquidity problem that should be avoided but a solvency problem. For this reason, and given the preference for clear rules, the German view is not opposed to the establishment of clear rules about how an exit from the currency union should be conducted. The German economist Hans-Werner Sinn even argued for a "breathing" union, where members could go in and out of the currency union, sometimes for a temporary adjustment period, following some specific rules—as this would keep necessary financial discipline. During the Grexit debate in 2015, the German finance minister Wolfgang Schäuble also made the case of a time out along these lines for Greece, but he did not go so far as to establish this as a general principle. Softness toward misbehaving periphery countries would mean that all rules are undermined, and so, in the long term, the euro-area project would be doomed to fail. In fact, in this view, the threat of exit can function as an effective disciplining device to ensure sustainable budget deficits and a stability-oriented currency union. In sum, some German economists were open to shrinking the currency union to create a more sustainable "core" ready to pursue deeper union and further integration.

An exit typically involves the imposition of capital controls and a cutoff of banks' funding. Hence, a country exit from the euro area invariably involves the ECB. The ECB continuously claimed that the exit decision is one that can only be taken by heads of governments. At the same time, however, the ECB, by cutting off its liquidity provision to banks—in particular in the form of emergency liquidity assistance (ELA), as described in chapter 15—de facto has the power to squeeze a country out of the union. With domestic banks unable to tap ECB liquidity, governments are unable to push their debt onto their banks, and so they are forced to print their own money to pay for their social programs, completing the exit.

An exit from a currency union causes large temporary costs. Almost every contract in the euro area (in particular all sorts of private and public debt contracts) is written in euros, so in case of an exit, it is not clear whether these contracts should continue to be enforced in euros or, alternatively, in the new currency of the exiting country. Of course, the exiting country could pass legislation dictating that all contractual payments will be translated into payments in the new currency. However, creditors would then presumably try to appeal to European and other international courts to ensure repayment in hard euros. If history (and in particular the recent Argentinian experience) is any guide, courts are likely to rule in favor of the plaintiffs, imposing yet more costs on the exiting country.[17]

Grexit Threats

The exit considerations added additional drama to the euro crisis, with two episodes taking center stage: the Grexit drama of 2012 and the Graccident fears of 2015.

FINANCIAL CONTAGION FEAR DURING THE 2012 GREXIT THREAT

In the summer of 2012, fears of a Greek exit—quickly dubbed "Grexit"—from the euro area reached new heights. Both France and the ECB saw the near certainty of large contagion spillover effects following an exit: there would be runs on Italian and Spanish banks as depositors feared that their assets would be converted overnight into a new and depreciating currency. The impact would be much worse than that of Deauville. Germans, in contrast, liked to repeat a rather hackneyed German chiasmus: that an end with terror was better than terror without end. These positions illustrate very well the fundamental economic trade-off described above: that of ex post multiple equilibria considerations versus ex ante discipline. Was Greece an infected leg that needed to be cut off to save the patient, or would the operation itself be fatal? Ultimately, the decision as to whether Greece should stay in the euro area was to be made in Berlin.

Initially, the German stance seemed to be very much open to a Grexit. Since early 2012, politicians and even government ministers such as Wolfgang Schäuble had been dropping hints that the crisis could be more easily solved if Greece were to exit. Indeed, German proponents of a Greek exit could draw on remarks coming from the Keynesian camp (especially from various US academics) that a Greek exit could be an attractive instrument to restore competitiveness. By June, according to *Reuters*, euro-area ministers were told to prepare for contingencies. On June 15, 2012, just before a parliamentary election in which radical opponents of the euro looked as if they might do well, Greeks withdrew over €3 billion from their bank accounts. European Commission and IMF officials worked secretly on a "Plan Z."[18] The Bundesbank stated publicly that a Greek exit would be better than a Greek default: "The challenge this would create for the euro area and Germany would be considerable but manageable. . . . By contrast, a significant dilution of existing agreements would damage confidence in all euro area agreements and treaties . . . calling into question the institutional status quo."[19]

Over the summer, however, the tide began to turn. Chancellor Merkel had throughout been closely guarded about her own stance, but, over time, it became clearer that, thanks to efforts from Commission officials and market participants, she had been convinced that a Greek exit would be too dangerous. Indeed, as Grexit fears increased, other peripheral spreads started to shoot up, giving credence to the contagion fears. Pressure from the United States also contributed: the Obama administration feared that a new financial crisis would sink its chances of reelection, and so Merkel was pressured to do away with any potential Grexit plans. In fact, at the end of July 2012, US treasury secretary Tim Geithner visited Schäuble at a holiday residence on the North Sea island of Sylt to press the case. (See chapter 13 for more details.)

The next steps toward avoiding Grexit were taken by the Greek government. Commission president José Manuel Barroso told the new Greek prime minister Antonis Samaras, "Don't start asking for new conditions; there's no way. The first message you have to convey to Germany: you have to say you are going to deliver."[20] Samaras made a tour of Europe, starting in Rome (the capital of the country most likely to be hit by Greek contagion), then to Madrid (the probable next domino), then Paris and Frankfurt. He proved to be a very effective communicator and convinced leaders across Europe on obvious grounds of self-interest to build a strong coalition lobbying to keep Greece in the euro area. Finally, he visited Angela Merkel in Berlin. He had practiced his pitch for hours in his hotel. "I can guarantee you, we will work day and night," Samaras said.[21]

This set the stage for Merkel to complete her U-turn, and she came out unambiguously in September in favor of a new Greek package and against any exit. No one in Germany had been able to assure her that it was really possible to limit the economic chaos of a Grexit. And nobody could predict how many more dominoes would fall if Greece were to exit the euro area. The contagion-discipline trade-off was thus, for the moment at least, resolved with a heavy slant toward contagion considerations. To conclude the policy shift, Merkel made a very visible trip to Athens (requiring immense police protection) in October 2012—her first since the start of the crisis. French officials were elated and saw the change in German attitude as a product and result of their close cooperation on that issue. By November, on the eve of an EU summit, there was an agreement to release a €34.3 billion aid installment.

Political Contagion and 2015 Graccident Possibility

In late 2014, Greece was plunged into an unexpected political crisis by the failure to elect a new president (a largely symbolic office). The Samaras coalition government dissolved Parliament, although its four-year term had not expired and called new elections. The clear winner was the leftist and populist Syriza movement, led by Alexis Tsipras. Tsipras—just like Rajoy in Spain (2011) and Hollande in France (2012)—had promised the electorate that he would undo various unpopular austerity measures and stimulate Greece out of crisis. Even before the election, tax receipts fell because of expectations of Syriza's victory and in anticipation that Syriza would cut unpopular taxes. These developments set the stage for the second incarnation of the Greek drama.

In an uncanny echo of the Samaras government's first steps, the new leaders, Tsipras and his charismatic and garrulous finance minister Yanis Varoufakis, went on a tour of European capitals (with Berlin coming last). The purpose of the tour was to drum up support for a general stimulus-based program that would apply to and, according to the new Greek government, rescue all of Europe. There appeared to be some moderate, polite interest and sympathy in London and Paris, while the Southern European countries were notably cooler. In fact, the tour overall began and ended with disasters: an icy confrontation of Varoufakis with the Eurogroup president, Dutch finance minister Jeroen Dijsselbloem, in Athens and between Varoufakis and Wolfgang Schäuble in Berlin.

Underlying these cool reactions was a much reduced concern about economic contagion. While in 2012 a Grexit was seen as a threat to all of the euro area, contagion risks were now regarded as contained. At the same time—and this explains the reaction from other Southern countries—there was more fear of political contagion. Too substantial a concession to Greece might not cost much, but it would destabilize the southern governments that had implemented reforms and which had shown initial signs of success. The most notable examples were Spain, where a new, powerful left-populist movement (Podemos) analogous to Syriza had emerged, and Ireland, where the old nationalist movement Sinn Fein was gaining support.

The Greek government, which had played with the threat of financial destabilization of all of Europe, consequently realized that its position was fundamentally weak. It thus accepted, on February 20, 2015, a four-month extension of the existing program, with some cosmetic changes but also a requirement that the Greek government submit an extensive reform agenda. Schäuble—already demonized in Athens—presented the outcome as a defeat for Greece: "Being in government is a date with reality, and reality is often not as nice as a dream."[22] The willingness of the European ministers (who were almost all deeply skeptical of the new Greek government) to reach an agreement also seemed to reflect a revival of the old Franco-German alliance. This revival, however, would prove temporary.

Syriza viewed the four-month respite as an opportunity to delay negotiations further, holding repeated meetings with the European creditors without producing any new results. This reflected a fundamental reluctance to enter a new bailout program on the terms of the creditors. The Greek negotiating style permanently undermined any semblance of trust between the troika and the Greek leadership. Interestingly, and unlike the Greek crisis of 2012, economic contagion was, as expected by the other European leaders, rather weak. Observers in part credited the ECB's quantitative easing program for this resiliency.

Still, French observers in particular continued to stress the threats posed by contagion, arguing that with a Grexit, the "genie of an exit" would be out of the bottle and possibly endanger the future stability of the currency union. The French finance minister, Michel Sapin, was especially eloquent on this point, as he had been finance minister already in 1993 when a speculative attack on the French franc forced France out of its exchange rate corridor in the European Monetary System. He now argued that any exit would hold out the possibility of liquidity attacks on other European governments.

The German side, however, favored a harsher treatment of Greece, and became less concerned about the consequences of Grexit. Thus, the German-French rift opened up more than ever before, with the French emerging as the euro area's "voice for Greece" and the German finance ministry as the steadfast believers in budgetary prudence. Given the erosion of trust between the Greek government and Germany, in particular, the creditors demanded, before any new negotiations were to be started, some sort of prior action from the Greek government. To recreate some trust, the Greek government needed to send some credible signal that it was willing to cooperate and undertake structural reforms.

It came to a showdown. After dragging on reform discussions for four months with little results, the Greek government called for a referendum in which a large majority of Greek citizens voted to reject the bailout terms on July 5, 2015. The ECB subsequently had to limit its emergency liquidity assistance (ELA), which led to bank closures and the imposition of capital controls. (See chapter 15 for details.) The economy came to a standstill and Grexit was near. Greek finance minister Varoufakis was replaced and, ultimately, a new agreement was reached: a third bailout for Greece, with strict conditionality for structural reforms, for example, going as far as to relax timings of shop opening hours. In April 2016 the IMF questioned the viability of this program and continued to call for further structural reforms combined with debt relief.

Policy Recommendations

As we have seen in this and the previous chapter, the Maastricht Treaty woefully neglected the modernization and internationalization of banking as well as the complexity of an unbalanced integration, and so it is unsurprising that the euro area was ill-equipped to deal with the complicated fallout from the global financial crisis. In particular, the threat of financial dominance—completely ignored in the Maastricht Treaty—gave rise to a second layer in the game of chicken between monetary and fiscal authorities.

European policy makers struggled to find solutions to these problems. In theory, most of them required further integration, but the political environment made it difficult to make progress on that aspect. Paradoxically,

France was willing to transfer resources but not power, especially budgeting power, to Europe, while Germany was reluctant to transfer more resources to Brussels to bail out (foreign) banks. As a consequence, a search ensued to find the minimal measures that limit the adverse implications of and spillovers from banking sector crisis, de facto pushing responsibility to act to the ECB, at least in the short term.

Liquidity-focused short-term responses raise long-term moral hazard issues, so policy makers at the same time needed to have a vision for a future institutional structure that would effectively deal with these problems. The basic idea of an adequate institutional environment that balances both forces is to *not* save the few worst performers and erect a firewall protecting the rest, in the hope of triggering a virtuous race away from the bottom that stabilizes the whole system. For the euro area, the recent move toward a banking union points in this direction. However, as we have seen, there is as of yet no area-wide safe asset, nor is any such asset on the horizon, even though precisely this will be indispensable for smooth functioning of the banking union.

One bold move forward could be to establish a European banking charter that makes the financial sector truly European, in other words, makes Europe like a county with respect to banks. All aspects of finance—regulatory and supervisory but also fiscal—would be moved to the European level. In good times, tax revenue from banks would thus accrue to a European budget, while in bad times, this taxing power could provide the necessary backstop to guarantee restructuring without adverse spillover and contagion effects. This would be unpopular with small countries with large financial sectors, but also politically impossible for the United Kingdom.

PART IV

OTHERS' PERSPECTIVES

12

Italy

The battle of ideas in Europe occurs between countries, but it also takes place within countries. Italy—which in many other respects replicates on a national level the problems of the European continent—also reproduces the European contrast in economic philosophies. Every aspect of the recent European tragedy has its equivalent in Italy's much longer historical experience. Italy is a microcosm of European experience. The country is often depicted as a near hopeless case, the sick man of Europe, with an ossified political and bureaucratic system, a stagnant economy, and a massive flight of talent. But the malaise is really an exaggerated version of problems prevalent throughout the Continent. It is inevitable that prescriptions to combat the deep malaise diverge.

This chapter addresses the following questions, all of which correspond to European as well as Italian debates:

- What were the different economic philosophies within Italy?
- Did the transfer union between the Italian North and South promote convergence or cement an income gap?
- How stable and long-lasting can a transfer union be within a nation-state?
- How did Italy cope with the exchange rate tool and which economic challenges does it face?
- How does politics respond to economic decline?

Battling Economic Philosophies within Italy

Italian economists were split between the major schools of thought outlined above as "German" and "French." The "German-style" liberals responded—as in Germany—to the aftermath of totalitarian economics under a strong and destructive state. The interwar economy—dominated by fascism and the attempt to apply corporatist principles—was also one increasingly cut off from the international economy. Postwar Italy was initially made by economic liberals such as Luigi Einaudi, an economics professor who became the first postwar president of the Banca d'Italia and then (in 1948) president of the republic. Einaudi's emphasis on the importance of rules in framing economic life had a clear similarity to the thought of the German Ordoliberals.

But there was also another tradition that stemmed from Italy's long concern with the role of the state in economic development. The corporatist practices of the interwar period remained quite powerful in postwar Italy, and many economists argued that there was a good way of thinking about how state action could overcome collective action problems. Keynesianism was at first best represented by two famous Italian economists who had fled from Mussolini's Italy: Piero Sraffa at Cambridge, who tried to combine Keynesianism and Marxism, and Franco Modigliani at MIT, one of the key architects of the new synthesis between Keynesian and neoclassical economics. The first Keynesian textbooks appeared in the late 1940s, and by the 1960s, the Italian orthodoxy, or mainstream, was Keynesian. Some of the Keynesian impetus went in a left-wing direction. Sraffa became a national symbol that radical political economists liked to invoke, with unions put Sraffa on strike placards. The left-wing tradition also derived support from some of the establishment. Some of the large Italian banks published economic journals that were substantially devoted to radical, nontraditional economics: the *Banca Nazionale del Lavoro Quarterly Review* (that from 1981 was edited by Alessandro Roncaglia) and the *Economic Notes* of the Monte dei Paschi of Siena.[1]

Some commentators have noted that there is a regional divide in the theoretic orientation of the first Italian economists: the great liberals, like Einaudi, or before him Costantino Bresciani-Turroni, come from the North, whereas the pioneers of practical Keynesianism in Italy, like Pasquale Saraceno or Marcello de Cecco, are Southerners.[2] The regional division seems appealing, in the simple sense that the South was poor and required development, and the North might well be eager to devise strategies that did not impose an endless cost on a prosperous and dynamic Italy.

Mezzogiorno: Convergence or Divergence within a Transfer Union

In Italy, since the unification of the county in the mid-nineteenth century, a drama has played out in which the North developed and the South became underdeveloped. (Some commentators like to make the point that Italy in the 1860s was like Germany and the United States: in each case, there was a civil war in which a more industrial and urbanized North defeated a more rural South that prided itself on its incarnation of traditional virtues.) In this sense, Italy anticipated a debate on the world stage in the mid-twentieth century, when a developed North seemed to be impoverishing an underdeveloped South or, in the euro crisis, where commentators liked to portray the contrast of North versus South in Europe.

Early Convergence from the 1920s to the 1960s

In the 1920s, the underdevelopment of the Italian South was accentuated by government policies; but after that, the Italian government—often in discussion with international institutions such as the World Bank—set out to try to implement a developmental strategy. From 1950 to 1980, state assistance was mostly channeled through the Cassa del Mezzogiorno, a public/national agency that was completely independent of government charged with formulating a new approach to development. In its first phase, a ten-year investment project was devoted to building up infrastructure, including land reclamation projects, hydroelectricity, and transportation. A 1957 law (Law 634/1957) then focused on industrialization, with the promotion of activity by state-owned corporations, which were required to devote a majority of their activity to the South.

The result of these initiatives was an apparent dramatic success. It looks analogous to the story of the 1990s and 2000s in Europe, when growth in the South was more impressive than growth in the North and when commentators claimed that this was an example of capital moving, and development proceeding, in the "right" or historically necessary direction. But in both cases, the development of the South was inherently fragile. As Iuzzolino, Pellegrini, and Vesti (2013) report, the gap in output per head in Southern Italy relative to the rest of the country fell from 53 percentage points in 1951 to 44 in 1961 and 33 in 1971.[3] Unlike in the 2000s in Europe, the Italian Southern miracle was not only due to an increase in capital and labor but was mostly a result of rising productivity, with workers moving from inefficient traditional agricultural activities into sparkling modern industrial plants, though some part also reflected a demographic shift as some workers and their families left.

Divergence from the 1970s Onward

The fragility became apparent with a European and global crisis in the 1970s, when the postwar exchange rate system broke down, inflation surged, and oil prices shot up. After 1971, the beneficent Italian convergence process stopped and then went into reverse, so regional disparities were greater at the end of the twentieth century. Public investment programs were curtailed in the wake of the oil price shocks, and the previous concentration on basic industries made the South particularly vulnerable. The Cassa del Mezzogiorno acquired the reputation for having promoted political infrastructure projects that became white elephants: for example, an unused airport at Lamezia Terme and what was billed as "Europe's largest film studio" at the instigation of the film producer Dino de Laurentiis, which only operated for two years. In general, public enterprises had been harnessed for political purposes, and as many were in the South, the problem of political capture was especially acute there.

After the Cassa was dissolved, a successor institution, the Agenzia per la Promozione dello Sviluppo ne Mezzogiorno, required projects to be submitted to the regional administration and then accepted by a central ministry for the Mezzogiorno before the Agenzia paid out on the project. Despite these schemes, productivity differences between North and South increased rather than decreased. The research institute EURISPES commented in its 1998 *Rapporto Italia*, "There has been waste, waste that generated a political underworld of clientelism and favours. In many cases, public spending, rather than offering the chance of growth and development (in the south), ended up contributing to the ascent and power of organised crime."[4]

The effect of public expenditure in furthering crime and corruption and decreasing economic as well as social well-being has been extensively documented. In a recent study, the economist Paolo Pinotti examines the

Southern Italian districts of Puglia and Basilicata and concludes that the surge in crime in the 1970s was pushed by public expenditure. The murder rate soared by a factor of four. Per capita income was cut by an estimated 20 percent, and the region was set on a lower growth trajectory. One-fifth of the Mafia's profits came directly from public investment. The costs in Sicily, where the Mafia had been longer established, could be reckoned to be higher.[5]

In 1992, when the European attempt to replace the Bretton Woods currency system, the European Monetary System, broke down, the shock again hit the South with particular brutality. As a consequence of the persistent criticism, the mechanism of regional support was Europeanized. In 1994, the European Union phased out a support scheme under which the central government had paid employers' social security contributions in the South.

The shocks of the 1970s and of 1992 did not reduce the amount of public money flowing in the cause of development. On the contrary, as later in the euro crisis, the flow of public funds actually increased while the developmental differential widened. From the beginning of the 1970s to 1992, net public resources transferred to the South increased from 11 to almost 12 percent of GDP.[6] The transfers did not appear to reduce the widening gap in performance and prosperity. The story of corruption and misallocation leads to some measure of skepticism about the stimulative and beneficial long-term effects of public sector investment.

Sustainability of a Transfer Union within a Nation-State

The Italian case demonstrates that there can be long-term account imbalances in a currency union, with the South running a persistent deficit largely financed by public transfers. There are striking cases elsewhere, and not just in the euro area: one example is the United Kingdom, where it was recently calculated that the London area had an 8 percent of GDP surplus in regard to the rest of the United Kingdom.[7] The standard response is that the current account does not matter if it is financed through a reliable fiscal system in a unitary state (and is not dependent on the vagaries of the capital market). But the Italian example demonstrates precisely how even such financing can lead to an exacerbation of regional differences and imbalances.

Italy's Economic Challenges

Wage Pressure and Recurring Exchange Rate Devaluation
prior to the Euro

At the moment of Italian state formation, a debate started on what to do to modernize and on why that might be worth doing at all. In Giuseppe Tomasi di Lampedusa's *The Leopard*, Prince Tancredi states, "If we want things to stay as they are, things will have to change."[8] The rest of the world was changing, and so Italy needed to adjust to preserve its identity. If that was the world of the last half of the nineteenth century, by the end of the twentieth century the same drama was played out on a global level. The world was being transformed by a new process termed *globalization* (the word was first used in its contemporary meaning by Italian radicals in the early 1970s). To preserve Europe, Europe needed some sort of radical transformation.

In the chaotic European currency conditions prevailing after the 1970s, wage pressure developed and made Italian producers relatively uncompetitive. The industrial pressure groups then mobilized to change the exchange rate to increase their share of export markets. Restoring Italian business performance required periodic devaluations of the Italian lira. Phases of living with an overvalued exchange rate were thus followed by an abrupt depreciation. Devaluation had an almost automatic quality as the exercise was repeated over and over again: like Catholics going to confession, the country could regularly relieve itself of its burden of sins.

In the 1970s and 1980s, some analysts had already come to a realization that this model was unsustainable. A profoundly political calculation then tipped the balance: giving up the exchange rate as an instrument of policy would dramatically increase fiscal credibility and reduce the cost of borrowing. That conclusion was always controversial, and, in particular, the well-regarded experts at the Banca d'Italia were skeptical of the advantages of tying one's hands—through the European Monetary System (EMS) and then later through the euro—and were worried about the dangers of a progressive loss of competiveness with no easily available adjustment mechanism.

The attraction of the European project in the 1990s was that it would also bring with it strong outside pressure to reform, which might overcome the domestic blockages. It was a larger scale version of policy initiatives in the mid-1970s, associated with the IMF package, and in the early 1980s, associated with the debate about membership in the EMS.

In the 1990s, the need for a European framework became more urgent because the political system had disintegrated: the two major parties of the postwar system collapsed. The Christian Democrats, who had consistently formed the governing party, were discredited by corruption scandals, and the reformist Communist Party lost its credibility after the disintegration of the Soviet Union. The parties that took the place of the old political system were too weak and internally inconsistent and depended too much on coalition arrangements to implement any real reforms. The center-left governments (notably that of Romano Prodi 1996–1998) formed a majority based on a range of support from ex-Christian Democrats to radical Marxist groups; on the right, Silvio Berlusconi (prime minister 1994–1995, 2001–2006, and 2008–2011) built a new political movement in large part to protect his business interests from competitive threats. Although he had initially cast himself as the Margaret Thatcher of Italian politics and promised to create a million new jobs, his reforms were blocked by the fractiousness of the coalition he headed, and in 2001, when he won an election victory based on the promise of a *Contratto con gli Italiani*, he disappointed again. The 2000s did not produce large capital inflows to Italy, and the result looks dramatically different than that of Greece or Spain.

The Labor Market

There are some quite specific institutional features that explain the Italian slowdown in the later years of the twentieth century, which continued into the 2000s. One lies in the restrictive labor practices that were very hard to reform because of social and political blockage. The problem was recognized for a long time, and in the 1990s and 2000s, there was a vigorous debate about reform. But it remained a largely theoretical debate.

POLITICAL HURDLES

Tackling the issue required real courage: indeed, just as Italian anti-Mafia judges and prosecutors were assassinated, there were two notorious cases in which economists were killed because of their identification with the cause of labor market reform. In May 1999, during the Romano Prodi administration, Massimo D'Antona, a center-left law professor who advised the minister of labor on reform, was killed in Rome. In 2002, under the center-right Berlusconi government, Marco Biagi was killed as he cycled to work in Bologna. He had been publicly calling for a reform of the pensions system but also for a reform of Article 18 of the 1970 Labor Statute, which required the reinstatement of dismissed workers if the dismissal was judged unfair by an adjudication panel. The Biagi case in particular highlighted the variety of the opposition to reform. Biagi, like D'Antona, was killed by left-wing terrorists, the so-called New Red Brigades; but Biagi had received multiple threats, and the minister of the interior withdrew the police protection a few months before the killing.

EDUCATION

The stasis and rigidity of labor markets was augmented by a deficiency in human capital. Educational attainment was poor in an international comparison: In 2000, only 36 percent of adults had finished secondary education, compared to an EU average of 42. For higher education, the figures were 10 and 20 percent, respectively (though there has been some improvement in the Italian figures since then: the respective proportions were 42 and 16 in 2012). Other indicators of skill levels demonstrated a lag compared with Northern Europe. Three-quarters of Italian enterprises carried out no vocational training.

INTERGENERATIONAL INEQUALITY AND DEMOGRAPHICS

The lack of skills has been amplified by the emigration of many of the most-skilled young people. About 60,000 emigrate annually, more than two-thirds of them with college degrees. The outflow of the young is driven in part by very high rates of youth unemployment, but also by a sense that society is organized to marginalize them. Italy, together with one other major industrialized country, Japan, has a wealth distribution that is highly skewed toward the elderly. Young people find it hard to afford housing, and, as a consequence, young men in particular often stay with "Hotel Mama" into their thirties. As young Italians start forming families very late in life they have very few children. As a consequence, one can't talk of the age "pyramid" anymore since the old vastly outnumber the young in Italy. The unequal wealth distribution is made worse by public sector transfers: old age pensions amount to 57 percent of social spending and 14 percent of overall GDP. Transfers that have to be borne by fewer and fewer young people.

This phenomenon was evident even before the euro crisis. In a widely discussed public letter to his son published in 2009 in the newspaper *La Repubblica*, the head of Rome's LUISS University, Pier Luigi Celli, wrote, "This country, your country, is no longer a place where it's possible to stay with pride. . . . That's why, with my heart suffering more than ever, my advice is that you, having finished your studies, take the road abroad. Choose to go where they still value loyalty, respect and the recognition of merit and results."[9] The exodus of the young is obviously a phenomenon that could be reversed: Ireland, for instance, suffered from this problem in the 1980s, but as the economy grew sharply at the end of the twentieth century, many skilled Irish workers returned and contributed to economic growth.

Reform of the Justice System

The complexity of Italy's legal system had often been a deterrent to investment, both by Italians and foreigners. The courts were blocked by often frivolous cases, and civil cases dragged on endlessly. Over 5 million cases were weighing down Italian courts. The large number of lawyers—the second highest in any European country with almost a quarter of a million lawyers registered at the bar (Spain has even more lawyers)—did nothing to speed up the cases.[10] A great deal of modern business school and legal literature stresses the enforcement of property rights as a key to modern economic success, and Italy looks as if its byzantine legal culture was a major obstacle to growth. Draghi frequently emphasized the need for legal reform in his speeches. Renzi in 2015 set out a reform agenda that involved speeding up civil cases and instituting new business units that would deal with civil cases, as well as facilitating out of court settlements.

Politics and Decline

Europeanization of Problems

Many Italians project their national malaise onto the European level, and Europeans, when they face the issue of long-term decline easily turn their thoughts to the grandeur that was Rome.[11] When he was governor of the

Banca d'Italia, before the financial crisis, Mario Draghi began a speech in Venice to an assembly of economists and economic historians with a statement that this was the future of Europe if there was no reform. Indeed, the Italian city-states were the most prosperous places on earth at the end of the Middle Ages. The moment of Italian decline can be dated quite precisely to the beginning of the seventeenth century. Italy only recovered its per capita income of that time in the late nineteenth century, when other European countries had already engaged in a major industrialization push.

As a government debt crisis erupted in 2010, it looked as if the old model of solving Italian questions by Europeanizing them had failed. By 2011, in private meetings with Merkel and Sarkozy, Prime Minister Silvio Berlusconi was suggesting that Italy might leave the euro. He was responding to the surge in yields on Italian bonds in July and August that threatened to make funding the Italian debt prohibitively expensive and to what he thought of as the aggressive letter of Trichet and Draghi of August 5 (see chapter 15). For their part, the German and French leaders treated Berlusconi with ill-concealed contempt and also pushed President Obama to express his impatience with the Italian prime minister. At the summit in October 2011, Merkel and Sarkozy smirked when they referred to Berlusconi. *Il Giornale*, a newspaper owned by the Berlusconi family, compared Sarkozy's gesture to Zinedine Zidane's notorious headbutt of Marco Matterazzi in the 2006 World Cup final.

Time for Technocrats

For a moment, the Greek and Italian crises moved in parallel. When the Greek prime minister George Papandreou surprised European politicians on October 31, 2011, by calling a referendum on the reform package and on euro membership, Sarkozy and Merkel warned about the dangers. Papandreou quickly canceled the referendum and called for a vote of confidence in the government. As it became clear that he had lost credibility, a cross-party coalition government was formed with a "technocratic" prime minister, Lucas Papademos, the former vice president of the ECB.

In Italy, with tension rising between Berlusconi and his finance minister, a similar solution emerged after Angela Merkel had been involved in telephone calls, on October 20, 2011, with President Giorgio Napolitano. Merkel had asked Napolitano to do what was "within your powers" to "nudge Berlusconi off the stage."[12] The technocrat in this case was Mario

Monti, a rather austere economist who was president of Bocconi University and had generally been seen as an exceptionally successful EU commissioner in charge of competition policy. He became prime minister on November 16, 2011.

Monti headed a purely technocratic or nonpolitical government. It implemented some fiscal measures to reduce the deficit but found it hard to tackle Italy's structural problems; the proposed labor market reforms fizzled out. He called new elections in December 2012, but when he decided to form a new political movement (Civic Choice), the limits of his popularity became very apparent. In a general election in February 2013, Civic Choice received only 8.3 percent of the vote. A new coalition government was headed by a social democrat, Enrique Letta. Letta looked too much like an old-school politician and in an internal party coup was forced out after less than a year in office by the dynamic young mayor of Florence, Matteo Renzi. Renzi then won a surprisingly large endorsement by voters in May 2014 in elections to the European Parliament, at a moment when voters in other countries had turned to radical and populist anti-European parties. A problem soon appeared as the introduction of labor market flexibility in the middle of a new downturn meant that it was easier to dismiss workers, but there was little new job creation.

Political Reforms

Tackling Italy's dilemma involves economic reform measures, but it also requires some political reform to remove the blockages in the political system. Renzi also proposed wide-ranging changes in the electoral law that would make it easy for the leading party to get a super majority of votes in Parliament even though it only had a relatively small proportion of votes in the election. (The party that had over 35% in the first round would get an 18% winner's bonus; if there was no such lead in the first round, there would be a run-off round between two parties in which the winner would obtain at least 53% of the seats.) In addition he pushed through a reform of the second chamber, which stripped it of its powers and ended what had been an American-style bicameral system.

After 2011, criticisms of the government focused on the monetary union as a source of Italian problems, and the most obvious way of attacking any government was to claim that it was too dependent on the outside, on Europe, on Germany, or on Merkel. By the beginning of 2014, according to a poll in *La Repubblica*, only 29 percent termed themselves pro-European, while 27 percent were anti-European, and 44 percent were "sceptical."[13] The separatist Liga Nord party published a pamphlet, *Basta Europa*, in which it compared the European debate to a boxing match between fighters of very different weights: "Of course the 'heavyweight,' i.e., Germany, is going to win, while everyone else loses."[14] The populist opposition party headed by a comedian, Beppo Grillo, called for a referendum on the euro, and an exit if necessary. In the summer of 2012, Berlusconi warned that the euro was a danger to an export-driven economy such as Italy's. Germany, he said, "should get out of the euro, or others will do so."[15] In another remark that he later claimed to be a joke, he stated that Italy should say "ciao, ciao" to the euro if the European Central Bank does not "start printing money."[16]

Renzi was disappointed when his reform initiatives appeared to bring little short-term gain, and when Italy's growth forecasts dipped again while Europe as a whole, including many crisis countries, were doing better. It was easy to think that the problem lay in the credit market, and in particular in bank problems prompted by the move to banking union (see chapter 10). As the economic data showed a darker picture, Renzi's rhetoric moved in an anti-EU and anti-German direction. At the end of 2015, he announced that "Europe has to serve all 28 countries, not just one."[17] He tried to insist on an Italian voice in the European debate. "The time when Europe could give us lessons or homework is over. Italy is back and will make itself heard."

The logic spelled out by Berlusconi, which he had begun to embrace in his last months of office as prime minister in 2011, is that of a game of chicken, with the hope of getting help from the outside. But that was a game that had played in the past and had no effect in turning around the broken Italian political economy. That fact was recognized by some observers, notably by the Italian who moved in to head the ECB. Mario Draghi, in one of his last speeches as governor of the Banca d'Italia, stated, "It is important that we should all understand that the salvation and the revival of the economy can only come from Italians themselves. An atavistic reflex, recorded by Alessandro Manzoni, is to wait until an initiative from beyond the Alps solves our problems. As in other moments of our history, today things are not like that. It is important that all citizens are aware. It would be a tragic illusion to think that successful interventions can come from the outside."[18]

Italy, like Europe, needs to be capable of generating its own solutions.

13

Anglo-American Economics
and Global Perspectives

The United Kingdom and the United States looked like outsiders in the euro drama, distanced by a different tradition of thinking about economics as well as by competing interests and the range of their geopolitical calculations. The United Kingdom was not in the euro and also not a signatory to the Schengen agreement, which provided for passport-free travel. In some ways, the United Kingdom was as detached from much of the European Union as the United States, and in June 2016 it would eventually vote for Brexit. With differences of interest, there can always be trade-offs and bargains: indeed, that is the essence of diplomatic negotiation. The same kind of compromising does not work with fundamental differences of view, and discussion often produces escalation rather than solution. Suspicions on both sides of the intellectual divide grew. In the increasingly acrimonious debate, Europeans detected what they held to be a fundamental lack of understanding of the European project as well as a self-oriented defense of a different interest. Americans wanted the Europeans to have more fiscal stimulus, more capacity to deal with problem banks, more currency flexibility, and more debt forgiveness—in short, a rather conventional old-style Keynesian solution. Europeans denounced this approach as "hyper Keynesianism."

Europeans felt frustrated that the major vehicles of international opinion, which set the terms of the debate, all came from the Anglo-American perspective. There are obviously major differences in political orientation and style between the *Financial Times*, the *New York Times*, the *Wall Street Journal*, and the *Economist*, but in their coverage of the European debt crisis, they all framed the issues in a similar way. Some American economists summoned up the ghost of Milton Friedman to confound the euro. But

Anglo-American critics have a wide ideological and intellectual range. Paul Krugman, Jeffrey Sachs, Joseph Stiglitz, Simon Wren-Lewis, and Martin Feldstein have major differences in their analyses, but they all appeared as vociferous and devastatingly articulate critics of what Europe was doing—or not doing. Some frustrated European officials in Brussels responded by resolving not to read the *Financial Times* until they had absorbed French, German, or Italian media.

Americans often felt that they had a moral and intellectual responsibility to save Europe. They rightly believed that many of the decisive European reforms after World War II—in monetary, fiscal, labor, and competition policy—had been inspired by American officials and by the American example. In the late 1940s, the United States had even seemed to back a project to create a unified Europe through the European Recovery Program and the Organization for Economic Cooperation in Europe.

The modern obstacles to a coordinated European response, along Keynesian lines, were in part organizational and institutional: to act decisively, Europe needed some capacity for effectively coordinated state action. The fundamental difference of vision from across the Atlantic, or across the English Channel, can be boiled down to Europe's lack of "statiness": Europeans had often liked to present their achievement as the practical realization of postmodern politics, in which the traditional idea of national sovereignty (which they thought had produced so much trouble in the European past) was dissipated and diffused. "Europe" as a framework was designed to supplant the traditional nation-state. A state as traditionally conceived, on the other hand, had sovereignty in economic policy: it could control a currency, adjust an exchange rate, deliver a fiscal stimulus, or recapitalize banks. The Europeans could do none of these things, and as a result, they were hopelessly stuck. They seemed obsessed with rules that had been deliberately devised to restrain national sovereignty by "tying their hands" (in the metaphor that many European economists frequently deployed).

The Anglo-American vision stood in fundamental opposition to German tenets of economic management, especially in regard to the German concern about basing economic activity on the principle of responsibility and a strong concern about moral hazard. Mostly it was quite aligned with the French view, but there were also some major differences that ensured that France could not always cite US economists as close allies.

This chapter addresses the following questions:

- How exactly do the French and Anglo-Saxon philosophies differ? In particular, how do they differ as regards the role of the state (for example, as the guardian of a currency), bankruptcy law, and the design of the global financial system?
- How did US policy makers try to influence the crisis response in Europe?
- How did the United Kingdom deal with the dilemma of seeing a tight fiscal union as the only possible solution to the crisis of the euro area, while at the same time not wanting to be a part of this fiscal union?
- What led to Brexit and how will it impact the relationship between the remaining powers in the European Union?
- How did China's push for a multipolar world impact the euro crisis? Why did it see its interests as being more aligned with Germany than with France, even though its economic tradition of pragmatism and adaptability as well as its push for a multipolar international monetary system might suggest to be more in line with French economic thinking?
- What role did Russia play in the euro crisis, and to what extent did the Ukrainian-Russian conflict strengthen the European spirit?

In sum, the differences across the Atlantic, and to some extent also across the Channel, concerned the role of the state, the appropriate response to financial stress and banking problems, the question of default and bankruptcy and how to manage it, and the international monetary order. We examine them in turn before addressing global perspectives.

Diverging Traditions

Many US and UK economists—in academia, in the private sector, and also in government and at the Federal Reserve—had long been skeptical about the European project of monetary integration. In a famous article in *Foreign Affairs*, Martin Feldstein had warned that the common currency would exacerbate tensions between European countries and might even lead to a European civil war. In apocalyptic tones, he warned that "The conflicts over economic policies and interference with national sovereignty could reinforce long-standing animosities based on history, nationality and religion. Germany's assertion that it needs to be contained in a larger European political entity is in itself a warning. Would such structure contain Germany, or tempt it to exercise hegemonic leadership?"[1] Two European economists, Lars Jonung and Eoin Drea, in 2009 on the eve of the euro trauma summarized the response of the American economics profession as "It can't happen, it's a bad idea, it won't last."[2] During the crisis, Feldstein and many others continued to insist on their old story and to underline how prophetic they had been.

The debate after 2010, however, looked quite different to that of the 1990s. At the inception of the euro, public discourse largely focused on whether there was enough mobility of labor (and to some extent other factors of production). After 2010, the central issue was one that had largely been neglected in the earlier debates: the role of banks in transmitting shocks (see chapters 9–11).

"Statiness"

The American critique started with the abstract argument that monetary union cannot work without political union, that a currency requires a state, and that the historical evidence points to failures of monetary unions between countries (such as the nineteenth-century Latin Monetary Union or the Scandinavian Currency Union). The most obvious evidence for this thesis is printed on every $10 bill: the face of Alexander Hamilton, the first American treasury secretary. Hamilton's 1790 negotiation of a federal assumption of the high levels of state debt in the aftermath of the War of Independence looks like a tempting model for European states groaning under unbearable debt burdens. It was cited as a precedent in Thomas Sargent's Nobel Prize acceptance speech and appeared prominently in Treasury Secretary Geithner's injunctions on how to save the euro (he gave Finance Minister Schäuble a copy of Ron Chernow's excellent biography of Hamilton). Hamilton became so popular in the United States that Lin-Manuel Miranda turned his life into a much lauded hip-hop musical that President Obama viewed not just once but twice.

Hamilton had argued in 1790—against James Madison and Thomas Jefferson—that the substantial debts accumulated by the states in the War of Independence should be assumed by the federation. There were two sides to his case, one practical, the other philosophical. Initially, the most appealing argument was that this was an exercise in providing greater security and thus reducing interest rates, from the 6 percent at which the states funded their debt to 4 percent. The historical case looks like an attractive precedent for the Europeans of today. Hamilton emphasized the importance of a commitment to sound finance as a prerequisite to public economy: "When the credit of a country is in any degree questionable, it never fails to give an extravagant premium upon all the loans it has occasion to make." Hamilton also insisted on a stronger reason for following good principles than merely the pursuit of expediency. There existed, he stated, "an intimate connection between public virtue and public happiness."[3] That virtue consisted of honoring commitments. Extended in a political body, it would build solidarity. Those principles made the fiscal union what he called "the powerful cement of our union." So a currency union, built around debt mutualization and a common fiscal source to pay off the debt, actually made a nation: the United States of America. (See also chapter 6 for a more detailed economic analysis of fiscal union and Eurobonds.)

A fiscal union can serve numerous purposes: in the United States in 1790, it was a way of dealing with legacy problems, and it was tempting to see state action as holding out a possibility of simply wiping the slate clean after the European debt crisis. But another role of fiscal union, as an insurance mechanism against asymmetric shocks or a transfer union, was rather alien to the spirit of 1790, but instead reflected institutional processes that arose in the United States only in the middle of the twentieth century.

So one side of the American argument rested on the ideas that a collective European fiscal project was needed and that it should take over more responsibilities and be able to act as an automatic stabilizer—in the same way as the US federal budget as well as the Social Security Administration does. Both US and UK officials repeatedly made this point, which sounded odder coming from the United Kingdom because it was also quite clear that the United Kingdom was unwilling to sign up for more European fiscal integration.

The French economic school is in principle more comfortable with a centralized fiscal power. French thinkers wanted large fiscal transfers all the time. For France, the state is a friend. Inconsistently with their economic tradition, however, French political leaders are reluctant to pass sovereign budgeting power to the European level. The Anglo-American view differs from the French view in that it considers the state as useful in times of crisis but otherwise has a negative attitude toward it.

The Bank Dynamic

A related difference between the Anglo-American and especially French economic thinking regards how the state should relate to the financial system. In the French tradition, credit allocation is a major political concern and hence involves the state. For Americans, state action is primarily a response to financial problems and instability and hence is not required in fair-weather conditions. In other words, the aspect of fiscal integration that looked especially important at first was the capacity to rescue banks. The other experience that shaped the US response was the domestic aftermath of the financial crisis and the experience with how the banking system could be stabilized. The turning point, when the fragile recovery set in, occurred in the spring of 2009. Some attributed the restoration of confidence to the display of international solidarity at the London G20 summit, but a more common view was that the financial system recovered because the regulators (chiefly the Federal Reserve System) carried out rigorous stress tests and insisted on the recapitalization of weak banks. The critical moment in the resolution of the financial crisis in the United States should thus be dated as May 7, 2009, when the stress test results for nineteen bank holding companies were released, and the Federal Reserve Board chairman conveyed a reassuring message: "The results released today should provide considerable comfort to investors and the public. . . . Our government, through the Treasury Department, stands ready to provide whatever additional capital may be necessary" to banks.[4]

The US experience stood in remarkable contrast with that of the Europeans. The first major European stress test results came much later, in 2011, because it took a long time to set up the European Banking Authority: there was thus a two-year lag over the United States.[5] Even worse, the 2011 tests were soon demonstrated to have been insufficient: Dexia, a Belgian-French bank that had been bailed out in 2008, passed the 2011 stress tests, but just three months later, in October, required a further rescue from the French and Belgian governments (and then again after another year). The European stress tests demonstrated all the weaknesses of the European construction: because there was no backstop—no government that could do "whatever may be necessary"—it was very dangerous to announce problematic results. In the United States, the government could simply respond by increasing capitalization; in Europe, the markets would respond by running. Moreover, there was a major debate about whether exposure to sovereign debt should be included in the tests: banks usually hold government bonds as a safe asset, but this was exactly where the problem lay in the case of Europe.

More fundamentally, the banking system was proportionally smaller in the United States, where bank assets amounted to 83 percent of GDP in 2013 according to the Federal Deposit Insurance Corporation. Using International Financial Reporting Standards (IFRS)–equivalent accounting, the US figure would be about 30 percentage points higher; including the assets held by Fannie Mae and Freddie Mac would add another 32 percentage points. Even with these two additions, total bank assets to GDP in the United States would be 145 percent—just half of the EU's tally of 334 percent. In some European countries, banking systems dwarfed the domestic economy (see figure 13.1).

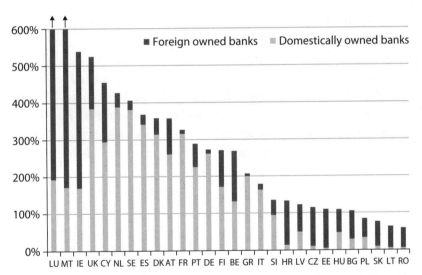

FIGURE 13.1. Total Consolidated Assets of Domestic and Foreign-Owned
Banks/GDP(%) in 2013
(Sources: ECB and IMF *World Economic Outlook*. The y-axis
is truncated at 600%: the value for Luxembourg is 1,719% and
for Malta is 798%.)

The contrasting successes of the stress tests on either side of the Atlantic gave US policy makers a feeling that they had managed the crisis well and that they had a right—even an obligation—to preach the truth at the Europeans.

Bankruptcy

Third, there were different attitudes to bankruptcy in the Anglo-American tradition. Especially in France, but also in other European countries where the great legal reforms of the Code Napoleon had had a major impact, bankruptcy was a terrible offense. Individuals who declared bankruptcy, whose names were written in red ink in the detailed ledgers kept in the offices of the Banque de France, found it almost impossible to recover their reputations and their credit. In practice, they often emigrated. By contrast, in the United States, bankruptcy at an individual level was often regarded as a badge of honor, worn by someone whose business ideas were innovative and essentially ahead of their time. Silicon Valley entrepreneurs treated bankruptcy as essentially a learning experience. Prominent individuals in American life, such as Donald Trump, owed their fortune and their position to the repeated use of bankruptcy provisions to escape liabilities to creditors.

American economists sometimes applied the same lessons to states, especially in a period in which state debt had accumulated to such an extent as to impose a severe fiscal burden on future generations. They had found it frustrating that the international system found it impossible to develop a bankruptcy regime analogous to that of chapter 11 in US domestic bankruptcy law, where the debtor is left in possession and subject only to court (not creditor) supervision, and where debtors can access new lending, which is given a priority in terms of the hierarchy of claims. The US administration, by contrast, had never embraced the more wide-ranging plans for a sovereign debt-restructuring mechanism proposed by the American first deputy director of the IMF Anne Krueger.[6]

The American perspective read the European problem as simply a bizarre variant in mature countries of developing country debt crises. Latin America in the 1980s and East Asia in the late 1990s had suffered from debt crises, and the only realistic way out was some write down of debt. This lesson had also been internalized by the IMF, which initially had resisted such an approach.

There is a fundamental time-inconsistency problem of sovereign default as a contingent insurance mechanism (outlined in chapter 5). Europeans were especially sensitive to this issue. They remember state bankruptcy as a fundamentally disruptive experience that destroys political capital. The French Revolution began with the bankruptcy of the ancient regime. After the end of the wars of the French Revolution, European countries tried to emulate the British example, where a revolution (the Glorious Revolution in 1688) worked because it set public finances in good order.

Americans then liked to reply: ah yes, but Europe did keep on going into default. In the debates about debt cancellation, the 1953 London Debt Agreement has become a constant reference point.[7] The simple argument, pushed vigorously by American economists, policy makers, and commentators, is that Germany was a serial defaulter in the twentieth century, with defaults in 1923, 1932–33, 1945, and 1953. In this view, German economic strength was built on a persistently cavalier attitude to debt, followed by a harsh legalistic attitude once Germany had become a creditor. According to these critics, Germany was trying to remove the ladder that allowed it to climb up the tree of economic development.

The reality is rather more complex. In fact, German history provides a powerful example of the time-inconsistency problem: Germany had become more unreliable and German politics ever more extreme in the wake of debt cancellations and defaults. The last cancellation, however, occurred in a setting of profound institutional reform and a binding into the international system: those were the conditions that ensured that, in peculiar circumstances, the solution of the debt issue could be linked to a more general cleaning up of the institutional foundations of economic activity. In 1923, there was an internal default conducted via hyperinflation that did long-term damage to German stability and weakened the German financial system so as to make it highly vulnerable in the Great Depression. The defaults of the early 1930s, during the Great Depression, became inevitable when Germany was not able to borrow any further on private capital markets and there was no longer any faith in the German future: J. P. Morgan started to refer to the Germans as "second rate people."[8] They did not set the stage for a sustainable economic recovery but contributed to the nationalistic poisoning of international discussions. The default of 1945 was the consequence of a lost war.

So there is only one "good" debt-cancellation exercise in German history—in 1953—and it is worth thinking more precisely about how it worked. It is not quite analogous to cancellations or write downs of developing country debt. As detailed studies of the London debt agreement by Tim Guinnane and others show, the cancellation related not to the principal but to accumulated interest arrears that had not been paid between the Great Depression and World War II.[9] The context of the negotiation is also important: the debt cancellation followed two other actions that set the stage for growth.

To start with, there was a completely different policy regime in Germany. After 1945, the Allied military authorities removed the people responsible for the destructive and destabilizing policies of the past. A new policy environment gave confidence that there had been a clean break and that from there things would go differently.

Moreover, before the debt conference, Germany had demonstrated that its policy makers were capable of absorbing and internalizing lessons from history. In 1950, after the outbreak of the Korean War, Germany had run into a severe balance of payments crisis. Some advisers recommended suspending the liberalization program that Ludwig Erhard had started, but instead the German government took a European Payments Union credit, accompanied it with a monetary tightening, and maintained the liberalization program. The operation, and its success, provided the intellectual basis for later IMF programs with conditionality. It showed that adjustment worked and that the contemporary critics of austerity (such as Thomas Balogh, who was the Joseph Stiglitz or Paul Krugman of those days) were wrong.

So the overall package of recommendations targeted at Europe over 2008–2012 and derived from the US philosophy involved some mix of greater fiscal action, coordinated action to save European banks, more currency flexibility to allow wage adjustment, an end to German or European trade and current account surpluses, and a willingness to write off government debt in the end. In this simple formulation, these policy measures are not coherent: in particular, the prospect of widespread debt write-offs would destabilize banks as long as capital movements across borders are permitted. The flexible exchange rate solution, in which deficit countries would recover their competitive position by devaluing and the surplus countries would be pushed to revalue, would have challenged the whole European integration project.

Global Financial System and Imbalances

The US tradition thought of the international monetary system as fundamentally a given, although Americans wanted other countries, in particular surplus countries, to take on more of the task of adjustment in the existing international monetary system. In France, by contrast, there was a long-standing suspicion of the US role as issuer of the global reserve currency (that went back to General de Gaulle's famous criticism of the US dollar). Consequently, French leaders wished that Europe could create a currency that would be more actively managed and supplant the United States' long-lived exorbitant privilege.

The US and UK view linked the inadequate European fiscal response to a long-standing debate about global financial imbalances, in which the United States had long worried about the distortions imposed on the world economy by countries running persistent current account surpluses. In the 1970s, the Carter administration had sent brilliant young economists to Europe to lecture the politicians on how Germany had a duty to act as an international "locomotive." But by the 2000s, the new generation of American policy makers put things in a different way. Initially, they had not been particularly concerned with Europe in general. The intellectual lens through which US policy makers interpreted the European crisis was shaped by a long-running narrative about global imbalances. In the 2000s, with a large US balance of payment deficits as an apparent counterpart to large Chinese (as well as other Asian and Middle Eastern) surpluses, Americans believed that there was a deliberate Chinese undervaluation of its currency designed to produce competitive advantages for exporters. There was continued US pressure for China to adopt a more realistic exchange rate, and the United States tried to use the IMF as an instrument for applying more suasion.

On June 15, 2007, after a substantial American campaign, the IMF came up with a Decision on Bilateral Surveillance over Members' Policies to replace the 1977 Decision on Surveillance over Exchange Rate Policies: it included measures against "exchange rate manipulation" and claimed to offer "clear guidance to Fund members on how they should run their exchange rate policies and on what is and is not acceptable to the international community."[10] China responded with great hostility and refused to cooperate. It was only a new managing director of the IMF, Dominique Strauss-Kahn, who managed to stage a strategic retreat on the Fund's claim to be an international policeman.

At that precrisis moment, the global imbalances story did not really include Europe because the overall current account of Europe was in balance: that did not mean, of course, that Europeans should feel secure, because there were massive imbalances in the financial sector (see chapters 9 and 10). But at that time not many people worried about the financial side, and the current account looked as if it were at the center of the debate. The supposed Chinese approach to the exchange rate was identified as a version of the export-oriented policies that Japan and West Germany had followed in the 1960s. A team of US-based economists working for Deutsche Bank dubbed the Chinese exchange rate model as "Bretton Woods II."[11]

But this analysis could easily be transferred to contemporary Europe as well, once Europe was treated not as a single entity but as a conglomeration of national economies. There it was a matter of surpluses on the part of Germany (and some other North European countries) and deficits in the periphery. The same logic that led to US pressure on China also now produced a demand that Germany should do more to expand the German economy and run down its large current account surpluses. At the Seoul G20 summit in November 2010, Treasury Secretary Tim Geithner launched an ill-fated proposal to limit current account balances to a 4 percent ceiling: the proposal was publicly criticized by Germany and Japan, with the German economics minister Rainer Brüderle speaking of a "fallback to economic planning."[12] Above all, the proposal brought China and Germany, whose objections were very similar, much closer together.

Some, but not all, American and British critics added a further dimension. Here the ideology from the outside appeared to take a different tack. Many conservative Americans were delighted by the imminent failure of what they saw as the European model of a tax-and-spend society, addicted to a costly and inefficient welfare state. They were not the only critics: there was a worldwide chorus of skepticism about Europeans' overly high expectations. The chairman of the China Investment Corporation, Jin Liquin, skeptically commented on ideas that China should bailout

Europe. It was "a worn-out welfare society" with "outdated" welfare laws that induced sloth and indolence.[13] Later on, other politicians added their version of Schadenfreude: authoritarian populist leaders such as Vladimir Putin, Christina Kirchner, and Recip Erdogan liked to think that their versions of a controlled economy or society (what they sometimes styled "illiberal democracy") built in the aftermath of default on foreign debt offered a more viable alternative to cosmopolitan international capitalism.

The United States: The Politics of Looking for Recovery

The United States had an overall geopolitical interest in seeing a Europe that would not be a source of additional worries. Europe should not contribute to a worsening of the global financial crisis but on the contrary should help to stabilize aggregate demand on the global level. For much of the crisis, there were other issues that seemed more pressing from the perspective of Washington politics: global terrorism, Iranian nuclear development, the economic and political rise of China, and, later, the new security challenge from Russia. There was also a lingering feeling, derived in part from the legacy of the Yugoslav crises and wars of the 1990s, that Europe was not very coordinated and required acts of leadership from the United States. The fact that the United States had a different economic philosophy augmented the tendency to lecture to the Europeans.

Fiscal Stimulus after Lehman

At the G20 London meeting in April 2009, the United Kingdom and the United States successfully pushed for a coordinated fiscal stimulus. Some continental Europeans were more skeptical; the Germans in particular argued that their powerful built-in fiscal stabilizers meant that public spending would rise automatically in a downturn, with support payments for short-term employment as well as welfare entitlements. So they thought that discretionary stimulus was not needed. And as the sovereign debt crisis hit, in Europe the nascent plan for fiscal stimulus looked increasingly problematic, in that new spending would increase debt levels and might trigger doubts about debt sustainability. When Spain was contemplating how to respond to the new situation, in May 2009, President Obama called the Spanish Socialist prime minister Zapatero to urge the adoption of an austerity program. There seemed to be an inconsistency in views about the kind of fiscal response that was warranted by the crisis.

The 2012 Grexit Fear: "Europe's Lehman"

The US impact on European development was felt most sharply at two turning points of the European debt crisis, when it looked as if radical or catastrophic possibilities were opening up. The most dramatic of these occurred in the summer of 2012, when there was a chance that the euro area might implode; some elements of the drama of 2012 were repeated in 2015.

In the spring and summer of 2012, Washington feared that the escalating euro crisis would trigger a new round of the global financial crisis. That would have a devastating effect on the United States, where there was something of a recovery from the depths of the 2008–2009 recession, but where there was still substantial fragility. A collapse of Europe would constitute a new "Lehman event." In addition, there was a sharp and urgent political edge to the debate: 2012 was a year of presidential and congressional elections. A new financial collapse could discredit the Obama administration and lead to a Republican victory.

There was thus from the perspective of Washington a need for very quick European action to resolve the crisis. The American policy makers had little time for Germans' worries about moral hazard or their concerns that large-scale measures would reduce the willingness of crisis countries to undertake reforms.

The US approach also rested on experience with previous international crises. Treasury Secretary Tim Geithner had been a critical member of the US Treasury team that responded in 1994–1995 to Mexico and in 1997–1998 to the Asian crisis. One lesson of the Asian crisis was that contagion in crises can spread very rapidly. In July 1997, when the first domino fell in Thailand, Korea was part of the group of countries participating in a rescue package; but by December, Korea needed its own rescue. There was, as a result, a need to put in firewalls to stop the spread of contagion: in particular, the United States was worried that a Spanish collapse would set off a new round of falling dominoes in Italy and France.

There existed, on the other hand, no reason why the United States should worry about Europe's long-term perspective, about improvements in the European governance structure, or in Europe's overall competiveness—all measures that might strengthen Europe relative to an America that itself was concerned about the possibility of long-term relative decline. The natural allies of the United States in the European bargaining game were thus politicians in crisis countries who were reluctant to undertake fundamental or structural reforms.

In repeated conference calls, Americans pushed the Europeans to "do something." The tensions reached a high point when Geithner joined the European finance ministers at a meeting in Wroclaw, Poland, in September 2011, and urged Europeans to increase the size of the EFSF. He warned, "What's very damaging is not just seeing the divisiveness in the debate over strategy in Europe but the ongoing conflict between countries and the [European] central bank. . . . Governments and central banks need to take out the catastrophic risk to markets." Not all his European colleagues responded enthusiastically to the American lecture. The pugnacious Austrian finance minister Maria Fekter, a moral hazard hawk who thought of herself as Austria's Margaret Thatcher, and who at the time voiced the German view more articulately than any German official, shot back: "I found it peculiar that even though the Americans have significantly worse fundamental [economic] data than the euro area, that they tell us what we should do."[14] The Polish host, Finance Minister Jacek Rostowski, claimed that the meeting showed "unity within the transatlantic family"; in fact, it demonstrated the opposite.[15]

In late July 2012, in the immediate aftermath of Mario Draghi's promise "to do whatever it takes to preserve the euro," Geithner had a bilateral encounter with German finance minister Wolfgang Schäuble at the Hotel Fährhaus Munkmarsch on the holiday island of Sylt. Again, Geithner pushed the Germans to act, primarily to allow a large monetary expansion program on the basis of bond purchases by the ECB. The rather anodyne statement issued after the meeting emphasized "the need for ongoing international cooperation and coordination to achieve sustainable public finances, reduce global macroeconomic imbalances and restore growth."[16] But this time the atmosphere was rather more cordial than it had been in Wroclaw, and it looked as if a basis for a way out of the European crisis was gradually taking shape.

US pressure was particularly decisive on one point. In the spring of 2012, a debate started up in the German government about whether there might be a suspension or an end to Greece's membership in the euro area, or what the markets quickly dubbed "Grexit." The ECB was working in secret on a contingency plan (code-named "Plan Z") coordinated by Jörg Asmussen, a new ECB board member who had just moved from a policy position in the German Finance Ministry. Schäuble in particular pushed for Grexit on the grounds that it was necessary to make an amputation to save the European patient: this became known as the "infected leg" argument. But the punishment of Greece would also have a demonstrational effect. One German official was later quoted in the press as saying, "You need to sacrifice one to scare the rest."[17]

For Americans, this type of argument looked like an exact replay of the frenetic discussions that had taken place in 2008. The rescue of Bear Stearns in March had created moral hazard; there was a need to demonstrate that there was no overall government guarantee for banks and that insolvent institutions should be allowed to fail in a market economy. Hence, when Lehman Brothers encountered a run in September 2008, the government would not help. And, in fact, the press on the Monday after the Lehman collapse almost unanimously welcomed the decision as a victory of market principles. When Lehman set off a global financial crisis, the sentiment was reversed, and the case turned into a powerful demonstration of the dangers of overemphasizing the moral hazard risk.

Angela Merkel thought about this point in the course of the summer of 2012 and made the final decision after a protracted period of balancing the arguments for and against Grexit. She never liked to make quick instinctive decisions but tried to remove herself from political pressures when contemplating her choice. When she came back from her summer vacation, she had convinced herself that the risks of an unanchored Greece were too high, and the bitter discussions in German political circles immediately stopped. Only academics went on questioning whether it was really a good idea to have Greece in the euro and insisting on the moral hazard threat. At the policy-making level, a more pragmatic American-style approach had prevailed, namely, that in a really bad crisis you cannot afford to think too much about moral hazard.

The debate about Grexit, and its outcome, indicates the way that the United States could influence the euro discussion: only through arguments carefully articulated behind the scenes. No US official ever made a set-piece speech on how to solve the euro crisis. When others used the same type of argument as the US government in a noisily public way, the result was probably counterproductive. The billionaire hedge fund operator, George Soros, for instance was filled with a deep and sincere belief that the civilized Europe that he had always passionately believed in was at the point of destroying itself; there was an emergency with only "three months to save the euro."[18] But his forceful advocacy, including interviews with Angela Merkel, only deepened German skepticism and provoked the argument that he had taken a substantial speculative position and was talking up his own book.

US Dollar Swap Lines

Did the United States have any financial leverage over Europeans? Because European banks had largely funded themselves by borrowing in dollars and had substantial currency mismatches on their books, they were dependent on dollar swap lines provided by the Federal Reserve to the ECB as well as to central banks in other industrial countries. The question of which central banks could access the swap facilities was the subject of very extensive discussion at the Federal Open Market Committee meetings in the immediate aftermath of the Lehman crisis. Another round of lending via the swap lines was required in 2010, with the outbreak of the debt crisis.

But these swaps were never made the subject of any policy conditionality because the self-interest of the United States was also quite clear: a collapse of any major global financial institution would be a catastrophe for the world and also for the United States, where the big European banks had a major presence.

The 2015 Grexit Possibility

The pattern of the dramatic crisis year 2012 was repeated in 2015. The United States—and US economists—warned more and more urgently that Europe needed to find an adequate solution. The Europeans were divided, with a clear intellectual gap between France and Germany. And the German government was also divided, with Finance Minister Schäuble pressing for a more radical course, involving Grexit as a way of saving the euro-area patient by amputating an "infected leg," and Chancellor Merkel worrying about the shock to European politics that might follow such a course. US pressure to conclude a deal was more gently applied to Chancellor Merkel and more forcefully to the hapless Greek prime minister. US treasury secretary Jack Lew, as well as Christine Lagarde from the IMF, urged Germany to include some measure of debt forgiveness. But as Lew formulated the point, the risks had shifted away from financial contagion, as in 2012, toward political contagion: a political disintegration would no longer plunge Portugal, Spain, or Italy into crisis, but it would strengthen President Putin's hand in Southeast Europe. "It's a mistake for the European economy, for the global economy, to take the risks involved with an uncontrolled crisis in Greece. It's geopolitically a mistake."[19]

American economists were more ferociously critical of Germany than ever, taking up the phrase of an EU official who was quoted as saying that, at a critical meeting in Brussels, Greek prime minister Alexis Tsipras was subjected to "extensive mental waterboarding."[20] Jeff Sachs tweeted: "I've never seen anything like this. Schäuble is dead set for Grexit, irrationally so." More radically, "Greece may be incompetent. The German leaders are cruel." In one tweet, Sachs declared that it was "time to leave the loony house."[21] Paul Krugman meanwhile blogged: "This goes beyond harsh into pure vindictiveness, complete destruction of national sovereignty, and no hope of relief. It is, presumably, meant to be an offer Greece can't accept; but even so, it's a grotesque betrayal of everything the European project was supposed to stand for. . . . Who will ever trust Germany's good intentions after this?"[22] German journalists in turn responded by claiming that Krugman and his colleagues were running an "anti-German hate campaign."[23]

The controversy was peculiar in the sense that both Krugman and Sachs on the one side, and Schäuble on the other, were sympathetic to the idea of a Greek exit from the euro. For the Americans, as well as for some Europeans (Germany's Hans-Werner Sinn took a similar position), the exit was justified because it would produce a devaluation, a return to competitiveness, and a surge in exports for the Greek economy. Krugman liked to refer to the Argentine experience of exiting a highly restrictive currency board in 2000–2001 as a major success. Schäuble's motivation was quite different, in that he increasingly saw the Greek problem as a barrier to further integration of the euro area.

The clash was also different as the financial landscape had shifted. By the summer of 2015, the alignment of financial interests was different to that of 2012. The threat of global contagion from the euro area had diminished. The question of Greek sovereign debt was largely an issue of who in Europe would absorb the losses, as most had been transferred to euro-area governments and EU institutions, including the ECB. European private sector financial institutions had largely succeeded in disengaging themselves. Only a few American and other hedge funds had engaged in high-yielding Greek debt as a speculative play on European solidarity. These interests inevitably pressed for a settlement that would *not* involve debt cancellation. In a remarkable e-mail that was photographed in the Greek Parliament on Greek finance minister Yanis Varoufakis's mobile phone, an American economist relayed a message from the financier George Soros. Soros apparently wanted "to communicate with my Prime Minister to urge him to remove me [Varoufakis] from gvt as I am the impediment to the agreement." In this message, Soros also urged Tsipras that it was "his duty to accept any deal, to forget about debt relief."[24]

By 2015, then, the urgent macroeconomic imperative had faded, but the intellectual pressure remained. Geopolitical interests seemed to play a more prominent role than they had in the initial stages of the crisis (and Greece certainly played them up on its side of the negotiating table as it made numerous approaches to Russia). When interests are more to the fore than ideas, the stress involved in bargaining is lowered, and the bargaining takes on a new complexion.

The United Kingdom:
Brexit and the Politics of Thinking Outside Europe

The United Kingdom played a starring role in the euro crisis—but not a constructive or a happy one. Shakespeare's most dynamic and attractive heroine, Imogen, refers to Great Britain as "in it but not of it, in a great pool a swan's nest." The British approach was the consequence of a long history of being apart from European dynamics but also from a central paradox of political economy: the recognition (following the basic lines of the Anglo-American approach) that monetary unions need fiscal unions to work, but at the same time a profound conviction that Great Britain did not want to participate in further European integration. So Great Britain alternately pushed Europe to do more and then stood back and opposed integration initiatives. Consequently, British policy seemed to combine preachiness ("simple steps to solve the euro crisis") with "I told you so" arrogance ("it was never going to work"). On occasions, the United Kingdom reenacted an old British sitcom (*Dad's Army*) set during World War II in which a gloomy Scotsman ran around repeating, "We're all doomed." The effects of the British stance were amplified because it was not just a matter of the government's position. The governor of the Bank of England, Mervyn King, believed that it was astonishing "that the people there [in the euro area] are not willing to face up to the fact."[25] Major newspapers and their commentators—above all Martin Wolf and Wolfgang Münchau in the *Financial Times*, Anatole Kaletsky in the *Times*, and Ambrose Evans-Pritchard in the *Daily Telegraph*—pursued the case that the euro was hopelessly doomed with relentless vigor. Anyone recalling their statements at the height of the crisis in 2012–2013 would be surprised that the euro had survived at all: if it continued, it must be some kind of malign and destructive zombie. As Evans-Pritchard put it, "If the project itself is rotten, surely what the euro area needs most is an undertaker."[26]

And what better undertaker than the Westminster government? The UK's view of Europe has always been both emotional and ambiguous. A Conservative government wanted to join the European Economic Community in the early 1960s but was rejected by French president Charles de Gaulle. The former general mocked the British ambition with a rendition of Edith Piaf's song about an English aristocrat left out on the street, "Ne pleurez pas, Milord." In the end, Great Britain came in from the cold, but British leaders always felt that they were not quite welcome in the European fold.

Underlying the British argument was the idea that Great Britain was simply much better at pursuing good economic policies than continental Europe and that the superiority stemmed from more clever economics but also from the possibility for greater policy discretion engendered by retaining one's own currency. The notion of a British special path, however, looked increasingly implausible in light of the severity of the British recession.

Gordon Brown's Initiatives after Lehman

The first phase of the global financial crisis occurred under the Labour government headed by Gordon Brown. Brown had been much admired as chancellor of the exchequer in the government of Tony Blair, where he had presided over a spectacular period of sustained growth in the wake of the financial deregulation that he had inherited from the Conservatives under John Major, but which "New Labour" had carried much further. Unlike Blair, who would have been keen to bring the United Kingdom into a

European monetary union, Brown was always hesitant and pushed the UK Treasury to devise a series of tests for euro-area membership that were so tough that Great Britain would probably remain on the sidelines for at least several Parliaments.

The fallout from the Lehman collapse was direct and dramatic in the United Kingdom. Brown very quickly and effectively put forward a bank rescue plan involving the de facto nationalization and recapitalization of large problematic banks that was conceptually simpler to the eventual US application of compulsory government recapitalization. Buoyed by the apparent success of the British effort to stabilize British banks, Brown set out to promote a plan for global action against the financial crisis. The G20 summit in London in April 2009 is undoubtedly a high point of international financial cooperation in the recent period. The London summit successfully nipped in the bud what might have been a destructively contagious financial crisis emanating from Central Europe (particularly from Hungary). The resources of the IMF were more than doubled, and the IMF's governance structure was adjusted to increase the representation of emerging markets. The World Bank was given resources to address the problem of unavailable commercial export insurance, which had played a part in the unprecedentedly steep collapse of world trade between September 2008 and April 2009.

In retrospect, perhaps the summit was not quite as successful as Brown initially thought. The other main platform beside IMF action as Brown conceived it was a coordinated global fiscal expansion, including in Europe, as an anticrisis measure. For countries such as Spain, where the cost of the real estate collapse and subsequent banking crisis had a heavy impact on public finances, this initial Keynesian stimulus did little to prevent the quick worsening of the crisis and eventually made the budgetary situation more severe and hence prompted sharper austerity. There was no attempt in London to work out the different capacities or room for fiscal maneuver of the various European countries. Later on, the London summit—and the process of summitry in general—also took a knock when it was revealed (as a result of the flight of a former US security analyst Edward Snowden) that British intelligence agencies had been conducting surveillance on the delegations at the London meeting in order for the United Kingdom and the United States to work out their negotiating tactics.

Brown's eventual defeat in the general election in May 2010 had nothing to do with his international activism. A major theme, that became even more critical in subsequent years, was British popular fear of immigration and the established parties' reaction to that fear. Brown himself suffered a direct hit when a hidden microphone caught him describing an elderly lady expressing anti-immigrant sentiment as "bigoted." The migration issue drove quite a large part of the British euro debate, in that it was realistic to fear that a major financial or economic collapse might prompt a flood of migrants to other countries, and particularly the United Kingdom. Indeed, the home secretary in the subsequent Conservative government even spoke of plans to suspend the mobility of persons in the event of a country such as Greece leaving the euro.

David Cameron's Dilemma: Closer Union Is the Only Way Out, but Also the Out for the United Kingdom

With no party commanding an overall majority in Parliament, Great Britain, in 2010, formed a surprisingly stable coalition government between the Liberal Democrats (the most clearly pro-European of the three major British parties) and the Conservatives, whose party was dominated by a powerful and articulate Eurosceptic wing. But the Conservatives had the upper hand, with the prime minister (David Cameron), the chancellor of the exchequer (George Osborne), and the foreign minister (William Hague). Cameron had deeply internalized the lesson of Margaret Thatcher: Great Britain needed to defend itself against budgetary claims from Europe. He and Osborne were also impressed by American economists who told them that a monetary union without a full fiscal union was inherently unstable, and, as a consequence, Europe could only save itself by going ahead quickly with a real fiscal union.

Unfortunately, this position made for an increasingly apparent policy incoherence that highlighted the anomaly of the British position. As signatories of the Maastricht Treaty, and as later accessories, all EU members without an opt-out (the United Kingdom and Denmark had obtained an exemption) had an obligation to eventually join the monetary union. The euro area itself had no fiscal capacity at all—only the European Union did. Thus, in pushing for an approach modeled on the early years of the American Republic, the United Kingdom was setting itself up for a potential existential choice about whether it should really be part of the ever-closer union on Hamiltonian lines.

In consequence, the relationship between the United Kingdom and the Continent looked more and more strained, and two gloomy summit meetings, both in Brussels, both in a gray and chilly December, drove Great Britain to contemplate something that even under Margaret Thatcher would have been quite unthinkable: a British exit from the European Union. On June 23, 2016, British voters drew the logical consequence and voted by a 52 to 48 percent margin for Brexit.

It all started optimistically and even cheerfully. On November 18, 2011, David Cameron went on what he believed was a successful trip to Berlin to negotiate a special deal for the United Kingdom. He had picked up from the United States the idea that a "big bazooka" was needed to deal with a big financial crisis and joked to the press: "My German isn't that good; I think a bazooka is a Superwaffe, am I right?"[27] Angela Merkel could not have been more forthcoming to the British plea for some economic reform, and her enthusiasm led Cameron to believe that Germany really needed Great Britain as the only reliable partner she could find in Europe: "Tell me what you want and I will find a way." "What about France?" inquired Cameron cautiously. "Nicolas will agree," the German chancellor emphatically retorted.[28]

But in fact, on December 8, at a meeting of the European People's Party (the center-right party grouping) in Marseilles, the day before the decisive European summit in Brussels, Merkel and Sarkozy struck a deal. Cameron was quite literally left out in the cold, with no European allies. Geithner was also present, and the appearance of an Anglo-American front pushed Sarkozy and Merkel to express their frustration with American "hectoring."[29] The tone in Brussels turned sharply against Cameron. In addition, he was tired and, though relatively young, lacked the iron constitution and perseverance of Angela Merkel.

In the early hours of Friday, December 9, Cameron "defiantly vetoed the proposed EU treaty changes, because as he claimed they did not contain his required 'safeguards' for the City of London."[30] That was waving a red flag in front of Merkel. Wasn't finance, and particularly its New York and London variety, at the root cause of the crisis, and why then should it be specially protected? Merkel at least tried to explain her position, that an exemption for the industry that caused the financial crisis was politically impossible. But she reflected that Europe had really broken down: "This is terrible—this is an existential issue for us. We can't go your way."[31]

Sarkozy was characteristically more confrontational: "David, we will not pay you to save the euro." Then he turned on the newly elected Danish prime minister Helle Thorning-Schmidt (by coincidence married to the son of the former British Labour leader and EU commissioner Neil Kinnock) when it seemed she was pushing for something all twenty-seven EU members could agree on: "You're an out, a small out, and you're new. We don't want to hear from you."[32]

Everywhere in Europe, the response was devastating. France's *Le Monde* newspaper concluded that "The Europe of 27 is finished," while Germany's *Der Spiegel* declared "Bye-Bye Britain."[33] The governor of the Banque de France, Christian Noyer, told a newspaper that based on economic fundamentals, the agencies should downgrade Great Britain rather than France because it had "higher deficits, more debt, higher inflation and less growth."[34] Europeans were appalled at how the last-minute injection of finicky points about bank regulation could stymie what was supposed to be a breakthrough on the regulation of budgets in Europe. Cameron's supporters in Great Britain cheered and presented the prime minister as a new Winston Churchill standing up to the threat of a vicious continental tyrant. Only Cameron's coalition partner hung back. The deputy prime minister, Liberal Democrat leader Nick Clegg, said that the result was "bad for Britain."[35] Tony Barber, the *Financial Times*'s Europe correspondent, wrote, "The nation that prides itself on a Rolls-Royce diplomacy appears triumphantly capable, at critical moments of EU history, of driving itself straight into a ditch."[36]

The "Brexit" Referendum

In consequence, Cameron seemed to steer back and argued that the United Kingdom did not in any way want a "multispeed" or "two-tier" Europe and that his government was aiming at continuing to be at the heart of all the European discussions. The full aftermath became clear only one year later.

SETTING THE STAGE FOR A REFERENDUM

The drama reached a new highpoint in the December 2012 negotiations for a treaty-based fiscal compact. Again, Cameron started with an optimistic spin that the proposed banking union would "lead to opportunities for the United Kingdom to make changes in our relationship with the EU." But for the first time, he raised the possibility of a British exit. "All futures for Britain are imaginable. We are in charge of [our] own destiny, we can make our own choices," he replied, adding that a British departure is "not my preference." He added a note of caution: "I believe the choice we should make is to stay in the European Union, to be members of the single market, to maximise our impact in Europe, but where we are unhappy with parts of the relationship we shouldn't be frightened of standing up and saying so."[37]

Then Cameron promised a big "Europe speech" that would stand along with the notorious speech Margaret Thatcher had once given in Bruges in 1988, when she had denounced the "European superstate exercising a new dominance from Brussels."[38] The speech was an embarrassment from beginning to end: it could not be given on the day originally scheduled, as that was the fiftieth anniversary of the historic Élysée Treaty, which had brought Germany in line with France; then it was further delayed because of the eruption of a hostage crisis in Algeria. The contents were widely leaked in advance:

> There is a growing frustration that the EU is seen as something that is done to people rather than acting on their behalf. And this is being intensified by the very solutions required to resolve the economic problems. . . . People are increasingly frustrated that decisions taken further and further away from them mean their living standards are slashed through enforced austerity or their taxes are used to bail out governments on the other side of the continent.[39]

The big message was that there would be negotiations to improve Great Britain's position in Europe, followed by a referendum in which Cameron would put the results to a popular test: but nobody could really say what results or "benefits" the British negotiators could possibly achieve.

The British initiative could certainly be given a positive twist, and there were certainly some people on the Continent who shared these sentiments. Unease about the development of the European Union, and its dubious anchoring in democratic legitimacy, is not uniquely a product of British peculiarity or insularity. In smaller Northern European countries, as well as in Germany, there seemed to be plenty of support, mostly for recasting the European Union along more economically liberal lines.

Cameron imagined that his speech was a helpful nudge to rethinking a more viable mix of liberal economics and a European fiscal regime that was in need of reform.

Before it had even been given, the Cameron speech had been condemned by the US assistant secretary of state Philip Gordon as well as by the German foreign minister and the Irish prime minister. Some European politicians rushed to express their profound worry about the bad consequences of a European Union without the United Kingdom. They should not really have bothered. The view of the friends of Great Britain, that the United Kingdom is a necessary part of Europe, rested on two quite contradictory cases, and they obviously both could not be right.

UK's Strategic Importance in Europe:
German-French Differences

For Germans, including Chancellor Merkel, Great Britain sometimes appeared as a valuable ally against Latin (and particularly French) statist proclivities. French and Southern European politicians articulated the exactly contrary position, that Great Britain is a necessary counterweight to prevent a German dominance of Europe. From the German perspective, the British are committed to the principles of the market. In the 1980s, Margaret Thatcher gave a major push forward to the idea of the single European market, and her successors have followed her fundamental approach to liberalization. The Latin hope is based more on classical Realpolitik lines about the balancing effect of the British presence. The idea takes up a favorite British interpretation of their own history: from the times of Charles V through Napoleon and Hitler, Great Britain, in the end, intervened to stop the domination of Europe by one power.

Neither of these arguments is really plausible. The Realpolitik line may offer a neat way of weighing up military potential, but it does not really convey the logic of peacetime bargaining about the optimal way of dealing with a complex economic problem. The market, especially in terms of a common labor market, is exactly what British voters found most terrifying. The biggest practical argument that drives the anti-European case in the United Kingdom is not concerned with the sometimes bizarre but often exaggerated effects of Brussels regulation, but rather with the inflows of foreign workers. Eastern European immigration may have made British businesses more effective and efficient, but the inflows had an impact on wages, especially during recessions. The British government responded with an advertising campaign to deter Bulgarians and Romanians from even thinking of crossing the Channel.

The only part of the Cameron strategy that ever made any sense was the idea that Angela Merkel needed and was looking around for a sympathetic ally in Europe. There were sometimes alternatives: in particular, Merkel soon began to think of Poland's prime minister Donald Tusk as the driver of a dynamic economy whose interests were closely aligned with Germany. Great Britain in the end largely isolated itself, and Poland acquired a new friend. However, the German inclination to build a new friend in the east did not survive the Polish elections of 2015, when, in elections for the presidency and the Parliament, Poles massively voted for the populist Law and Justice Party that staked a large part of its appeal on resistance to German hegemony.

UK's STRATEGIC REORIENTATION

The British government could calmly drop the European ball because it was looking elsewhere. It interpreted the aftermath of the 2008 financial crisis as shifting the economic geography of the world. In particular, British politicians made a special effort to court the new giant, China. Sometimes it even appeared as if relations with the new economic superpower were more important than the old cross-Atlantic or cross-Channel ties. At the beginning of 2015, Chancellor of the Exchequer Osborne pressed for British membership of a new China-led Asian Infrastructure Investment Bank at a meeting of the British National Security Council. British diplomats and the Foreign Office had warned that Japan and the United States would see the British step as a hostile move, and the Obama administration indeed promptly indicated the extent of its objections. Later in the year, Osborne visited China, announcing a "golden decade" of British-Chinese relations and of Britain as China's new "best partner in the West." Then the Chinese president Xi Jinping came on a state visit to London, which was crowned with a controversial deal to buy Chinese nuclear power plants. At the same time, Cameron followed a much softer line than the United States on issues such as China's human rights record or its push into the South China Sea. Xi took up Osborne's language and referred to his "visionary and strategic" hosts. Britain was looking for a new global role, in which new partners would step into the places of the economically and politically challenged older industrial countries.[40]

British isolation in Europe increased as a consequence of a referendum on EU membership promised by Cameron: the aim was fundamentally to defang the euroskeptic UKIP party, which threatened to perform very well in elections to the European Parliament scheduled for June 2014. The maneuver did not stop a powerful UKIP surge in the European Parliament elections but contributed to stymying UKIP in the May 2015 general election. Winning an absolute majority of seats in Parliament allowed Cameron to remain prime minister and shake off the previous coalition partner. Cameron's loneliness in Europe was emphasized when in the aftermath of the European Parliament elections he participated in a summit in Sweden and attempted to block the appointment of Jean-Claude Juncker as Commission president. The futility of the negotiation was captured by a press photograph that showed him sitting at the back of a rowing boat on a lake by the Swedish prime minister's summer house at Harpsund with three other leaders of conservative parties (with Chancellor Merkel in a commanding position in the middle of the boat).

A Symbolic Deal with Brussels

Cameron committed himself to hold the referendum by 2017, but it looked increasingly unrealistic that there could be any fundamental constitutional or treaty change that would satisfy British demands. He engaged in vigorous diplomacy, visiting more European capitals than any previous British prime minister before announcing the date of the referendum on European Union membership (June 23, 2016). The results of the initiative were meager. There was one very large emotional issue in the United Kingdom—migration: as in the United States, many workers, especially those with lower incomes, fear being displaced by immigrants. They also see immigrants as a cultural deep challenge, even when outsiders might see cultural complementarity. As an example, some British Catholics get upset when their churches seem to be taken over by devout Poles. The negotiated deal contained the possibility of an "emergency brake" on employee benefits (often referred to as "in-work benefits" in the United Kingdom) to European Union migrant workers. The deal involved a partial limit on current government child support payments to migrants (welfare benefits are paid to children of European Union nationals in the United Kingdom, even when the children themselves may not live there). These measures were a watered-down version of what Cameron had originally wanted and will not have any great effect on migration at all. Another big issue was the protection of the financial sector in the City of London from European regulation. There was a new mechanism allowing the United Kingdom to challenge new European measures and also a firm acceptance of the principle of nondiscrimination (i.e., that United Kingdom financial institutions may offer financial services to the whole of Europe in accordance with the principles of the Single Market); but there was no change to the EU voting rules.

The details of the deal hammered out in Brussels really mattered less than the symbolic parts. And those more rhetorical elements were at the core of the referendum campaign: the recognition that the euro is not the only European Union currency and the specific British exemption from the ever-closer union, or in Cameron's phrasing, the acknowledgment that "Britain will never be part of a European super-state."[41] The problem is that all of that was actually clear long before: the Maastricht Treaty of 1992 gave the opt-out possibility, non-eurozone members are represented on the European Central Bank's admittedly not-very-active General Council, and in any case, almost no one thinks that Europe is going to be a super-state. As a result, Cameron went into the campaign with a fundamentally defensive and negative message, whose kernel was that leaving the European Union would produce an unpredictable shock and lessen the United Kingdom's capacity for international power projection.

Other Europeans accused Cameron of blackmail; some started to express the sentiment that the European Union might be better off without a continuous British irritant. The Belgian prime minister, Charles Michel, told Cameron, "If you want to go, just go."[42] Even negotiating a modest restriction of EU migrants' rights to benefits proved very difficult, though the British position clearly addressed the fears of many Europeans over the threats posed by large-scale migration. So the British prime minister locked himself into a position from which it would be difficult to recommend continued membership in the European Union. On June 24, 2016, a day after the lost referendum, David Cameron announced that he would resign as prime minister within about three months.

"Brexit" Advantages and Dangers

Proponents of "Brexit" believed that leaving the European Union will produce two major benefits: the UK would be able to control migration more effectively and it would free itself of intrusive legislation and regulation, especially in regard to financial services. Sometimes Brexiteers cast their argument more generally, as a defense of sovereignty. They also believed that nothing much else would change, and that Britain and Europe would continue peacefully and prosperously trading with each other.

But, there is a big but here. One effect of Brexit is that it could unravel statehood and sovereignty within the United Kingdom. The United Kingdom is not really a conventional nation-state, but rather a composite. The question of sovereignty and self-determination arises most immediately in the case of Scotland, where the Scottish National Party (SNP) came close to achieving a positive vote in a referendum on independence. The SNP leadership has already made it clear prior to the referendum that it will not be bound by a Brexit vote that did not include a majority in Scotland (as well as in other units, Wales and Northern Ireland). So the exit process that will be launched in a two-year frame by a NO vote would also begin the undoing of the 1707 Act of Union, which brought Scotland together with England and Wales. Indeed, in Scotland a clear majority of 62 percent voted to remain in the European Union. Just a few days after the Brexit referendum, the Scottish first minister announced a plan for how Scotland can remain in the European Union. Similarly, the future of Northern Ireland is also not clear, as the majority in Northern Ireland also voted to remain in the European Union.

There is also a profound shock to the rest of Europe, which just like the United Kingdom could have its own unraveling. Brexit has been interpreted as a signal to many countries of a Europe that is turning in a wrong direction. Italians, already restive about German fiscal and banking rules, would see a chance to escape. Sweden, Denmark, the Netherlands, and perhaps even Germany would see a Europe in which rules are being broken as a Europe that they too need to leave. Indeed, immediately after the Brexit vote was announced, Dutch right-wing populist Geert Wilders called for a "Nexit" and France's National Front for a "Frexit." Negotiations about special deals are like a game of pick-up sticks (or Mikado). Players hope that they can pull a stick out of the pile without disturbing it; but some sticks are in a crucial position, and their removal destroys the stability of the whole system. Voters may be about to pull out the stick that keeps Europe's pile together. When stability collapses, nothing is certain, politics are radicalized, and people flee collapsing and impoverished states. It is unclear that even an independent and sovereign Britain—or England—would be in a position to contain or exclude those movements.

If the British departure has any positive effect on Europe, it will be to push the euro area into closer fiscal cooperation. The issue surfaced already during the Greek rescue package in 2015, when Cameron refused to participate in the financing via the EFSM, and Chancellor George Osborne emphasized that "the euro area needs to foot its own bill."[43]

Great Britain's position on most of the economic debates was intellectually close to that of the United States rather than to the European vision. But the United States also consistently pushed for the United Kingdom to play a constructively engaged role in Europe. The more the United Kingdom was willing to raise an existential challenge to Europe, the more distanced the United States became. With the Brexit referendum, the United States has to look for a different main strategic parter within the European Union. Germany is in the pole position for economic issues, while for security and military aspects France might play a more important role.

China and Russia

If the intellectual world of Great Britain and the United States is alien to Europeans and pushed an increasingly wider gap over the Atlantic and the Channel, there are forces that are both stranger and stronger operating in the world. Responding to geopolitical challenges has a different political logic and requires a pragmatism and flexibility that does not characterize the reaction to different visions of how economies operate.

China's Push for a Multipolar World

The financial crisis appeared to shake up the world economic order. Many interpreted the story of the crisis as marking a shift of economic power toward Asia, and especially toward China. China traditionally had a quite different philosophy in respect to economic arrangements than either Europe or the United States. Since Deng Xiaoping's reforms of the 1980s, Chinese policy makers had emphasized the need for pragmatism and adaptability, "passing a river by touching the stone," or experimenting with reforms to see which one worked in practice. There was no worry about moral hazard, and a confidence that the state would always be able to direct or control financial markets. The stock market was originally created in the 1990s as a way of directing finance to state enterprises. When the world was shaken by a financial crisis in 2008, China's leaders interpreted it as an opportunity to restructure the international financial system and to reduce the dependence on the hegemonic role of the US dollar. It was this feature that initially made for a greater propensity to look to Europe as a potential ally.

The 2007–2008 financial crisis also brought a resurgence of zero-sum thinking—a style of politics that had last been seen during the Great Depression. In this worldview, there are few or no cooperative games, and everyone who gains must do it at the expense of someone else. Cooperation is an exercise that only fools undertake. European countries suffered from the new antagonistic and uncooperative thinking, and so did the world as a whole. With the zero-sum mentality goes another widely prevalent instinct. One of the most widely used Chinese terms of recent years is 幸灾乐祸 (xìng zāi lè huò), not easily translated into English but well rendered by the German word *Schadenfreude*. Somebody else—some other society—has simply tripped on an enormous political banana skin. At first, in 2007–2008, the crisis looked like an American crisis that discredited American capitalism, then like a European crisis that revealed the failings of the European model. People in many countries started to think about what made their economic way of life unusual, peculiar, or prone to crisis.

CHINA'S PURCHASE OF BONDS AND INDUSTRIAL ASSETS

For European governments suffering in the aftermath of a debt crisis, selling bonds to China looked like a perfect way out. There had long been a debate about the extent to which China had trapped itself through its accumulation of large dollar holdings: it could not sell US government securities in a crisis without setting off a precipitated price collapse that would hurt China more than it would hurt the United States. So the financial crisis offered a perfect opportunity for China to diversify its assets. In late 2010 and early 2011, during a period of euro weakness on the exchange markets, China very publicly bought Portuguese and Spanish bonds, and the deputy governor of the People's Bank of China explained that "We will do our best to be a stabilizer in this process and support further integration of the EU."[44] China also looked like a major upholder of the euro rescue mechanisms when it (along with Japan) bought large numbers of EFSF bonds at a time when most

Anglo-American investors were worried about the imminent breakup of the European currency and consequently stood on the sidelines.

These were polite expressions of interest, but China was really more interested in acquiring industrial and other business assets in Europe at cheap prices. The problems of Europe's banks and the drying up of bank lending pushed some European companies to look for overseas purchasers. Other factors played a role: in family firms, the always problematic question of transfer between generations prompted a desire to sell.

FROM FRANCE'S GRAND INTERNATIONAL VISION
TO GERMAN CONCRETE INVESTMENTS

As Chinese economic links with the European economy intensified, China became less interested in enlisting Europe in a grand project of restructuring the international financial architecture and more interested in case-by-case pragmatic intervention. The debate about big visions came at the early stage of the financial crisis. In March 2009, the governor of the People's Bank of China, Zhou Xiaochuan, published a paper titled "Reform the International Monetary System," laying out the case for a greater role of special drawing rights (SDR; a synthetic basket currency managed by the IMF) in the international financial system and arguing that the basket of the SDR should also include major emerging market currencies.

In 2011, France picked up the idea of including the renminbi in the SDR basket and organized a meeting in China with academics and officials. Sarkozy started the meeting with a gentle provocation that irritated the United States but did not earn a great deal of Chinese sympathy: "We must accompany the inevitable internationalization of the major global currencies. This does not mean, cher Tim [Geithner], challenging the role of the dollar, nobody would think of doing that, and the euro, which must be stable currencies."[45] But commentators paid more attention to Secretary of the Treasury Geithner's remarks, in which he set out conditions (including the removal of capital controls) that would in practice mean that the SDR was unlikely to include the renminbi for some considerable time. At the November 2011 G20 summit in Cannes, the final communiqué excised a reference to a broader SDR basket: a defeat for the French concept. In the end, in 2015 the IMF agreed to include the renminbi in the SDR basket, but the move did not appear as a major upgrade of the SDR and its role. The American dollar is still the world's major currency.

In place of the rather futile international financial architecture debate, China became more involved in concrete steps to internationalize the renminbi and increase China's influence. That meant talking primarily with Berlin. Many European observers were struck by the way in which Chinese officials treated Brussels and the EU authorities as an irrelevance, but also by the closeness of the Beijing-Berlin relationship. Prime Minister Li Keqiang's first trip abroad in May 2013 was to Berlin; President Xi Jinping's first European trip in March 2014 had its highpoint in his visit to Berlin. There was also some Chinese discussion of the similarities of the Chinese and the German approach to economic management, with the notion of a socialist market economy being redefined as simply a variant of Germany's celebrated postwar model of the social market economy.

Germany accounted for 38 percent of all Chinese investments in Europe in 2012, far exceeding the United Kingdom (22%) and France (5%). In 2013, the Chinese Social Science Academy reported that Germany was the safest country in the world for Chinese investment. Some of the most famous purchases were the Zhejiang Geely Group's acquisition of Volvo (Sweden) in 2010, Lenovo's of Medion (Germany) in 2011, Sany's of Putzmeister (Germany), Wolong's of ATB Drive Technology (Austria), and the Weichei Power Group's of the Kion Group AG (Germany). Most of the purchases were by private Chinese firms (with less than 20% public participation), although there were also some public stakes built up, such as China Investment Corporation's buying of a 10 percent stake in Heathrow Airport and the 2011 sale of a 20 percent stake in Energias de Portugal to China's Three Gorges.

The increasingly German-centered approach of Chinese policy makers reflected not just a new surge of investment but also a realization of the importance of the Chinese market (and of emerging market economies more generally) for Germany's export performance. In the course of the global financial crisis, German trade experienced a substantial reorientation. Before 2008–2009, there had been large German bilateral surpluses with peripheral Europe. As those economies contracted, the slack was taken up by orders for machine tools and engineering products as well as high-end automobiles from the emerging market economies that experienced no contraction and, on the contrary, represented the major locomotive of the world economy: this was one of the most important reasons why the Great Recession was restricted to the advanced economies and why there was no global repeat of the interwar Great Depression. By the early 2010s, Chinese demand was estimated to account for about 0.5 percentage points of Germany's growth.

Russia

Russia, like China, immediately interpreted the global financial crisis as the beginning of a momentous shift in power relations. Whereas before 2008 President Putin had been a cooperative player in the international system who realized how dependent and interlinked Russia had become, there was now a decisive shift. After the 2008 crisis, Putin saw a disintegrating global governance framework. The financial crisis looked first like the end of American capitalism and then as a demonstration of European ineffectiveness and division. Putin saw both as an opportunity to extend Russian power and influence: at some moments, he even—like China's leaders—thought of refashioning the global economic order. President Putin, speaking in Sochi in September 2008, conspicuously revived de Gaulle's language criticizing the preeminence of the dollar: "Regarding the global financial crisis, we should pause and think up ways to change the architecture of international finance and to diversify risks. The world economy cannot be supplied 'from one currency-printing press.'"[46] A major point of the Chinese-Russian gas deal in 2014 was the non-dollar pricing.

RUSSIAN FINANCIAL INVESTMENTS

While Chinese firms were buying stakes in European enterprises, Russian activity was more narrowly focused on the financial sector and on energy. A consequence of the severity of the European banking crisis was that many European banks needed to improve their capitalization; they could not easily raise new capital, and so they sold off assets. In many countries, there was also official encouragement to dispose of foreign holdings. Italian and Austrian banks had few domestic problems but massive losses as a consequence of earlier large-scale purchases of banks in Central Europe.

Those Central European banks offered a buying opportunity for Russian financial interests. In particular, Sberbank Europe AG (until 2012 named Volksbank International) built up a substantial position with banks in Slovakia, Czech Republic, Hungary, Slovenia, Croatia, Bosnia and Herzegovina (including Republika Srpska), Serbia, and Ukraine. In 2012, it bought the East European assets of ÖVAG for €505 million and injected new capital. But ever larger injections of new capital were required, and, in total, Sberbank has so far put in €1.3 billion. VTB and Gazprombank also have major Eastern European holdings. Gazprom and Transneft have large investments in energy infrastructure, mostly in the form of joint ventures. Some geostrategic theorists in Russia promoted such strategic investments as a way of building up a gradually increased command over what Lenin had dubbed the "controlling heights" of the economy of Russia's Western neighbors and hence for an increased extension of influence.

Europe's Dependency on Russian Energy

But the most obvious instrument for Russian control came from its energy sector. The resource curse—in which abundant natural resources (above all energy) promote rent-seeking behavior—means that many large energy exporters are prone to corrupted politics and unstable policies and have a proclivity to blackmail.

For modern Europe, the most obvious threat is posed by the extent of dependence on Russian gas. Although there were incidents in which disputes between Russia and Ukraine overpricing of long-term gas contracts led to a cutoff of supplies to some areas, notably in January 2009, when there were major shortages and cutoffs in Bulgaria and Romania, the issue only reached political and popular salience as a strategic threat to Europe in the aftermath of the collapse of the Yanukovych regime in Ukraine and the subsequent Russian annexation of the Crimea and destabilization of Eastern Ukraine.

Europe's dependence on imported gas, by far the cleanest fossil fuel, has increased. EU domestic production of gas has fallen since the late 1990s, as the resources of the United Kingdom and the Netherlands in the North Sea were depleted. Only the Netherlands and Denmark are net gas exporters. There are some shale gas resources, but a large part of these are unlikely to be useable, for economic as well as political reasons (including worries about the environmental consequences of shale extraction). Of European countries, only Poland has the potential to become a major producer of shale gas. The share of gas imports in the European Union has been rising steadily from the mid-1990s (when it was around 40%) to about 70 percent today. In 2013, 39 percent of extra-EU imports (in volume) came from Russia, followed by Norway (34%), Algeria (13%), and Qatar (7%). Most of the gas comes through pipelines, most notably the newly constructed Nord Stream; the Baltic states and Finland are exclusively dependent on a single (Russian) source.

The history of discussions about gas supply is fraught with suspicions that a monopoly (or near monopoly) supplier is attempting to cut special deals with individual countries in a divide-and-rule strategy. Russian president Vladimir Putin cultivated strong ties with Italian prime minister Silvio Berlusconi. Berlusconi, in signing a project for a pipeline that would send substantial quantities of Russian gas to the Italian state-owned firm ENI, advised Brussels to "cultivate the same kind of good relations that Rome enjoys with Moscow."[47] In Germany, Chancellor Gerhard Schröder cultivated an analogous relationship with Putin, and after he retired from politics took a position with the energy giant Gazprom. When Russia negotiated the construction of a new sea pipeline in the mid-2000s (North Transgas, then Nord Stream) to bring Siberian gas to Northwestern Europe, despite the higher costs and potential environmental threat of an underwater line, the Baltic states and Poland felt that they were being cut out and would consequently be vulnerable to Russian pressure over their own supplies. The then Polish defense minister Radek Sikorski, in 2006, made the extreme comparison between the German-Russian negotiations on Nord Stream and the Molotov-Ribbentrop Pact, the pact wherein Germany and Russia divided Poland among themselves.

Geopolitics: Russian-Ukraine conflict and the Refugee Crisis

Until 2014, comparatively few Europeans worried about a geopolitical threat from Russia. Those that did were concentrated in Poland and the Baltic states. The Russian response to the revolution that overthrew the Yanukovych regime in Ukraine changed this perception. In 2014, the dynamics of the European debate also changed and made it much clearer that the European project brought security benefits for the Continent as a whole. At the beginning of 2013, Luxembourg's prime minister Jean-Claude Juncker was widely ridiculed for evoking the shades of 1913 and Europe's last prewar year of peace as a warning of the dangers of the escalation of national animosities and rivalries within Europe. One year later, he looked prophetic. By 2014, as the security situation in the South China Sea deteriorated, Japanese prime minister Shinzo Abe cast China as the equivalent to Kaiser Wilhelm's Germany; and the outbreak of fighting in Eastern Ukraine, as well as in Iraq and in Gaza, was a sharp reminder of the dangers of conflict escalation. The escalation of conflict in Syria in the summer of 2015 prompted a large flow of refugees into Europe and divided Europeans in a new east-west split, with Eastern Europeans worrying about the cultural impact of Muslim refugees and attempting to limit the inflow. By 2015, the links between security issues and the European crisis discussions became very evident, and the main fear about a Greek exit from the euro area was less about financial contagion than about geopolitical vulnerability.

Conclusion

Three sets of very different outside interventions shaped the course of the euro crisis. The United States tried to preach and laid out economic theoretical reasons why Europe needed to coordinate more. The more direct the warnings were, the less impact they had. The general message about the need for more fiscal coordination was appropriate, but the idea of moving quickly along Hamiltonian lines was always a political nonstarter. China did not directly try to influence European policy but had a general interest in the strengthening of alternative and multiple poles of the global system to replace what had been seen as an unfair American unipolarity, a version of the "exorbitant privilege" that French policy makers had castigated in the early postwar period. Both American and Chinese policies tended—despite their intent—to polarize Europe and to drive more wedges between different European countries. In that sense they helped to encourage the European proclivity to play games of chicken.

The United States made German policy makers feel threatened and beleaguered; the Chinese made many European governments feel powerful and offered a powerful allure of new commercial contracts. By contrast, Russia's more obvious and politicized attempt to shape European politics and to develop what its geostrategic thinkers termed "Eurasia" as a counterweight to American unipolarity was not an effective strategy as far as Russia's interests were concerned, and, by 2014, Russia was more isolated from Europe than it had ever been in the post–Cold War, post-Gorbachev era. But it had an immediate impact in drawing Europe closer together and in reemphasizing the political desirability of a shared concept of pluralism and defense of European values. Vladimir Putin provided a powerful reminder that Europe had something in common: he may thus have contributed (in a negative way) to rescuing the European model in a world that was increasingly thinking in zero-sum terms.

14

The International Monetary Fund (IMF)

The involvement of the International Monetary Fund (IMF) altered the course of the European sovereign debt crisis. Although some might argue, from a purely formal perspective, that the Fund is simply an agent of the national governments of the world that own it, in practice, the IMF took a position that was distinctly its own and that reflected a particular *weltanschauung* ("worldview"). The management of the Fund, above all the managing director, and the staff of professional economists define policies that are often intended to nudge governments in a particular direction. Its economists have developed a reputation for technical competence and for standing above day-to-day politics. In 2010, it was the demand for technical outside competence that drove the European governments to change their minds about the desirability of involving the Fund. In that sense, the involvement of the Fund was a response to a clear recognition that Europe did not have the competence or the authority to solve its own problems: it needed an outside doctor to make the prescriptions.

The kind of expertise that the Fund had developed was however problematic for the Europeans. First, the most technical attention in the IMF had been given to the issue of debt management and debt sustainability because of its extensive and painful involvement with overindebted countries: low-income countries, Latin American emerging markets in the 1980s, and East Asia in the later 1990s.

Second, the Fund had evolved an approach to the politics of economic reform that made it uncomfortable with the enforcer or whipping boy role that it had traditionally been given by the international community (i.e., the big and powerful states). Since the 1990s, it had begun to emphasize more and more the idea of "ownership": reforms do not work unless they are carried by a deep political consensus. But the Europeans' idea in calling in the Fund was precisely to find a substitute for the lacking consensus about economic reform.

As an international economic policy think tank (as well as a funding organization), it was inevitable that the IMF was a principal forum in which the disagreements between the different worldviews would be fought out. It had always had a strong orientation toward Europe and a particularly close relationship with French policy making. Meanwhile, Germans often complained that the structure and training of their civil service made it difficult to get high-level representation in international institutions, including the IMF. Since the IMF was created at the International Monetary Conference of the United Nations in 1944, held in Bretton Woods, New Hampshire, there have been eleven managing directors (heads of the IMF), all of them European. The fact that all managing directors (MD) were European was a matter of chance: the principal American architect of the Bretton Woods agreement, Harry Dexter White, was the obvious candidate to be the first MD, but he was accused of being a Soviet spy, with the result that an American became head of the World Bank and a non-American—in practice always a European—headed the IMF. Of the eleven, five were French, and all of them profoundly influenced the development of the Fund in transitional moments: when the fixed exchange rate system broke down, during the Latin American debt crisis, after the collapse of communism, and then during the euro crisis. By contrast, four of the six non-French European MDs did little to shape the Fund: the first two postwar MDs, a Belgian and a Swede, presided over a rather marginal institution, and the first two MDs of the twenty-first century, a German and a Spaniard, also saw their institution slipping into irrelevance and left before completing their terms of office. In short, the IMF looked like France's chance to shape the world. Indeed, in the late 1990s, during the Asian crisis, the popular magazine *Paris Match* carried a photo of the managing director with a caption reading, "The most powerful Frenchman in the world."[1] During the euro crisis, the Fund was led by two powerful and charismatic French political figures: the first, Dominique Strauss-Kahn, was widely believed to be the likely (and probably successful) socialist candidate for the presidency of the Republic. His successor, Christine Lagarde, had been the French minister of finance.

In this chapter, we attempt to answer the following questions:

- What is the IMF's philosophy toward crisis management? Why was the IMF increasingly focused on debt sustainability?
- Why did the IMF start its engagement in Europe in 2010?
- Why did the IMF's involvement prompt unprecedented tensions in the IMF, in its board, and in its management?
- How was the IMF torn between taking a French view (on relaxing fiscal rules) and a German view about strict policy conditionality?

The IMF's Philosophy and Crisis Management

This section pictures the IMF's economic approaches. First, we study its approach toward international capital flows: in its young history, the Fund came to change it drastically. Next, we explore the three ways for the IMF to make debt sustainable: first, as the international lender of last resort to overcome a temporary liquidity shortage; second, to commit countries to long-lasting structural reforms and assume the role as a whipping boy; and, third, to extract coordinated concessions from creditors and help to overcome the holdout problem. Finally, we explore the remaining crisis management techniques of the Fund.

The IMF's Attitude toward International Capital Flows: A Swinging Pendulum

Initially, the IMF was designed as an institution that would enable the application of the ideas of the founding fathers of Bretton Woods—the British economist John Maynard Keynes and American assistant treasury secretary Harry Dexter White. Keynes had been asked by the British government to prepare a counterscheme to the German economics minister Walther Funk's remarkable (but insincere) plan of 1940 for European prosperity (and for a sort of monetary union). He rejected very decisively the idea that a return to 1920s internationalism might be attractive as a pattern for postwar relations. It would not be enough, he said, to offer "good old 1920–1921 [the postwar slump] or 1930–1933 [the Great Depression], i.e., gold standard or international exchange laissez-faire aggravated by heavy tariffs, unemployment, etc., etc."[2] In his proposals, Keynes spoke of "the craving for social and personal security" after the war.[3] The essence of Keynes and White's approach was that capital flows had been the culprit in interwar instability and thus should be limited for the sake of international stability. Keynes repeatedly asserted his skepticism about the benefits of both capital exports and capital imports. He wrote, "There is no country which can, in future, safely allow the flight of funds for political reasons or to evade domestic taxation or in anticipation of the owner turning refugee. Equally, there is no country that can safely receive fugitive funds, which constitute an unwanted import of capital, yet cannot safely be used for fixed investment."[4] The possibility of a sudden reversal makes countries that use these funds for long-run investment projects with low market liquidity vulnerable to a crisis.

But the pendulum swung, and capital movements resumed. In the 1980s, in the new "Zeitgeist" of deregulation, the new "Washington Consensus" emerged—a consensus that shares many similarities with the German Ordoliberalism discussed in chapter 4. In the international arena, the IMF was at the forefront of designing a system in which rules were developed for a new era of economic but also financial globalization. Free international capital and trade flows were the guiding North Star of a new global architecture. This view was consistent with German economic thinking. Paradoxically, the international civil servants who at that time worked on devising rules for liberalization and globalization were all French nationals: Jacques Delors in the European Commission and Pascal Lamy at the World Trade Organization, but above all Jacques de Larosière and Michel Camdessus at the IMF.[5]

By the mid-1990s, the IMF was championing the idea of a third amendment to its Articles of Agreement, in which international capital mobility would be specified as a commitment of countries engaged in the Fund (in a way analogous to the original commitment in the 1940s to establish convertibility for current account transactions, i.e., payments for goods and services, but not foreign investment). But that third amendment never became a reality, as the 1997–1998 Asian crisis demonstrated quite how dangerous the interaction of unregulated capital flows and immature financial systems might be. Malaysia, which was (negatively) branded for imposing capital controls by the IMF and the international community, fared better than countries that kept their current accounts open. The pendulum started to swing back again. Even in the late 1990s, some Fund research documents warned against the dangers of capital mobility: some of the worries that had originally driven Keynes and White came back.

The IMF on Debt Sustainability

The IMF had developed substantial expertise in dealing with sovereign debt crises. Before 1982, as private capital flowed into Latin America, many analysts saw the IMF as losing its intended role. When a debt crisis started in Mexico and then rapidly spread to other large Latin American countries, Brazil and Argentina, the IMF stepped in as a crisis manager. Initially, it solved the crisis by supplying new money from its own resources, conditional on private banks also agreeing to lend more, and negotiating reform programs designed to return the borrowing countries to sustainability. It was only seven years after the outbreak of the original 1982 crisis that creditors started to accept debt write-offs under the Brady Plan.[6]

The primary aim of the IMF's crisis management program is to make a country's debt sustainable. That is, the country's future projected tax revenue minus its expenditure should be large enough to ensure that the country is able and willing to service its debt. In most cases, however, there is no clear-cut answer to the question, "Is debt sustainable?" Debt may be sustainable in some states of the world (strong growth, low interest rates) and unsustainable in others.

There are three ways for the IMF to make debt sustainable: first, as international lender of last resort to overcome a temporary liquidity shortage; second, to commit countries to long-lasting structural growth-enhancing reforms and to take on the blame for unpopular measures; and, third, to extract coordinated concessions from creditors and help to overcome the holdout problem.

IMF AS LENDER OF LAST RESORT

First, the IMF functions as an international lender of last resort when a country faces rollover risk. This can occur in countries that issue short-term debt denominated in foreign currencies. The central bank may not have enough foreign reserves to overcome a temporary liquidity shortage. High interest rates may become self-fulfilling. The IMF's financial assistance can lower a country's interest burden, thereby making the overall debt level sustainable. In general, growth and interest rates depend on whether debt is judged by creditors as sustainable. This creates indeterminacy with possible feedback loops and multiple equilibria. The success of the IMF programs has become heavily dependent on *confidence effects*: if markets believe that the debt/GDP ratio will be stabilized, they will provide the necessary funding at a low interest rate, thereby allowing growth to resume, and their belief will be self-fulfilled. In the reverse case, the country will be caught in a downward spiral of low growth and increasing debt/GDP ratio.

Some critics argued that the possibility of a rescue constituted a moral hazard risk and that the insurance provided by the IMF was actually stimulating unproductive and dangerous capital flows. That criticism became especially powerful in the aftermath of the 1994–1995 Tesobono crisis in Mexico, where it was articulated most powerfully by free-market economists such as Milton Friedman. As Friedman put it, "The Mexican bailout helped fuel the East Asian crisis that erupted two years later. It encouraged individuals and financial institutions to lend to and invest in the East Asian countries, drawn by high domestic interest rates and returns on investment, and reassured about currency risk by the belief that the IMF would bail them out if the unexpected happened and the exchange pegs broke."[7] On the IMF board, the moral hazard worry was articulated most forcefully and consistently by the German representatives. It was also Germany that successfully blocked a proposal in October 1994 at the annual IMF meeting in Madrid to undertake a general issue of the IMF's reserve currency, the special drawing right (SDR). As the Germans argued, there was no evidence of a general liquidity shortage that was the condition in the IMF's amended Articles of Agreement for a new issue.[8]

The IMF's liquidity assistance alone is typically not enough to turn a country around by itself and make its debt level sustainable. The Fund's lending has to be leveraged or, as the Fund often puts it, "catalytic": it needs to persuade investors that a sustainable debt level has been reached and that their future investment will be secure. The second element of the Fund's crisis management is to offer the crisis country a commitment device for implementing future growth-enhancing structural reforms. In addition to extracting concessions from the country, the Fund serves as coordinator among existing creditors to reduce the existing legacy debt and to overcome holdout problems.

IMF AS ENFORCER

More specifically, the IMF's second crisis management tool is to act as an enforcer and "whipping boy." The Fund's conditionality imposed on a country provides a commitment device to implement structural reforms. There was a strong political economy argument for that: entrenched interests blocking reform and sustainable adjustment could only be overcome by a diktat from the outside. In the last major European engagements of the IMF, with the United Kingdom and Italy in 1976–1977, such outside pressure had been a crucial part of shifting the balance of policy toward reform. But the most devastating examples of the outside imposition of reform had come in the course of the Asian crisis in 1997 and 1998, where they had generated immense resentment in the program countries. In particular, the very detailed conditionality of the Indonesia program, which was suspected to be part of a broader political plan to force the Suharto regime out of power, generated discussion of whether Fund conditionality had gone too far. The alternative to the outside pressure position was then formulated as a doctrine of ownership: Fund programs could really only hope to succeed if they were supported by a genuine and deep reform consensus in the country concerned.

The two contrasting visions, on the one hand of the Fund as an outside agent, the whipping boy who took the blame for the unpleasant aspects of reform and adjustment, and the Fund as a promoter of country ownership, had always alternated with each other throughout the Fund's history. Even in the late 1950s, the then managing director Per Jacobsson had told a television audience in Spain, "I must emphasize that such programs can only succeed if there is a will to succeed in the countries themselves. The Fund has always found people in these countries who know very well what needs to be done. The Fund does not impose conditions on countries; they themselves freely have come to the conclusion that the measures they arrange to take—even when they are sometimes harsh—are in the best interests of their own countries."[9] Since the Asian crisis, in response to widespread criticism of excessively intrusive conditionality, the Fund had moved back to the ownership model and did not want to be seen as a harsh imposer of austere adjustment policy.

IMF AS COORDINATOR

Third, the IMF plays a coordination role among creditors to extract concessions from them. To make debt levels sustainable, existing creditors have to be convinced and often "arm-twisted" to forgo some of or at least stretch the maturity of their debt claims. Of course, each individual creditor is reluctant to make concessions and hopes that other creditors forgive some of their claims to make the overall debt level sustainable. Strategically, each individual creditor has an incentive to wait and hold out, even though a coordinated effort by all creditors could make the debt sustainable and everyone better off. The role of the IMF is to overcome the hold-out problem by brokering a coordinated solution.

The 1980s crisis in retrospect looked easy to resolve because a relatively small number of large international banks held the debt in the form of syndicated bank loans. In the 1990s and 2000s, the development of capital markets and bond financing of sovereign debt made infeasible the 1980s-style solution of forcing lenders to make concessions and continue lending. With increased capital flows, bondholdings become increasingly dispersed. Strategic hedge funds and vulture funds showed no appetite for a coordinated debt restructuring, and the holdout problem became more severe. The IMF started to engage in a discussion of how creditors might contribute to reform programs by writing down some share of the debt.

In 1996, the G10 recommended including collective action clauses (CACs) for sovereign bond contracts that are denominated in foreign currency. CACs automatically commit all creditors to consent to a specific debt-restructuring proposal if a critical threshold of holders of the issue vote in favor. In the early 2000s, in the wake of the Asian crises, and of crises in Russia and Turkey, the issue arose again. In 2001, First Deputy Managing Director Anne Krueger suggested a general principle procedure, treaty based, of debt reduction analogous to a domestic bankruptcy procedure, the Sovereign Debt Reduction Mechanism (SDRM). However, the proposal ran into the sand.[10] The United States preferred to rely on the market to resolve the issue.

FURTHER COMPLICATIONS

Sovereign bondholdings not only became more dispersed but the overall size of the sovereign bond market has significantly increased since the 1980s. The IMF adjusted to the new world characterized by sovereign debt crises by adopting, in 2002, a new policy of "exceptional access," significantly increasing the resources available to a single country (in proportion to its quota). This exceptional access was subordinated, however, to an assessment of the country's external debt sustainability, which had to be positive with a "high probability." In nonsystemic countries—Pakistan and Ukraine—debt maturities were extended as an accompaniment to IMF programs; for Uruguay, in 2003, there was a modest haircut in a range of 5–20 percent, depending on the security.[11] The two larger cases were Argentina and Russia, which began with unilateral defaults and where an outcome was later negotiated that provided for substantial haircuts: over 50 percent for Russia (2000) and over 70 percent for Argentina (2005).

As countries became increasingly integrated in (and sometimes dependent on) global capital markets, restoration of market access became a primary objective of the Fund's programs and a major benchmark to judge their efficiency. In turn, restoration of market access required that debt be judged sustainable by existing and future creditors. Otherwise, the efforts made and the resources spent would have been in vain. If the debt was judged unsustainable, any program would have to include an element of debt reduction.

Moreover, open and active capital markets create new channels of financial contagion between countries. This became a concern when dealing with sovereign debt, as it was feared that debt reduction in one country would trigger broader systemic consequences for other economies. That is why the trial balloons on debt reduction as a part of Fund programs had occurred in nonsystemic countries. These missing elements in the 2002 framework came back to haunt the Fund when it had to deal with Greece in 2010, and ultimately led to the introduction of the systemic exemption undermining the debt-sustainability criterion.

The IMF's Initial Involvement in the Euro Crisis

When the debate about the involvement of the Fund in the European crisis began, the IMF looked as if it were in one of the periodic down phases of its long history. Capital markets were working very well, large amounts of capital were flowing internationally, and the demand for Fund programs had fallen. As one of the principal ways the IMF finances its activity is through interest on lending, it looked as if the Fund was no longer able to pay for itself. When French president Sarkozy nominated the socialist economist and politician Dominique Strauss-Kahn as the tenth IMF managing director in 2007, he probably thought that he was sending his main political rival to a position in which he was bound to fail. Strauss-Kahn's first major task in Washington in fact was to downsize the institution dramatically.

With the onset of the global financial crisis, the IMF again became a central institution in the discussion of global economic cooperation and coordination. A $15.7 billion IMF program for Hungary that was concluded in November 2008 helped to prevent a contagious crisis that for some time threatened to spill over to Austria and then to other European countries via the banking system, and that might have constituted a replay of the Central European causes of the Great Depression. At the G20 crisis summit in London in April 2009, the world's major countries agreed on a doubling of the IMF's resources and a governance reform that would give a greater weight to dynamic emerging economies. The IMF also pushed for a coordinated fiscal stimulus after November 2008 to counteract the sharp contraction of the world economy.[12]

While the Hungarian rescue operation looked like a major success and did not seem any different from the IMF's normal mode of operation, when similar difficulties appeared one year later in Greece, a member of the euro area, everything was more complicated. The euro area is a monetary union, and it was natural for euro countries to consider themselves as a single entity in the IMF. True, individual countries are, legally, the sole members of the Fund. The ECB has an observer at the board, with no voting rights. Ambitious proposals to create a "euro chair" never materialized.

Euro countries are dispersed among many constituencies, pooling their influence and voting power with non-euro or even non-European countries (Ireland is part of the Canadian constituency). The IMF executive board comprises twenty-four members. Most are elected by countries regrouped into constituencies. The largest five countries (by quota size)—the United States, Japan, Germany, France, and the United Kingdom—appointed their own executive director until the implementation of a quota reform in 2016. The privilege perpetuated the perception of European overrepresentation. The euro identity progressively materialized in the IMF as well as other international forums. The euro area has its own Article 4 surveillance procedure (a sort of regular economic health check) that progressively took more importance and drew more administrative resources than those of member countries. Inside the G20, euro countries tried to appear as a bloc, resisting any discussion of the external position and current account of individual countries (which suited Germany well as its surplus was diluted in the overall balance of the euro area).

When the Greek fiscal crisis first erupted after the October 2009 election, all policy makers assumed that they could find a European solution. For some time, the IMF contemplated a European program rather than a specific Greek action, but legally there was no way of doing this, as neither the EU nor the euro area were members of the Fund (and hence ineligible to conclude Fund programs or draw Fund resources). In December 2009, the Greek government committed to a stability program with the European Commission that was submitted in January 2010. The official line in Brussels was that financial assistance from the Fund was not "appropriate or welcome."[13] This was echoed by major policy makers such as Axel Weber, the Bundesbank president, quoted by the *Financial Times* on December 9 as saying, "Within the stability and growth pact there is no role for the IMF—rightly."[14] A few days earlier, the Greek minister of finance had declared that it was "out of the question" that Greece would turn to the IMF. He later recalled that Sarkozy had said very emphatically that "I will never allow the IMF in Europe."[15]

That stance became harder to keep as market pressure intensified, financing conditions deteriorated, doubts surfaced over the reliability of Greek public finance data, and the necessity of ample external support became apparent. The first German response—coming from Finance Minister Wolfgang Schäuble—was to call for a European Monetary Fund. Angela Merkel shifted her position in part because she thought that the IMF would come from the outside and be a tough cop, imposing strict conditions that the Europeans on their own might not be able to agree. "Europe in and of itself is not in a position to solve such a problem," according to Merkel. "The IMF simply has more experience."[16] In addition, involving the IMF provided a bolster against a possible challenge to the Greek rescue in the German Constitutional Court.[17]

Initially, France and the ECB resisted the German call for IMF involvement. Greece, on the other hand, seemed to be happy. Petros Christodoulou, the head of Greece's public-debt authority, argued that the involvement of the IMF "eliminates the default risk and the refinancing risk and definitely raises the credibility of the government's austerity package."[18] In fact, as the IMF's MD Strauss-Kahn later revealed, the Greek prime minister had been talking to him in secret about involving the IMF since November or December 2009, and Strauss-Kahn had a team briefing the Greeks on how to deal with Europe: "All that because the Greeks themselves wished an intervention of the IMF even if [Prime Minister George] Papandreou for political reasons would not say that."[19]

Strauss-Kahn had obviously wanted to get involved. He had strong ideas about what was needed to save Europe, and he also wanted to show how active the IMF could be and how he was presiding over a "new IMF." At a policy speech at the Brookings Institution, where he laid out his vision for a new IMF, he began by quoting Keynes: "At the end of his magnum opus, *The General Theory*, Keynes stated the following: 'The outstanding faults of the economic society in which we live are its failure to provide for full employment and its arbitrary and inequitable distribution of wealth and incomes.'" He went on to conclude that "employment and equity are building blocks of economic stability and prosperity, of political stability and peace."[20] Strauss-Kahn wanted the IMF to be in the loop and indeed at the center of any discussion of the world economy. He consistently pushed for significant support for Greece and was very confident in his ability to influence Germany.

The Fund program for Greece turned out to be absolutely extraordinary. Although the IMF was providing only 30 percent of the financing, or €30 billion, that amounted to 3,212 percent of Greek quota, the largest Fund program ever in relation to quota (by comparison, the largest Asian program in 1998 for Korea, the previous record holder, had been under 2,000%).

The Fund circumvented its own requirement of debt sustainability, a framework that had been imposed in 2003 in the aftermath of the East Asian and Argentine programs, when a widespread criticism held that the Fund had exceeded its mandate. Taking into account the special circumstance that Greece was part of a monetary union, the IMF introduced a *systemic exemption* (a code word for the risk of contagion inside the euro area) that in reality waived any condition related to debt. Thus, as requested by European authorities, the first Greek program did not comprise any debt reduction. This exemption was very hard to accept by the board and the membership. It was the first time that the Fund dramatically changed a key element of its lending framework without prior deliberation and to fit the specific constraint of a program.

When the IMF executive board discussed the program on May 9, 2010, all the representatives of emerging markets (as well as Switzerland) voiced severe reservations. As the subsequently leaked minutes revealed,

> The exceptionally high risks of the program were recognized by staff itself, in particular in its assessment of debt sustainability. . . . Several chairs (Argentina, Brazil, India, Russia, and Switzerland) lamented that the program has a missing element: it should have included debt restructuring and Private Sector Involvement (PSI) to avoid, according to the Brazilian Executive Director (ED), "a bailout of Greece's private sector bondholders, mainly European financial institutions." The Argentine ED was very critical at the program, as it seems to replicate the mistakes (i.e., unsustainable fiscal tightening) made in the run up to the Argentina's crisis of 2001. Much to the "surprise" of the other European EDs, the Swiss ED forcefully echoed the above concerns about the lack of debt restructuring in the program, and pointed to the need for resuming the discussions on a Sovereign Debt Restructuring Mechanism. The Swiss ED (supported by Australia, Brazil, Iran) noted that staff had "silently" changed in the paper (i.e., without a prior approval by the board) the criterion No. 2 of the exceptional access policy, by extending it to cases where there is a "high risk of international systemic spillover effects."[21]

But at the time, there was substantial pressure from the management, and from the United States as well as the big European governments, to agree. The first deputy managing director, the American John Lipsky, bullied the meeting with the words, "Let me be clear on a couple of things. There is no Plan B. There is Plan A, and a determination to make Plan A succeed, and this is it."[22]

As noted by the IMF Independent Evaluation Office in 2012, the systemic exception seems to have continued to be justified at each review, although the risks of contagion declined somewhat as more Greek government debt shifted to official hands.[23]

Obviously, the systemic exception stemmed from the absolute opposition of European authorities—especially the ECB—to consider any form of debt restructuring. In the eyes of many of the Fund staff, it considerably undermined the program's credibility. That skepticism leaked immediately after the board's decision, contributing to a further loss of confidence and negative market dynamics.

The IMF had to share the definition of conditionality with other European actors that did not pursue the same objectives and did not possess the appropriate expertise to the same degree. The Fund's finances and reputation were engaged while it had only partial control over the programs, and that made failure, when it came, more difficult to accept and absorb.

The IMF and the Troika

From the start, it was agreed that country programs would be constructed in a partnership between the European Commission and the IMF, with contributions from the ECB. The troika was born from this cooperation. Bureaucratic tensions inevitably arose between the three but did not constitute the main source of difficulty. The formal troika arrangements worked reasonably well. They obviously introduced an additional layer of complexity: positions had to be agreed upon between troika members before being presented to program countries. There was also an asymmetry of expertise: the IMF was very experienced in adjustment programs and conditionality, but the European Commission was on a steep learning curve. Even when visions were not significantly different (such as structural reform), overlap of competences caused complications. To quote from a later IMF staff report on the Greek program, "From the Fund's perspective, the EC, with the focus of its reforms more on compliance with EU norms than on growth impact, was not able to contribute much to identifying growth-enhancing structural reforms. In the financial sector, the ECB had an obvious claim to take the lead, but was not expert in bank supervision where the Fund had specialist knowledge."[24]

That sentence points to the real source of difficulty: the three members of the troika had fundamentally different mandates and objectives. The IMF, concerned with restoring viability and growth, wanted to take a rather pragmatic view, whereas the Commission was bound in its approach by specific rules. Moreover, in its financing activities (not in surveillance), the IMF is "genetically" oriented toward saving one particular country and may not be inclined to internalize the needs of the broader system. This was exactly the opposite from the ECB, whose only concern was to preserve the euro area from an irresistible—and lethal—systemic shock.

Strauss-Kahn always also knew that although he would like to push the Fund into the leadership position on European issues, it needed to take a backseat in the troika and provide only one-third of the funding. He told Commission president Barroso, "I want to be the leader myself. I cannot, because for political and logical reasons, I cannot take over the ECB. We will give technical assistance, and some financial resources, but you are leading."[25] As a consequence of its need to play down its leadership, inside the troika, the IMF faced three big fights: fiscal policy, banking, and the question of debt reduction.

First Fight within the Troika: Structural Conditionality

The first tussle with the European Commission occurred over fiscal policy and, to a lesser extent, over the character of structural conditionality. On fiscal policy, the IMF was more progressive in its approach to consolidation and was perceived as being softer in the program countries. IMF staff members enjoyed being heroes rather than villains of a reform drama. The European Commission was mainly preoccupied with the application of its fiscal rules (and the negotiation of delays to reach the 3% deficit target). The ECB was even tougher: personal factors may have played a role here, as the ECB's chief economist, the hardline German Jürgen Stark, was mainly in charge of this aspect of policy. The IMF could not efficiently make its case because it was mired in an academic debate between researchers on the level of fiscal multipliers (the IMF argued that they were higher than expected, so fiscal consolidation should be more moderate and stimulus might prove more efficient). The fiscal debate provoked German anger, and a clear policy framework did not emerge. That clash followed another IMF "transgression" when its Research Department, and in particular the IMF's chief economist Olivier Blanchard, pushed for a 4 percent inflation target as a way of giving monetary policy more leverage. This was another move that was very poorly received in Germany, where inflation worries are a major part of the political consensus.

Structural policy was also a problem, as the IMF and the European Commission did not have the same priorities. The IMF took a hard line on structural reforms, and the ECB liked its toughness. The conciliation of the different positions of the troika resulted in numerous requirements—a shopping list—most of which could not be met.

Second Fight within the Troika: The Banking Sector

A second fight for the IMF, on the banking sector, was fought against all the EU institutions. The IMF was systematically more pessimistic—and vocal—about the situation of the euro banking sector. Its attitude was judged irresponsible in Europe, particularly during the summer of 2011 when there were market pressures on the banking sector, especially on French banks. There was a substantial European pushback in response to the IMF's call for a substantial recapitalization of banks seeking private resources first and, if necessary, also public funds.[26] Overall, the IMF was seen in Frankfurt as amateurish, stirring market volatility, and very much under US influence. Most of the IMF's dire predictions on the euro banking sector, especially in Spain, did not immediately materialize. There was a dilemma: it was true that European banks were not in a good shape, but the IMF continually pointed to that fact without having the authority to fix it. This stance on the part of the IMF could in consequence be perceived as heightening uncertainty and pessimism, and thus holding back the possibility for growing out of the situation.

The IMF relationship with the ECB was fraught with ambiguity. The IMF customarily builds programs around a fiscal and monetary policy mix. Here, it had no control over any aspect of monetary policy. Nevertheless, both the IMF and the ECB shared the same philosophy and approach to conditionality. The ECB proved ready to fill ex post any financing gap resulting from program failures, through relaxation of collateral policies and growth in Emergency Liquidity Assistance (ELA). In effect, the gaps were financed through an expansion of TARGET2 balances, which the ECB argued served monetary policy and not financing purposes, a position that triggered a ferocious debate in Germany. But, ex ante, the ECB fiercely resisted any attempt to get its collateral and other policies involved in discussions or monitoring by the IMF.

Third Fight within the Troika: Treatment of Debt

The biggest fight in the troika was over the treatment of debt. The ECB permanently resisted any attempt by the IMF to promote sovereign debt restructuring. From the beginning, there were strong tensions within the IMF, as the European Department, under the former Polish prime minister Marek Belka, was close to its "client" and ruled out debt restructuring, while the counsel general, Sean Hagan, who had extensive involvement in the saga of Argentine debt, and above all the influential Strategy Policy and Review Department under Reza Moghadem pressed that bondholders should be bailed in. IMF staff were also concerned that if there were to be a debt restructuring, a very large firewall would be needed for the rest of Europe as a protection against the financial damage following debt write-off. Extraordinarily, just a few days after the IMF executive board approved the Greek program, Strauss-Kahn called in the alternate executive director from Greece, Panagotis Roumeliotis, and told him that there was indeed an urgent need for debt restructuring, perhaps as early as September 2010.[27] By July 2011, the IMF staff paper on euro-area policies in effect warned that the debt level was unsustainable and that the reform policies were not working:

> The focus should be on strong program implementation, with sufficient proceeds from privatization, adequate financing from other official sources on terms supporting debt sustainability, and private sector based solutions to banking problems (such as cross-border takeovers). This strategy, however, might be difficult to reach given the scale of the targeted adjustment, its possible social repercussions, as well as unfavorable financial market circumstances.[28]

Conflict also arose on bank debt, in discussions of the Irish program, and, more specifically, on the treatment of unsecured senior creditors who held around €19 billion. Compared to the volume of the program (€85 billion), the amounts were not decisive. But the debate was very fierce and public up to the emergency summit on July 21, 2011, pitting the ECB against the IMF. After the summit the ECB accepted the political decision that had been in favor of debt restructuring in Greece.

The IMF increasingly and openly urged the European Union to use the bailout fund (the ESM) to reduce the large bank debt that the government had assumed in the course of the blanket bank guarantee given—almost certainly unwisely—by the Irish government in September 2008. The guarantee covered all bank loans, deposits, bonds, and other liabilities. At the time, the Irish press commented that senior bank executives must have been "rubbing their hands with glee."[29] A few years later, tapes of the dramatic and expletive-ridden conversations of the leading bankers were revealed, with the chief executive of Anglo-Irish Bank David Drumm explaining the negotiating strategy with the central bank to his senior colleague John Bowe: "Get into the f**king simple speak: 'We need the moolah, you have it, so you're going to give it to us and when would that be?' We'll start there."[30] The Dublin government had to pay €31 billion over ten years to cover the cost of the promissory notes issued to cover the cost of winding up the Anglo-Irish Bank. In September 2012, the IMF announced in its review of the Irish program that "Material investments in Irish banks by the ESM (European Stability Mechanism) could transform the public debt outlook, cut the bank-sovereign link, and cement a needed win for Europe."[31] That was not to be. Ultimately, the ECB won as the US Treasury reportedly changed its position and stopped supporting the IMF.

The IMF position on Greek debt, which looked unsustainable by all calculations in the later stages of the crisis, evolved slowly. In April 2011, when the German finance minister dropped hints that Greek debt should be restructured, Strauss-Kahn denied in public that this was needed: "I understand how painful it is for the Greek people but I think Greece will make it."[32] On May 6, 2011, European finance ministers and Trichet discussed the idea of a debt restructuring in a secret meeting in Senningen Castle in Luxembourg, but both the ECB and the IMF were officially opposed. Strauss-Kahn privately had developed a completely different view at this point and was preparing to push for restructuring, but then a completely unanticipated event altered the course of Fund negotiations.

A Change in the IMF's Leadership

The negotiations for a second Greek IMF agreement became more complex because of the arrest of Strauss-Kahn in a New York airport on a charge of sexual assault. He was about to fly to Europe to convince Chancellor Merkel to move on the debt issue. In the Brussels negotiations over the Greek program, the IMF was represented by a new and very young deputy managing director, Nemat Shafik, who had only been in office for a few weeks. The first deputy managing director John Lipsky stayed in Washington but found it much harder than Strauss-Kahn had to bring the executive board into line. He insisted that the IMF could not agree to a new program before Europe reached an agreement. Herman Van Rompuy complained of "a lack of leadership in solving the Greek crisis."[33] In his first interview after he had resigned and returned in disgrace to France in September 2011, Strauss-Kahn said that euro countries should have "cut their losses" and rescued Greece early in the process.[34]

If Strauss-Kahn was enthusiastic about the prospect of helping Europe, a considerable part of the IMF board was not. Well before the crisis, Europe's role and place in the IMF had been a matter of difficulties and conflict. Strauss-Kahn had only been appointed in November 2007 after a near rebellion by emerging markets economies' representatives, who argued forcefully for the appointment of a very popular former first deputy managing director, Stanley Fischer, who had been born in Zambia (although he was a US and Israeli citizen). The atmosphere was poisoned by the discussion on quotas and the composition of the board. Europe's quotas (the EU countries had 32% of the votes in the Fund) were judged excessive, and all the quota negotiations occurring during the global financial crisis were implicitly aimed at reducing Europe's share. There was outrage at the number of chairs held by Europe in the executive board (in earlier discussions, the United States had threatened not to allow a "routine" expansion of the board from twenty-two to twenty-four chairs to extract a commitment by Europe to reduce its number of chairs by two). On both grounds, Europe was seen as overrepresented and blocking the emerging world from taking its legitimate place. On this question, there was a remarkable convergence between the staff (which wanted to regain credibility in Asia), the United States, and the big emerging markets economies. An agreement on new quota shares was painfully achieved in the G20 in 2009–2010, but its ratification by the United States was delayed by congressional politics.

The large emerging markets economies (EMEs) and some advanced countries could not understand why the second-richest and most integrated area in the world needed to go to the IMF for support. This was the "old world," defending its past position but still very rich in comparison to most of the members, showing an inability to deal with an internal crisis and coming for help. The IMF involvement in Europe was even more difficult to stomach for EMEs when it became clear that significant amounts would be drawn by Greece, in violation of the principle of equality of treatment that, formally at least, was supposed to inspire the Fund's actions.

Europe's ability to still defend its hegemonic position was vividly illustrated by the election of a new managing director in June 2011, on the eve of the conclusion of the second Greek program. Europe's arguments were intellectually indefensible. For sixty years, it had claimed the top job as the major contributor to the IMF's resources. Now, reversing that logic, Europeans let it be said that they must head the Fund because they were beneficiaries of the biggest IMF program ever. EMEs could not exploit the inherent intellectual weakness of the European case, however, as they proved unable to rally behind a single candidate. Agustin Carstens, the Mexican central bank governor and former IMF deputy managing director, did not elicit support from Latin American countries because he was perceived as too close to the United States. China seemed uninterested in putting up an Asian candidate. By contrast, all Europeans (including the United Kingdom) were able to rally behind French finance minister Christine Lagarde in less than a week in a rare and very efficient show of unity (even though there was a shadow of possible judicial proceedings in relation to a French corruption scandal hanging over her). US support, according to the informal power-sharing arrangement with Europe, was enough to ensure election, and Lagarde quickly also garnered the votes of China and Russia. However, in private, she was still quite skeptical about the second Greek program and predicted that within three years the IMF would have to put up more money.[35]

Loss of Credibility: Muddling Through, Delayed Greek PSI

Looking back on the successive IMF programs for Greece, the Fund's staff reached a devastating conclusion in June 2013: "Market confidence was not restored, the banking system lost 30% of its deposits and the economy encountered a much deeper than expected recession with exceptionally high unemployment."[36] The fundamental problem, according to this diagnosis, was that there had been insufficient country ownership: the Greeks had not been convinced that they needed to take the necessary reforms, and such a conviction could only have emerged on the basis of a realistic approach to debt reduction. The Fund now implied that it had championed that course from the beginning, a position that was immediately rejected by the European Commission. The EU economic and monetary affairs commissioner Olli Rehn again emphasized how disastrous a debt reduction would have been at the outset of the crisis ("Europe's Lehman moment," as Rehn put it). He also acidly commented, "I don't recall the

IMF's managing director Dominique Strauss-Kahn proposing early debt restructuring, but I do recall that Christine Lagarde was opposed to it."[37]

The IMF was thus forced to muddle through in its successive debt-sustainability assessments and lost credibility in the process. PSI for Greece—which Angela Merkel and Nicolas Sarkozy agreed upon during their walk in Deauville in October 2010—was only accepted by the European authorities, especially the ECB, in July 2011 as part of the second €130 billion package, after significant delays. Private creditors were able to significantly reduce their exposure, and there was a large-scale substitution from privately held to publicly held debt. To compensate, the Fund took an increasingly tougher approach and pressured the governments into numerous concessions on their official loans.

Each program review led to either new official commitments from euro countries or softening of existing loans (through interest rate reduction and lengthening of maturities). The governments that had originally insisted on IMF involvement found themselves piling up huge official claims and other commitments to Greece. Germany alone had given €116 billion in fiscal credit to peripheral Europe and to Greece. But, in addition, there were the large claims that had accumulated in the ECB as a result of TARGET2. German officials were stunned when confronted with the amounts of official money necessary to enhance the Greek debt exchange in 2012.

Other initiatives to draw the IMF into a solution of the European crisis faltered. At Cannes in November 2011, France suggested that the central banks in the Eurosystem might pawn their total foreign exchange reserves of 50–60 billion euros to the trust of the European crisis fund in the form of special drawing rights (SDRs) at the IMF. The Bundesbank issued a terse statement: "We know this plan and we reject it."[38] In a letter to Merkel, Bundesbank president Jens Weidmann had argued that using foreign reserves would be financial trickery and would only make markets more nervous. The Bundesbank controlled Germany's reserves, including the SDRs, and could not allow a bad precedent to be set. Merkel only found out about the Bundesbank letter at Cannes, and she felt cornered by the other European leaders and by US President Obama. According to some news reports, this confrontation produced the moment when she broke into tears. Obama laid on the pressure: "Germany has one-fourth of all [euro-area] SDR allocations. . . . If you have all the EU countries together but not Germany, ... it starts losing credibility." To this, Merkel responded, "That is not fair. I cannot decide in lieu of the Bundesbank. I cannot do that." And then she added, "I am not going to commit suicide."[39] There would be no use of the IMF.

The IMF programs—particularly for Greece—left an unpleasant aftermath and discredited the Fund. The results for Ireland and Portugal might be seen as more satisfactory, in that the countries regained market access. In the case of Portugal, this may have been due more to the general world environment of low interest rates and the aftermath of Draghi's "whatever it takes" speech.

It was clear early in the implementation that most of the assumptions about growth and debt sustainability were overly optimistic and that targets would be missed by significant margins. In a few weeks, Greece's situation deteriorated, with capital outflows, deteriorating growth, debt scenarios losing any credibility, and constant revisions in the program and debt-sustainability assessments. Figure 14.1 shows the way the IMF staff recalculated downward the projected development of the Greek economy in the original package (standby arrangement in IMF terminology or SBA) whenever it came up for review and compares the projections with the actual dismal outcome. The problem was one that the IMF staff gradually began to think was at the heart of the difficulties: to regain competitiveness, Greece needed some deflation to reduce costs, but deflation raised the real value of debt and made debt levels increasingly unsustainable—the "Devaluation Dilemma" we described in chapter 6. Several IMF officials began to draw parallels with the debt deflation that Irving Fisher, in 1933, had found to be at the root of the Great Depression.[40] The implication was that the IMF should have been more straightforward about the need for debt restructuring in 2010 and that it had lost an opportunity to have a positive influence on European developments.

For Europeans, the lesson of Greece was clear. For the creditor countries, the IMF had at first appeared as a way of exerting increased leverage. The large European governments tried to use the international institution to strengthen their own approach to crisis management. Germany had originally turned to the IMF because it wanted to be sure that discipline was enforced with sufficient rigor, but the IMF started to push for a different approach to the debt crisis. At a later stage, France proposed

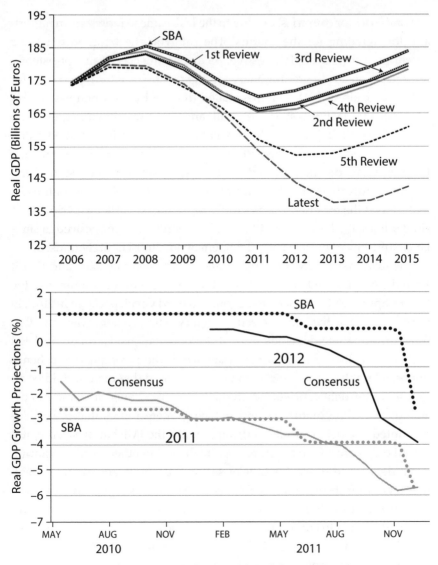

FIGURE 14.1. Real Greek GDP Level and Growth Projections
(Source: IMF, "Greece: Ex Post Evaluation")

to use the IMF as a vehicle to "leverage" the EFSF: first, by developing bilateral contributions to increase IMF resources, and, second, by trying to use the SDR to directly increase the EFSF lending capacity. The initiative failed as the Bundesbank held a position on the IMF governing body that could block the SDR proposal.

For the debtor countries, turning to the IMF came to represent an import-ant downgrading for the country. The catalytic effect turned out to be absent or, rather, strongly negative. As a consequence, Spain consistently refused to consider a precautionary arrangement. The reform programs for Italy and Spain in 2011 were negotiated directly by the Commission and ECB, with no IMF involvement at all, and there was in consequence no formal ESM/EFSF program. In November 2011, the IMF instituted a Pre-cautionary and Liquidity Line (PLL) facility, as a way of tackling the stigma issue, but this did not succeed in making the idea of the use of Fund resources attractive to potentially crisis-hit countries. On the contrary, it looked as if the experience was simply repeating an earlier experiment on similar lines, the Flexible Credit Line (FCL), which was introduced in simi-lar circumstances in 1999 and which remained almost entirely unused.

The idea that the IMF's initial strategy had been mistaken and that it should have insisted on debt reduction as a condition dominated the Fund's approach to the need to negotiate a third Greek package in 2015, in the aftermath of the Syriza election victory. The problem was now that three incompatible demands framed the negotiations. Germany insisted that without IMF consent a new plan would be incomplete and hence impossible; at the same time, Germany demanded that there should be no official sector debt cancellation (though it seemed open to some discus-sion of extending maturities and reducing interest rates that in practice amounted to a debt cancellation); and, finally, the IMF emphasized that it would only agree if the program was "realistic," in other words, requiring some debt write down for official sector (European government) debt, though not for its own claims on Greece. At the end of June 2015, Greece defaulted on its debt payment to the IMF, though eventually it was paid.

The IMF tried to cut through this Gordian knot by releasing an analysis on July 2, 2015, as the negotiations were entering a critical phase, which elaborately documented the case that Greek debt was not sustainable. The message was cast in terms of a presentation of Greek reform failures: there had not been enough structural reform to spur growth; not enough assets had been privatized to pay off outstanding government debt; and the Greek government was unable to undertake sufficient fiscal austerity. The European governments tried to suppress the report, but the Fund staff worked hard to convince Christine Lagarde that she should stand up to the German pressure to agree to a program without (official sector) debt relief.[41]

At the beginning of 2016, the IMF formally ended the systemic exemption that had been the basis of the Greek program. The Fund staff had been unhappy with the process that seemed to allow for Fund programs in circumstances when excessive debt made for a failure of the program. But some countries had resisted, as they did not want to rock the boat and let the IMF leave Europe. The resolution of the clash came from a political process, as a result of negotiations in the US Congress, where the Republican majority was persuaded by some US economists, in particular by Stanford's John Taylor, to insert this measure (rather than some domestic content, such as ending Obamacare) into the legislative package that increased the IMF quotas in response to the global financial crisis. Taylor had first floated the idea as a *Wall Street Journal* article.[42]

The IMF was not sorry to see the end of the exemption. In a devastating retrospective judgment, it acknowledged that the bending of the usual and traditional IMF rules had delayed "remedial measures risks impairing the member's prospects for success and undermining safeguards for the Fund's resources."[43] It also increased private sector risk by subordinating private claims to Fund credit, and it had thus not achieved its stated goal of minimizing contagion. In announcing the end of the exemption, the IMF also acknowledged the difficulty of making the calculation of debt sustainability and allowed for a new fudging of the issue: it examined the conditions that might arise "when a member's debt is assessed to be sustainable but not with high probability, requiring a definitive debt restructuring could incur unnecessary costs."[44] There might be a need for reprofiling the debt: maturity debt would be put on a standstill and not repaid until a sustainable path is figured out. In an ungainly sentence, the IMF set out a roadmap for such a situation, in which other public sector institutions (i.e., the European Union or the member states) would need to bear a higher part of the risk: "In such situations, it would be appropriate for the Fund to grant exceptional access so long as the member also receives financing from other sources during the program on a scale and terms such that the policies implemented with program support and associated financing, although they may not restore projected debt sustainability with a high probability, improve debt sustainability and sufficiently enhance the safeguards for Fund resources."[45] By 2016 the Fund was outraging not only the creditor governments but also the debtor government. Tsipras responded to a leaked discussion of the possibility of an

IMF-induced bankruptcy with the accusation that the IMF was planning to "politically destabilize Europe."[46]

Why did the Fund look to push for confrontation with the European governments in 2015 and 2016? It could, of course, be a case of a victory of solid economic reasoning; but there was also a sense of growing frustration stemming from the increasingly vocal non-European membership of the Fund, especially Asia and particularly China. In 2015, relations with China looked more and more critical as the Chinese economy slowed down and financial turbulence hit. The experience of the euro crisis reinforced the criticism that this was an excessively Europe-focused institution that had not successfully or completely adapted to the major structural changes of the world economy. The prospect that as official credit replaced private credit and as the discussion turned more and more to debt write-offs, pressure would develop to haircut IMF as well as European government support credits and threaten the whole underlying concept of the Fund as a credit cooperative, whose claims had absolute seniority. The aftermath of the euro discussion accelerated the move of large emerging market economies to look for alternatives to the Bretton Woods institutions, such as the New Development Bank (NDB) (popularly called the BRICS bank) to finance infrastructure and sustainable development projects, as an alternative to the World Bank, and a \$100 billion Contingent Reserve Arrangement (CRA) to tide over members in financial difficulties, as an alternative to the IMF. By the time the institutions came to mark their seventieth birthday in 2014, no one thought it an anniversary worth celebrating anymore. The Fund had been born in the last stages of a great European war, and it looked as if another European quasi war (this time a war of ideas) was threatening its effectiveness and its influence.

15

European Central Bank (ECB)

When Mario Draghi rose to give a speech at the Global Investment Conference in London on July 26, 2012, his audience did not really expect any surprises. Market tension was extreme, with capital and deposit flights from Spain and Italy threatening at panic levels. His rather anodyne prepared remarks contained nothing new. But then, reading from hand-written notes, Draghi uttered the two famous sentences: "Within our mandate, the ECB is ready to do whatever it takes to preserve the euro. And believe me, it will be enough."[1]

Draghi's two sentences proved a game changer for the markets, the politics, and the dynamics of the crisis. No specific measures were announced at that time, and even later in the year when the ECB unveiled its Outright Monetary Transactions (OMT) program to buy bonds of European countries with a reform program in place, no OMT measures were actually carried out. It looked like an illusion, but it was stunningly effective. Within weeks of Draghi's remarks, Italian and Spanish spreads had fallen dramatically, and the OMT program was seen as marking the end of the euro crisis. A few weeks after the July conference, a number of analysts and politicians, somewhat prematurely, proclaimed that the crisis was over. This turn in sentiment provided an obvious illustration of the ECB's power and its unique ability to shape events. Political leaders had repeatedly said that they would do everything to save the euro, but the markets knew that they couldn't, and any positive market impact evaporated within days—or in some cases hours. But when a central banker said exactly the same words, the markets knew that the promise was credible.

Central banks had in fact become the stars of the global financial crisis. They knew they needed to respond decisively and innovatively to problems that could not easily be tackled by governments, finance ministries, and politicians. In the aftermath of the collapse of Lehman Brothers in September 2008, the US administration and the Congress were paralyzed by the upcoming presidential election, and consequently the government lacked the possibility to act. But the Federal Reserve System could be very decisive. It injected liquidity into the banking system. The New York Fed intervened in a very unorthodox way to prop up a systemically vital financial institution whose collapse would have destroyed the global financial system: it lent AIG $85 billion in return for 80 percent of its stock as well as providing $20.9 billion in the commercial credit program and a $38 billion facility providing liquidity for the company's securities. Federal Reserve chairman Ben Bernanke was explicit about how a historical lesson drove the policy response. As he put it, "History teaches us that government engagement in times of severe financial crisis often arrives late, usually at a point at which most financial institutions are insolvent or nearly so."[2] The theoretical point is that monetary policy can shift expectations about future and, hence, current asset values. That affects the question of the solvency or insolvency of agents. In a world of multiple equilibria, the central bank can in the short term bring agents back into a good equilibrium. Monetary policy appears as very powerful mechanisms to restore short-run growth prospects. In the longer run, the extent to which they can affect overall growth rates is more restricted.

In the course of the crisis, the ECB remade itself as an institution. To emphasize this change better, this chapter starts by describing the ECB before the crisis: its institutional design, its philosophy, and its mechanics. The following section then describes the ECB at the onset of the crisis: its reaction to the 2008 financial crisis and the political pressures (notably at Deauville) that shaped the euro crisis. These developments brought a political involvement for the ECB via the so-called troika, and the third section of the chapter examines the new problems posed by policy conditionality.

The ECB also changed—because it needed to change—its approach to monetary policy, lending (or issuing money) against a much wider range of securities through numerous asset purchase and lending programs. In a sense, it changed the European definition of money. This chapter thus also covers the debates about the implementation of new bond-purchasing programs. In particular, it looks at how monetary policy was influenced by the old differences in national approaches outlined earlier in the book, in which Germans were worried about conducting a quasi-fiscal policy through monetary means, and the French were inclined to think that that was just what was needed—just what the doctor prescribed. It also examines the move of the ECB into a completely new area of banking supervision, a function that before the crisis had been managed by some (but not all) central banks and where again there was a substantial initial German-French disagreement about the appropriateness of that function.

This chapter examines the following questions:

- How did the ECB's institutional structure and economic philosophy affect its decision-making capacity? Did it evolve or adjust to answer the complexity of the crisis?
- How did the ECB's approach to monetary policy change with the euro crisis, notably in light of the German-French dichotomy?
- Which tools did the ECB develop to implement its decisions during the euro crisis? Was the ECB forced into developing these new tools? Which debates did their creation spur?
- The ECB was soon forced into banking supervision. How important was such a move? Who pushed it, and who opposed it? What were the reasons?

The ECB before the Crisis: Institutional Design and Philosophy

The ECB as an Institution

The ECB is an unusual central bank in that, unlike the Fed, the Bank of Japan, or the Bundesbank, it does not have a single government as a counterpart. Indeed, until the new EU Lisbon Treaty came into force in October 2010, in the middle of the financial crisis, it was not even, legally speaking, an institution of the European Union. However, like other modern central banks, it used operations with government securities (issued by euro-member countries) as a standard tool of monetary operations.

The ECB is, arguably, the most powerful central bank in the world. Its independence is not simply a result of a domestic law but is enshrined in an international treaty. The bank is managed, on a day-to-day basis, by an executive board of six persons (including a president and a vice president), all appointed by the European Council for a single eight-year term. The executive board, together with the governors of all the national central banks of the euro area, forms the governing council, which makes the policy decisions and meets twice a month. Although appointed, directly or indirectly, by national governments, members participate as individuals, not as representatives of specific countries. At its first meeting, the head of the German Bundesbank, Hans Tietmeyer, a sturdily built man with a somewhat bullying manner, made the point of insisting that members sit in the alphabetical order of their names, rather than of the countries whose central banks they headed. The council members are legally prohibited from accepting instructions from any political authority (and Trichet had built a reputation rejecting any attempt by the French president to influence ECB decisions). All members of the council are equal. Except for so-called patrimonial matters, affecting the distribution of profits and losses, decisions are taken with a simple majority on the basis of "one man one vote."[3] In practice, in the early and successful years, there were few votes, and decision making operated by a process of consensus, largely built by the president.

Economic Philosophy

The ECB entered the euro crisis basking in the glory of stability and success. The euro's tenth anniversary had been celebrated in Frankfurt with appropriate restraint and modesty but also with a sense of pride and accomplishment. Even some of its strongest critics saluted the single currency as a remarkable success. The ECB's representatives—and at the fore its president Jean-Claude Trichet—were most proud of their record in delivering an inflation performance superior to even the historic legacy of the stability-focused German Bundesbank.

Perfectly in line with the ECB's primary mandate of price stability, inflation had averaged 1.97 percent during the euro's first decade. This illustrates a defining factor of the ECB's economic principles: its primary objective, as written in the Treaty on the Functioning of the European Union, is to maintain price stability. This contrasts with the US Fed, for example, which has a dual mandate of both price and economic stability. This focus on price stability is a clear heritage from the Bundesbank, which adopted a hawkish position after the previous historical inflation episodes that Germans had experienced. Hence, historically at least, the ECB hasn't been built around the principle of stabilizing the economy beyond prices: yet, as we will see, the crisis forced the ECB toward a move in that direction. In that sense, the development of the ECB represented a compromise—a necessary one—with the most simple version of the German vision.

Another important defining factor of the ECB's economic principles is that by design it necessarily sees the euro area as one unit. Indeed, even this success at maintaining a 2 percent figure contained something of a problem: the figure is an average, with substantially higher rates in Southern Europe and lower rates in the North, as figure 15.1 illustrates.

These imbalances were not only reflected in prices but also in trade balances: while Germany, for example, ran large surpluses, southern countries often imported beyond their means—with the consequences that we know now. These heterogeneity issues were not ignored by the ECB. Almost any single policy statement issued by the governing council called for greater convergence in nominal wages and inflation rates, pointing to the increasing gap in competitiveness between core and peripheral countries. Trichet himself would regularly produce graphs highlighting the divergences in unit labor costs and growing internal imbalances. But

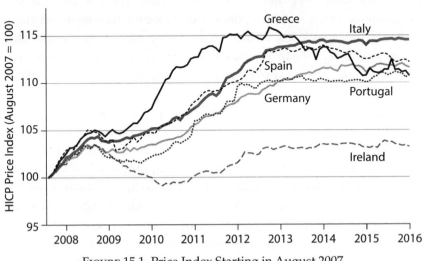

FIGURE 15.1. Price Index Starting in August 2007
(Source: Eurostat)

financial markets were working well, deficits were financed, and those calls were met with polite indifference by markets and policy makers alike.

The ECB's strategy was to extend the Bundesbank's excellent reputation as an inflation fighter to the ECB.[4] At the beginning, in 1998 the ECB set out a simple objective of price stability that was implicitly defined as a range between 0 and 2 percent. Later Otmar Issing, the first chief economist of the ECB, came from the Bundesbank and was instrumental in setting up the ECB's monetary strategy, including the two-pillar monetary policy approach. The first pillar, called *monetary analysis*, followed the approach of the Bundesbank by assigning a prominent role to money aggregates and their evolution, as compared to nominal income. While the Bundesbank had an explicit target for money growth, the ECB used a reference value that was less directly binding on policy decisions. The reason was that, with many heterogeneous countries, the relationship between income and money (the money demand) was less stable and harder to predict. The second pillar looked more like the approach followed by other major central banks. It consisted of an economic analysis largely based on a dynamic stochastic general equilibrium (DSGE) model, a large-scale model with price rigidity assumptions that allowed the governing council to look through a whole range of data sets to assess the short- and medium-term prospects for inflation. This data does contain monetary aggregates. Although, they never admitted it, and actually resisted any suggestion to that effect, ECB policy makers were following an inflation-targeting framework inside the second pillar. Also, they thought that proper attention of the first pillar to monetary developments in medium-term price movements would provide an antidote against the pitfalls of exceedingly forward-looking rules that are part of inflation (forecast) targeting.[5] The objective of targeting money growth was to ensure price stability in the short and medium term, building on the premise that in the long term the quantity theory of money holds. The reference value of the first pillar was money growth—in particular the growth of M3 (money supply, widely defined as including time and savings deposits as well as money market mutual funds). That was a series that the US Fed stopped publishing in 2006, given its preference for a focus on DSGE models.

In the 2000s, M3 growth consistently overshot projections, and, as a consequence, the prominent role of money growth in the ECB's monetary policy framework resulted in serious communication challenges. After a review of the ECB's monetary policy framework in 2003, the ECB decided on an important revision.

First, the hierarchy between the two pillars was inverted: the economic analysis became the first pillar and monetary analysis came second. Also, and more importantly, the publication of a reference value for the growth of money was abandoned. The monetary analysis was demoted to a cross-checking role. The ECB relied on the monetary analysis to extract long-run inflationary signals from monetary aggregates to cross-check the information from the economic pillar. The emphasis shifted first to credit growth, which was also seen as an early-warning indicator of financial imbalances, and then to a broad range of monetary and financial variables.[6] The search for a new approach became evident in a high-level conference organized in 2006.[7]

Finally, the ECB restated its definition of price stability. When the euro was created, the ECB had taken the initiative of quantifying its definition of price stability, which the Maastricht Treaty left to the ECB's Governing Council. It thus "took control" over that definition, whereas, for instance, in the United Kingdom that power belongs to the executive (the chancellor of the exchequer). The ECB initially decided that price stability would be achieved if inflation was below 2 percent. It was immediately confronted with a barrage of questions by economists and market participants. Did the definition imply that any number below 2 percent was acceptable? Was zero inflation consistent with price stability (the discussion of the harmonized index of consumer prices simply assumed that there would be some increase)? There was some embarrassment in Frankfurt, and for some years the ECB avoided the question. Underlying the whole debate was one fundamental issue: was the inflation objective symmetric or not? Or, put differently, would the ECB react with equal force if inflation was too low rather than too high?

Many major central banks—including the Bank of England—had adopted another definition: they referred to a range around a midpoint. For the Bank of England, it was (and still is) 2 percent with a band of 1 percent on either side. The objective was clearly symmetric, all the more so as the governor is obliged to write a letter to the chancellor if inflation rises over 3 percent or falls below 1 percent. In 2003, therefore, the ECB decided to move to more symmetry and redefined price stability as below but close to 2 percent. That formulation clearly indicated that very low inflation would not be acceptable. On the other hand, it sounded somehow awkward initially, so many self-appointed ECB watchers started to speculate on whether the (unannounced) objective was 1.8 percent or 1.9 percent. The debate progressively disappeared until 2012, when the ECB was vindicated when the Federal Reserve adopted, for the first time, a quantified definition of price stability that coincided with the 2003 ECB formulation.

An unspoken part of the ECB's philosophy became apparent during the crisis. As the only truly federal institution in the euro area, the ECB felt an ultimate, if never explicit, responsibility for keeping the monetary union intact and working. In the minds of most of its governors and its two presidents, that responsibility allows the ECB to take all necessary actions to preserve the euro as long as the primary objective of price stability is achieved. That broad interpretation of the mandate is consistent with the treaty. And, whenever they had to take exceptional and sometimes controversial actions, ECB policy makers took great care to mention they were acting "in line with our mandate." (Draghi's famous pronouncement on July 26, 2012, opened with that phrase.) This philosophy also inspired Trichet, who deeply believed that the ECB's price stability mandate included securing "monetary transmission," and that financial instability would destroy that mechanism by disrupting government debt markets.[8] Avoiding default, or even the possibility of government default, was essential in his view to ensure the cohesion of the euro area and prevent disruptive contagion. Draghi had exactly the same concern: his initiatives were bolder, although he would not justify them with the same visionary zeal as his predecessor.

For the sake of preserving the euro, both presidents embarked on very contentious programs of government bond purchases that were strongly opposed by their main shareholder, the Bundesbank. Both Trichet and Draghi felt they were perfectly in line with their mandate, which allowed them to do whatever it took to preserve the euro as long as price stability was maintained. But, of course, this was not exactly the German vision, which implicitly defined price stability in a broader context, a culture of stability that avoided any action posing future (if remote) risks to the integrity of policy making. Clearly, purchasing government debt fell into that category and should not be envisaged. That difference in the meaning of *stability* was the source of many misunderstandings, divergences, and conflicts during the course of the crisis.

The Inner Workings of the Eurosystem

The ECB is part of the Eurosystem, a network that includes the national central banks (NCBs) of member countries. Those NCBs are responsible for implementing monetary policy, and all banks still have their accounts with the Eurosystem in their home countries.

The Eurosystem is a complex structure. Although well designed, it came under strong pressure during the crisis. Some technical features and elements, up to then viewed as benign and commonplace, came to play a crucial political role and have triggered very contentious debates. Nobody had heard about "collateral eligibility" or "TARGET2 balances" before 2010. Both have been at the center of intense public discussions and difficult decisions inside the Eurosystem in 2010–2012. This section explains why and how this could happen.

One can start with the banks. Banks hold liquidity in the form of reserves deposited at the ECB in order to make payments to other banks or to face cash withdrawals. If they need more reserves, they can borrow from other banks in the interbank market. Alternatively, they can borrow from the ECB. This is called *refinancing*. In technical terms, refinancing is done through an operation called a *repo*. Economically speaking, a repo transaction is just a loan by the ECB to a bank (for a certain period of time, normally between one day and three months) against a security. The security is called collateral. When the repo expires, the bank pays back its loan and repossesses the collateral.

Two important points should be noted here. First, the ECB does not own the collateral. It does not purchase it. And, second, the ECB strictly limits its risk in the operation because if the bank fails to pay back its loan, the ECB keeps the collateral and sells it. To reduce the probability that losses will be incurred in the process, the ECB asks for a higher (sometimes much higher) value of collateral than the liquidity it provides. For instance, it may require a collateral valued at €150 to provide an amount of €100 in liquidity. The difference (in that case €50) is called a *haircut*. Government bonds, because they are deemed safe, are the most valued and frequently used collateral. So, in ordinary times, haircuts on government debt are minimal.

But these were not ordinary times, and, in many occasions, government debt in peripheral (and some core) countries came to be downgraded by rating agencies. So government bonds could not be considered as safe any-more. Technical parameters such as haircuts became vehicles for extremely important policy decisions. By deciding on which collateral it would accept—and with which haircut—the governing council could, in effect, cut off banks or, for that matter, entire countries, from access to liquidity and external finance. This was an extraordinarily powerful weapon that could only be used with great care. But choices could not be avoided. In effect, the ECB had to develop its own doctrine and framework to decide on collateral policy and its conditions. Collateral became one central support for conditionality, and, as will become clear in later sections, that conditionality was exercised with great force to the point that, at least in two cases, it led to a change of government in member countries.

When rating agencies started to downgrade many of the assets in the wake of the Lehman crisis, eligible collateral for some banks became scarce. The first response of the ECB was to lower the collateral requirements and broaden the set of possible collateral assets. For example, in the month after the Lehman failure, the rating requirement for collateral was reduced from A– to BBB–. An analogous crisis-driven radical extension of the range of securities acceptable as collateral occurred in the case of other central banks, including the Federal Reserve, and the Bank of England. In May 2010, the ECB removed any minimum standard for Greek government paper and then, in March 2011, carried this exemption over to Irish and, in July 2011, to Portuguese government debt. Instead of relying on agencies' ratings, the ECB accepted bonds from crisis countries as long as they were compliant with the troika assistance program. As the crisis continued, German commentators became increasingly critical of the softening of collateral standards.[9]

Banks in a country whose collateral was not eligible could no be refi-nanced directly from the ECB. They still had, however, an ultimate recourse. They could obtain emergency liquidity assistance (ELA) from their own central bank. Technically, ELA is, like refinancing, a repo. There are three differences. First, low-quality collateral can be accepted in ELA but not in refinancing. Second, as a consequence, the risk of ELA not being reimbursed stays with the national central banks (whereas losses coming from refinancing operations are mutualized inside the Eurosystem). And third, ELA funding is often more expensive for banks.

Still, ELA creates liquidity and could, therefore, interfere with the implementation of monetary policy. For that reason, the ECB's governing council can cap a national central bank's ELA provisioning with a two-thirds majority. Again, conditions had to be defined, and ELA became, for distressed banks and countries, an extremely powerful tool for implementing conditionality. During the most acute phase of the 2015 Greek crisis, ELA was approved on a daily basis. The ECB managed very subtly to provide the necessary liquidity to Greek banks and still keep the pressure to get an agreement on a program while studiously avoiding interference with the content of the program itself.

When implementing monetary policy, the Eurosystem is a single entity. It is composed, however, of many elements, and its architecture can be best described as a network where different entities—the ECB and the NCBs—constantly interact according to predetermined processes and rules.

The financial relationship between the ECB and national central banks is the backbone and the lifeblood of the euro. Cross-border payments between countries are ultimately settled between central banks under the TARGET2 multilateral payments system (in 2007 TARGET2 replaced the similar TARGET system).

Prior to the crisis, large sums of cross-border capital flows were channeled through the interbank market. Many banks in the periphery of Europe, such as Spain, refinanced the loans they granted short term in the interbank market, for example from a German bank. When the interbank market dried up, that source of credit dried up as well, and the Spanish bank borrowed from the Spanish central bank, the Banco d'España, instead. The German bank on the other side of the transaction parked its excess savings with the German Bundesbank. To balance the system, the Banco d'España had a liability in the settlement system (TARGET2) to the German Bundesbank.

TARGET2 claims also rise when, for example, a Greek depositor closes his account at a Greek bank and transfers the sum to a German bank. The Greek bank has to borrow from the Bank of Greece to replace the missing demand deposits, and the Bank of Greece takes a debit in the clearing system; the German bank deposits the new money with the Bundesbank, which has a clearing claim.

TARGET2 measured the extent to which the European System of Central Banks (ESCB), that is, the ECB working with the national central banks, stepped in as an intermediary. A similar buildup of central bank imbalances as with TARGET2 occurred in the United States in the interdistrict settlement account (ISA) of the Federal Reserve System after 2008, with large liabilities of the San Francisco and Richmond banks and large asset balances in New York. They are comparable to European TARGET2 imbalances in that they arose from very large movements of funds out of some commercial banks that operate across the whole of the United States but have their headquarters (and thus their financial home) in a particular place within one of the twelve Federal Reserve districts.

The development of the TARGET2 imbalances has been subject to quite varied interpretations. On the simplest level, they are a substitution of official (central bank) claims for claims that would normally be built up in the private system. Private claims always have an element of uncertainty and are subject to creditors agreeing to hold the debt of an agent who may or may not repay it, whereas the modern monetary system is built on the ability of the central bank to create absolutely secure claims. In a sense, absent any exchange rate movements, the TARGET2 imbalances took on a similar role within the euro area as the swap-line arrangement across central banks did for the international monetary system.

The accumulation of TARGET2 imbalances (see figure 15.2) would have no consequences if the Eurosystem returned to normal operations, and indeed, in the US system, the ISA balances started to decline after 2011. Importantly, however, they represented a substantial blackmail potential

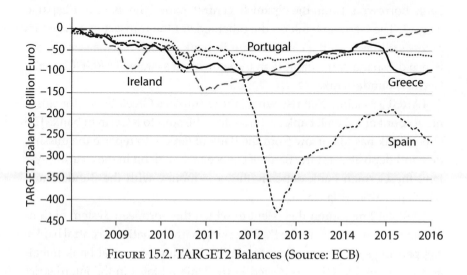

FIGURE 15.2. TARGET2 Balances (Source: ECB)

in that, if the system were to break up, they would impose major costs on the participants. It was that blackmail potential that was at the heart of the concerns of a former Bundesbank president, Helmut Schlesinger, which he then communicated to the contemporary leadership of the Bundesbank. In a series of articles published in early 2011, Hans-Werner Sinn drew public and popular attention to the previously ignored phenomenon.[10] For Sinn, the large creditor position of the Bundesbank and the debtor position of Southern central banks was a sign that something had gone deeply wrong and that Germany was vulnerable.[11] He presented the growth of the imbalances as measuring net payments orders, in other words, the part of the current account imbalance that was not financed by the private capital market. In that sense, in his view, the claims under this system were functionally the equivalent to an unconditional and publicly funded balance of payment financing. Even dramatic improvements in the sense of reductions of TARGET2 deficits, such as that which occurred in Spain after mid-2012, were interpreted not as a return of confidence to the banking sector and an increase in private deposits but as a consequence of payments made through the official bank rescue packages, that is, another form of public sector financing.[12]

At the end of 2015, the issue of national central banks purchasing large quantities of assets (outside the ECB's balance sheet) attracted attention, especially in Germany. The Banque de France increased its holdings of euro-denominated securities issued by euro-area residents (including by the national government) from under €10 billion in 2012 to €90 billion in 2014 and the Banca d'Italia from €35 billion in 2006 to €80 billion by 2014. These portfolios, operating under the Agreement on Net Financial Assets (ANFA), are part of a standard process of market management, but they could also be presented as offering NCBs a way of providing regionally limited stimulus packages.

The ECB's Early Successes and Defeats

ECB's Early Glory

When the world financial crisis erupted, the ECB was quick to act, famously allocating an exceptional €95 billion liquidity provision on August 8, 2007, at a time when the Bank of England was more hesitant and worried about moral hazard issues. The ECB followed up with a succession of increasingly bolder moves, culminating, in October 2008, in a shift to an unlimited liquidity-provision regime. That is, funds were not auctioned off to the banks that offered the best rates but granted unlimited at a fixed rate subject to collateral constraints. This extremely proactive crisis management was intended to dispel the perception of the ECB as a slow and rigid institution (as compared with the supposedly more flexible Fed). Allusions to the ECB being behind the curve, which flourished in market analyses for its first years of existence, initially faded after 2007. The ECB's approach to monetary policy indeed looked more innovative and capable of responding to the crisis than that of the Fed. The Fed faced the problem that the discount window, by which banks had access to emergency funds, seemed to carry a stigma, and banks were unwilling to declare themselves weak and in need of central bank support. By contrast, the European system extended support to banks quietly, and the support operations for individual banks were not revealed to the public. Moreover, before the crisis the Europeans worked through auctioning off liquidity potentially to 9,000 banks, while Fed operations needed to be channeled through a handful of banks, referred to as primary dealers.

But there was a wrinkle to the ECB's policy performance. In the summer of 2008, financial conditions on international markets seemed to be improving and the threat to financial stability receding. There was also a surge in commodity prices, including oil. Some commentators argued that the commodity boom was fueled by cheap central bank credit. In these circumstances, a rate increase in July 2008 looked fully justified. But it was criticized very severely in retrospect, after September 2008 and the Lehman crisis prompted everyone to rethink their views on financial stability.

The ECB's next rate increase in April 2011 was like a déjà vu moment of the 2008 rate increase. The measure also came in response to signs of economic recovery and to a continued surge of commodity prices, but it was heavily criticized in retrospect as it seemed to accentuate the divergence of government bond yields. However, at that time it came in part as a reaction to the German criticism of the ECB. The debate about the 2011 hike eventually resulted in a major rethinking about the way inflation expectations should be inferred by the central bank.

The euro area had of course not been immune from the effects of the global crisis after the Lehman collapse, and the major economies (especially

Germany as the world's largest exporter) suffered from dramatic output contractions in 2008–2009. Overall, however, in the early phase of the world crisis, Europe and the euro area had shown great resilience, and its banking sector's fragility seemed, at that stage, to be manageable.

ECB Opposition to IMF Involvement in February 2010

By January 2010, it became apparent that Greece might need financial help. Were Greece to request assistance, euro members knew they would be confronted with a major difficulty: there was no financial instrument available. As noted earlier, the no-bailout clause of the Maastricht Treaty prevented euro members from directly supporting each other. The treaty also prohibited any financial help from the EU budget to a euro country. This was ironic as non-euro members could obtain balance of payment support from the European Union. Later on, in June, a way was found around this legal restriction, allowing the EU budget to issue guarantees for borrowing up to €60 billion. But at the beginning of the Greek discussions, this legal constraint was considered absolutely binding.

Euro-area governments and their leaders were thus faced with an unpleasant choice in which some sort of innovation was required: either they reneged on the no-bailout clause, or they created new instruments, or they called for external support, which could only come from the IMF. But there was considerable opposition to the latter, most strikingly in France (see chapter 14) but also initially in Germany, until Chancellor Merkel changed her mind.

No one was more determined to avoid the IMF than ECB president Trichet. He had big ambitions for Europe. He would frequently mention, in public speeches as well as in private, the size of the euro area and its weight in the world. He always insisted that it should be treated and considered as a single entity within institutions such as the G7 and G20 and saw the ECB as an institution with a global governance role. As he put it in July 2010, "Beyond our role as guardians of the euro, we also have to deliver on our responsibilities as part of European and global economic governance."[13] He also knew that he was by far the euro-area policy maker most experienced in problems of international finance. As president of the Paris Club, he had personally dealt with, and solved, numerous debt crises in poor countries. He mastered perfectly the technique of program negotiations and knew how best to balance, in difficult circumstances, the needs for adjustment and financing. He had constantly fought with non-European governments to push them toward stronger adjustment. There was no doubt in his mind that the euro area could, and should, deal with its own problems and that it did not need an external monitor or enforcer.

Consequently, Trichet resisted the German initiative to bring in the IMF until the last moment. On March 4, 2010, using the regular ECB press conference, he told journalists that he did "not trust that it would be appropriate to have the introduction of the IMF as a supplier of help."[14] He still thought it possible, at that time, to limit the IMF in a role of a technical adviser for constructing programs and defining conditionality. On March 26, on the eve of one decisive meeting of government leaders, he declared to French public radio that calling for help outside the euro area would be "very, very bad."[15]

Despite its initial opposition, the ECB energetically threw itself into the negotiations of the Greek program, including its fiscal and structural components. The package, as agreed at the May 9, 2010, Ecofin Council, involved three elements: a two-part European Stabilization Mechanism that consisted of the European Financial Stability Facility (EFSF) with €440 billion raised on the basis of joint and mutual government guarantees allocated on the basis of shares in the ECB capital as well as a smaller €60 billion facility run by the European Commission, the EFSM; IMF support; and the engagement of the ECB through an innovative program to provide liquidity to stop crisis contagion. The EFSF would borrow on the capital markets and lend the proceeds to countries that agreed on a reform program. It could also intervene in the primary and secondary bond markets, act on the basis of a precautionary program, and finance recapitalizations of financial institutions in nonprogram countries through loans to governments.

This became institutionalized as the troika of Commission, IMF, and ECB, a term originally coined by Greek journalists but then widely used by all participants.

ECB's Opposition to Deauville

The second shock to the ECB's vision of how the world should operate was more devastating. When Sarkozy and Merkel met in Deauville on October 18, 2010, they conjured private sector involvement (PSI) out of their magician's hat. They thought they had produced a beautifully simple solution: by asking creditors, especially banks, to potentially take losses on government debts, they would kill several birds with one stone. They would instill a sense of responsibility among lenders and limit excessive risk-taking. They would also react to a public opinion that was growing increasingly hostile to the idea of bailing out the banks. And, finally, they would protect their own taxpayers from the costs of such bailouts.

Trichet could easily see the likely response of the market. When the result of the Deauville walk on the beach became known, the ECB president was deeply shocked. He expressed in private his strong opposition to PSI, which he believed would destroy financial stability in the euro area. At the following European summit, he passionately tried to persuade the politicians to reverse course and give up PSI. Trichet had multiple reasons for considering PSI to be highly dangerous. First, he thought that the Greek case could be resolved with the traditional mix of financing and adjustment that he had practiced and seen practiced over several decades with emerging economies with income levels much lower than that of Greece.

Second, and most important, there was a matter of principle and integrity of debt markets. Only totally distressed (and second grade) countries would consider reneging on their sovereign obligations. Advanced countries should never create any doubts about their willingness to pay. It was a huge loss of status and a source of enormous dangers. He would often say in private "contracts must be honored" and would lament the fact that, once PSI had become official policy, sovereign CDSs for Spain were higher than Egypt or Pakistan. That development to him seemed to prove the absurdity of the Merkel-Sarkozy decision.

Finally, the ECB president was strongly influenced by his long experience in dealing with debt problems as chairman of the Paris Club. The standard practice was rescheduling the debt together with implementing a strong adjustment program with concessionality and conditionality imbedded in an IMF program. Debt reduction was only accepted as a possible solution very late in the existence of the club and was considered as a very last resort remedy reserved for countries that had lost market access, which they would not recover for many years.

Trichet was immediately and vigorously rebuffed at Deauville by the French president, Sarkozy, who was reported as telling him that technical officials should not criticize elected leaders and that "It was us, the heads of state and government, who took the vital decisions." In other words, the political leaders felt estranged from the ECB, which was now seen as part of the banking world, and they now wanted to punish the bankers for their excesses.[16] The rebuff by President Sarkozy to the ECB president made clear that the French side did not anticipate the consequences that PSI would bring for sovereign euro-debt markets. At the time of Deauville, it seemed to offer an easy way out of the request for stronger budget discipline. It was also intended to facilitate the financing of the Greek program, which was becoming more and more difficult every day.

Trichet's gloomy predictions proved correct. Soon after PSI was decided in principle, and even before it became official policy, spreads started to increase for peripheral countries' debt (as well as sovereign credit default swaps) and the gap between long-term interest rates inside the euro area widened. This was especially spectacular for Ireland, Spain, and Italy. Before Deauville, those countries could still be considered immune from the crisis (although a small divergence in interest rates had appeared). After Deauville, the spreads started to diverge from Germany, France, and other core countries.

The aftermath of Deauville was intense confrontation between the ECB and many euro-area governments on the possibility of a Greek default. Default, in any form, was opposed by the ECB, which explicitly threatened, on many occasions, to cut off financing to Greece by not accepting Greek collateral in the event of a default. Such a step would have forced the European governments to take over the totality of Greece's financing needs.

There were plenty of analogies for such a process from the history of emerging market debt crises: in 1982, in the Latin American debt crisis, Mexico, Argentina, and Brazil did not formally default, but payment terms were stretched out. The first two of these countries never defaulted; only Brazil went into a formal default, but in 1987, five years after the outbreak of the crisis.

The ECB's refusal to contemplate any kind of default obliged the governments to negotiate a voluntary restructuring with private creditor banks (represented by the Institute for International Finance, chaired by Josef Ackermann of Deutsche Bank). Long and painful interactions took place through the second quarter of 2011. The negotiations were complicated by technicalities and ambiguities about rating agencies' qualification of different possible scenarios. It took some time for participants to agree that a voluntary restructuring would lead to a selective default (SD), a misnomer in the sense that it was not a credit event but the ultimate step of a downgrading.

Finally, a compromise on the Greek issue was reached at the July 21, 2011, EU Summit in Brussels. As usual, the summit meeting was anticipated in a bilateral Franco-German meeting on July 20. At the same time, the ECB governing council was meeting in Frankfurt (July 21). While chairing the governing council, the ECB president received an invitation to join the political leaders in Brussels. It was clear there were serious disagreements between Berlin and Paris, especially on PSI. President Sarkozy took the initiative in inviting the ECB president with the hope that he could act as a referee. The request was discussed in the ECB governing council, after which the president decided to immediately go to Brussels on the basis of a precise mandate: to eliminate PSI.

The summit decision appeared as a mixed success for the Trichet principle. The summit declaration stated: "We reaffirm our commitment to the euro and to do whatever is needed to ensure the financial stability of the euro area as a whole and its Member States."[17] For Greece, PSI was to be implemented through a voluntary restructuring, and the ECB accepted the idea of a selective default. The ECB obtained some additional protection with the governments pledging €35 billion (in the form of EFSF notes) as a guarantee toward its exposure to Greece. Trichet managed to ensure the insertion of a statement in the communiqué to the effect that Greece was an exceptional case. For all other countries, their governments committed to fully respecting their signatures: in other words, there would be no further PSI.

Overall, the PSI agreed upon by the heads of state during the summit was favorable to creditors. For this reason, it was modified considerably by the troika before it was finally implemented in March 2012 amounting to a 79 cent per euro haircut of original principal. Even after that modification the Greek debt level still was not sustainable.[18]

The ECB and Conditionality

Since the outbreak of the global crisis in 2008, banks have had unlimited access to ECB liquidity. There was one condition: they had to provide adequate collateral, and the ECB ultimately decided what "adequate" meant.

In normal times, this is not an issue. Good quality collateral is abundant, principally in the form of highly rated government debt. But the old guides to central banking emphasize how monetary policy in crises needs to be made with unusual assets: Bagehot quotes a director of the Bank of England in 1825 as saying, "we were not on some occasions over-nice."[19] Not being over-nice in the glare of politics and public opinion is, however, a tough job.

Starting in 2010, rating agencies had embarked on a cycle of constant downgrading of peripheral countries' government debts (and bank debt as well). Very soon, the statutory limits enshrined in the ECB rules were reached. Collateral was not adequate anymore. Strict implementation of the rules would lead to interruption in the financing of banks and, by consequence, their economies and their governments. The governing council had to take over and discretionally decide what collateral would be acceptable. Did the ECB take more risk upon itself because of its collateral changes as well as the much larger lending during the crisis? The answer to this question is an obvious yes, if one takes the risk management approach of a private institution, which must regard prices and general market conditions as exogenous to its action. The answer is most likely no, if one takes into account that, unlike a private institution (think of the small country assumption in international economics), market equilibrium is endogenous to central bank action.[20]

These considerations highlight that, after the ECB played the role of lender of last resort for banks when the financial crisis emerged, the European debt crisis forced it to think about its role as a lender of last resort for governments. As the Maastricht Treaty technically prevented the ECB from monetary financing—printing money to support government debt—it was forced to find its own way in the policy sphere. Large debates emerged about the exact role the ECB ought to have regarding fiscal policy, most notably, to what extent should it be involved in the decision whether a country is solvent? This section aims at surveying these debates.

Sovereigns and Liquidity Risk Revisited

Government debt should normally not be subject to liquidity risk, as any temporary shortfall of funds can be made up by its central bank. In other words, the central bank can smooth out funding needs. However, countries in the euro area did not have their own central bank, and hence their debt was essentially subsovereign debt. Therefore, they were subject to liquidity and run risk (as we discussed in detail in chapter 7), and as a consequence peripheral sovereign debt carried an extra liquidity-risk premium.

As risk premia rose in 2011–2012, a debate emerged about whether the ECB should become a lender of last resort, freely purchasing government debt of various membership countries.[21] The Dutch economist Willem Buiter, in a series of papers, even proposed that the ECB should become a market maker of last resort, as the ECB was de facto already fulfilling this duty through indirect asset purchases of sovereign debt (to be discussed in the next section of this chapter) and through financial regulation designed at requiring banks to hold more sovereign debt, particularly from peripheral countries. Making the duty official would only increase its effectiveness, he advocated.

Yet, beyond breaking the treaties, purchasing government debt exposes the ECB to default risk should a government not fully pay back its debt. The risk would be even larger if the sovereigns did not conduct politically unpopular but necessary structural reforms. ECB intervention that lowers interest rates has indeed two effects: First, the lower interest cost increases the sustainability of debt. Second, the removal of the pressure for governments to implement reforms reduces the debt sustainability—a classic moral hazard issue. Losses incurred by the ECB would then be monetary financing of government deficits, which would surely exceed the ECB's original purposes. The Germans, in particular, were intent on avoiding the use of their taxpayers' money potentially paying for the reluctance of the South to undertake reforms.

Game of Chicken and Conditionality

In essence, the ECB and the governments were playing a classic game of chicken (see chapter 5 for details): if the ECB did not intervene in buying government debts, the governments would have more incentives to enact structural reforms to save the country, but if the ECB intervened and the governments did nothing (fiscal dominance), the default risk would not decline despite the ECB's intervention. With government bonds on its balance sheet after an intervention, the ECB is exposed to default risk that constitutes monetary financing. The game was even more complicated as the ECB faced not one but eighteen (and after the inclusion of Lithuania nineteen) governments, with often conflicting views on adjustment. They wanted to save the euro, but they did not want to pay the price for it by either providing financial help (the creditors) or carrying out macroeconomic adjustments (the debtor countries).

So how could the ECB provide liquidity support and yet ensure that governments do their part to reduce default risk? The route it took has been labeled "conditionality." In essence, conditionality involved the provision of liquidity conditional on reform measures being undertaken, and the ECB became a quasi-fiscal player in the European crisis.

Given the inaction of governments, the ECB had no choice but to become deeply involved in the management of policy conditionality. Early on, it took partial responsibility for devising the first Greek adjustment program. That function became permanent and institutionalized as the ECB, together with the Commission and the IMF, became part of the troika defining and monitoring conditionality in program countries inside the euro area. Trichet was naturally at ease with this configuration, which seemed to him like a logical extension of his Paris Club work, and saw a possibility of coordinating with the Ecofin in devising and implementing conditionality for program countries. Not all members of the governing council were fully comfortable with a role in implementing conditionality, even if it would allow for a better protection of the institution's financial interests.

Italian Tensions: ECB's Conditionality in Action

The ECB pushed the application of conditionality to the extreme, in the case of Italy, which now took center stage in this phase of the European crisis. The Deauville decision had affected Italian and Spanish yields. As the cost of financing debt increased because the euro area no longer had a single interest rate for government debt, it looked as if Italy needed a new approach to its budget. Italy had a very large stock of debt stemming from large-scale government borrowing before the introduction of the euro. Unlike Greece or Spain or Ireland, there had been no spectacular property boom in the 2000s, and indeed growth was very low. The government was operating a primary surplus: that is, the cost of government except for debt service was more than met by revenue. But it was extremely sensitive to an increase in borrowing costs.

Tensions rose between the Italian prime minister, Silvio Berlusconi, and the finance minister, Giulio Tremonti, in the summer of 2011, who insisted on the need for budget cuts. The spat was overshadowed by a backdrop of judicial inquiries: Italian magistrates had charged Berlusconi with tax offenses as well as with involvement with underage prostitutes, and Tremonti was investigated for living in a rent-free apartment. But the clash between the two men also indicated the problems of running democratic regimes in a Europe of austerity and budgetary orthodoxy. Berlusconi seemed to reject Tremonti's plans and stated that he needed to think about winning elections. As the crisis escalated, Tremonti raised the stakes by asserting, "If I fall, Italy falls. And if Italy falls, then the euro falls."[22]

The ECB inserted itself into this debate in 2011, with a demand for greater budgetary austerity as part of the conditionality of the extension of the Securities Markets Program (SMP) to Italy (and Spain). The letter was signed by Trichet as well as the governor of the Banca d'Italia, Mario Draghi, who had also been nominated as Trichet's successor. Draghi was in a difficult position. Originally, there had been substantial opposition to his candidacy for the presidency of the ECB. There was French opposition because he had worked for some time at Goldman Sachs, which was regarded as the ultimate incarnation of Anglo-Saxon finance and Wall Street greed and evil. Populists in Germany, on the other hand, pointed to the fact that he was Italian, and the German tabloid *Bild Zeitung* screamed "Mamma Mia," adding that inflation belonged to Italy as surely as tomato sauce to spaghetti.[23] (The *Bild* later made amends and presented Draghi with an honorary Pickelhaube, the Prussian spiked helmet, as a sign of his commitment to the principles of austere Prussian rectitude.)

Market analysts had known about the ECB letter after a few days, but its content was kept secret. Berlusconi refused repeated calls to make it public. A full text was finally leaked and published in English by the *Corriere Della Serra* on September 29, 2011. The political backlash was immediate and strong. Umberto Bossi, the leader of the populist Northern League, a coalition partner of the Berlusconi party, lambasted the ECB's letter as "an attempt to overthrow the government."[24] In a clear reference to Draghi, he added, "I fear that this letter was done in Rome. He's gone from here into Europe, but he's always in Rome." Bossi also refused to support many of the measures included in the letter, especially pension cuts. From that moment, the coalition government was probably doomed.

An analogous letter by the ECB, and countersigned by the governor of the Bank of Spain, addressed to the Spanish government also laid out the details of a reform program. Unlike the Italian letter, it received no publicity at the time, and its existence was only revealed a few years later in the memoirs of Spain's then prime minister Zapatero. Berlusconi had clearly made himself more vulnerable than his Spanish counterpart.

On November 4, 2011, Berlusconi went to the G20 summit in Cannes and had a private joint meeting with Merkel and Sarkozy, during which he was strongly urged to act decisively. Berlusconi saw the meeting as a public humiliation, especially as Merkel and Sarkozy seemed to grin or smirk at a press reference about him. In Parliament, Berlusconi had lost his majority and would not survive a vote of confidence. But the manner and mechanism of his fall gave rise to the suspicion that Germany was imposing its demands and its choices on Italy. Chancellor Merkel talked on the telephone with the president of the republic, Giorgio Napolitano (whose office was mainly symbolic but played a considerable role at moments of governmental instability), on November 7, 2011. The next day, November 8, Berlusconi announced his resignation, just days after the fall of Greek prime minister Papandreou in Greece. His successor, Mario Monti, was an academic and a devout Catholic with a personally blameless life that contrasted with the morass of fiscal and sexual scandal that emanated from Berlusconi, but he was also someone who as a highly successful former EU commissioner with responsibility for competition policy had the confidence of Europe's elites.

The ECB's conditionality policy also played a major role in Greece, eventually contributing to the dismissal of Papandreou in November 2011. As in Italy, a technocrat became the new prime minister. In the case of Greece, the former vice president of the ECB, Lucas Papademos, became prime minister of Greece on November 11, 2011, for six months.

ELAs in Ireland, Cyprus, and Greece

Already in the early phase of the crisis, the interbank market, where banks normally lend funding surpluses and meet their borrowing needs, froze up as banks no longer trusted each other and wanted to deal only with the central bank as a counterparty. Many European banks thus became heavily dependent on the ECB and the NCBs for meeting their funding needs.

As good quality collateral ran out, banks primarily relied on emergency liquidity assistance (ELA) from their own NCBs, which could employ more lax collateral standards. ELA provides support at a penalty rate after a vote of the ECB council to "prevent or mitigate potential systemic effects on financial institutions, including repercussions for market infrastructure such as the disruption of payment and settlement systems." The risk from these credits was retained by the NCB and ultimately by its government. However, Article 32.4 of the ECB statute implied de facto that a two-thirds majority in the ECB general council could impose a cap on a single NCB's emergency liquidity assistance. For all practical purposes, the country would in effect be excluded from the euro.

Although apparently technical, those decisions had vital consequences for the member countries. With private capital flows all but interrupted, in effect, the ECB took full control over financial inflows in peripheral countries. Circumstances had placed the ECB as the ultimate manager of financial stability in the euro area. It became the referee on individual countries' financial viability. And beyond, it had the last word on the survival of the euro. A decision by the ECB to stop financing banks from one specific country would shut off its financial system from the rest of the euro area. Deprived of liquidity, its banks could no longer transfer funds.

This mechanism played a major role during the crisis, most notably in Ireland, Cyprus, and Greece. We now turn to these three cases.

IRELAND

After years of sustained economic growth, Ireland was severely hit by the financial crisis. As Patrick Honohan, the governor of the Central Bank of Ireland, put it, "The Irish banking system was, in effect, on a life-support system since September 2008. Complacency resulted in the banks fueling the late stage of an obvious construction bubble with massive foreign borrowing, leaving them exposed to solvency and liquidity risks which in past times would have been inconceivable."[25] Although many had warned that the banking sector might prove insolvent in the face of a downturn in housing prices, this eventuality was not adequately forecasted by relevant economic actors. On top of that, debt overhang prevented the recovery of growth, and as Jörg Asmussen (then a member of the executive board of the ECB) pointed out in a speech given in Dublin, the Celtic Tiger also suffered from a serious lack of competitiveness.[26]

The Irish government stepped in to save the financial sector: it decided on September 30, 2008, to guarantee (for two years) bank liabilities and later committed to large recapitalization programs. These unilaterally taken decisions were not approved by the ECB, which expressed its disapproval in two published opinions in October 2008. It particularly worried about the negative externalities caused by the guarantees that the banks were given, that a diabolic loop between sovereigns and banks would take place, and pointed out the lack of coordination with European partners and institutions, notably the ECB. The negotiations on Ireland produced a substantial amount of tension and animosity. Many European countries resented the long-standing Irish low-tax regime, and they thought that the blanket guarantee given by the Irish government to bank deposits in the wake of the Lehman failure was a hostile competitive act that would suck deposits out of other euro-area countries. In March 2010, the Irish government had to issue a promissory note of €30.6 billion to fund the bailout of the Anglo-Irish Bank and the Irish Nationwide Building Society, a move that pushed up the debt and the financing needs of the Irish government. At one point in the discussion, France insisted (unsuccessfully) that Ireland increase the very low rate of corporate taxation (12.5%), which it saw as a race to the bottom.

As the bank guarantee was set to expire in 2010, interest rates in Ireland started to spike and diverge from the euro-area average rate. Ireland and its banks soon lost market access. The Irish bank problems then forced the ECB to step in significantly: its liquidity provisions (including ELAs) amounted to €90 billion in January 2010 and €140 billion in November 2010—85 percent of the Irish GDP at that time and a quarter of the total ECB lending.[27] This represented at that time the largest exposure to a single country the ECB had ever taken.

Trichet and the vice president of the ECB, Vitor Constâncio, implied that Irish banks, which depended very heavily on the ECB, could no longer rely forever on funding from the Eurosystem.[28] At first, the Irish response was that no external help was needed, but the banks began to suffer from a rapid withdrawal of deposits. By November 18, 2010, the governor of the Irish Central Bank, Patrick Honohan, said that his government was "definitely likely" to ask for a support operation, and the official demand came on the weekend of November 20–21, 2010.[29] In Ireland, extending the bank guarantee was controversial. When the final rescue package of €85 billion was worked out on November 27–28, it produced a new controversy. The fact that German and French banks were substantial creditors of the Irish banking system, and that the ECB was pressing against any haircut for senior bank bondholders, was interpreted as evidence less of a theoretically coherent position on PSI than as a sign that the ECB had been captured by the German and French governments and their banks.

In an infamous exchange of letters between Jean-Claude Trichet and Brian Lenihan (then minister of finance) recently declassified by the ECB, the former recalled that the ECB's support for Ireland was not unlimited and subject to specific rules. In particular, the second letter (dated November 19, 2010) described conditions under which the provisions of liquidity, ELAs in particular, would be continued.[30]

1) The Irish government shall send a request for financial support to the Eurogroup;

2) The request shall include the commitment to undertake decisive actions in the areas of fiscal consolidation, structural reforms and financial sector restructuring, in agreement with the European Commission, the International Monetary Fund and the ECB;

3) The plan for the restructuring of the Irish financial sector shall include the provision of the necessary capital to those Irish banks needing it and will be funded by the financial resources provided at the European and international level to the Irish government as well as by financial means currently available to the Irish government, including existing cash reserves of the Irish government;

4) The repayment of the funds provided in the form of ELA shall be fully guaranteed by the Irish government, which would ensure the payment of immediate compensation to the Central Bank of Ireland in the event of missed payments on the side of the recipient institutions.

The provision of extra capital to Irish banks at that time helped primarily the ECB and the Central Bank of Ireland. The Irish Central Bank had accumulated a very large exposure to the Irish banking sector as a result of an earlier move that allowed French and German banks as well as US money market funds to reduce their Irish exposure at favorable prices. In a reply two days later, Lenihan agreed to meet these conditions. The ECB granted cheap funding through depository notes for Ireland and maintained ELA access, which succeeded at calming financial tensions. The ECB even participated in the four-year economic strategy that the Irish government formulated to spur economic growth. However, the involvement of the ECB inside the political process clearly demonstrated that the ECB had to deal with policy makers and impose its conditions to conduct its monetary policy successfully.

CYPRUS

Cyprus is a small country with a small economy and should not have been capable of blowing up the whole euro area. It also looked as if it was another version of the overbloated expansion of a financial system that had done damage in small countries such as Iceland and Ireland as well as in Great Britain and Switzerland. Two sets of arguments converged: the belief that overlarge banks were dangerous and the analysis of debt dynamics that suggested that there were limits beyond which too much government debt could be dangerous and would destroy financial stability.

The growing worries about a transfer union in the Northern European states meshed with an acute aversion to using taxpayers' money to potentially bailout Greek, Ukrainian, and Russian oligarchs. But a full bailout, which would have required some €17 billion, would have raised the government debt to an unsustainable amount. The IMF pushed for a smaller sum and for a bank contribution. Using what the Icelandic government had done as a model, it suggested a scheme that played well with the German government: a merger of the two large Cyprus banks and a new bank that would save the deposits of small depositors (with accounts under €100,000) and put large deposits in a bad bank.

In an initial negotiation, on the night of March 15–16, 2013, the Cyprus government feared that this would lead to an end of its banking model as Russian and other foreign depositors were severely punished. So the government proposed a tax (not a debt restructuring with a haircut) of 6.75 percent on small deposits and 9.9 percent on large deposits (on the assumption that anything over 10% would be interpreted as punitive). But the measure set off violent demonstrations and was rejected by the Cyprus Parliament.

It is in the next week of negotiations that the ECB largely tried to influence the plan. Although the ECB's exposure to Cyprus was much smaller than to Ireland, ELAs were technically the only reason allowing the two banks to survive, as Wolfgang Schäuble duly acknowledged.[31] But as the solvency of these institutions was put into question, the ECB was forced to act. On March 21, 2013, it issued a press release that was quite explicit:

> The Governing Council of the European Central Bank decided to maintain the current level of Emergency Liquidity Assistance (ELA) until Monday, 25 March 2013. Thereafter, Emergency Liquidity Assistance (ELA) could only be considered if an EU/IMF program is in place that would ensure the solvency of the concerned banks.[32]

After a week of tense negotiations, another version of the original plan was finally accepted by Cyprus, involving both a rescue for small savers and a harsher loss for the large bank deposit holders. But once again, the push of the ECB was instrumental in making it happen.

GREECE

Greece encountered serious economic problems after the financial crisis, which revealed cracks in public accounting and led to a severe debt crisis that peaked on two occasions, in 2012 and 2015 (see figure 15.3), with a

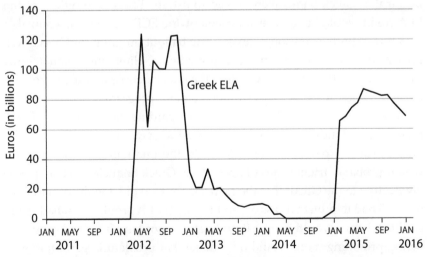

FIGURE 15.3. Size of the Greek Emergency Liquidity Assistance (ELA)

debate about the possible departure of Greece from the monetary union (Grexit). Both of these crises were covered in the previous chapters from a broad European perspective, but it is informative to focus on the contentious role the ECB played in 2015 in this section.

In January 2015, Greeks elected Alexis Tsipras as the new prime minister. The head of the far-left party Syriza promised to take a pro-stimulus stand and refused to keep the austerity that had plunged Greece into a severe depression. Both he and his finance minister Yanis Varoufakis believed that their stance might swing the whole of Europe toward anti-austerity. But insolvency fears for both Greek banks and the Greek government started to rise again, potentially threatening the financial stability of the country. It soon became clear that Greece would need a further bailout program, and harsh negotiations regarding the terms and conditions followed.

On February 4, 2015, the governing council of the ECB, which they state was "based on the fact that it is not currently possible to assume a successful conclusion of the review of the European Union/International Monetary Fund programme for the Hellenic Republic, and in line with existing Eurosystem rules," decided to lift the waiver affecting marketable debt instruments issued or fully guaranteed by the Hellenic Republic.[33] These waivers previously weakened credit rating requirements for Greek banks, which allowed them to obtain liquid central bank assets; their removal meant that Greek banks were forced to ask for ELAs. The ceiling of the ELA credit would have to be approved by the ECB's governing council.

A four-month extension of an existing bailout program for Greece was finally adopted, but tensions soon grew again, climaxing when Tsipras caught Europe by surprise by calling the Greek people to directly vote on the acceptance of the newly negotiated bailout program.

This put the ECB in a difficult position regarding the pursuance of ELA financing, and the debate that it had to deal with was very much along the lines already explored in this book. On the one hand, stopping ELAs would probably trigger the collapse of the Greek financial system, possibly leading to the Grexit that the ECB sought to avoid. On the other hand, the ECB had to protect its assets, and the large ELA provisions it had given to Greek banks would be lost if no fiscal bailout (and a Grexit) occurred; hence, providing more would only make that problem larger. Moreover, the ECB also had to deal with a government deemed unreliable and whose ultimate objective might have been to run up TARGET2 claims. Higher TARGET2 claims increased the losses the rest of Europe would suffer in the case of Grexit and hence would improve Greece's bargaining power.

These tensions were reflected in the behavior of the ECB before the referendum and also after the latter was refused. The ECB did not formally threaten Greece with removal of the ELAs, but glimpses of discourses from its leaders suggested that it was considering it as an option. Ultimately—after Greek banks were closed for a couple of days—a fiscal bailout program was accepted and the ELA provision maintained, but for some, the ECB's behavior had once again exceeded its mandate. Martin Hellwig, one of the most acclaimed German economists, notably stated that the ECB should not have the right to put political pressure on member states and argued how the provision of ELAs to Greek banks did not break any rules of its mandate.[34] In a powerful analogy, he recalled the 1931 episode in Germany when the then German central bank, the Reichsbank (at the insistence of foreign central bank creditors, the Bank of England and the Federal Reserve Bank of New York), ceased to support German banks, triggering an economic crisis that featured a 20 percent drop in output and pushed 2 million Germans into unemployment, contributing to the rise of the disaster that followed.[35] On the other hand, one might also argue that the ECB had no other choice, as a generous liquidity provision to banks with insufficient collateral could have set a dangerous precedent of effectively helping a euro-area government that conducted short-sighted and non-sustainable policies with negative spillover effects on other countries. In sum, the ELA debate renewed the worry about the political character of the policy impositions of Europe's central bank.

Lending and Asset Purchase Programs

As mentioned earlier, lending against collateral (in the form of repo operations) is a standard practice of central banks for implementing monetary policy. Those operations primarily affect short-term interest rates.

The global financial crisis created an exceptional situation that called for extra monetary stimulus. Central banks reacted by bringing their (short-term) policy rates to zero. That proved insufficient. Confronted with the zero lower bound, central banks had to invent new ways of creating monetary accommodation. They started to implement unconventional monetary policies through various means. One important approach was to try and bring down long-term rates by acting directly on the long-term bond market. That could only be achieved through buying securities, notably long-term government bonds. Those long-term asset purchases are commonly known as *quantitative easing.*

There are two crucial differences for the ECB between refinancing operations (taking securities as collateral in a short-term repo transaction), the conventional way, and purchasing securities, the unconventional way.[36] First, with refinancing operations, the central bank provides liquidity to the banks. In contrast, when it purchases government bonds, it still directly provides liquidity to the banking system, but their actions mean that the ECB is also indirectly providing liquidity to governments. And, second, refinancing carries little risk in principle (if value of collateral assets is sufficiently high, i.e., if the haircut is large enough). Purchases, on the contrary, are inherently risky, as the government issuing the bonds may default on its debt. This would create losses for the central bank. Of course, in the case of the ECB, which is indirectly owned by all euro-area governments, the risk taken on by the ECB is in fact carried by all the others. And, as the ECB occasionally pointed out, central banks can create money and as a result can operate with negative equity. They are thus protected from insolvency.

Those two differences explain the absolute and irreducible German hostility to the purchase of government bonds by the ECB. Germany considers any direct support by the central bank to a government as a violation of the prohibition of monetary financing. The 1924 Reichsbank Law, in the aftermath of the disastrous Great Inflation, and the 1953 law establishing the Bank Deutscher Länder, the predecessor of the Bundesbank, both contained ceilings (but not an absolute prohibition) for the purchase of government debt by the central bank. In addition, for Germans, such monetary financing exacerbates moral hazard problems as it reduces the incentive of governments to adjust their fiscal stance and reduce their debt. Finally, piling up risk in the ECB's balance sheet creates the possibility of fiscal transfers between member states, a violation of the no-bailout clause. The Bundesbank has shown that it is prepared to go very far to expand liquidity-provision programs. It never could bring itself to support and accept public debt purchases. This is the case as long as those purchases take place on the (secondary) market and not directly at issuance and as long as the bond-purchasing program does not discriminate between countries.

Asset purchases started with the Covered Bond Purchase Programme (CBPP), announced in July 2009, in which the ECB and the national central banks purchased covered bonds for a total of €60 billion to stabilize these troubled markets and recapitalize banks indirectly. These were purchases of private assets and, therefore, not contentious. Covered bonds are traditional bonds covered by earmarking of (usually) first-class mortgages or public sector loans: hence, these purchases were viewed as free of default risk.

The chasm between Germany and the ECB opened when the governing council decided to start purchasing government debt. This happened in May 2010, well before there was any project of quantitative easing in the euro area. The first ECB asset purchase program was the May 2010 Securities Markets Programme (SMP), which for the first time allowed National Central Banks (NCBs) to "conduct outright interventions in the euro-area public and private debt securities markets."[37] The ECB embarked on purchases of some government debt for reasons not directly related to monetary accommodation. The purposes of the first programs were different from quantitative easing. The stated objective was twofold: preserve financial stability and allow efficient implementation of monetary policy in all parts of the euro area.

In May 2010, the central banks of the Eurosystem were allowed for the first time to purchase government bonds on secondary markets on a large scale. This change of position, supported by ECB president Jean-Claude Trichet, sparked harsh discussion among German academics and policy makers—eventually leading to the resignation of Axel Weber, then president of the Bundesbank. Germans saw in the SMP the shadow of indirect monetary financing, even though purchases of Southern public bonds (Greece, Portugal, etc.) were "sterilized," that is, they were accompanied by operations withdrawing liquidity through offering interest bearing deposits to banks, thus draining money from financial markets.

The very long-term refinancing operations (VLTROs) began in 2011, a traditional refinancing through collateral—although with exceptional maturity: banks were given financing for a period of three years (instead of three months for LTROs, the longer-term refinancing operations). This was supported by the Bundesbank, although it was somehow expected that banks would start to again buy long-term government debt from their home countries, seen, by some analysts, as implicit monetary financing.

It is with this in mind that one needs to analyze Draghi's 2012 London speech and the outright monetary transactions (OMT) program that followed. The OMT was a vast asset purchase program whose objective was to bring down interest rates on peripheral bonds. The increase in value of these government bonds, which were mostly held by peripheral banks, should lead to capital gains and indirectly recapitalize and reduce funding costs of peripheral banks. The hope was that this would also attenuate the segmentation of credit markets and eliminate the redenomination risk (discussed in chapter 11) that was appearing inside the euro-area capital markets. Like the SMP, the OMT was conditional.

Quantitative easing was launched in 2015. This time the conditionality was very limited, which ultimately only ruled out Greece. This ultimate stretch was accepted because the official objective was not to provide liquidity or funding for governments but to increase inflation expectations, which were desperately low—including in Northern countries such as Germany. In addition, it was targeted at the entire euro area and not to only a part of it, like the SMP or the OMT. The success of the program along this dimension is still a matter of discussion, but there is evidence that it provided a useful firewall against contagion during the Grexit threat in 2015.

The rest of this subsection lays out the details of the programs, in particular of the different actors involved in their creation, deliberation, and criticism.

Securities Markets Programme

The initiation of the Securities Markets Programme (SMP) in May 2010 triggered both publicity and dissent. On May 6, Trichet stated that the ECB was not considering buying bonds, but just four days later, on May 10, in the aftermath of the May 9 Ecofin meeting, he announced the Securities Purchase Program. That announcement was seen as an unprecedented reversal and a major surprise. The policy environment had suddenly changed with the "flash crash" on the New York Stock Exchange that took place on May 6, introducing a new element of market uncertainty. The 1,000 point fall in the Dow Jones Industrial Average was a chaotic computer-generated response to a single large trade in an atmosphere of nervousness created by the Greek crisis.[38] The ECB wanted to act promptly, before the Eurogroup started to debate the issue, so as not to give the impression they were engaged in any sort of negotiation or trade-off with governments. The members of the ECB council may have had the feeling, from previous internal conversations, that they could reach consensus on launching that program. They also took great care in explaining that the new initiative did not constitute monetary financing of governments, as all monetary impact would be instantly and fully sterilized.

Whatever discussions occurred prior to the ECB decision on securities markets purchases, there was no mention in the communication of any deep disagreements inside the governing council. Five members of the council had opposed the initiative, but only one spoke publicly about the issue. The president of the Bundesbank, Axel Weber, was extremely unhappy and said in a newspaper interview that the SMP posed "significant stability risks."[39] This was the first time a member of the governing council publicly dissented from a major decision. This highlighted another difference between the German and French views. German central bankers think that ECB council members are personally accountable for their decision and their sole loyalty is to the ECB's mandate, while from a French perspective the loyalty is to the ECB president and the governing council.

Meanwhile, the crisis was widening. The August ECB council was immediately followed by a surge in Irish bond yields, and central bank governor Patrick Honohan spoke of "a setback for our hopes of a narrowing to reflect the fiscal credibility of the country."[40] Portugal had been downgraded by the rating agencies in the summer of 2010 and in September concluded an austerity package with tax hikes and cuts in civil service pay.

Other governors may have shared Weber's views but kept silent in public. That set him apart from the rest of the group and triggered the chain of events that ultimately led to his withdrawal from the race for the ECB president. Sarkozy, in particular, was less than enthusiastic about the German central banker and deployed much energy in identifying alternative candidates. Weber was also aware that his stance on the SMP had estranged him from his colleagues in the governing council. As he put it himself, his "clear position" on major decisions had "not always been beneficial for my acceptance by some governments."[41] Sticking to his principles, Weber informed the ECB board and the German chancellor that he would not consider the ECB job and also that he would resign from the Bundesbank presidency, effective on April 30, 2011. Weber's withdrawal was a blow for German influence on European monetary policy making, though Merkel never really believed that a German should take the top position at the ECB.

Yet, these asset-purchase decisions were not just a question of personalities: this was a moment in which a substantial part of conservative opinion in Germany turned against the ECB and the monetary union. The influential leading center-right paper, the *Frankfurter Allgemeine Zeitung*, concluded, "Since a transfer union has been effectively introduced and the central bank is now under political command, the fate of the euro as a soft currency and the failure of the monetary union are certain."[42] Some of the German academics who in the 1990s had tried to stop the monetary union now emerged again with a new challenge to the constitutionality of the rescue package that would be decided by the German Constitutional Court.

Despite these troubles, the ECB pushed on with the SMP. A teleconference of the governing council took place on the evening of Sunday, August 7, 2011. A communiqué was issued later by the president stating that the governing council considered "fundamental that governments stand ready to activate the European Financial Stability Facility (EFSF) in the secondary market," and on the basis of the above assessments that the ECB would actively implement its Securities Markets Programme with respect also to Italy and Spain, without a formal program and consequently with substantially looser conditionality.[43]

Around that time, the Belgian economist Paul de Grauwe called attention to a destabilizing phenomenon that arises when a country with large amounts of sovereign debt does not have its own central bank. As discussed in chapter 7, a national central bank within a currency union cannot simply counteract a possible liquidity squeeze or run. Hence, this country's sovereign debt is subsovereign—using Charles Goodhart's terminology—and its interest rate is higher as it also carries a liquidity-risk premium.[44] De Grauwe advocated direct support to governments on the part of the ECB acting as "lender of last resort to governments," a concept the ECB strongly resisted.

The concept found a ready echo outside the euro area. Non-euro countries were afraid that contagion could spread and affect major peripheral economies: Spain and Italy. Using the G7 and G20 forums, they provided open and increasingly vocal policy advice on the necessity for the euro area to build up a strong firewall or, to use the British prime minister's words (borrowed from US discussions of the appropriate response to the financial crisis), a "big bazooka." The idea of the central bank as a "lender of last resort to governments" was quickly adopted by market analysts as well as some non-euro governments. Most kept their recommendations private, with the sole exception of United Kingdom, whose ministers called openly for ECB interventions.

Not surprisingly, those ideas were rejected by German authorities (the government and the Bundesbank) as being in contradiction with the prohibition of monetary financing. There was also no support by the Eurosystem, which had for many months insisted that it was the governments' responsibility to ensure liquidity of the debt markets and that the EFSF and ESM should be adapted accordingly. There were also doubts that providing such a safety net at a time when solvency or willingness to pay was in doubt was inviting "real money" outside investors to offload their positions.

December 2011: The Three-Year VLTROs

Draghi Replaces Trichet

On November 1, 2011, Mario Draghi took office as the new president of the ECB. Two days later, on November 3, the governing council lowered interest rates by 0.25 percent to 1.25 percent, the first reduction in two years and coming only four months after an increase justified by heightened inflationary expectations. This move was followed one month later by another decrease of the same amount. In five weeks, two previous increases that occurred in 2011 had been reversed and rates were brought down to 1 percent. For Draghi, it was clear that the euro area was now confronting a new recession.

Markets were duly impressed. In just a few days, the new president managed to project an image of decisiveness and hint at a different style from his predecessor, while at the same time affirming continuity in inspiration and proclaiming respect and admiration for his actions. Those moves aimed at communicating a new style, trying to shake off the gloom that had engulfed the markets and the European process and breaking with an endless process of mutual recrimination and paralysis. Trichet reveled in long deliberations, deep collective introspections, careful examination of data, intense exchanges of arguments, and progressive emergence of consensus. Draghi hated long meetings, quickly showed impatience with lengthy statements, and would rather settle divergences and arguments in long, bilateral phone conversations.

There was however a real continuity in policies. Trichet had not shied away from bold and unexpected moves in the past, antagonizing in the process some of the ECB's most faithful supporters in the German establishment. And the situation had changed, fully justifying a quick reversal of the previous tightening stance. Markets were getting paralyzed, and the economic situation deteriorated rapidly. Euro interest rates were the highest in advanced economies while growth was weak and inflation risks minimal. By moving fast and decisively, Draghi was no doubt responding to circumstances as much as seeking to create a new image for himself and for the ECB.

There was more to come. At the same December meeting, the ECB governing council took a major, unprecedented move. It announced two exceptional operations of liquidity provision to the banks for unlimited amounts with a three-year maturity. Those VLTROs came as a total surprise and solidified the reputation of the new ECB president as a bold operator.

Crucially, the governing council unanimously agreed to the VLTROs, with the explicit consent of its German members: the new Bundesbank president Jens Weidmann and chief economist Jürgen Stark—although the latter came to publicly criticize the measure a few months later, after he had resigned from the executive board, as he found it strongly at odds with his own philosophy. Actually, the decision was taken at the last governing council in which Stark participated, and Germany then gave up the position of chief economist, with Jörg Asmussen taking the responsibility for international and European relations on the executive board.

That the Bundesbank agreed to the VLTROs is both surprising and instructive. It was a surprise considering that the liquidity provided to the banks was widely expected to fuel the purchase of government debt in peripheral countries. So the ECB was indirectly encouraging some monetary financing of the governments. Banks seemed wary of possible stigma effects. Many hesitated before subscribing to the first VLTRO auction, and some (including Deutsche Bank) waited for the second one.

The ECB had two major reasons for taking this exceptional step. First, as was obvious for everyone to see, European government bond markets were still completely paralyzed. For many months, banks had been the sole buyers as "real money" was fleeing peripheral countries. Now, following the latest wave of stress tests, they were asked to take up front a new capital charge, in addition to the intrinsic credit risk attached to peripheral countries. For the first time, European regulators were publicly sending a clear signal that buying government debt was bad. That message was in sharp contrast with the implicit and more discrete opposite encouragements they were receiving from their own national authorities. Issuances of debt met with increasingly low demand, and by the end of November, Italian ten-year bonds were yielding almost 8 percent, the highest level ever attained since the creation of the euro. Governments had to resort to short-term borrowing in the hope that long-term rates would return to more manageable levels.

The ECB could not eliminate the perception of risk attached to peripheral countries, nor did it wish to do so at that stage, as the fundamentals of fiscal policy were still hotly debated in those countries and adjustment was highly uncertain. But the central bank could make it more attractive to take those risks by providing the necessary financing on a stable and predictable basis.

"The Wall of Funding"

The second reason for the VLTRO was less visible but even more important. The crisis had forced all European banks into borrowing on the private market with shorter maturity in 2009–2010. As a result, refinancing needs accumulated for the years 2012 to 2014. Banks had to roll over an unprecedented €700 billion for each of those calendar years, an almost impossible task in view of the doubts about their perceived resilience and creditworthiness. This coming "wall of funding" was already creating financing tensions and inhibiting credit and risk taking. With one stroke of a pen, the ECB wiped out all those fears and uncertainties by providing unlimited financing to banks for the whole critical period. In case any doubts persisted as to the ability of banks to take advantage of this facility, eligible collateral was broadened by the creation of a second category of private claims that could be brought to the national central banks.

The take up of VLTRO's initial impact was very positive. Subscriptions were enormous; €489 billion were allotted in the first VLTRO and €529.5 billion in the second. The ECB received bids from 523 bidders in December and 800 banks in February. The market impact was spectacular. The yields on ten-year Italian and Spanish government bonds fell to around 5–5.5 percent by late February. Credit default swap (CDS) spreads for leading euro-area banks fell by more than 150 basis points. Banks started to issue new bonds again, something they had been unable to do for more than six months. The first VLTRO alone had been sufficient to cover nearly 70 percent of total bank debt maturing in 2012, bringing confidence and stability to potential investors by eliminating imminent funding risks.

However, the basis for improvements remained fragile. The VLTROs acted more through pure confidence effects than removing fundamental imbalances in government bond markets. One negative side effect was the reinforcement of the link between banks and their sovereigns. Banks, especially struggling ones, could load up on their home country's sovereign debt. There was no funding risk as the ECB ensured long-term funding. Second, from a regulatory perspective, government debt was treated as totally risk-free, and hence no (costly) equity capital had to be put aside. Hence, banks had an incentive to substitute away from loans to the real economy toward holding government bonds—a worry that Jens Weidmann also expressed. In addition, an increased exposure of banks to government debt makes banks and the sovereign vulnerable to the diabolic loop. As explained in more detail in chapter 10, an adverse shock drags banks and governments down together. However, if government bond prices were to rise, that is, interest rates were to fall, then the diabolic loop would turn into a divine loop. Banks would enjoy capital gains, and banks would be recapitalized.

In 2014 the ECB introduced a new lending program, the Targeted LTRO (TLTRO), which favors banks that extend their lending to the real economy. We discuss this program after the next subsection.

The London Speech and Outright Monetary Transactions (OMT)

WIDENING OF THE CRISIS

Conditions in bond markets started to deteriorate again around mid-March 2012. Risk aversion was first fueled by uncertainty coming from Greece. Based on the personal credibility of the prime minister, Lucas Papademos, a former vice president of the ECB, other euro governments had agreed to significant adjustments in the program financing. Specifically, they had accepted a retroactive lowering of the interest rates of their bilateral loans to the Greek government. They also had agreed that some revenues emanating from bond purchases by their central banks would be allocated to further improving the sustainability of Greece's public debt. Nevertheless, the parliamentary elections in May 2012 had produced a stalemate, with no clear majority, and there was a fear that a new election, scheduled on June 17, 2012, could lead to Greece leaving the euro area.

The main driver, however, was Spain. The change of government in November 2011 brought a significant change in crisis management: the style became more adversarial, less predictable. In February 2012, the prime minister announced that Spain would not meet its fiscal targets and hinted he was not prepared to agree on binding new restrictions. The statement struck a tone of defiance vis-à-vis the Commission and the troika. In the following weeks, that communication strategy backfired and fueled permanent uncertainty. European officials started airing private complaints about the behavior of Spanish authorities, which later found their way into a remarkable *Reuters* dispatch about the prime minister's radical and eccentric chief economic and European adviser.

Financial tensions were compounded by regional and banking problems. Several Spanish regions were asking for central government assistance. Uncertainty also prevailed about the recapitalization process for Spanish banks. Rumors about possible haircuts to be demanded from holders of senior bank debt did not help.

Major results were achieved during the euro-area leaders' summit on June 28–29, 2012, which made it much easier for Spain to access the ESM. In particular, loans to Spain from the ESM would not have seniority over debt from private creditors, and ESM would be able to directly recapitalize banks (with appropriate conditionality) once the single bank supervisory mechanism was established. That brought a temporary improvement, but it was only short-lived. During that period, negative market sentiment was constantly fueled by a succession of rating downgrades that raised doubts about the ability of Spain to issue debt in the future. In turn, those moves increased expectations that the country would soon need a full-fledged EU-IMF program.

The same dynamics were at work in Italy. Sovereign credit had been downgraded by Moody's in view of contagion risks from Spain and Greece. Subsequently, thirteen Italian banks were also downgraded.

From that point on, the crisis changed in nature. Up to then, financial tensions mainly resulted from a sudden stop in cross-border capital flows in the euro area. Southern countries could not finance their deficits, but there was no sign of significant capital or deposit flights, even from Greece. Starting in March 2012, there were signs of cross-border capital flight as deposits were being moved from the periphery back to the core of the euro area.

REDENOMINATION OR CONVERSION RISK

Several indicators of increased convertibility risk appeared during the spring of 2012: an increase in spreads; deposit flows reflected in the surge of TARGET2 imbalances; and divergences in benchmark indicators of financial conditions across countries and, more generally, of credit conditions for the same borrower. Assets and liabilities were managed on a country basis by banks, and there was thus a renationalization or fragmentation of European banking. Many bankers tried to hedge the risk that might result from a possible Greek exit, which then could be followed by other countries (the details of redenomination risk are covered in chapter 11).

LONDON SPEECH AND BERLIN'S BACKING

Draghi's landmark London speech of July 26, 2012, was very much his own initiative. It had not been preceded by deliberations with the governing council or with the German or French government. Only subsequently did Draghi circulate the transcript of his remarks to the ECB council, asking them to agree that the words were not at variance with the previous stance of the ECB. Draghi, after the speech, placed phone calls to Jens Weidmann, and Wolfgang Schäuble, who was vacationing. Draghi asked for help and a public defense of the ECB. Schäuble agreed to Draghi's request, overriding finance ministry officials who advised him not to comment on the decisions of the central bank. The German chancellor was slower in responding, but eventually agreed to issue a joint statement with the new French president, François Hollande, stating that the governments were "determined to do everything to defend . . . the integrity of the euro area." The member states and the European institutions should "fulfill their obligations to this end, each according to their prerogatives," the statement continued.[45] The political statement was not directly related to Draghi's speech, but it helped to increase its impact.

On the morning after Draghi's speech, the Bundesbank attacked bond buying as "problematic" and "not the most sensible" way to tackle the crisis.[46] In an innovative piece of defiance, the Bundesbank also published its resistance to the ECB measure in its monthly *Bulletin:* "The Bundesbank holds to the opinion that government bond purchases by the Eurosystem are to be seen critically and entail significant stability risks."[47] The new program "could be unlimited," and decisions about potentially far greater sharing of solvency risks should be taken by governments or parliaments, not by central banks, the Bundesbank stated.

Judged by market criteria, the new Draghi initiative was brilliantly successful. It was easy to conclude that he understood the psychology of markets more intimately than Trichet. The market psychology had pushed most of Wall Street and the City of London into taking large positions against the euro. But it was immediately obvious that in theory the central bank could intervene endlessly—and indeed do what it takes. As a consequence, many firms realized that they could not hold on to their short positions and had to unwind them.

Merkel seemed to have been impressed by the abrupt change in market sentiment: she had become convinced that she needed independent advice on the behavior of markets that the bureaucratic German establishment was incapable of giving. She talked instead to some non-German experts who were more familiar with the mentality of the City and Wall Street. On September 16, Merkel firmly restated her endorsement of Draghi's plan to intervene in the euro-area sovereign bond markets—under strict conditions—to keep down borrowing costs for the most indebted member states. "The German government has made it clear it believes that monetary stability issues justify the ECB's latest decisions," the chancellor declared. "If the ECB comes to the conclusion that money supply is difficult . . . then the central bank must take corresponding measures to ensure monetary stability. We don't lay down limits for that."[48] Berlin had broken with the Bundesbank and provided Draghi with the cover he wanted. The lesson on the need for harmony between the ECB, the Bundesbank and the Berlin government was underlined by Jörg Asmussen, a member of the ECB Governing Council who at this time provided a crucial link between Frankfurt and Berlin in working out the details of OMT: "Nobody should try to create the impression that the Bundesbank or its president are isolated."[49]

That harmony was quite short-lived, as a fight over public opinion in Germany broke out. Bundesbank president Weidmann made a number of high-profile statements that created the impression that he was trying to sway the German public against the government. Like Axel Weber in May 2010, Jens Weidmann thought that the ECB had stretched its mandate and felt obliged to express his discomfort in public. In an interview with *Der Spiegel* on August 28, he broke with the taboo of commenting on internal ECB discussions. Weidmann defended his step stating that the ECB governing council was "not a politburo. In the US, the minutes of Federal Reserve sessions are even published."[50] In the past, the ECB had believed that minutes should not be published, in large part because that would mean a higher degree of politicization and would bring the danger of seeing policy decisions as cast in terms of conflicts between the priorities of different countries in the euro area.

On September 19, 2012, Weidmann seemed to compare the ECB's unlimited bond-buying program to a scene from Goethe's *Faust*, the play that more than any other defines the German national spirit and culture. The two-century-old play also seems to hold a fascinating modern political parallel, as Weidmann realized. Goethe's Mephistopheles took Faust to observe an emperor ruling over a polity in crumbling chaos in which criminality and corruption prevail. Political parties do not function as they used to, politicians aren't trusted, nobody wants to help their neighbor, and everyone just looks out for number one. Goethe could be describing most modern political orders, and all of his criticisms of the imaginary medieval empire apply to the European Union.

The poet himself was experiencing the moribund political order of an *ancien régime* Germany that was about to disintegrate completely. Faced with the long litany of complaints about inefficiency and uncompetitiveness, Mephistopheles leaps to a simple conclusion: there had been too much deflation and austerity and what was lacking was money. There is, he says, plenty of gold and silver beneath the earth; the emperor simply needs to issue pieces of paper in the form of claims against the underground metallic treasure. The emperor is suspicious of the very clever advice and ominously remarks that Satan is always making golden chains. But everything in the empire improves as a consequence of the introduction of paper money. The generals are pleased because the soldiers are paid once more, the treasurer finds that he can pay off all the debts, tailors are busily making new clothes, ladies become more willing to embark on well-paid romantic adventures, the property market booms, and simpletons can buy big houses. Loose money produces a big boom (and that kind of state has always worried the Bundesbank).

Weidmann's excursion into the German literary past was interpreted by many commentators as an allusion to the workings of the ECB. Just two weeks earlier, on September 6, 2012, the governing council had formally agreed on the modalities of the OMT.[51] Draghi made it clear that there was a single dissent. That move did not seem to have been expected by Weidmann. On October 19, Draghi invited himself to the Bundestag and spoke to the finance and EU committees, where around a hundred parliamentarians listened to the ECB's defense against Bundesbank criticism.

RECAPITALIZATION OF BANKS

Despite these disagreements, Draghi's London speech was very effective in bringing the interest rate of peripheral sovereign debt down. Surprisingly, this appreciation in government bond prices had already occurred before the details of the OMT program were made specific in September 2012. The VLTRO in December 2011 and February 2012 and the regulatory framework had incentivized banks to load up on government bonds and turned into a stealth recapitalization of the banks. As government bond prices appreciated in value, banks made capital gains and their balance sheets improved. A "divine loop" (the opposite of the feared "diabolic loop") was at work. These capital gains also made it easier for banks to pass subsequent stress tests.

CONDITIONALITY OF OMT

The OMT was also subject to conditionality. The bond-buying program would only involve countries that were part of an ESM program, that is, the troika program countries and also Spain. Conditionality was there to ensure that fiscal and structural reforms would also be undertaken, with the aim of minimizing the risk for the ECB of a default by obtaining a sustainable path, fiscally speaking. With OMT, a more efficient and explicit conditionality framework based on the EU financial assistance program was developed. Lessons learned from earlier shortcomings of the SMP were incorporated. Of course, another motivation was to dispel German concerns about monetary financing.

GERMAN CONSTITUTIONAL COURT IN KARLSRUHE

Nevertheless, the bond-buying programs of the ECB were the subject of constitutional challenges that were carried to the German Constitutional Court in Karlsruhe by opposing economists and lawyers, who conscripted the wider public into a general mobilization of pressure against the central bank. A further challenge against the OMT program was endorsed by some 37,000 German citizens: the organizers were trying to turn a version of direct democracy against the government's assent to European rescue measures. The OMT challenge was already the second attempt. The first of these challenges was filed in 2011 and dismissed by the German Constitutional Court with a ruling that stated that the actions of the ECB were legitimate but had reached a political limit.

The initial ruling of the court in the OMT case, the second challenge, was ambiguous and after long consultations was only made public in February 2014. Some read it as an endorsement of the constitutional challenge—especially the critics of the ECB—in that the court stated that "weighty grounds" spoke for the claim that the ECB had exceeded its competence and that the court "was bending to the conclusion that the action was ultra vires."[52] But this was calculatedly not a ruling, and the court's second senate that issued its decision with a 6:2 majority almost certainly felt that it did not want to be directly responsible for setting off a financial panic that might jeopardize the euro and the European Union. Indeed, the preamble of the German Basic Law especially committed the German people to seek unity in the context of European integration.

Instead, the German court asked for an opinion from the European Court of Justice (ECJ) as a "pre-decision" (*Vorentscheidung*), so the court looked as if it were handing over some of its law-making power to a European institution. When the ECJ produced a clear ruling that the ECB had not exceeded its powers "in relation to monetary policy" and that the OMT program did not contravene the prohibition on monetary financing, the financial community believed that Mario Draghi and the ECB were vindicated. The German critics were furious, with the veteran Bavarian politician Peter Gauweiler calling this a "declaration of war against Karlsruhe" and Hans-Werner Sinn predicting a major constitutional crisis, as the European Court was interfering with German democracy, and his successor as head of the CESifo think tank, Clemens Fuest, more soberly stating that OMT was fiscal and not monetary policy.[53] In the end, it looked as if, in a decision of supreme political importance, German judges were not confident of being able to assess the economic consequences of their rulings and inevitably worried about a decision that might plunge Europe into turmoil.

Quantitative Easing (QE) and Extraordinary Measures

NEGATIVE INTEREST RATES, TLTRO, AND ASSET-BASED SECURITIES

In 2014, it became increasingly clear that the ECB would miss its inflation target of below but close to 2 percent. Even inflation in Germany—an economy that was in full employment—fell far short of the 2 percent mark. The German price response mattered to Europe because it made adjustment in Europe harder: to remove the competitive difference that had built up in the first decade of the twenty-first century, Germany needed some inflation and the Southern countries some deflation.

It was unclear at first what the appropriate policy response should be, as there were many uncertainties. Was the threat of deflation an illusion produced by a temporary commodity shock? Some part of the low-inflation outcome was the result of falling oil prices. The worry was that the decline in oil prices would lead to second-round effects: lower oil prices, lower inflation expectations, lower wage growth rate, lower inflation for all products, and so on.

In June 2014, the ECB embarked on three measures: First, it ventured in the area of negative interest rates. The ECB cut the rate paid on bank deposits to a negative rate, −0.1 percent, moving later in September to −0.2 percent. The Danish central bank had already introduced a negative rate in 2012, to stop capital inflows at the height of the euro crisis; and the Swiss National Bank made the same move in December 2014 in a vain bid to halt the appreciation of its currency. In February 2015, the Swedish Riksbank followed. The motivation of the ECB cut was primarily to avoid deflation and raise inflation closer to the 2 percent that constituted its mandate. However, many commentators quickly noted the most obvious effect of the move would be to lower the exchange rate of the euro. One way this process worked was that borrowers in other countries—largely emerging markets—found it attractive to borrow in a low cost and depreciating currency. The carry trade lowers the value of the euro. The prospect of currency wars seemed to recall the worst aspects of the 1930s Great Depression experience, but in fact the period of euro depreciation soon came to an end.

Second, the ECB agreed to targeted longer-term refinancing operations (TLTROs) that were designed to prompt European banks to lend more in support of economic activity (rather than simply refinancing government debt): the four-year credits were based on the banks' outstanding loans and secondly on their net lending.

Third, in the summer of 2014, the ECB also started off with the purchase of private assets, so-called asset-backed papers. The purchase of private assets was seen by some as less controversial as it is further removed from the danger of government funding by central banks. The ECB in particular wanted to use the program to affect business conditions and was worried that the small and medium enterprise (SME) sector that was vital to the economy in many European countries (especially in Northern Italy and Spain) had been locked out of bank lending by the effects of the bank crisis. An asset-based securities purchasing program might thus be a way of galvanizing the European financial sector. Overall, however, the asset-backed securities markets stayed small, and the quantitative impact of the program remained limited.

The Jackson Hole Speech

A decisive turn was taken by Mario Draghi at the end of August 2014, in a speech that he gave in Jackson Hole, Wyoming, a scenic meeting ground where senior central bankers from across the world meet every year. As in his June 2012 London speech, the ECB president inserted crucial remarks at the last moment that were not included in the prepared (written) text. With great clarity and vigor, Draghi focused the analysis on long-term inflation expectations.[54] Central bankers know they have little influence on short-term movements in the inflation rate. Their main objective is to control inflation in the medium term. At this horizon, expectations are the major driver of inflation. If people believe that the central bank will fulfill its mandate, if the central bank is credible, then long-term expectations are stable or, in the jargon, "anchored." That had constantly been the case for the ECB since its creation. Long-term inflation expectations had stayed close to 2 percent, the definition of price stability. But, for the first time, they were drifting down and getting close to 1.6 percent. This was considered very worrisome, and Draghi made it clear that it could be a reason to act.

Inflation expectations can be measured in many ways. They can be inferred from surveys of consumers and professional forecasters or they can be extracted from financial market data: First, survey-based inflation expectations focus on households, which are typically very stable and mostly driven by prices of specific highly visible products such as gasoline, milk, or chocolate. The price increase of these products also affects the public's perception of inflation and thus has a disproportionately large political impact. Second, there is also traded inflation that can be ascertained from the many financial products that allow one to infer the inflation expectations of traders. The ECB, as many other central banks, paid special attention to the "five years in five years" expectation, that is, the inflation rate that financial markets project from year five to year ten, starting from now. This specific indicator has always played an important role in internal policy deliberations. By virtue of the Jackson Hole speech, it has almost become an intermediate objective of ECB monetary policy.

QE ANNOUNCEMENT BY THE ECB

In January 2015, amid continued deflationary pressures, the ECB announced its own large-scale QE program. The size of the program turned out to be larger than the market expected: €60 billion bonds per month were to be purchased, comprising €45 billion of sovereign debt, €5 billion of bonds issued by institutions and agencies, and €10 billion for asset-backed securities and covered bonds (an extension of the previously existing program). The price movements during the minutes of the QE announcements revealed the extent to which markets perceived the impact of the program. The German bund (ten year) yield dropped by 0.13 percentage points (even though the announcement was widely expected). More interestingly, the US Treasury (ten year) also dropped by 0.10 percentage points. That was a clear sign of spillovers, in which easier borrowing in the euro area made it easier to finance debt elsewhere in the world.

The program started in March 2015 and was supposed to run at least until September 2016, so that total purchases would amount to €1.1 trillion. If the inflation target was at that point not yet within reach, QE could be extended beyond September 2016. The purchases would be made in proportion to the capital that each member's central bank contributed to the ECB. National central banks make 80 percent of the purchases and also take on any risk they carry. As a consequence, the loss sharing that the Germans worried about would be limited to 20 percent. The limitation of loss sharing amounted to a concession to German interests, but it still looked as if the QE program would in effect amount to the introduction of a Eurobond through the backdoor. Some critics, however, noted that the limitation of loss sharing meant that the idea of a single monetary policy had taken a hit. And, critically, the QE purchases did not include Greek government bonds, as Greece did not satisfy some technical requirements (in place precisely to limit Greece's access to the program).

Possible Transmission Mechanisms of QE

The transmission mechanism of QE is not fully understood. Bernanke famously claimed that "The problem with QE is it works in practice, but it doesn't work in theory."[55] Many channels are at work. The most frequently mentioned is the portfolio rebalancing channel. When the central bank buys long-term debt, it gives cash to portfolio managers and creates an incentive for them to buy other riskier assets. In this way, long-term rates tend to decrease over a wide spectrum of financial asset classes. If this rebalancing takes place toward foreign assets, the exchange rate depreciates and that would stimulate exports through the exchange rate channel. Interestingly, a very large fraction of bonds were purchased from foreign sellers allowing foreigners to sell their holdings at an enhanced price. Moreover, QE may have a signaling effect: by showing its determination to act, the central bank could directly hit long-term inflation expectations. Finally, there is a redistributive channel, as QE redistributes wealth between different sectors. If balance sheet–impaired parts of the economy are assisted in this way, the result should contribute to macro economic stabilization.

There were a number of paradoxes that this action produced. Generally, the IMF was supportive of QE. But the most immediate effect of the measure would be a further increase of German exports, and both the IMF and the United States were strongly critical of the German trade surplus, which they saw as the major cause of global imbalances and consequently of deflationary pressure on deficit countries.

But this exchange rate effect could have been what the ECB implicitly sought. Monetary authorities could intervene in bond markets with the intended or unintended effect of weakening the currency: this strategy has constituted the only real success of Abenomics in Japan. Europeans had always suspected that it was the weaker dollar that boosted the United States after 2009. Moreover, the worry about the world economy would shift to emerging markets, where corporations could embark on a new carry trade and fund themselves in euros. As they did that, they would need to sell the euros they had borrowed to undertake local investments, with the effect that the exchange rate of the euro would be lowered further and the carry trade of borrowing in a low-interest, undervalued currency would become even more lucrative.[56] No central bank would admit that it is implicitly targeting the exchange rate, the reason being that the action would be seen as a beggar-thy-neighbor policy, as it obviously isn't possible for everybody to depreciate at the same time. Indeed, in late 2010, when the Federal Reserve Open Market Committee discussed QE, Governor Kevin Warsh stated that this policy would not be seen as politically correct: "I think there's a good reason for that. I think it's a dangerous policy. I think it is risky pool playing in the foreign exchange markets, asking them to do so much of our work when the world's recovery is resting on this."[57]

The other, more traditional channel through which QE was held to work was through domestic demand. If that was the case, and if the problem was lopsided low inflation or deflation within the euro area, then the appropriate stance would have been to buy German securities (especially government bonds, bunds) so as to push German demand and inflation. This would have made Germany less competitive and close the wage gap that emerged in the first decade of the twenty-first century. Such a policy would have led to an increase in the spreads between German and peripheral bonds—an outcome that the ECB wished to avoid.

The redistributive channel view emphasizes that correctly designed QE can redistribute wealth toward balance sheet–impaired entities in crisis countries. This interpretation suggests that the ECB should purchase assets from crisis countries only, and not from the core. As such a program would be clearly and openly redistributive, it would invite the objection that the ECB was in effect acting as a European fiscal central planner. It would have the effect of lowering yields and pushing up the value of government bonds that are held to a large extent by banks in crisis countries. Hence, QE essentially was a form of recapitalizing banks in crisis countries.

GERMAN OBJECTIONS TO QE

As mentioned above, Germany, and the Bundesbank in particular, has deep-seated objections toward any kind of public asset purchase by the ECB. There are good reasons to think that Weidman opposed the decision in the governing council. German opposition was articulated in the public debate along several lines.

A first issue was whether inflation and inflation expectations are measured in the right way. It is not clear that inflation expectations inferred from financial products, such as the five year/five year inflation swap, should be the target. Applied to the world of 2014, the German view saw the problem as coming mostly from the collapse of oil (and some other commodity) prices. That development amounted to a real increase in income for oil-importing countries (including the European-crisis countries) and should correctly be thought of as a windfall gain or even as a stimulus package. Low oil prices were something to cheer about, not something to deplore.[58]

A second question is whether nonconventional measures are effective. As the interest rate was already set to its minimum level (known as the zero lower bound), monetary stimulus had to take a different form than interest rate reductions. The model was the United States, where the Fed implemented three rounds of quantitative easing measures involving the purchase of government bonds and mortgage-backed securities. The Fed's approach was widely judged to have been a success that had allowed the US economy to recover while Europe was still stagnating. Overall, the first and third round of QE in the US, QE1 and QE3, largely involved purchases of mortgage products and, hence, propped up housing prices. This helped the balance sheet–impaired housing sector to recover. The success of the part of US QE operations that involved government debt is less obvious. This suggests that the redistributive channel toward balance-sheet constrained sectors in the economy is more effective than the signaling effect. In the same vein, there were also unsuccessful versions of QE in the history books. Japan had played with a version of QE back in the 1990s, but it was undone after some few years and, hence, not very effective. In 2013, quantitative and qualitative monetary easing (QQE) was implemented, which led to large price swings in the exchange rate and the stock market. Consequently, some observers interpreted the main effect of QE as being on the foreign exchange market.

Third, the story of falling inflation and the risk of deflation was interpreted in different ways. The German position was that declining prices do not necessarily go hand in hand with declining consumer expenditures and that consumers do not necessarily delay the purchase of a good because it will be cheaper (or better) tomorrow. The most obvious example is consumer electronics, such as computers or televisions. Despite steadily falling prices, people continued to buy electronic products.[59]

Finally, the position that some kinds of deflation are not inimical to growth is also supported by the historical record. Especially in the nineteenth century, there were long periods of "good" deflation, when falling prices reflected improved productivity and demand was sustained. In a recent study, the BIS examined thirty-eight economies over 140 years and found that low inflation did not correspond to low growth.[60] The historical argument about bad or vicious deflation is based on one very dramatic and dangerous case, but it is a rather exceptional one: the Great Depression.

The counterargument rests on the point that there is real wage rigidity: in other words, it is hard to reduce wages as prices fall, and thus workers will price themselves out of jobs. There is some evidence for this effect, even in the alleged episodes of good deflation from the nineteenth century.[61] In Europe's periphery, nominal wages declined while prices were more sticky (see chapter 6).

On the QE program in particular, the Germans believed that there was an inappropriate mixing or conflation of monetary with fiscal policy. QE helps to recapitalize, especially, peripheral banks by generating capital gains on their existing government bond holdings. In addition, the ECB is taking credit risk through the purchase of bonds from fiscally weak countries, and if these countries default, the ECB would suffer losses that in the end have to be borne by (German) taxpayers. So, in effect, the ECB's QE policy amounts to transfers from core to periphery. German policy makers also feared that QE could de facto introduce Eurobonds and joint liability through the backdoor, and they worried that the ECB's measures would weaken incentives to cut deficits and debts in the peripheral countries. In addition, there were specific technical issues that might mean that QE would not work as well as in the United States. The corporate bond market is relatively small and illiquid (compared to the United States), so European interventions are much harder.

Impact of QE on Inflation Expectations

Figure 15.4 shows the evolution of the five year/five year inflation swap rate. From summer 2014, and especially after Mario Draghi's Jackson Hole speech, the inflation expectations declined. The evolution of the inflation expectations after January 2015 can be interpreted in two ways: either QE stops the downward trend or QE is not very effective. In any case, QE helped to contain potential spillover effects that might have emerged from the Grexit threat in the summer of 2015. This significantly lowered the bargaining power of the Greek government as it could no longer threaten causing havoc to the rest of peripheral Europe. Paradoxically, even though Germany was opposed to QE, the measure helped Germany because Greece couldn't threaten with adverse spillover effects.

In March 2016 the ECB cut its deposit interest rate further to -0.4 percent and expanded its QE program, amid continued subdued inflation and credit growth numbers. It increased the monthly QE purchases of sovereign bonds from €60 billion to €80 billion a month. In addition, a new series of four targeted longer-term refinancing operations (TLTRO II), each with a maturity of four years, would be launched, starting in June 2016. Borrowing conditions in these operations can be as low as the negative interest rate on the deposit facility.

FIGURE 15.4. Inflation Expectations Inferred from the Five Year/Five Year Swap Contract and Size of ECB's Balance Sheet

Alternatives to Lending and Purchase Programs

What are potential alternatives to asset purchase programs? Recently, some economists began taking up Milton Friedman's old idea of a "helicopter drop of money," that is, a stimulus that would be in effect fiscal. The modern version of helicopter money is sometimes termed "People's QE," as it supposedly benefits everyone equally rather than banks and investors. The intrusion of central banks into direct redistribution, however, looks dangerous to many in the German tradition. Otmar Issing stated that the proposal simply reflected intellectual confusion.[62]

Another alternative to QE would have been a communication policy by the central banks targeted at influencing wage bargaining. Such a policy would directly address the competitiveness gap between peripheral and core countries that builds up through wage restraints in the core countries. While nominal wage cuts in the peripheral countries would also close this gap, it is problematic as debtors would not be able to repay their debts—the "Devaluation Dilemma" discussed in chapter 6. A wage rise in the core countries avoids this debt deflation. In this sense, Germany's introduction of a minimum wage in 2015 was helpful. The German Bundesbank made some initial steps toward such a communication strategy but was not sufficiently determined and shied away from presenting it as a serious alternative to QE. The Bundesbank has a long tradition of managing inflation expectations and through it wage bargaining. The most effective help Germany can provide is to have strong wage growth in Germany and avoid negative second-round effects from the current low-inflation environment (which is partially due to the low oil price.) The shock of falling oil prices in 2014–2015 can be seen as exactly the opposite to the oil price increases of 1973–1974 and 1979. In the 1970s the Bundesbank tried to avoid the second-round effects of high oil prices on wage bargaining. From 1974, when the Bundesbank moved to monetary targeting, its representatives also insisted that a major goal in setting the monetary target was to give employer and worker representatives a sense of how the economy was developing, and consequently of what would be an appropriate wage settlement. Today, an equivalent communications policy would nudge wages up—in an environment in which, in Germany at least, there is already some wage growth.

Single Supervisory Mechanism (SSM) for European Banks

With the onset of the euro crisis, Mario Draghi saw an opening, an opportunity to establish a strong banking union within the euro area. The decision to involve the ECB in banking supervision and regulation was, next to the founding of the ESM, major institutional change in Europe's financial governance. The decision was taken very fast, and only three months elapsed between the first discussion in 2012 and the formal agreement in the euro leaders' summit. The ECB's central role was quickly recognized, including by the Commission, and 1,000 new positions were created in Frankfurt, a significant increase in the staffing of the ECB.[63] This large change was controversially discussed by policy makers and academics of euro-area countries.

Historical Background

The question of whether the ECB should be involved in banking supervision and regulation has a long history that goes back to the early days of thinking about the institutional logic of monetary union. The penultimate draft of the 1989 Delors Report, the founding document of the economic and monetary union, specified in paragraph 32 that the "system would participate in the coordination of banking supervision policies of the national supervisory authorities."[64] But in the final report, "national" was deleted, leaving the implication that the supervisory authorities would be European. In the original draft of the ECB statute produced by the governors' alternates, the "tasks" of the ECB included "to support the stability of the financial system," and Article 25 on "Prudential Supervision" included the following tasks for the ECB, which were placed in square brackets to indicate that they were not yet consensual:

25.2. [The ECB may formulate, interpret and implement policies relating to the prudential supervision of credit and other financial institutions for which it is designated as competent supervisory authority.]

25.3. [The ECB shall be entitled to offer advice to Community bodies and national authorities on measures which it considers desirable for the purpose of maintaining the stability of the banking and financial systems.]

25.4. [The ECB may itself determine policies and take measures within its competence necessary for the purpose of maintaining the stability of the banking and financial systems.][65]

The Bundesbank consistently wanted to avoid references to an explicit role for the ECB in supervising banks, "especially in the context of maintaining the stability of the banking and financial system and the delicate question of moral hazard. These two Articles could be misinterpreted as a lender of last-resort function."[66] As a consequence, the items in square brackets were in the end excised from the draft. In October 1990, when the alternates discussed the Banking Supervision Subcommittee's proposals on draft articles for the central bank statute, Hans Tietmeyer restated the skeptical position of the Bundesbank, which was consistently worried about the moral hazard implications of central bank involvement in supervision. If the central bank took on the responsibility of regulating, it would also deliver an implicit commitment to rescue banks should there be bad developments that it had overlooked. Tietmeyer provided a neat encapsulation of the German philosophy of regulation: "This did not mean from the view of the Board of the Deutsche Bundesbank that the ECB should not support the stability of the financial system, but that it should never be written down; this would be moral hazard."[67]

By the time the proposal about ECB involvement in banking supervision was included in the Maastricht Treaty's provisions on monetary policy (Article 105, section 6, now Article 127 of the Lisbon Treaty), it was accompanied by so many provisos that it looked as if the hurdles to effective European banking supervision could not be set higher. The intrusion of politics had thus resulted in a fundamental flaw in the new European monetary order.

Institutional Debates

A major debate regarding the creation of a euro-wide banking union was whether the agency responsible for this role of bank supervision would be under ECB management—or even part of the ECB—or a separate institution in Brussels. A main concern was the potential conflict of interest involved in having the central bank as the major bank supervisor. To some, including the Bundesbank, this could create an incentive to deflect monetary policy from its main objective of price stability and make decisions based on the necessity to preserve the health of the banking sector—or worse, enter a world of financial dominance where the central bank would be forced to print money to preserve the stability of the financial system. Moreover, mistakes in banking supervision may hurt the credibility of the central bank—a negative spillover.

On the other hand, positive complementarities also existed, others argued. Information flows are a major one. Indeed, during the crisis, the ECB had very little information about the value of collateral held by banks, for example, yet was supposed to act as a lender of last resort to them. (Many collateral assets were marked to model, as many loans are not traded.) Information sharing was very limited, and NCBs were generally reluctant to pass it on to the ECB, which had already taken away a hefty share of their former power. The positive aspect of centralizing banking and market supervisions can also be understood when contrasting it with US regulation. There, many regulators coexist with often conflicting interests; the SEC, for example, is or used to be controlled by lawyers with an emphasis on investor protection but not financial stability. An alphabet soup of regulators exists: SEC, CFTC, Fed, and so on. De facto, financial firms are or were able to pick their favorite regulators, resulting in moral hazard problems—to which the Fed is or was powerless.

Another important debate about a euro-wide banking union was the scope of the supervisory mechanism. While Germans insisted that the scope should be limited, leaving national supervisory boards some powers, notably over small banks, such as savings and loans, France also wanted to put small banks under European supervision. It argued that small banks can also be systemic, like Northern Rock in the United Kingdom. The fact that most banks in France are large banks, that is, national champions, may have also played a role in this position.

Another debate was whether and to what extent macroprudential regulation should be Europeanized. While the crisis regulation had previously focused on the soundness of each bank separately, after the crisis, the focus shifted to the soundness of the whole financial system. Microprudential regulation was complemented with macroprudential regulation. Macroprudential regulation is closely interlinked with monetary policy. Indeed, in many Asian countries, price stability is conducted with macroprudential instruments. For example, Hong Kong has a currency board with the United States, that is, the exchange rate is fixed. Hence,

Hong Kong cannot use the interest rate as a policy tool. Hong Kong is instead using macroprudential tools, such as loan-to-value ratio regulation, to achieve its inflation objective. Given the close link between macroprudential policies and monetary policy, some observers found it natural to also extend the ECB's sphere of influence to macroprudential policy.

This is especially the case because this would allow the ECB to smooth out regional policies and lean against national bubbles and credit imbalances. Indeed, as was mentioned before, the ECB used as a main instrument for its monetary policy a unique, euro-area-wide interest rate—which caused regional imbalances. Differential macroprudential policies are one way to lean against these imbalances. More generally, such an arrangement could optimize a nonoptimal currency area.[68]

Compromises

In light of these debates, appropriate governance arrangements had to be negotiated. The scheme agreed upon in December 2012, which led to the creation of the Single Supervisory Mechanism (SSM), reflected the concerns of all parties. Supervision decisions would be taken by a new supervisory board, separated from the governing council, but subordinated to it. The chair of the board (currently Daniele Nouy) would be independent from the ECB's executive board, although the vice chair (currently Sabine Lautenschläger) would come from the latter—again, to facilitate information flows while keeping linkages to a minimum to preserve the ECB's reputation. A single resolution authority (the SRM) and a joint deposit insurance fund were also created as part of the banking union—as we discussed in detail in chapters 10 and 11. It is not clear that this complicated governance structure will stay the same in the long run.

In terms of scope, a certain division of tasks had to be decided between the SSM and the corresponding national authorities. Systemic banks were to be supervised directly by the ECB. National authorities would take care of banks judged nonsystemic, but, importantly, the SSM would keep the right to supervise any bank it deemed to be systemically important. Moreover, the SSM would also have the rights to conduct on-site inspections, grant and withdraw banking licenses, set up capital requirements, and make some adjustments to banks' balance sheets if it deemed such actions necessary. Another important task involved stress tests or, more generally, comprehensive assessment of the health of the banking sector in the euro area.

Overall, the SSM was granted a sizable share of power. Some actually discussed whether the ECB could end up with too much power and dominate other institutions in the euro area, or even the European Union. Indeed, granting it supervisory authority would in some sense challenge the importance of other institutions (discussed in chapter 11) that were created at a European level to deal with banking issues, notably the European Banking Authority (EBA) and the European Systemic Risk Board (ESRB). This is especially so because the SSM, in terms of staffing, turns out to be much larger in size than the EBA and the ESRB, and nonmember states of the European Union have the right to enter it if they want to. As of now, this is still an open issue, but there definitely exists a tension between the euro area and the rest of the European Union—what some have labeled "two-speed Europe."

Taking Stock: Where Does the ECB Stand?

The ECB appears both as a hero and a victim of the crisis—a tragic hero. It has been heroic in many ways: taking initiatives and risks, facing and resisting the pressures, and finally saving the day at a moment when all hope seemed to be lost. Why did it have a "good" crisis—unlike the IMF, whose prestige suffered? Unlike the IMF, the ECB is not directly owned by governments, and the possibilities for political intervention are more limited. But the major initiatives outlined were backed by the political authorities—including and especially Germany—and that backing made the initiatives credible and effective.

According to some observers, the ECB came out with its reputation enhanced, its independence fully intact, and near universal respect from both inside and outside the euro area. As an institution, however, it suffered significant collateral damage. Its internal cohesion has been badly shaken. Trust has repeatedly been broken between its members. It was hit by two successive resignations from its governing council. And it has been bitterly attacked in Germany from one side and in peripheral countries from the other side.

To some extent, the controversy, the plaudits, and the blame are all just a consequence of the new postcrisis role of central banks: despite the power shift away from EU institutions (see chapter 2), the ECB is the only one that grew in power (in addition to the newly created ESM). The enhanced influence of central banks is not confined to Europe but is really common in all big industrial countries. The European discussion has its parallels in the United States, where the Fed and especially its chairman were attacked by Republicans in the 2012 election. Unorthodox policies required choosing to buy particular assets, with a redistributional conse-quence. There was a move from monetary policy to credit policy and, in effect, for the central bank to be making fiscal policy.[69] This same criticism has been made in Europe and comes from some powerful and influential former policy makers. The well-regarded former ECB chief economist, the German Otmar Issing, for instance, responds to questions about the ECB by first stating that as a former ECB official, he feels that he should not make comments on monetary policy: but then he adds that because the ECB is now doing fiscal policy, he can indeed speak (and speak critically).

It was frequently claimed, in the context of the bitter divisions in Europe, that the central banks were the only grownups in the room. But it was not just a question of acting efficiently: it was also a matter of generating new approaches. The ECB was more of an effective policy laboratory during the euro crisis than the European Commission. It needed to reconcile concep-tually opposite theories. Sometimes its officials liked to joke that they were two-handed economists, constantly saying on the one hand, on the other hand. When the Europe an Commission produced plans for greater fiscal integration, they were smiled at. But the ECB developed an approach that in effect amounted to greater fiscal integration and then set about thinking of ways in which that might be formalized. During the course of the crisis, the ECB became a central European institution. As outlined in this chapter, three major innovations changed the course of the crisis response: policy conditionality, the prospect of OMT, and the move toward a banking union (the latter two occurring in the summer of 2012).

All the initiatives needed to be justified by reference to the mandate created by the Maastricht Treaty. From the point of view of the ECB, mon-etary easing was justified simply by reference to the mandate of price sta-bility. The ECB's policymakers did not think that their actions, effectively lowering borrowing costs in debtor countries, had any effect on the will-ingness of those countries to embark on structural reforms. Many of the needed reforms—simplification of over-complex regulation, streamlining of voting procedures, labor market reforms—could not really be said to be induced by the need to respond to a fiscal crisis. By contrast, creditor governments, especially in Germany, equally firmly believed the idea that only crisis could induce reform in a fundamentally blocked society and policy, and that without crisis there would be no reform. That case was most clearly made in respect to pensions policy, a subject of ferocious political contestation particularly in Greece and Spain. So on one side, or on the French or southern hand, there was a belief that reform needed a conducive policy environment; on the German or northern hand, the opposed belief that reform arose out of inclement circumstances. The ECB tried to alleviate inclemency.

Presidents Trichet and Draghi spoke about completing the European Union. They—and other board members, such as Benoît Coeuré, who spoke of the need for a European Finance Ministry—were driven by a sense that the ECB had been overextended by the crisis and that it urgently needed to have a counterpart in strengthened EU institutions.[70] But in becoming more powerful, the ECB also had become more vulnerable. An independent central bank just seemed to be making too many decisions.

16

Conclusion: Black and White or Twenty-Eight Shades of Gray?

At the heart of this book is the story of diverging concepts of how economics works. They have polarized and divided Europe and made responses to the financial crisis weaker and the crisis in consequence more intense. The problem of differing views of how economics works is not, of course, confined to Europe. The United States is famously divided between freshwater (Chicago, Minnesota) and saltwater (MIT, Harvard, Princeton, Berkeley) economics, a division that has some affinity—but not a complete identity—with the political division between "red" and "blue" states. For a long time, the economics world in the United Kingdom was sharply differentiated between Cambridge and the London School of Economics. Economists in fact often present quite different imaginative simplifications of how the world works—models. Sometimes, they believe that their creation is a universal model, applicable in all circumstances. Recently, Dani Rodrik made a plea that economists should have a more modest view of the universalizability of their models and instead should proceed rather pragmatically to "carry multiple models in their heads simultaneously" and "build maps between specific settings and applicable models."[1]

In the previous chapters, we have investigated how different models, broadly conceived, have led to a nondialogue in Europe, especially between France and Germany, while politics should be all about dialogue and the reconciliation of views and differences. At the moment, each side does not understand the other. As a consequence, they misinterpret what the other side is arguing and impute, instead of well-intentioned and constructive motives, egoistical desires and sinister master plans. The old strategy in European debates was to paper over these differences, to pretend that they weren't really there. Meetings would produce agreement about only a vague outcome, and everyone would go home thinking things were well and then find out in a few days or weeks that actually the fundamental problems were still there.

The aim of our book is to make readers—including, we hope, Europe's decision makers—aware of the different ways of economic thinking. There needs to be a deeper understanding of the differences before there can really be any reconciliation of the different positions. One of the facts that the book has demonstrated is that these differences are not written in stone; they are not eternal, and they may, especially in crisis situations, be quite fluid.

Toward an "Economic Ideas Union"

Today, everyone is talking at a political level about "completing the European Union."[2] There has been progress on establishing the banking union; there is a debate about a capital markets union, with capital markets substituting for banks as a source of funding; the coordination of refugee policy is an urgent issue, requiring a migration union; and the coordination of energy policy has also and already for a long time been a focus of political attention. These financial and economic themes are at the core of the recent *Five Presidents' Report*, though the report observes that "In significant policy areas, such as goods and services, as well as in areas with untapped potential, such as energy, digital and capital markets, the Single Market is still incomplete."[3]

How can that incompleteness be tackled? Our answer to the European problem would be to have an economic ideas union.

In the examples of the United States or the United Kingdom, differences in economic views are played out in terms of attempts to influence national politics. Europe would need to go further and have a political debate union. Having the *Spitzenkandidaten* for the European presidency in 2014 was a first step. There are obvious linguistic barriers, but it is conceivable that in a relatively short space of time they might be overcome by automatic translation. Social media with such translation enabled could effectively create a common European political space, a common framework for analysis. China and India also have multiple languages but manage a shared political culture, as does Switzerland in the middle of Europe.

At the moment, a great deal of the European debate occurs in English, which creates plenty of possibilities for misunderstandings. It also can easily contribute to two very undesirable outcomes. First, the American and British participants in debates may think that they are superior because their accents are a little bit more authentic or their grammar a little less defective. A great deal of the interpretation of the course of the euro crisis was shaped by the British and American press—the *Financial Times*, the *Economist*, the *New York Times*, and the *Wall Street Journal*—and that outside vision was filtered through a sort of condescension about Europeans not really getting it.

Second, the international debate in an elite language—English—has fostered the idea that there is a large gap between the technocracy in governments and central banks on the one hand and ordinary people on the other. A large part of the response to the various European crises is thus increasingly driven by a populism that portrays itself as defending citizens against the cosmopolitan elite.

Overcoming National Thinking

The economist and political scientist Mancur Olson identified what he termed a logic of collective action, in which powerful sectoral groups frustrate attempts to find an overall collective solution that corresponds to a general or overarching interest. His analysis offers a helpful way to understand Europe's contemporary stasis. Obviously, the complex political construction of a mechanism for integrating and coordinating the positions of twenty-eight national governments lends itself to blockage by particular interests. In modern Europe, there is really no clear way of articulating and politically representing the general interest of Europeans.

Some contemporary issues that have been tearing Europe apart should in principle not be difficult to resolve if they are seen in aggregate terms. The euro area as a whole has a lower public sector deficit (as a share of GDP) than the United States, the United Kingdom, or Japan: for 2015, the IMF estimates are 2.0 percent for the euro area, but 3.7 percent for the United States, 4.4 percent for the United Kingdom, and 5.2 percent for Japan.[4] The net debt levels show a similar position of greater European sustainability: 69.4 percent of GDP for the euro area, but 80.6 percent for the United States, 80.7 percent for the United Kingdom, and 128.1 percent for Japan. Few outsiders argue that the United States or the United Kingdom have an impossible fiscal position. Similarly, the European Union, with a population of over 500 million, should not have a problem integrating much larger numbers of refugees than the 160,000 that the European Commission is planning on distributing throughout Europe. Energy coordination and the greater integration of energy markets would deal effectively with an important aspect of the security threat.

However, when these same issues are treated exclusively within the framework of national politics, they look insuperable. When the problem is framed nationally, no one can produce an answer. The clashes between national approaches generate conflicts that threaten to tear Europe apart.

After 2008, national politics everywhere—not just in Europe—have become more important for two reasons: as an emotional reaction to crises and as a financial or fiscal reaction that then shapes the kind of response to the challenge that can be envisaged.

First, then, there is a new unease or uncertainty about the world as a whole, specifically about the consequences of globalization. National politics are sometimes presented as a way of defending local populations against threats that come from the outside. The state looks like a defense mechanism in the age of globalization.

Globalization pulls people together over long distances. But the participants do not always like the results. They find the cultures of others too strange: there are different cuisines, different languages, and different religions. Islam in particular looks strange to many modern Europeans, and its theocratic tendencies run counter to expectations of a secular or nonreligious state. There is as a consequence a strongly national element to the populist parties that have arisen in the wake of the financial crisis and the euro crisis.

Globalization inevitably exposes people to problems in faraway countries. They often respond by thinking of ways to be more self-sufficient. In the twentieth century, the most common form of the response was to demand trade protection, but that is now a more remote threat because large numbers of consumers are used to the idea of cheap clothing and cheap electronics.

But the story of bad reactions to globalization is not just confined to the trade policy response. The most obvious human side of globalization is the way it generates large flows of people. In some of the large emerging markets that are hitting the economic buffers, the political response is that a new or more intense authoritarianism could cure the problem of dysfunctional economics. There are also more wars. As a result, many people are afraid in the face of substantial violence. And people who are afraid are even more inclined to migrate.

Second, there are more immediate financial reasons why a crisis makes people look more closely at the national political framework. Managing the aftermath of major financial crises, as opposed to trying to prevent them from developing, always involves the mobilization of substantial fiscal resources. That task remained in the hands of national governments, as the European Union had only a very small fiscal capacity of its own. So inevitably, when it comes to demands for state action, people focus on the national states, and these are the wrong framework for dealing with many of today's problems.

Focusing on the national unit and its fiscal capacity has had further consequences for the way in which people view Europe. Not all the twenty-eight member states are the same size; and in the course of the crisis, it has become clearer that many solutions are hammered out essentially between two countries, France and Germany—and even then Germany is substantially more powerful and effective than France. So a great deal of the crisis turned out to be a debate about the new German question, about the extent of German power and whether modern Germany had the capacity or the willingness for leadership in Europe. Almost every sort of German leadership is deeply problematic, however. Thus, the nationalist right in other European countries will even see the positive response to the refugee crisis as an egotistical attempt to exploit the cheap labor opportunities following increased migration. Marine Le Pen of the French National Front speaks of Germany creating a new empire based on slave labor. The Brexit campaign had a strongly Germano-critical component.

There is, in other words, a need for a mechanism for seeing the big picture issue, for zooming out from the obsession with the national and onto the aggregate, to the big picture, to Europe as a whole. But how can Europeans get this larger picture, and how can it stop seeing the world primarily in terms of national interest, national advantage, and national egotism?

The "Rhine-Divide": Four Key Differences

This book has described a mental world in which the policy approach on either side of the River Rhine is sharply differentiated by fundamentally contrasted outlooks. We have examined four poles along which these differences lie. The first is rules versus discretion. The German tradition of federalism, like federalism elsewhere, requires a carefully formulated and legally binding system of rules. The long French tradition of a central state means that the ruler—the heir to the great monarchs of the ancient regime—has initiative and flexibility.

The second pole is liability versus solidarity. The German tradition requires a strong principle of liability: if you break the rules, you are responsible for the consequences. The French tradition, coming from the French Revolution, has by contrast a principle of solidarity, of sharing the burdens of the weaker and disadvantaged.

The third pole is solvency versus liquidity. In managing sudden crises or shocks, German see fundamental solvency issues when bad behavior has resulted in liabilities exceeding assets and there is little chance of rescue except through a radical alteration of behavior. On the other side of the Rhine, and of the English Channel, and of the Atlantic, values are subject to big fluctuations and an effective and appropriate action can ensure that temporary liquidity issues are resolved and that there is no long-term insolvency.

And, fourth, there is a difference in the appropriate response. On the one side of the debate, austerity provides big incentives to improve behavior, to reform, or to remove institutional imperfections. On the other side, austerity perpetuates and makes worse the liquidity problems and threatens to really produce insolvencies, so monetary or fiscal stimulus is required. The first approach is emphatically not Keynesian, the second is.

This book has also examined the moments at which these differing concepts have clashed most strikingly: first, in regard to the first Greek crisis in May 2010 and especially in the formulation of a strategy for private sector involvement in October 2010; second, in thinking about the appropriate central bank (ECB) response to the threat of euro-area disintegration in the summer of 2012; third, in respect to the general issues raised by the crisis in the Cyprus banking system in 2013; and, finally, in respect to a renewed uncertainty about the Greek program and the threat of Grexit in 2015, as well as to the prospect of Brexit in 2016.

The discussions, and clashes of views, were played out in different forums. October 2010, which we argue shaped the euro crisis, was a bilateral deal between the French president and the German chancellor. There were many other meetings of the European Council, in which the two large countries played a dominant role. The European Commission struggled to make effective suggestions. The IMF was brought in, despite enormous initial resistance in France and Germany, to bridge the incompatibilities, but the result strained relations between the IMF and European institutions and probably also damaged the reputation and effectiveness of the Fund. The ECB proved to be the most effective forum in which policy initiatives emerged, above all in July 2012 and again with the move to a QE program. In that sense, the ECB was engaged in an intellectual endeavor to make sense of Europe's crisis. But there are obviously limits to which policy initiatives, especially with large potential fiscal implications, can be delegated to a central bank whose mandate is primarily concerned with monetary stability.

Geopolitical Threats: Ukraine-Russian Conflicts and Refugee Crisis

As the euro crisis seemed to settle into an acerbic routine, new crises erupted, which complicated the solution. There was a security challenge of a kind not imagined in the calm years after the end of the Cold War. On February 27–28, 2014, pro-Russian gunmen seized key positions in Crimea, part of Ukraine, and in the middle of March, after a referendum with a massive pro-Russian vote, Russia declared the annexation of Crimea. There was continuing fighting in Eastern Ukraine, with the involvement of Russian soldiers.

Then, in the summer of 2015, the long-standing issue of refugees from conflict zones and migrants seeking a better life in Europe suddenly became acute, with a dramatic surge of migration in August. A great number of the migrants wanted to settle in just two European countries, Germany and Sweden. On August 25, the German Federal Office for Migration and Refugees tweeted that it was de facto (*faktisch*) not implementing the EU's Dublin protocols, and a few days later, Chancellor Merkel's spokesman said that Germany would not refuse refugees. Merkel in the subsequent weeks emphasized again and again that Germany was a strong and prosperous country, with a duty to assist the victims of war and violence, and that "we can do it" (*Wir schaffen das*). To some, this seemed an echo of Barack Obama's confident election motto, "Yes, we can."

But the German announcements antagonized many other Europeans, who saw them as a unilateral breach of European agreements. Especially in Central and Eastern Europe, there was widespread hostility to the idea of taking migrants. It looked as if the north-south divide created by the euro crisis was being supplemented by an east-west divide.

These new problems facing Europe were interconnected. At the root of the refugee problem is a previous failure of foreign policy and the destabilization of North Africa and the Middle East. Unsolved security issues are continuing to feed into the challenge for European governments. The Russian attack on anti-Assad forces in Syria has destabilized large areas of the country and driven more victims of violence to flee to look for shelter in Europe.

The security issues also became entangled with the discussion of Islamic terrorism. Like the Russian attack on Crimea and Ukraine, terrorism had the immediate effect of pulling France and Germany closer together. In part, this is because it is clear in the military and security spheres that there is an obvious bargain to be made between France and Germany: France has a military tradition and capacity that Germany lacks. The ties between Hollande and Merkel became much closer after Crimea. After the terrorist attack on the satirical magazine *Charlie Hebdo* in Paris on January 7, 2015, Merkel rushed to demonstrate solidarity with France, and Hollande continued to support Merkel over the refugee crisis, even though his stance attracted the opprobrium of the French nationalist right. After the flaring up of the refugee crisis, Hollande and Merkel made a joint appearance before the European Parliament, the first such occasion since Helmut Kohl and François Mitterrand had spoken in the dramatic circumstances after the fall of the Berlin Wall. Hollande said that "more Europe" was needed. And Merkel explained, "We must not fall prey to an inclination to want to act nationally on these matters. We must, to the contrary, act together."[5]

Brexit Referendum

There is an additional issue, perhaps an even more fundamental European crisis, that is highlighted by the polarization in French politics but also the Brexit vote in June 2016. All of Europe is confronting the fundamental issue of democratic legitimacy, which continually appears in new forms and in new places. Authoritarianism, left-wing populism, separatism, right-wing populism, fascism—all are back. For the first half of 2015, democracy in Greece seemed to be pitted against Europe. Later in 2015, the same drama was replayed in Portugal, with a notional majority in Parliament for a left coalition that included politicians deeply hostile to Europe.

The Brexit vote was also a revolt against experts, and especially against economists, from a middle and lower class that felt excluded. That result can also be partially attributed to the European Union losing touch with its citizens, especially the elderly (young British people voted for Europe). The initial ideals of Europe had lost their power to attract—and they need to be reinvented and revived.

During the Brexit negotiations, which the new British government will strategically delay, the European Union faces a challenge. On the one hand, a lenient behavior toward the UK might invite moral hazard behavior by other countries asking for special treatment and for Nexit, Dexit, Frexit, and other exit referenda. This would erode the base for a stability-focused rule-driven framework and might even threaten to unravel the whole European Union. On the other hand, an excessively harsh stand toward the UK might fuel further anti-European and especially anti-German resentment.

The Many European Crises and Monnet's Error

There are, in short, many crises in Europe. One widely held theory argues that the overload of crisis is destructive because there is a limited amount of political capital, or psychic energy, that can be used in addressing Europe's problems. In this view of the world, Europe's capacity to respond to the refugee crisis is limited by the exhaustion produced by the euro crisis. There are simply not enough fresh ideas to solve yet another new problem that was unanticipated, even though the flow of refugees across the Mediterranean had been going on for years.

The European Union was actually built on the idea of needing crisis as an instrument of further cooperation and integration. Jean Monnet, Europe's secular saint, repeatedly went back to the thought that Europe would be built by responding to new challenges. As he put it, "Europe would be built through crises, and [...] would be the sum of their solutions."[6] But this approach requires that each problem—each crisis—be sufficiently small to be manageable. An excessive load would by contrast lead to breakdown.

In Shakespeare's *Hamlet*, Claudius contemplates Ophelia's deteriorating mental state: "When sorrows come, they come not single spies, but in battalions."[7] Ophelia, of course, broke down and while mad drowned herself. But Claudius is a murderer and a tyrant and not necessarily the font of all wisdom. There exists in fact a radically different approach to the issue of multiple crises. Problems that appear almost insoluble on their own can be tackled if they are seen as a giant bundle.

Countries can calculate that they might lose out on the solution to one of the issues but gain on another. For instance, Germany might have to pay something in terms of debt relief for Southern European countries but also might quickly benefit from a European solution to the refugee crisis. The presence of migrants—some from within, some from without—raises the case of how social security is provided. Military integration could raise the effectiveness of defense while cutting costs, especially in those countries with a high military budget. Europe would appear as an arena in which trade-offs and compromises were negotiated, rather than a place where precious concepts of sovereignty were destroyed.

The association of many different questions is most familiar in the international arena from trade negotiations. Big breakthroughs have also been difficult to achieve there but have in the end resulted in generalized gains for all the participants. In the French language, issue linkage is known as *globalisation*: this is the kind of globalization that Europe now requires. In this perspective, a large-scale crisis prompts a deep need for rethinking.

In short, Europe needs to recover something of the mentality of 1989, when large movements of people across borders—initially on the Hungarian-Austrian frontier—prompted reform and openness rather than a silo mentality. At that time, protesters who were looking for new freedom thought in terms both of Europe and their nations. The strengthening of the one was integrally associated with the legitimacy of the other.

The Ukraine-Russia conflict and then the humanitarian catastrophe of 2015 have increased the European stakes: like 1989, when communism disintegrated, Europe is at a foundational moment—a moment of a potential new ordering in international affairs.[8] The events of 1989 caused an unanticipated shock that could not have been prepared for; in 2016, we know that there will be many more shocks. The year 1989 delivered the lesson that the nation-state was a sort of psychic insurance mechanism in an era of turbulence; 2015 indicated the need for a much larger sort of insurance system that exists on a European level. Like any insurance, it requires careful design and a system of rules to guard against abuse.

Finding the Optimal Balance

At the end, then, we might ask whether there is a view that can break down, on a more comprehensive basis, the world of opposites, of black and white, and push Europe to live with, if not fifty, twenty-eight shades of gray. Thinking of the provision of public goods such as monetary and fiscal stability as equivalent to an insurance contract might be a way of combining the demand for solidarity in a political community with global responsibilities—in the European Union—with a rules-based approach.

What is the optimal balance between the French and the German positions, between rules and discretion? Policy makers need to strike the right balance between an optimal immediate policy response and the creation of a robust, sustainable long-term economic framework.

A key feature of an adequate rules-based environment is the operational independence of monetary policy making, in other words, of central bank policy. However, as it emerged in the European debt crisis, this independence will be (and should be) weakened in times of crisis, as fiscal and monetary authorities necessarily work together. The most striking example of this cooperation was Berlin's implicit backing of Draghi's "whatever it takes" London speech at a critical moment of the crisis in the summer of 2012.

In the presence of extreme adverse events, an excessive emphasis on individual liability is counterproductive. In such extreme circumstances, the solidarity principle should dominate. The European community thus needs a discussion of the extent to which it is willing to assume tail risk for its members. A commonly acceptable cutoff needs to be identified, agreed upon, clearly communicated, and enforced in future crises. A common liability for extreme crisis events must then go hand in hand with some kind of common control. That process is already reflected in the nascent moves toward a more credible imposition of budget discipline in the euro area.

The existing discussion, however, is generally limited to the case where governments refinance themselves through debt, and when there are two options, either they repay or they default. In principle, it is possible to go beyond the limitations inherent to debt instruments and move to something more akin to government equity: GDP bonds. The basic idea is simple: GDP-linked bonds pay nothing if GDP is sufficiently depressed relative to some benchmark, and pay high returns when the economy is booming. This would make payments procyclical and ensure that borrower and lender incentives are aligned.

Fiscal Policy

Many of the responses required are fiscal. There is a good case to be made for delaying fiscal consolidation if credibility is already strong. Intuitively, the confidence arguments at the heart of the austerity case do not really apply to countries with a strong reputation on international financial markets. Highly indebted countries, in contrast, are faced with a dilemma. Immediate fiscal retrenchment may well prove to be counterproductive, but similarly fiscal lenience now will undermine the credibility of promises for future prudence. Without credible commitment devices for future consolidation, highly indebted countries are, as far as austerity now is concerned, "damned if they do, and damned if they don't." Institutional arrangements and credible ex ante rules might help to overcome this dilemma. At present, for the highly indebted countries of the euro-area periphery, many of the new institutional provisions designed in the course of the crisis are simply an unnecessary straitjacket, sacrificing growth at the altar of credibility.

Stimulus measures should, particularly in the current environment of high-debt burdens, always be designed so that they can be reversed rather easily. Otherwise, the credibility of long-term consolidation plans would be undermined. One key difference between Europe and the United States is that in Europe temporary stimulus measures are politically more difficult to reverse.

Moreover, it may be a good idea to combine much-needed structural reform with some extra government spending. Naturally, fundamental structural change begets uncertainty, and uncertainty weighs down consumer spending (as precautionary savings rise) and investment. In the language of our simple Keynesian multiplier analysis, the marginal propensity to consume falls, and so output slumps even further. In such an environment, government spending can pick up some of the slack, push up demand, and so stabilize output. And if the underlying structural reforms are wide-ranging enough, in these particular circumstances credibility issues should not loom as large.

Monetary and Macroprudential Policy: Financial Crisis Management and Prevention

There are also responses needed for the financial sector crisis that has been at the heart of the euro area's difficulties. How can we prevent crises or at least reduce their severity should they happen? This focus on the ex ante rules-based environment is very much in keeping with the German tradition. Redistribution toward sectors with impaired balance sheets, via monetary policy intervention, the granting of monopoly rights, or outright bailout, can be useful immediate ex post crisis management tools, but these measures include a host of problems, both in the immediate term and in the longer run. Insolvent zombie and vampire banks are not dealt with. Lending to the productive real economy will contract, and aggregate output could suffer for decades after the initial crisis (as in Japan from the 1990s). Furthermore, the provision of insurance will—as time and time again pointed out by adherents of the German philosophy—give rise to standard moral hazard problems. Banks know that the monetary and fiscal authorities will do everything in their power to redistribute income toward the banking sector in times of crisis, and so banks start behaving imprudently.

The central bank should first act to limit the fallout from these moral hazard issues. Redistribution through interest rate cuts is a very blunt tool. Within any given distressed sector, the benefits of the policy intervention accrue mostly to those firms that behaved (in comparative terms) the least imprudently. In other words, the insurance has embedded in it an extra reward for good behavior, and this can give rise to a beneficial race to the top. Second, the central bank could reduce its redistribution bias through a rigid ex ante commitment to a policy rule. Alas, the economy is too complicated for a rigid, fully ex ante specified rule to be optimal. Third, the central bank can try to build up a reputation for prudent use of its stabilization tools in times of crisis. If such a reputation is built up credibly, then households, the corporate sector, and above all banks will think twice before accumulating excessive amounts of debt and risk, and so the central bank may never actually come into a position where it is forced to use its stabilization tools. Even more so than in the case of the classical inflation bias, however, it is very hard to build up a reputation for such monetary restraint in times of crisis. Finally, and most importantly, the central bank can combine its insurance policies with strict rules that limit aggregate risk-taking. For example, strict limits on loan-to-value ratios or stringent haircut rules—the so-called macroprudential approach—can quite effectively put brakes on banks' risk-taking behavior.

The macroprudential toolkit allows the monetary authority to provide more tail insurance without the associated moral hazard complications. In short, macroprudential tools are a perfect complement to and closely interwoven with conventional monetary policy. This distinguishes macroprudential regulation from microprudential policy measures, which are often seen as quite divorced from the rest of the financial sector. Macroprudential regulation of the sort we just discussed is an effective response to the time series dimension of systemic risk. Systemic risks typically build up below the surface in times of tranquility and then materialize during the crisis. Effective macroprudential regulation captures this buildup and acts against it. Nevertheless, macroprudential policy measures are no panacea: By their very nature, they are targeted and so invite regulatory arbitrage. Macroprudential measures may thus well turn out to be powerless or, worse yet, induce undesirable side effects.

The Maastricht Treaty did not anticipate the quick-paced modernization and internationalization of banking, and it also underestimated the complexity of an unbalanced integration. Thus, it was unsurprising that the euro area was ill-equipped to deal with the complicated fallout of the global financial crisis. In particular, the threat of financial dominance—completely ignored in the Maastricht Treaty—gave rise to a complex game of chicken between monetary and fiscal authorities.

European policy makers struggled to find solutions to these problems. In theory, most of them required further integration, but the political environment made it fairly difficult to make progress on that aspect. Paradoxically, France was willing to transfer resources but not power, especially budgeting power, to Europe, while Germany was reluctant to transfer more resources to Brussels to bail out (foreign) banks. As a consequence, a search was made to find the minimum compromises that limit the adverse implications of and spillovers from banking sector crisis—de facto pushing responsibility to act to the ECB, at least in the short term.

Liquidity-focused short-term responses raise long-term moral hazard issues, so policy makers at the same time needed to have a vision for a future institutional structure that would effectively deal with these problems. The basic idea of an adequate institutional environment that balances both forces is to not save the few worst performers and erect a firewall protecting the rest with the hope of triggering a virtuous race away from the bottom that stabilizes the whole system. For the euro area, the recent move toward banking union points in this direction. However, as we have seen, there is as of yet no area-wide safe asset, nor is any such asset on the horizon—even though precisely this will be indispensable for smooth functioning of the banking union.

European Banking Charter and ESBies

One bold move forward could be to establish a European banking charter that makes the financial sector truly European. All aspects of finance would be moved to the European level. In good times, tax revenue would accrue to a European budget, while in bad times, this taxing power could provide the necessary backstop to guarantee restructuring without adverse spillover and contagion effects. The insurance principle might usefully be extended to a common European old age and insurance scheme, but that would require some significant departure from long ingrained habits of thinking about existing countries as the best forum for the organization of insurance.

Insurance cannot function if the risks are inadequately calculated and the rules badly designed and if there are incentives for the insured to extract resources from the insurer without well-defined limits. But insurance when properly designed can make the insured stable and successful. In general, we need a search for creative solutions that balance the provision of insurance and the German liability principle. A European bond structure in the form of ESBies avoids any joint liability but would still redirect destabilizing cross-border capital flights and reduce the diabolic loop between government debt risk and banking risk.

Agreed Cut-off Rule When Society Should Insure "Tail Risk"

Irrespective of the specifics of the ultimately agreed-upon optimal policy rule, society will in the end provide some tail insurance for extreme events that its leveraged sectors or individuals may face. How much tail risk society—or, better said, nominal claim holders—should assume is a political question and depends very much on the underlying economic philosophy of the country. One of the main points of this book is that Europe has, up until now, avoided giving an answer to this question. There clearly is no agreement among member states, with countries in the German tradition very aware of the moral hazard problems, while those dominated by French thinking call for more insurance and aggressive interventionism in times of crisis. And these calls for crisis interventionism are yet another source of conflict. For countries in the French tradition, emergency measures are part of the standard crisis-fighting toolkit; the German philosophy interprets every intervention as setting a precedent, and so it creates a new, permanent rules-based environment for the euro area.

Insurance—the pooling of risk—helps to establish predictability. That is an essential element in allowing the establishment of ever more complex social interactions, involving more people, across longer distances, and with new and innovative and inherently unforeseeable technologies. It is in fact on this basis that the modern world, and the modern view of the world, has been built. One of the reasons that premodern farmers and artisans—and those living today in poor countries—are vulnerable is that they cannot insure themselves against disasters such as harvest failures, which posed and continue to pose a threat to their means of existence. Experimental psychology has produced an increasing amount of evidence that shows that very poor people under tight resource constraints make poorer quality decisions, take fewer risks, and that momentary poverty depresses measured intelligence levels.[9] Well-being and an increased ability to make rational choices are closely connected with each other and with a sense of preparedness and of certainty about the future. The instinct to insure is linked to and derived from the instinct to organize and to evolve more and more complex and interlinked structures of mutual support. That support, which is central to the French tradition, can only work if it is credible and does not distort incentives—a point firmly made by the German tradition. In short, what we have characterized as the German view and the French view actually need each other to be sustainable.

Acknowledgments

We would like to thank the following for their helpful advice and criticism of drafts of the manuscript: Mark Aguiar, Jörg Asmussen, Leszek Balcerowicz, José Manuel Barroso, Michael Bordo, Gerald Braunberger, Margaret Bray, Claudia Buch, Marco Butti, Elena Carletti, Christophe Chamley, Vítor Constâncio, Giancarlo Corsetti, Benoît Cœuré, Tyler Cowen, Giovanni Dell'Ariccia, Mario Draghi, Tom Ferguson, Jesus Fernandez-Villaverde, Eugenio Gaiotti, Gabriele Galati, Luis Garicano, Thomas Gehrig, Pierre-Olivier Gourinchas, Helmut Herres, Fédéric Holm-Hadulla, Patrick Honohan, Otmar Issing, Nobu Kiyotaki, Yann Koby, Jan Pieter Krahnen, Christine Lagarde, Philip Lane, Sam Langfield, Wolfgang Lemke, Stefan Luck, Klaus Masuch, Falk Mazelis, Sebastian Merkel, Ashoka Mody, Andrew Moravcsik, Stephen Morris, Jerry Z. Muller, Martin Mühleisen, Stijn van Nieuwerburgh, Christian Noyer, Marco Pagano, Francesco Papadia, Filippos Papakonstantinou, Jean Pisani-Ferry, Peter Praet, Stephen Redding, Klaus Regling, Ricardo Reis, Massimo Rostagno, Alexander den Ruijter, Matthias Rupprecht, Yuliy Sannikov, Tano Santos, Massimo Sbracia, Ludger Schuknecht, Chris Sims, Frank Smets, Larry Summers, Istvan-Pal Szekely, Leopold von Thadden, David Thesmar, Axel Weber, Jens Weidmann, Benjamin Weigert, Faith Witryol, Dimitri Vayanos, Christian Wolf, Wei Xiong, Jeromin Zettelmeyer, and three anonymous referees. They are not, of course, responsible for any interpretations or errors in the book. We are also grateful for financial support from Princeton University's Bendheim Center for Finance and the Julis Rabinowitz Center for Public Policy and Finance.

Heike Berleth, Hongbum Lee, and Emily Riley provided invaluable research assistance. We would also like to thank Andrew DeSio, Seth Ditchik, Peter Dougherty, Terri O'Prey, and Caroline Priday at Princeton University Press, and our project manager, Pete Feely.

Special thanks goes to our families, Smita, Anjali, and Priya Brunnermeier and Marzenna, Marie-Louise, Maximilian, and Montagu James.

Notes

CHAPTER 1

1. Peter Spiegel, "Draghi's ECB Management: The Leaked Geithner Files," *Financial Times*, November 11, 2014. Last accessed January 4, 2016, from http://blogs.ft.com/brusselsblog/2014/11/11/draghis-ecb-management-the-leaked-geithner-files.

2. His standard example of the use of the concept of "ideal type" was the economist's assumption of rational (ends rational: *Zweckrational*) action, even though in the real world it was obvious that all sorts of influence—including traditions, effects, mistakes, and the influence of noneconomic ends—would influence economic actions. Weber insisted that an abstraction that allowed a coherent sense was necessary and analogous to some scientific experiments that also would not work perfectly except if conducted in an absolute vacuum. Max Weber, *Wirtschaft und Gesellschaft: Studienausgabe* (Stuttgart, Germany: J.C.B. Mohr [Paul Siebeck], 2014), 13–14.

3. Shahin Vallée, "How the Greek Deal Could Destroy the Euro," July 27, 2015. Last accessed January 4, 2016, from http://www.nytimes.com/2015/07/28/opinion/how-the-greek-deal-could-destroy-the-euro.html.

4. See, for instance, Jeffrey A. Frieden, "The Political Economy of Adjustment and Rebalancing," paper at JIMF-U.S.C. Conference on Financial Adjustment in the Aftermath of the Global Crisis, Los Angeles, April 18–19, 2014; see also Jeffrey A. Frieden, *Currency Politics: The Political Economy of Exchange Rate Policy* (Princeton, NJ: Princeton University Press, 2014).

5. Claudio Borio and Piti Disyatat, "Capital Flows and the Current Account: Taking Financing (More) Seriously," BIS Working Paper 525, 2015.

6. Max Weber, "The Social Psychology of World Religions," in *From Max Weber: Essays in Sociology*, edited by Hans H. Gerth and C. Wright Mills (London: Routledge and Kegan Paul, 1948), 280.

7. John Gray, *Men Are from Mars, Women Are from Venus: A Practical Guide for Improving Communication and Getting What You Want in Your Relationship* (New York: HarperCollins, 1992).

8. Robert Kagan, *Of Paradise and Power: America and Europe in the New World Order* (New York: Alfred A. Knopf, 2003).

9. Paul Krugman, "The Conscience of a Liberal," *New York Times*, January 27, 2009. Last accessed January 4, 2016, from http://krugman.blogs.nytimes.com/2009/01/27/a-dark-age-of-macroeconomics-wonkish/?_r=0.

10. Karl Lamers and Wolfgang Schäuble, Überlegungen zur Europäischen Politik, September 1, 1994.

11. James Politi, "*Financial Times* interview: Matteo Renzi," *Financial Times*, December 22, 2015. https://next.ft.com/content/c6ab59e2-a8c1-11e5-955c-1e1d6de94879.

CHAPTER 2

1. For a similar analysis of what he calls the EU2 where "the real power lies," see Anthony Giddens, *Turbulent and Mighty Continent: What Future for Europe?* (Cambridge, UK: Polity Press, 2013), 6–7.

2. Peter Spiegel, "Varoufakis Unplugged: The London Call Transcript," *Financial Times*, July 27, 2015. Last accessed January 4, 2016, from http://blogs .ft.com/brusselsblog/2015/07/27/varoufakis-unplugged-the-london-call -transcript.

3. Jean Monnet, *Memoirs*, translated by Richard Mayne (New York: Doubleday & Company, 1978), 417.

4. Carlo Bastasin, *Saving Europe* (Washington DC: Brookings, 2012), 166.

5. "Who Will Rescue Greece's Rescuers?" *Wall Street Journal*, March 28, 2010, http://www.wsj.com/articles/SB100014240527487041006045751454501 47500816.

6. Bastasin, *Saving Europe*, 166–67.

7. Ibid., 193.

8. The Commission took the initiative at first, stating in a document titled "Reinforcing Economic Policy Coordination" that in order to make the EFSF "fully operational," there would need to be a permanent crisis-resolution mechanism. This would in turn require improving the functioning of existing mechanisms under the Stability and Growth Pact, with national fiscal frameworks, incentives, and sanctions (a requirement to make interest-bearing deposits as well as more rigorous use of the Cohesion Fund Regulation) to comply with the rules of the Stability and Growth Pact, strengthened macroeconomic surveillance based on indicators, and a "European Semester" for better ex ante integrated fiscal policy coordination. (European Commission, "Communication from the Commission to the European Parliament, the European Council, the Council, the European Central Bank, the Economic and Social Committee, and the Committee of the Regions: Reinforcing Economic Policy Coordination," *COM (2010) 250 final* (May 12, 2010).) However, the intergovernmental character later became apparent in the governance arrangements: all of the then sixteen members of the euro area were to designate board members. All disbursements would be decided by unanimity of members. By July 9, the creation of the EFSF was formally approved by 90 percent of its membership and it became operational.

9. "Merkel Warns of Europe's Collapse: 'If Euro Fails, So Will the Idea of European Union,'" *Spiegel Online*, May 13, 2010. Last accessed January 4, 2016, from http://www.spiegel.de/international/germany/merkel-warns-of-europe -s-collapse-if-euro-fails-so-will-the-idea-of-european-union-a-694696.html.

10. Deutscher Bundestag, Stenografischer Bericht, 17/42. Sitzung, Berlin, Mittwoch, den 19. Mai 2010.

11. Ulrich Beck, *German Europe* (Cambridge, UK: Polity Press, 2013), 54.

12. "France, Germany Split on Automatic EU Budget Fines," *EUbusiness*, September 28, 2010. Last accessed January 4, 2016, from http://www.eubusiness.com/news-eu/finance-economy.6an.

13. Jan Strupczewski and John Irish, "Berlin, Paris Seek EU Treaty Change to Handle Crises," *Reuters*, October 18, 2010. Last accessed January 4, 2016, from http://www.reuters.com/article/euro area-crisis-resolution-idU.S.LDE 69H2DD20101018.

14. Erik Nielson, "Euro Area Bond Haircuts Must Look Appealing," *Financial Times*, November 9, 2010. Last accessed January 4, 2016, from http://www.ft.com/intl/cms/s/0/59e597dc-ec15-11df-b50f-00144feab49a.html#axzz3v4IOkBH2.

15. Bastasin, *Saving Europe*, 225.

16. Jeff Black and Rainer Buergin, "Weidmann Says ECB Council Skepticism about Bond Buys Growing," *Bloomberg Business*, December 14, 2011. Last accessed January 4, 2016, http://www.bloomberg.com/news/articles/2011-12-14/weidmann-says-ecb-council-growing-more-skeptical-about-bond-buys.

17. Simeon Djankov, *Inside the Euro Crisis: An Eyewitness Account* (Washington DC: Peterson Institute for International Economics, 2014), 84.

18. Angelique Chrisafis, "François Hollande: Look Past Austerity or Risk Falling Out of Love with Europe," *Guardian*, October 17, 2012. Last accessed January 4, 2016, from http://www.theguardian.com/world/2012/oct/17/francois-hollande-interview-eu-france.

19. "L'intransigeance égoïste de la chancelière Merkel," *Le Monde*, April 26, 2013. Last accessed January 4, 2016, from http://www.lemonde.fr/politique/article/2013/04/26/le-ps-denonce-l-intransigeance-egoiste-de-la-chanceliere-merkel_3167068_823448.html.

20. *Guardian*, Monday, January 26, 2015. Retrieved from http://www.theguardian.com/world/2015/jan/26/spain-podemos-syriza-victory-greek-elections.

21. See Ashifa Kassam, Henry McDonald, Stephanie Krichgaessner, and Anne Penketh, "Syriza's Election Victory in Greece—How Europe Reacted," *Guardian*, January 26, 2015, http://www.theguardian.com/world/2015/jan/26/-sp-syriza-election-victory-greece-europe-reacted?CMP=share_btn_link.

Chapter 3

1. Madame de Staël: "*On pourrait dire avec raison que les Français et les Allemands sont aux deux extrémités de la chaîne morale, puisque les uns considèrent les objets extérieurs comme le mobile de toutes les idées, et les autres, les idées comme le mobile de toutes les impressions. Ces deux nations cependant s'accordent assez bien sous les rapports sociaux; mais il n'en est point de plus opposées dans leur système littéraire et philosophique.*" Madame de Staël, *De L'Allemagne* (London: John Murray, 1813).

2. Alexis de Tocqueville, *The Old Regime and the Revolution* (New York: Harper & Brothers, 1856), 253.

3. Thomas Mann, *Doktor Faustus: Das Leben eines deutschen Tonsetzers* (Frankfurt: Fischer, 1971; originally 1947), 86–7.

4. Massimo Morelli, Helios Herrera, and Luigi Guiso, *A Cultural Clash View of the EU Crisis*, Working Paper, 2013. See also Luigi Guiso, Paola Sapienza, and Luigi Zingales, "Long Term Persistence," National Bureau of Economic Research Working Paper 14278, 2008.

5. de Staël, *De L'Allemagne*: "*Néanmoins on a vu souvent chez les nations latines une politique singulièrement adroite dans l'art de s'affranchir de tous les devoirs; mais on peut le dire à la gloire de la nation allemande, elle a presque l'incapacité de cette souplesse hardie qui fait plier toutes les vérités pour tous les intérêts, et sacrifie tous les engagements à tous les calculs. Ses défauts, comme ses qualités, la soumettent à l'honorable nécessité de la justice.*"

6. Le Meunier Sans-Souci, in François-Guillaume-Jean-Stanislas Andrieux, *Oeuvres* (Paris: Chez Nepveu, 1818, Vol. III.), 208.

7. Eugénie Bastié, "Article 49-3, vote bloqué : les armes de Manuel Valls contre les frondeurs du PS," *Le Figaro*, July 1, 2014. Last accessed January 4, 2016, from http://www.lefigaro.fr/vox/politique/2014/07/01/31001-20140701 ARTFIG00397-article-49-3-vote-bloque-les-armes-de-manuel-valls-contre-les -frondeurs-du-ps.php.

8. Michael Maurice Loriaux, *France after Hegemony: International Change and Financial Reform* (New York: Cornell University Press, 1991).

9. Christian Noyer, A propos du statut et de l'indépendance des banques centrales, *Revue d'économie financière*, 1992, 13–18. See also Susanne Lohmann, "Federalism and Central Bank Independence: The Politics of German Monetary Policy, 1957–92," *World Politics* 50 (3), 1998, 401–446.

10. David Howarth, *The French Road to Monetary Union* (London: Palgrave, 2001), 131.

11. Gary Herrigel, *Industrial Constructions: The Sources of German Industrial Power* (New York: Cambridge University Press, 1996).

12. Robert Putnam, *Bowling Alone: The Collapse and Revival of the American Community* (New York: Simon & Schuster, 2000).

13. Mancur Olson, *The Logic of Collective Action*, 2nd edition (Cambridge, MA: Harvard University Press, 1971).

14. Axel Weber, *Monetary Policy over Fifty Years: Experiences and Lessons*, edited by Heinz Herrmann (New York: Routledge, 2009), 6.

15. Karl Klasen, Committee of Governors, Meeting 108, Basel (February 8, 1977); BIS archive, Basel.

16. Peter Andrew Johnson, *The Government of Money: Monetarism in Germany and the United States* (New York: Cornell University Press, 1998), 3.

17. Wilhelm Haferkamp, Committee of Governors, Meeting 98, Basel (February 10, 1976).

CHAPTER 4

1. Sudhir Hazareesingh, *How the French Think: An Affectionate Portrayal of an Intellectual People* (New York: Basic Books, 2015).

2. Pierre Nicole De Chanteresne, *De l'éducation d'un Prince* (Paris: Veuve Charles Savreux, 1671), 204.

3. John Law, *Idée générale du nouveau Système des Finances*, [1719 or 1720], reproduced in John Law, *Oeuvres complètes*, vol. 3 (Paris: Sirey, 1934), 82. On Law's view of the world, see Arnaud Orain, "John Law's System in France 1717–1720," Princeton University Paper (2015).

4. See Jesús Fernández-Villaverde, "Magna Carta, the Rule of Law, and the Limits on Government," University of Pennsylvania Paper (2015).

5. François Perroux, Des mythes hitlériens à l'Europe allemande (Paris: Librairie Générale de Droit et de Jurisprudence, 1940), 45, 291–292 (the texts quoted were written in 1935).

6. Friedrich Hayek, *The Road to Serfdom* (London: Routledge, 1944), 129.

7. Erinnerungen Hans Schäffers an Ernst Trendelenburg.

8. Friedrich A. Hayek, *The Road to Serfdom* (London: Routledge and Kegan Paul, 1944), 55.

9. Hayek, *Road to Serfdom*, 55, 94.

10. Harold James, *The German Slump: Politics and Economics 1924–1936* (New York: Oxford University Press, 1986) 353.

11. Walter Eucken *The Foundations of Economics: History and Theory in the Analysis of Economic Reality*, translated by Terence Wilmot Hutchison (Berlin; Heidelberg: Springer-Verlag, 1992), 316.

12. Text of Joint Chiefs of Staff Directive Regarding the Military Government of Germany, April 1945, available at http://usa.usembassy.de/etexts /ga3-450426.pdf.

13. Franz Böhm, "Western Germany," in *Monopoly and Competition and their Regulation*, edited by Edward Chamberlin (London: MacMillan, 1954), 154.

14. Ludwig Erhard (1952), quoted in Tony A. Freyer, *Antitrust and Global Capitalism 1930–2004* (New York: Cambridge University Press, 2006), 270.

15. Quoted in Christopher Allen, "Ordo-liberalism Trumps Keynesianism: Economic Policy in the Federal Republic of Germany and the EU," in *Monetary Union in Crisis: The European Union as a Neo-liberal Construction*, edited by Bernard Moss (New York: Palgrave Macmillan, 2005), 199–221.

16. Albrecht Ritschl, "Der späte Fluch des Dritten Reichs: Pfadabhängigkeiten in der Entstehung der bundesdeutschen Wirtschaftsordnung," *Perspektiven der Wirtschaftspolitik* 6(2) (2005): 151–70.

17. Olaf Sievert, "Geld, das man nicht selbst herstellen kann—Ein ordnungspolitisches Plädoyer für die Europäische Währungsunion," in *Währungsunion oder Währungschaos? Was kommt nach der D-Mark*, edited by Peter Bofinger, Stephan Collignon, and Ernst-Moritz Lipp (Wiesbaden: Gabler), 145; also Lars Feld, Ekkehard Köhler, and Daniel Nientiedt, "Ordoliberalism, Pragmatism and the Euro Area Crisis: How the German Tradition Shaped Economic Policy in Europe," paper at conference at Schloss Ettersberg, Weimar (January 2015).

18. Wolfgang Münchau, "The Wacky Economics of Germany's Parallel Universe," *Financial Times*, November 16, 2014. Last accessed January 4, 2016, from http://www.ft.com/intl/cms/s/0/e257ed96-6b2c-11e4-be68-00144feabdc0 .html#axzz3wf2Kdzlw.

19. Mark Blyth, *Austerity: The History of a Dangerous Idea* (New York: Oxford University Press, 2013), 142; see also Feld, Köhler, and Nientiedt, "Ordoliberalism, Pragmatism and the Euro Area Crisis."

20. Christian Reiermann, Michael Sauga, and Anne Seith, "The Bundesbank against the World: German Central Bank Opposes Euro Strategy," *Spiegel Online*, August 27, 2012. Last accessed January 4, 2016, from http://www.spiegel.de/international/europe/german-bundesbank-opposes-euro-crisis-strategy-a-852237.html.

21. "Schwarz-Rot contra Weise," *Handelsblatt*, February 2, 2015, 13.

22. Karl Albrecht Schachtschneider, *In Sachen der Verfassungsbeschwerde gegen die Währungspolitik der Bundesrepublik Deutschland wegen Verletzung der Grundrechte der Beschwerdeführer aus Art. 38 Abs. 1, Art. 14 Abs. 1 und Art. 2 Abs. 1*, 2010. Last accessed January 4, 2016, from http://www.kaschachtschneider.de/files/Rettungsschirm_Klage_06062010.pdf.

23. "Protestaufruf: Der offene Brief der Ökonomen im Wortlaut," *Frankfurter Allgemeine Wirtschaft*, 2012, July 5. Last accessed January 4, 2016, from http://www.faz.net/aktuell/wirtschaft/protestaufruf-der-offene-brief-der-oekonomen-im-wortlaut-11810652.html

24. "Staatsanleihen-Ankäufe: Verfassungsgericht wendet sich erstmals an EuGH," *JUVE*, Feburary 7, 2014. Last accessed January 4, 2016, from http://www.juve.de/nachrichten/verfahren/2014/02/ankaufe-von-staatsanleihen-bundesverfassungsgericht-wendet-sich-erstmals-an-eugh.

25. See Jurgen Reinhoudt, *Jacques Rueff's Theory of Order in the Context of Early Neo-liberal Political Thought*. Dissertation, University of Pennsylvania, 2014.

26. Jens Weidmann, *Crisis Management and Regulatory Policy*, Walter Eucken Lecture, Walte Eucken Institut, February 11, 2013. Last accessed January 4, 2016, from http://www.bundesbank.de/Redaktion/EN/Reden/2013/2013_02_11_weidmann_eucken.html.

27. Karsten Wendorff, *Challenges for Public Finances in and after the Crisis*, Deutsche Bundesbank, April 24, 2012.

28. Ibid.

29. Robert King and Charles Plosser, "Money, Deficits, and Inflation," *Carnegie-Rochester Conference Series* 22 (1985), 147–96; Thomas Sargent and Neil Wallace, "Some Unpleasant Monetarist Arithmetic," *Federal Reserve Bank of Minneapolis Quarterly Review* 5(3) (1981): 1–17; Michele Fratianni and Franco Spinelli, "Fiscal Dominance and Money Growth in Italy: The Long Record," *Explorations in Economic History* 38 (2001): 252–72.

30. Dennis Snower, Johannes Burmeister, and Moritz Seidel, "Dealing with the Euro Area Debt Crisis: A Proposal for Reform," *Kiel Policy Brief No. 33*, Kiel Institut für Weltwirtschaft. Last accessed January 4, 2016, from http://www.ifw-kiel.de/wirtschaftspolitik/politikberatung/kiel-policy-brief/kiel_policy_brief_33.

31. Michael Hüther, "Es steht auf Messers Schneide in Athen," interview in *Münchener Merkur*, May 10, 2012.

32. Maurice Allais, "Nobel Prize Acceptance Speech," in *A History of the Mont Pelerin Society*, Max Hartwell (Indianapolis: Liberty Fund, 1995).

33. Marion Fourcade, *Economists and Societies: Discipline and Profession in the United States, Britain, and France, 1890s to 1990s* (Princeton, NJ: Princeton University Press, 2010), 231.

34. Cecil Smith, "The Longest Run: Public Engineers and Planning in France," *American Historical Review* 95 (1990): 657–92; Charles Gillispie, *Science and Polity in France: The End of the Old Regime* (Princeton, NJ: Princeton University Press, 1980); Richard Kuisel, "Technocrats and Public Economic Policy: From the Third to the Fourth Republic," *Journal of European Economic History* 2 (1973): 53–99; Richard Kuisel, *Capitalism and the State in Modern France: Renovation and Economic Management in the Twentieth Century* (New York: Cambridge University Press, 1981), 202–12.

35. Jean-Baptiste Say, *A Treatise on Political Economy* (Philadelphia: Grigg and Elliott, 1834), 417.

36. Frédéric Bastiat, *La Loi* (London: Institute of Economic Affairs, 2001; originally 1850).

37. Jack Hayward, "The Nemesis of Industrial Patriotism: The French Response to the Steel Crisis," in Yves Mény and Vincent Wright (Eds.), *The Politics of Steel: Western Europe and the Steel Industry in the Crisis Years (1974–1986)* (Berlin: de Gruyter, 1986), 502–533.

38. Jack Hayward, "The Nemesis of Industrial Patriotism: The French Response to the Steel Crisis," in *The Politics of Steel: Western Europe and the Steel Industry in the Crisis Years (1974–1984)*, edited by Yves Mény (Berlin: Walter de Gruyter), 502–33; Jean Padioleau, *Quand la France s'enferre: La politique sidérurgique de la France depuis 1945* (Paris: Presses Universitaires de France, 1981), 32, 34.

39. Gabrielle Hecht, *The Radiance of France: Nuclear Power and National Identity after World War II* (Cambridge, MA: MIT Press, 1998).

40. Jean G. Padioleau, *Quand la France s'enferre* (Paris: Presses Universitaires Françaises, 1981), 33.

41. Padioleau, *Quand la France s'enferre*, 33, 79.

42. Charles Maier, "The Politics of Productivity: Foundations of American International Economic Policy after World War II," in *In Search of Stability: Explorations in Historical Political Economy*, edited by Charles Maier (New York: Cambridge University Press), 121–52.

43. Pierre Bauby, *L'Etat-stratège*, (Paris: Les éditions ouvrières, 1991), 195.

44. Jean-Jacques Laffont and Jean Tirole, *A Theory of Incentives in Regulation and Procurement* (Cambridge, MA: MIT Press, 1993). In Germany, Hans-Werner Sinn also made a significant contribution to the analysis of the provision of public goods and built this position up as the basis for a critique of many of the Euro rescue mechanisms.

45. Thomas Piketty, *Capital in the Twenty-first Century* (Cambridge, MA: Harvard University Press, 2014), 32.

46. Obituary: Raymond Barre, *Independent*, August 26, 2007, http://www.independent.co.uk/news/obituaries/raymond-barre-5334901.html.

47. Jacques Sapir, *Les Économistes contre la démocratie: Pouvoir, mondialisation et démocratie* (Paris: Albin Michel, 2000).

48. Bernard Maris, *Lettre ouverte aux gourous de l'économie qui nous prennent pour des imbéciles* (Paris: Albin Miche, 1999).

49. John Thornhill, "France Reforms Its Anglo-Saxon Attitudes," *Financial Times*, September 22, 2008, available at https://next.ft.com/content/9e839a34

-88c5-11dd-a179-0000779fd18c; and Sarah Waters, *Between Republic and Market: Globalization and Identity in Contemporary France* (London: Continuum, 2012), 1.

50. Joseph Stieglitzand and Jean-Paul Fitoussi, *Report by the Commission on the Measurement of Economic Performance and Social Progress*, 2009. Last accessed January 4, 2016, from http://www.stiglitz_sen_fitoussi.fr/documents/rap port_anglais.pdf.

51. Philippe Askenazy, Thomas Coutrot, André Orléan, and Henri Sterdy-niak, "Manifesto of the Appalled Economists," *Real-world Economics Review* 54 (2010): 19–31. Last accessed January 4, 2016, from http://www.paecon.net /PAEReview/issue54/Manifesto54.pdf; Sarah Waters, *Between Republic and Market: Globalization and Identity in Contemporary France* (New York: Continuum, 2012).

52. Maurice Obstfeld, Jay C. Shambaugh, and Alan M. Taylor, "The Tri-lemma in History: Tradeoffs among Exchange Rates, Monetary Policies, and Capital Mobility," *Review of Economics and Statistics* 87 (2005): 423–38.

53. See Michael Bordo and Harold James, "Capital Flows and Domestic and International Order: Trilemmas from Macroeconomics to Political Econ-omy and International Relations," NBER Working Paper, 2015

54. For a historical description of the crisis, see for instance Willem Buiter, Giancarlo Corsetti, and Paolo Pesenti, "Interpreting the ERM Crisis: Country-specific and Systemic Issues," *Princeton Studies in International Finance* 84 (1998). Last accessed January 4, 2016, from https://www.princeton.edu/~ies /IES_Studies/S84.pdf.

CHAPTER 5

1. Quoted in Ashoka Mody, "Greece and the André Szász Axiom," *Bruegel*, February 25, 2015. Last accessed January 4, 2016, from http://bruegel.org /2015/02/greece-and-the-andre-szasz-axiom-2.

2. Douglass C. North and Barry R. Weingast, "Constitutions and Commit-ment: The Evolution of Institutional Governing Public Choice in Seventeenth-century England," *Journal of Economic History* 49 (1989): 803–32, provides the classic account of the new institutional alignment.

3. Barry Eichengreen, *Golden Fetters: The Gold Standard and the Great Depres-sion, 1919–1939* (New York: Oxford University Press, 1992).

4. See for instance Daniel Gros, "Why Greece Is Different," *Project Syndi-cate*, May 13, 2015. Last accessed January 4, 2016, from http://www.project -syndicate.org/commentary/greece-export-problem-by-daniel-gros-2015-05.

5. Kydland and Prescott (1977) initially pointed out the time-inconsistency problem in the context of inflation. Finn Kydland and Edward Prescott, "Rules Rather Than Discretion: The Inconsistency of Optimal Plans," *Journal of Politi-cal Economy* 85 (1977): 472–92. They received the Nobel Prize in Economics later for this insight. Barro and Gordon (1983) and Rogoff (1985) proposed to delegate monetary policy to conservative central bankers. Robert Barro and David Gordon, "Rules, Discretion and Reputation in a Model of Monetary Policy," NBER Working Paper No. 1079, February 1983; and Kenneth Rogoff,

"The Optimal Degree of Commitment to an Intermediate Monetary Target," *Quarterly Journal of Economics* 100 (1985): 1169–189. Lohmann (1992) shows that after an extreme adverse event the independence of central can be temporarily broken. Susanne Lohmann, "Optimal Commitment in Monetary Policy: Credibility versus Flexibility," *American Economic Review* 82 (1992): 273–86.

6. For more details, see Mauricio Drelichman and Hans-Joachim, *Lending to the Borrowers from Hell: Debt, Taxes, and Default in the Age of Philip II* (Princeton, NJ: Princeton University Press, 2014).

CHAPTER 6

1. Johann Wolfgang Goethe, Zahme Xenien 9, Bürgerpflicht, *"Ein jeder kehre vor seiner Tür, und rein ist jedes Stadtquartier."*

2. Peter Kenen, "The Theory of Optimum Currency Areas: An Eclectic View," in *Monetary Problems of the International Economy*, edited by Robert Mundell and Alexander Swoboda (Chicago: University of Chicago Press, 1969).

3. See Paul Krugman, "Florida versus Spain," *New York Times*, June 2, 2012. Last accessed January 4, 2016, from http://krugman.blogs.nytimes.com/2012/06/02/florida-versus-spain.

4. Some developing countries, such as India, form a currency union across different economies as well that are not divided by national boundaries. The relevant consumption basket in the countryside is very different than in big cities.

5. French Finance Ministry, "An Unemployment Insurance Scheme for the Euro Area," *Trésor-Economics* 132 (June 2014); Italian Ministry of Economics and Finance, "European Unemployment Insurance Scheme" (October 2015).

6. James Politi, "Italy Pushes for Euro Area Jobless Insurance Scheme," *Financial Times*, October 3, 2015. Last accessed January 12, 2016, from http://www.ft.com/intl/cms/s/0/f96fa2e8-6b63-11e5-8171-ba1968cf791a.html#axzz3x47DDAYM.

7. László Andor (European Commissioner for Employment, Social Affairs and Inclusion), "Basic European Unemployment Insurance: Countering Divergences within the Economic and Monetary Union," speech at Vienna University of Economics and Business, September 29, 2014, http://europa.eu/rapid/press-release_SPEECH-14-635_en.htm; Henrik Enderlein, Jann Spiess, and Lucas Guttenberg, "Blueprint for a Cyclical Shock Insurance in the Euro Area," *Notre Europe Studies and Reports*, September 17, 2013, http://www.delorsinstitute.eu/011-16659-Blueprint-for-a-Cyclical-Shock-Insurance-in-the-euro-area.html.

8. Sebastien Dullien, (European Council on Foreign Relations blog), October 13, 2013, http://www.ecfr.eu/blog/entry/what_happened_to_the_idea_of_a_european_unemployment_insurance.

9. Robert Mundell, "A Theory of Optimum Currency Areas," *American Economic Review* 51 (1961): 657–65. Robert Mundell, "Uncommon Arguments for Common Currencies," in *The Economics of Common Currencies*, edited by

Harry Johnson and Alexander Swoboda (Cambridge, MA: Harvard University Press, 1973).

10. See Steven Davis and John Haltiwanger, "Labor Market Fluidity and Economic Performance," NBER Working Paper No. 20479 (September 2014); *Economic Report of the President* (February 2015), 134–41. Last accessed January 4, 2016, from http://www.whitehouse.gov/sites/default/files/docs/cea_2015_erp.pdf.

11. See Markus Brunnermeier and Yuliy Sannikov, "A Macroeconomic Model with a Financial Sector," *American Economic Review*, 104(2) (2014): 379–421, for an exact description of endogenous risk dynamics and volatility paradox.

12. See for instance Emmaneul Farhi and Iván Werning, "Fiscal Unions" (March 2013). Last accessed January 4, 2016, from http://scholar.harvard.edu/files/farhi/files/fiscal-unions_july_2014_0.pdf?m=1410354615.

13. Robert I. McKinnon, "Optimum Currency Areas." *American Economic Review*, 53(4) (1963): 717–724.

14. Defined as GDP per person employed.

15. Enrico Marro, "La corsa contro il tempo per investire i dodici miliardi stanziati dall'Europa," *Corsiera della Sera*, August 3, 2015. Last accessed January 4, 2016, from http://www.corriere.it/economia/15_agosto_03/corsa-contro-tempo-investire-dodici-miliardi-stanziati-dall-europa-0beefc18-39a3-11e5-b49b-ae37d5ff3efe.shtml?refresh_ce-cp.

16. Daniel Gros, "The Fate of Greece in a 'Genuine Economic and Monetary Union': Lessons from a Small Island State," CEPS Policy Brief, 2015.

17. Enrico Marro, "Bismarck und seine Griechen," *Frankfurter Allgemeine Sonntagszeitung* (March 2015). Harold James, *Monetary and Fiscal Unification in Nineteenth Century Germany: What Can Kohl Learn from Bismarck?*, Essays in International Finance No. 202, Princeton University, 1997.

18. Jacob von Weizsäcker and Jacques Delpla, "Eurobonds: The Blue Bond Concept and Its Implications," Bruegel, March 21, 2011. Last accessed January 4, 2016, from http://www.bruegel.org/publications/publication-detail/publication/509-eurobonds-the-blue-bond-concept-and-its-implications and http://www.europarl.europa.eu/document/activities/cont/201103/20110321ATT15948/20110321ATT15948EN.pdf.

19. "Der Europäische Schuldentilgungspakt—Fragen und Antworten," *Sachverständigenrat zur Begutachtung der gesamtwirtschaftlichen Entwicklung*, 2011. Last accessed January 4, 2016, from http://www.sachverstaendigenrat-wirtschaft.de/fileadmin/dateiablage/download/publikationen/arbeitspapier_01_2012.pdf.

20. Thomas Phillipon and Christian Hellwig, "Eurobills, Not Euro Bonds," *Vox*, December 2, 2011. Last accessed January 4, 2016, from http://www.voxeu.org/article/eurobills-not-euro-bonds.

21. "European Commission Green Paper on the Feasibility of Introducing Stability Bonds," European Commission MEMO/11/820, November 23, 2011. Last accessed January 4, 2016, from http://europa.eu/rapid/press-release_MEMO-11-820_en.htm.

22. Ibid.

23. Alex Barker, "Barroso Warns Fate of the Euro at Stake," *Financial Times*, November 23, 2011. Last accessed January 4, 2016, from http://www.ft.com /intl/cms/s/0/c7323b36-15dd-11e1-a691-00144feabdc0.html#axzz3vBTXBpxK.

24. For details, see www.euro-nomics.com, or Brunnermeier et al., "ESBies: A Realistic Reform of Europe's Financial Architecture," VoxEU, October 25, 2011, http://voxeu.org/article/esbies-realistic-reform-europes-financial-architecture. One coauthor, Markus Brunnermeier, is a member of the Euro -nomics group.

25. "Merkel zur Schuldenpolitik: 'Keine Euro-Bonds, solange ich lebe,'" *Spiegel Online*, June 26, 2012. Last accessed January 4, 2016, from http://www .spiegel.de/politik/ausland/kanzlerin-merkel-schliesst-euro-bonds-aus-a -841115.html.

26. Tony Cross, "Hollande-Merkel Fail to Agree on Eurobonds Ahead of Euro-summit," *RFI English*, June 28, 2012. Last accessed January 4, 2016, from http://www.english.rfi.fr/economy/20120628-hollande-merkel-fail-agree -eurobonds-ahead-euro-summit.

CHAPTER 7

1. See, with an application to the Euro discussion, Jean Pisani-Ferry, *The Euro Crisis and Its Aftermath* (New York: Oxford University Press, 2014), 102–3.

2. Why do governments issue short-term debt and thereby expose themselves to rollover risk? The reason is that long-term debt financing is typically more expensive, as existing debt may be diluted through the issuance of new bonds. In particular, new bond holders could be given higher priority by issuing very short-term new debt, which matures prior to most outstanding debt. Because investors are aware that long-term debt might well be diluted in this fashion, a "maturity rat race" could occur. Brunnermeier and Oehmke show that nobody wants to buy long-term bonds, ultimately making only short-term funding possible. Markus Brunnermeier and Martin Oehmke, "The Maturity Rat Race," *Journal of Finance* 68 (2013): 483–521.

3. Charles Goodhart, "Global Macroeconomic and Financial Supervision: Where Next?" in *Globalization in an Age of Crisis: Multilateral Economic Cooperation in the Twenty-first Century*, edited by Robert C. Feenstra and Alan M. Taylor (Chicago: University of Chicago Press, 2013), 343–63. Available online. Last accessed January 4, 2016, from http://www.nber.org/chapters/c12599.pdf.

4. Speech by Mario Draghi, President of the European Central Bank at the Global Investment Conference in London, July 26, 2012, available at 2012 https://www.ecb.europa.eu/press/key/date/2012/html/sp120726.en.html.

5. David Marsh liked to make this analogy.

6. See Elena Carletti, Paolo Colla, Mitu Gulati, and Steven Ongena. (2016) "No Mere Walk on the Beach: Are Collective Action Clauses Introduced in European Sovereign Bonds Actually Priced?" Working Paper Bocconi University, http://ssrn.com/abstract=2686879.

7. Council of the European Union, "Statement by the Heads of State or Government of the Euro Area and EU Institutions," July 21, 2011. Last accessed January 4, 2016, from https://www.consilium.europa.eu/uedocs/cms_data/docs/pressdata/en/ec/123978.pdf.

8. Tony Barber, "Has Europe Been Rescued?" *Financial Times,* July 22, 2011. Last accessed January 4, 2016, from http://www.ft.com/intl/cms/s/0/8b1caeee-b48d-11e0-a21d-00144feabdc0.html#axzz3Pwey00Q1.

9. "Tatra Tiger on the Ropes," Economist blog, October 12, 2011, available at http://www.economist.com/blogs/eastern-approaches/2011/10/slovakia-and-euro-crisis.

10. The ESM members agreed that ESM loans under a macroeconomic adjustment program and recapitalization facilities would enjoy preferred creditor status in a similar fashion to those of the IMF while accepting preferred creditor status of the IMF over the ESM. This would, however, not apply to ESM financial assistance in the form of ESM loans following a European financial assistance program existing at the time of the ESM Treaty's signing. The decision to forgo preferred creditor status in the case of the recapitalization of Spanish banks was one-off in nature, as the Financial Assistance Facility Agreement (FFA) was negotiated by the EFSF. This FFA was be transferred to the ESM with rights and obligations, including the EFSF's pari passu status. The loss of preferred creditor status in this instance made it look as if taxpayers, who would ultimately be liable, were being sacrificed for the sake of the banks.

11. Moody's Investors Service, "Rating Action: Moody's Assigns Aaa/Prime-1 Rating to European Stability Mechanism (ESM); Negative Outlook." Last accessed January 4, 2016, from http://www.moodys.com/research/Moodys-assigns-AaaPrime-1-rating-to-European-Stability-Mechanism-ESM--PR_256438.

12. Anträge auf Erlass einer einstweiligen Anordnung zur Verhinderung der Ratifikation von ESM-Vertrag und Fiskalpakt überwiegend erfolglos, Bundesverfassungsgericht, Pressemitteilung Nr. 67/2012, September 12, 2012.

13. White House, "Press Conference by President Obama after G20 Summit," November 4, 2011. Last accessed January 6, 2015, from https://www.whitehouse.gov/the-press-office/2011/11/04/press-conference-president-obama-after-g20-summit.

CHAPTER 8

1. See "Währungsunion: Drei Komma Null," *Der Spiegel,* 6, February 3, 1997, http://www.spiegel.de/spiegel/print/d-8653515.html.

2. Milton Friedman, *A Theory of the Consumption Function* (Princeton, NJ: Princeton University Press, 1957).

3. The multiplier is typically above zero even in neoclassical models because a reduction in consumption induces people to work more, which boosts output.

4. See, for example, Jonathan Parker, Nicholas Souleles, David Johnson, and Robert McClelland, "Consumer Spending and the Economic Stimulus Payments of 2008," *American Economic Review* 103 (2013): 2530–53.

5. See, for example, Olivier Blanchard, Eugenio Cerutti, and Lawrence Summers, "Inflation and Activity: Two Explorations and Their Monetary Policy Implications," *Peterson Institution for International Economics Working Paper Series*, wp15-19 November 2015.

6. Paul Krugman, http://www.nytimes.com/2010/07/02/opinion/02krugman.html.

7. Valerie A. Ramey, "Can Government Purchases Stimulate the Economy?" *Journal of Economic Literature*, 49(3) (2011): 673–85. See also Valerie Ramey, "Macroeconomic Shocks and Their Propagation," Handbook of Macroeconomics (forthcoming).

8. Alan Auerbach and Yuriy Gorodnichenko, "Fiscal Multipliers in Recession and Expansion," in *Fiscal Policy after the Financial Crisis* (Cambridge, MA: National Bureau of Economic Research (NBER), 2013).

9. Robert Hall, "By How Much Does GDP Rise if the Government Buys More Output?" *Brookings Papers on Economic Activity*, 2009: 183–231.

10. Olivier Blanchard and Daniel Leigh, "Growth Forecast Errors and Fiscal Multipliers," IMF Working Paper 1301, January 2013.

11. Emi Nakamura and Jon Steinsson, *Fiscal Stimulus in a Monetary Union: Evidence from U.S. Regions*, unpublished manuscript, 2012. http://www.columbia.edu/~en2198/papers/fiscal.pdf.

12. Vito Tanzi, paper on "Public Finance and Public Debt," CESifo conference, January 22, 2016.

13. For an important contribution to this discussion, see for example Alberto Alesina and Silvia Ardagna, "Large Changes in Fiscal Policy: Taxes versus Spending," in *Tax Policy and the Economy*, vol. 24, edited by Jeffrey Brown (Chicago: University of Chicago Press; NBER, 2010).

14. See for instance Paul Krugman, "Getting Trendy," *New York Times*, July 23, 2010. Last accessed January 4, 2016, from http://krugman.blogs.nytimes.com/2010/07/23/getting-trendy.

15. John Cochrane, "How Big Is the Random Walk in GNP?" *Journal of Political Economy* 96(5) (1988): 893–920.

16. Blanchard, Cerutti, and Summers, "Inflation and Activity."

17. Lawrence Summers, in a speech at an IMF research conference on November 8, 2013, http://ftalphaville.ft.com/2013/11/18/1696762/summers-on-bubbles-and-secular-stagnation-forever/.

18. For recent empirical studies see, for example, Mathias Drehmann, Claudio Borio, and Kostas Tsatsaronis, "Characterising the Financial Cycle: Don't Lose Sight of the Medium Term!", 2012, Bank of International Settlement Working Paper 380, and Moritz Schularick and Alan Taylor "Credit Booms Gone Bust: Monetary Policy, Leverage Cycles and Financial Crises, 1870–2008." *American Economic Review*, 102(2): 1029-1061 (2012).

19. Source: Eurostat.

20. Claudio Borio, Enisse Kharroubi, Christian Upper, and Fabrizio Zampolli, "Labour Reallocation and Productivity Dynamics: Financial Causes, Real Consequences," BIS Working Papers No 534, January 2016.

21. Jean-Claude Juncker, "The Quest for Prosperity," *The Economist*, March 15, 2007, http://www.economist.com/node/8808044.

22. For an empirical analysis see Alessandra Bofinglioli and Gino Gancia, "Economic Uncertainty and Structural Reforms," Barcelona GSE Working Paper 847, October 2015.

23. *The Economist*, November 17, 2004, http://www.economist.com/node/3352024.

24. See Simeon Djankov, *Inside the Euro Crisis: An Eyewitness Account* (Washington DC: Peterson Institute for International Economics, 2014).

25. Katy Barnato, "Krugman Can't Admit He Was Wrong on Austerity: Latvia PM," CNBC, March 15, 2013. Last accessed January 4, 2016, from http://www.cnbc.com/id/100558455.

26. Horand Knaup and Christian Reiermann, "Out of Balance? Criticism of Germany Grows as Economy Stalls," *Spiegel Online*, October 14, 2014. Last accessed January 4, 2016, from http://www.spiegel.de/international/germany/germany-and-finance-minister-schaeuble-under-fire-as-economy-slows-a-996966.html.

27. Geoff Cutmore and Jenny Cosgrave, "Summers, Schäuble Go Head to Head on Ailing Europe," CNBC, October 9, 2014. Last accessed January 4, 2016, from http://www.cnbc.com/2014/10/09/summers-schauble-go-head-to-head-on-ailing-europe.html.

28. MEMO/10/288, Brussels, June 30, 2010, "A toolbox for stronger economic governance in Europe," europa.eu/rapid/press-release_MEMO-10-288_en.doc.

29. (a) European Council, "Council Regulation (EU) No 1177/2011 of 8 November 2011 Amending Regulation (EC) No 1467/97 on Speeding Up and Clarifying the Implementation of the Excessive Deficit Procedure," *Official Journal of the European Union* L 306 (November 23, 2011): 33–40.

(b) European Council, "Council Directive 2011/85/EU of 8 November 2011 on Requirements for Budgetary Frameworks of the Member States," *Official Journal of the European Union* L 306 (November 23, 2011): 41–47.

(c) European Parliament and European Council, "Regulation (EU) No 1173/2011 of the European Parliament and of the Council of 16 November 2011 on the Effective Enforcement of Budgetary Surveillance in the Euro Area," *Official Journal of the European Union* L 306 (November 23, 2011): 1–7.

(d) European Parliament and European Council, "Regulation (EU) No 1174/2011 of the European Parliament and of the Council of 16 November 2011 on Enforcement Measures to Correct Excessive Macroeconomic Imbalances in the Euro Area," *Official Journal of the European Union* L 306 (November 23, 2011): 8–11.

(e) European Parliament and European Council, "Regulation (EU) No 1175/2011 of the European Parliament and of the Council of 16 November 2011 Amending Council Regulation (EC) No 1466/97 on the Strengthening of the Surveillance of Budgetary Positions and the Surveillance and Coordination of Economic Policies," *Official Journal of the European Union* L 306 (November 23, 2011): 12–24.

(f) European Parliament and European Council, "Regulation (EU) No 1176/2011 of the European Parliament and of the Council of 16 November 2011 on the Prevention and Correction of Macroeconomic Imbalances," *Official Journal of the European Union* L 306 (November 23, 2011): 25–32.

30. "Germany's Debt Brake: Tie Your Hands, Please," *Economist*, December 11, 2011. Last accessed January 4, 2016, from http://www.economist.com/node /21541459.

31. "Merkel, Sarkozy Agree on EU Treaty Change to Handle Crises," http://www.euractiv.com/future-eu/merkel-sarkozy-agree-eu-treaty-c-news -498902 (October 19, 2010).

32. Tony Patterson and John Litchfield, "Rain on Francois Hollande's Parade as New President Celebrates Inauguration," *Independent*, May 16, 2012. Last accessed January 4, 2016, from http://www.independent.co.uk/news/world /europe/rain-on-his-parade-then-fran-ois-hollande-flies-into-a-storm-7754459. html; and *Daily Telegraph*, May 16, 2012. Last accessed January 4, 2016, from http://www.telegraph.co.uk/news/worldnews/europe/france/9267144/Rain -on-Francois-Hollandes-parade-as-new-president-celebrates-inauguration.html.

33. Wolf demanded "more financing, ideally via some sort of euro area bond; collective backing of banks; less fiscal contraction; more expansionary monetary policies; and stronger German demand." Martin Wolf, "The Riddle of German Self-Interest," *Financial Times*, May 30, 2012, https://next.ft.com /content/4fe89d8c-a8df-11e1-b085-00144feabdc0; Summers stated, "Fiscal contraction reduces incomes, limiting the capacity to repay debts. It achieves only limited reductions in deficits once the adverse effects of economic contraction on tax revenue and benefit payments are accounted for." Larry Summers, "Austerity Has Brought Europe to the Brink Again," *Reuters*, April 30, 2012, http://blogs.reuters.com/lawrencesummers/2012/04/30/austerity-has -brought-europe-to-the-brink-again/.

34. Ian Traynor and Kate Connolly, "Hollande and Merkel Clash Looms Over Euro Area Austerity," *Guardian*, April 27, 2012. Last accessed January 4, 2016, from http://www.theguardian.com/world/2012/apr/27/francois -hollande-angela-merkel-clash-euro area.

35. James Angelos, "Germany Warns on Currency Depreciation," *Wall Street Journal*, February 8, 2013. http://www.wsj.com/articles/SB1000142412 7887324590904578291540790587804.

36. The German chancellor Angela Merkel refers to this standoff in her TV ZDF summer interview on August 16, 2015. "Angela Merkel im ZDF Sommer-interview," August 16, 2015. Last accessed January 4, 2015, from http://www .zdf.de/ZDFmediathek/beitrag/video/2468958.

37. See for example Alberto Alesina, Carlo Favero, and Francesco Giavazzi, "The Output Effect of Fiscal Consolidations," NBER Working Paper 18336, March 19, 2014; and Alberto Alesina and Veronique de Rugy, "Austerity: The Relative Effects of Tax Increases versus Spending Cuts," Mercatus Working Paper (2013).

CHAPTER 9

1. One notable exception was the monetary expert Charles Goodhart from the London School of Economics.

2. ECB, *Monthly Bulletin*, April 2009. See also Sam Langfield and Marco Pagano, "Bank Bias in Europe: Effects on Systemic Risk and Growth," *Economic Policy*, 31(85) (2016): 51–106. Last accessed January 23, 2016, from

http://economicpolicy.oxfordjournals.org/content/31/85/51.full?ijkey=hn
1dRzXNYnT1zpa&keytype=ref.

3. "U.S. Will Lose Financial Superpower Status: Germany," Reuters, September 25, 2008, available at http://www.reuters.com/article/us-financial
-germany-steinbruecknews-idUSTRE48O2L020080925.

4. For a more detailed description, see the teaching notes by Brunnermeier
and Reis, "A Crash-course on the Euro Crisis" (2015), Working Paper, Princeton University. http://scholar.princeton.edu/markus.

5. Note, however, that banks usually keep some residual risk on their
books, ensuring that they still have some "skin in the game."

6. See for instance Anat Admati and Martin Hellwig, *The Bankers' New
Clothes* (Princeton, NJ: Princeton University Press, 2013).

7. Harald Hau and Marcel Thum, "Subprime Crisis and Board (in-)Competence: Private vs. Public Banks in Germany," *Economic Policy,* vol. 24(60) (2009):
701–51.

8. See European Economic Advisory Group, "The EEAG Report on the
European Economy 2016: What next?"Munich: CESIfo, 2016.

CHAPTER 10

1. For a formal analysis of these two amplification spirals, see Markus
Brunnermeier and Yuliy Sannikov, "The I Theory of Money," Working Paper
Princeton University, 2016. http://scholar.princeton.edu/markus.

2. The term "Paradox of Prudence" was coined in Brunnermeier and Sannikov's "I Theory of Money."

3. Mehreen Kahn and Isabelle Fraser, "Greece News Live: Bail-out Talks
Collapse without Agreement Forcing Leaders into Emergency Weekend Summit," *Daily Telegraph,* July 7, 2015. Last accessed January 4, 2016, from http://
www.telegraph.co.uk/finance/economics/11725393/As-it-happened-Greek
-turmoil-on-Tuesday-July-7.html.

4. See Brunnermeier and Sannikov, "A Macroeconomic Model with a
Financial Sector," *American Economic Review,* vol. 104(2) (2014): 379–421.

5. This definition is based on Markus Brunnermeier and Valentin Haddad,
"Safe Assets," in preparation, 2015. See also https://www.newyorkfed.org
/medialibrary/media/aboutthefed/pdf/FAR_Oct2014.pdf.

6. For a tractable formal model of the diabolic loop, see Markus Brunnermeier, Luis Garicano, Philip Lane, Marco Pagano, Ricardo Reis, Tano Santos,
David Thesmar, Stijn Van Nieuwerburgh, and Dimitri Vayanos, "The Sovereign-banking Diabolic Loop and ESBies," *American Economic Review Papers and
Proceedings,* vol. 106(5) (2016).

7. See also Carlo Altavilla, Marco Pagano, and Saverio Simonelli, "Bank
Exposures and Sovereign Stress Transmission." SSRN Working Paper No.
2640131, 2015.

8. For more details see Markus Brunnermeier, "Financial Dominance,"
Banca d'Italia Baffi Lecture, 2015 (2016).

9. See for instance Katie Linsell, "Spanish Credit Risk Surges to Record on
Bankia 'Zombie' Peril," *Bloomberg Business,* May 9, 2012. Last accessed January

4, 2016, from http://www.bloomberg.com/news/articles/2012-05-09/sover eign-corporate-bond-risk-rises-credit-default-swaps-show.

10. See for instance Martin Hellwig, "Financial Stability, Monetary Policy, Banking Supervision, and Central Banking," Max Planck Institute for Research on Collective Goods (2014). Last accessed January 4, 2016, from https://2014 .ecbforum.eu/up/artigos-bin_paper_pdf_0304507001401014475-683.pdf.

11. Alexander Möthe, "Cristiano Ronaldo geht—zur EZB," *Handelsblatt*, July 27, 2011. Last accessed January 4, 2016, from http://www.handelsblatt .com/finanzen/maerkte/boerse-inside/kurioses-kreditgeschaeft-cristiano -ronaldo-geht-zur-ezb/4438824.html.

12. Vincent Browne, "Let's Own Up to Our Part in the Burst Bubble," *Irish Times*, April 6, 2011, http://www.irishtimes.com/opinion/let-s-own-up-to -our-part-in-the-burst-bubble-1.564844.

13. Luis Garicano, "Five Lessons from the Spanish Cajas Debacle for a New Euro-wide Supervisor," *Vox*, October 16, 2012. Last accessed January 4, 2016, from http://voxeu.org/article/five-lessons-spanish-cajas-debacle-new -euro-wide-supervisor.

14. Andreas Hadjipapas and Kerin Hope, "Cyprus Nears €2.5bn Russian Loan Deal," *Financial Times*, September 14, 2011. Last accessed January 4, 2016, from http://www.ft.com/intl/cms/s/0/655a3fd2-de31-11e0-9fb7-00144feab dc0.html#axzz3Lvk7ym2N.

15. Rachel Cooper, "Cyprus Bailout: Timeline," *Daily Telegraph*, March 25, 2013. Last accessed January 4, 2016, from http://www.telegraph.co.uk /finance/financialcrisis/9951858/Cyprus-bailout-timeline.html.

16. "Bail-Ins: EU Deal Protects Taxpayers in Bank Bailouts," *Spiegel Online*, June 27, 2013. Last accessed January 4, 2016, from http://www.spiegel.de /international/business/eu-deal-would-require-bail-ins-in-future-bank-rescue -plans-a-908175.html.

17. Council of the European Union, "Council Agrees Position on Bank Res-olution," Press Release 11228/13, June 27, 2013. Last accessed January 4, 2016, from http://www.consilium.europa.eu/uedocs/cms_data/docs/pressdata /en/ecofin/137627.pdf.

18. Mario Draghi, "Banking Communication—Treatment of Subordinated Debt in Precautionary Recapitalization," Letter to Joaquin Almunia, July 30, 2013. Reproduced in *El Pais* and *The Daily Telegraph*. Last accessed January 4, 2016, from http://ep00.epimg.net/descargables/2013/10/21/e4c63829a1ef61 f17a50533be5a2e3a9.pdf and from http://blogs.telegraph.co.uk/finance/files /2013/10/letter-full.jpg.

19. For a more detailed account, see Miles Johnson and Peter Wise, "Banco Espírito Santo: Family Fortunes: Bank Chief Ricardo Espírito Santo Salgado Faces Allegations That His Group Engaged in a Fraud," *Financial Times*, Sep-tember 11, 2014. Last accessed January 4, 2016, from http://www.ft.com/intl /cms/s/0/a63a4a56-32c0-11e4-93c6-00144feabdc0.html#axzz3D6OCJLme.

20. Axel Bugge, "Update 1—Portugal's Novo Banco Completes BESI Sale to China's Haitong," *Reuters*, September 7, 2015. Last accessed January 4, 2016, from http://www.reuters.com/article/2015/09/07/novobanco-haitong-idU.S .L5N11D32720150907.

21. "BES Rescue Saves Senior Bondholders," *Financial Times*, August 4, 2014. Last accessed January 4, 2016, from http://video.ft.com/v/3712187340001.

22. "Wie Bankberater ihre Kunden ausnehmen," *Focus* 43 (October 20, 2008): 144f.

23. Tom Beardsworth and Loreenzo Totaro, "Italy Plans Fund to Help Savers of Four Rescued Banks," *Bloomberg News*, December 11, 2015. http://www.bloomberg.com/news/articles/2015-12-11/italy-plans-fund-to-help-savers-of-four-rescued-banks.

24. Ibid.

25. http://www.mef.gov.it/focus/article_0001.html.

26. See for example Martin Sandbu, "Free Lunch," *Financial Times*. Last accessed January 27, 2016, from https://next.ft.com/content/8984288c-c43c-11e5-b3b1-7b2481276e45.

CHAPTER 11

1. Martin Hellwig, "Yes Virginia, There Is a European Banking Union! But It May not Make Your Wishes Come True," preprints of the Max Planck Institute for Research on Collective Goods, Bonn 2014/12 (August 2014).

2. Steve Schifferes, "Can Banking Regulation Go Global?" BBC, March 18, 2009. Last accessed January 4, 2016, from http://news.bbc.co.uk/2/hi/business/7950758.stm.

3. Broner, Martin, and Ventura outline why foreigners sell government debt to domestic investors to ensure that default becomes less likely. Fernando Broner, Alberto Martin, and Jaume Ventura, "Sovereign Risk and Secondary Markets," *American Economic Review* 11 (2010): 1523–555.

4. Yet, note that this does not go the other way around: creditor countries still have incentives to treat liquidity problems as such because they may turn into insolvency problems if left untreated.

5. Remarks by President Herman Van Rompuy following the European Council, June 29, 2012. Last accessed January 15, 2016, from http://europa.eu/rapid/press-release_PRES-12-309_en.htm.

6. European Commission, "Commission Proposes New ECB Powers for Banking Supervision as Part of a Banking Union," Press Release Ref IP/12/953, September 12, 2012. Last accessed January 15, 2016, from http://europa.eu/rapid/press-release_IP-12-953_en.htm.

7. Ibid.

8. For a nice timeline, see *Wikipedia*, "Single Supervisory Mechanism." Last accessed January 4, 2016, from http://en.wikipedia.org/wiki/Single_Supervisory_Mechanism.

9. In the United States, the ceiling for insured deposits had been raised in the financial crisis from $100,000 to $250,000 as a result of a calculation of the typical cash balances of small and medium-sized enterprises.

10. See "EU-Einlagensicherung in weiter Ferne," *FAZ*, September 13, 2015. Last accessed January 4, 2016, from http://www.faz.net/aktuell/wirtschaft/eurokrise/finanzminister-treffen-eu-einlagensicherung-in-weiter-ferne-13800544.html.

11. European Commission, "Capital Markets Union: Unlocking Funding for Europe's growth." Last accessed January 4, 2016, from http://ec.europa.eu /finance/capital-markets-union/index_en.htm.

12. "Merkel zur Schuldenpolitik: 'Keine Euro-Bonds, solange ich lebe,'" *Spiegel Online,* June 26, 2012, http://www.spiegel.de/politik/ausland/kanzlerin -merkel-schliesst-euro-bonds-aus-a-841115.html.

13. Brunnermeier et al., "ESBies: A Realistic Reform of Europe's Financial Architecture," 2011, VoxEU, http://voxeu.org/article/esbies-realistic-reform -europes-financial-architecture.

14. For a formal analysis, see Brunnermeier et al. 2016, "The Sovereign-Bank Diabolic Loop and ESBies," *American Economic Review Papers and Proceedings, 106*(5), pp. 508–512.

15. Rather, German euros would offer a redenomination opportunity, as a new Deutschmark would appreciate.

16. The run-up in TARGET2 liabilities prior to an exit might be so large, such that the central bank's liabilities exceed their assets. This is okay to an extent because central banks can operate with some negative equity.

17. See Sebastian Edwards, "Currency Changes and Contracts: Lessons for Greece," *Vox,* August 16, 2015. Last accessed January 4, 2016, from http:// www.voxeu.org/article/currency-changes-and-contracts-lessons-greece.

18. Peter Spiegel, "Inside Europe's Plan Z," *Financial Times,* May 14, 2014. Last accessed January 4, 2016, from http://www.ft.com/intl/cms/s/0/0ac 1306e-d508-11e3-9187-00144feabdc0.html#axzz3Lvk7ym2N.

19. Ian Traynor and Patrick Wintour, "Euro Area Crisis: Germany and France Clash over Eurobonds at Summit," *Guardian,* May 23, 2012. Last accessed January 4, 2016, from http://www.theguardian.com/business/2012 /may/23/euro area-crisis-france-germany-divide.

20. Spiegel, "Inside Europe's Plan Z."

21. Marcus Walker, "Inside Merkel's Bet on the Euro's Future," *Wall Street Journal,* April 23, 2013. Last accessed January 4, 2016, from http://www.wsj .com/articles/SB10001424127887324695104578418813865393942.

22. George Georgiopooulos, "Greece Readies Reform Promises," *Reuters,* February 22, 2015. Last accessed January 4, 2016, from http://www.reuters .com/article/2015/02/20/us-euro area-greece-idU.S.KBN0LO0O620150220.

CHAPTER 12

1. J. E. King, *A History of Post Keynesian Economics Since 1930* (Northampton, MA: Edward Elgar, 2002), 156.

2. Pier Luigi Porta, "Italian Economics through the Postwar Years," in *The Post-1945 Internationalization of Economics,* edited by Alfred William Coats (Durham, NC: Duke University Press, 1997), 165–83; Ivo Maes, "The Spread of Keynesian Economics: A Comparison of the Belgian and Italian Experiences," National Bank of Belgium Working Paper No. 113, 2007.

3. Giovanni Iuzzolino, Guido Pellegrini, and Gianfranco Viesti, Convergence among Italian Regions, 1861–2011, Economic History Working Papers #22, 2011, Banca d'Italia.

4. EURISPES. http://www.eurispes.eu/content/rapporto-italia-1998.

5. Paolo Pinotti, "The Economic Costs of Organized Crime: Evidence from Southern Italy," *Economic Journal* 125 (August 2015): F203–F232.

6. Nicholas Crafts and Marco Magnani, "The Golden Age and the Second Globalization" in Italy. Edited by Gianni Toniolo, *The Oxford Handbook of the Italian Economy Since Unification* (Oxford: Oxford University Press, 2014), 69–107, see in particular p. 92.

7. Deutsche Bank, 2013. http://www.efxnews.com/story/21864/uk-currency-area-penny-pound-deutsche-bank.

8. Giuseppe Tomasi di Lampedusa, *The Leopard*. (New York: Pantheon, 1960), 40.

9. Stephen Faris, "Arrivederci, Italia: Why Young Italians Are Leaving," *Time*, October 18, 2010. http://content.time.com/time/magazine/article/0,9171,2024136,00.html.

10. From 2015 statistical database of CCBE (Council of Bars and Law Societies of Europe). http://www.ccbe.eu/index.php?id=29.

11. Alberto Alesina and Federico Giavazzi, *The Future of Europe: Reform or Decline* (Cambridge, MA: MIT Press, 2006).

12. Michael Day, "Merkel under Fire over Phone Bid to Oust Berlusconi," *Independent*, December 30, 2011. Last accessed January 4, 2016, from http://www.independent.co.uk/news/world/europe/merkel-under-fire-over-phone-bid-to-oust-berlusconi-6283345.html.

13. Ferdinando Giugliano, "Italy's Love Affair with Brussels Cools," blog, March 13, 2014. http://blogs.ft.com/the-world/2014/03/italys-love-affair-with-the-euro-wanes/.

14. Ibid.

15. John Hooper, "Silvio Berlusconi Hints at Comeback Bid," *Guardian*, June 24, 2012. http://www.theguardian.com/world/2012/jun/24/berlusconi-plans-comeback; "Italy Minister Worried at Euro Exit Campaign," *Reuters*, June 19, 2012. http://www.reuters.com/article/us-italy-euro-minister-idUSBRE85I17C20120619.

16. John Hooper, "Silvio Berlusconi Hints at Comeback," *Guardian*, June 24, 2011. Last accessed January 4, 2016, from http://www.theguardian.com/world/2012/jun/24/berlusconi-plans-comeback.

17. James Politi, "Eurozone Austerity Fanning Popuist Flames, says Renzi," *Financial Times*, December 21, 2015, http://www.ft.com/intl/cms/s/0/08ba78f8-a805-11e5-955c-1e1d6de94879.html#axzz48HV6SPpG.

18. Mario Draghi, "L'Italia e l'economia internazionale, 1861–2011," October 12, 2011, speech.

Chapter 13

1. Martin Feldstein, "EMU and International Conflict," *Foreign Affairs* (Nov/Dec 1997): 72.

2. Lars Jonung and Eoin Drea, "The Euro: It Can't Happen, It's a Bad Idea, It *Won't* Last. U.S. Economists on the EMU, 1989–2002," European Commission

Economic Papers 395 (2009). Last accessed January 4, 2016, from http://ec .europa.eu/economy_finance/publications/publication16345_en.pdf.

3. See for instance Alexander Hamilton, "Report on Public Credit," the Founders' Constitution Article 1, Section 8, Clause 2, in *The Papers of Alexander Hamilton*, edited by Harold C. Syrett et al., 26 vols. (New York and London: Columbia University Press, 1961–79). Last accessed January 4, 2016, from http://press-pubs.uchicago.edu/founders/print_documents/a1_8_2s5.html.

4. Statement by Chairman Ben S. Bernanke, May 7, 2009. Last accessed January 9, 2016, from http://www.federalreserve.gov/newsevents/press/bcreg /bernankescap20090507.htm.

5. There was also a European stress test conducted in 2010 by CEBS, the predecessor to the EBA: http://www.eba.europa.eu/risk-analysis-and-data/eu -wide-stress-testing/2010.

6. Anne O. Krueger, *A New Approach to Sovereign Debt Restructuring* (Washington DC: International Monetary Fund (IMF), 2002). Last accessed January 4, 2016, from https://www.imf.org/external/pubs/ft/exrp/sdrm/eng/sdrm.pdf.

7. See for instance Benjamin M. Friedman, "The Pathology of Europe's Debt," *New York Review of Books*, October 9, 2013. Last accessed January 4, 2016, from http://www.nybooks.com/articles/2014/10/09/pathology-europes-debt.

8. James, *German Slump*, 17.

9. Timothy Guinnane, "Financial Vergangenheitsbewältigung: The 1953 London Debt Agreement," Yale University Economic Growth Center Discussion Paper No. 880, 2015.

10. Landmark Framework for IMF Surveillance, IMF Survey, June 21, 2007. https://www.imf.org/external/pubs/ft/survey/so/2007/POL0621B.htm.

11. Michael P. Dooley, David Folkerts-Landau, and Peter Garber, "An Essay on the Revived Bretton Woods System," NBER Working Paper 9971, September 2003. Last accessed January 4, 2016, from http://www.nber.org/papers /w9971; and "The Revived Bretton Woods System: The Effects of Periphery Intervention and Reserve Management on Interest Rates & Exchange Rates in Center Countries," NBER Working Paper 10332, March 2004. Last accessed January 4, 2016, from http://www.nber.org/papers/w10332.

12. Cho Jin-seo, "Geithner Calls for '4% Rule,'" *Korea Times*, October 22, 2010. Last accessed January 4, 2016, from http://www.koreatimes.co.kr/www /news/biz/2014/07/299_75069.html.

13. Andrew Rettman, "Chinese Fund Manager Lambasts EU 'Sloth, Indolence,'" *EU Observer*, November 7, 2011. https://euobserver.com/china/114195.

14. "Geithner Warns EU against Infighting over Greece," BBC, September 16, 2011. Last accessed January 4, 2016, from http://www.bbc.com/news /business-14943320.

15. Stephen Castle, "Meetings on European Debt Crisis End in Debate, but Little Progress," *New York Times*, September 17, 2011. Last accessed January 4, 2016, from http://www.nytimes.com/2011/09/18/business/global/meetings -on-european-debt-crisis-end-in-debate-but-little-progress.html?_r=0.

16. U.S. Treasury Press Release, July 30, 2012. https://www.treasury.gov /press-center/press-releases/Pages/tg1657.aspx.

17. Peter Spiegel, "Inside Europe's Plan Z," *Financial Times*, May 14, 2014. https://next.ft.com/content/0ac1306e-d508-11e3-9187-00144feabdc0.

18. See for instance Michael Day, "Soros Warns of Three-month Window to Save the Single Currency," *Independent*, June 4, 2012. Last accessed January 4, 2016, from http://www.independent.co.uk/news/world/europe/soros-warns -of-three-month-window-to-save-the-single-currency-7815164.html.

19. Ian Talley, "U.S., IMF Step Up Calls for Europe to Restructure Greece's Debt," *Wall Street Journal*, July 8, 2015. Last accessed January 4, 2016, from http://www.wsj.com/articles/u-s-treasury-secretary-europe-must-restructure -greek-debt-1436367143.

20. Ian Traynor, Jennifer Rankin, and Helena Smith, "Greek Crisis: Surrender Fiscal Sovereignty in Return for Bailout, Merkel Tells Tsipras," *Guardian*, July 12, 2015. Last accessed January 4, 2016, from http://www.theguardian .com/business/2015/jul/12/greek-crisis-surrender-fiscal-sovereignty-in -return-for-bailout-merkel-tells-tsipras.

21. Tweets by Jeffrey Sachs, July 12, 2015. Last accessed January 4, 2016, from https://twitter.com/jeffdsachs/status/620201786561986561; see also Ulrich Schäfer, "Twitter-Gewitter gegen Merkel und Schäuble," *Süddeutsche Zeitung*, July 12, 2015. Last accessed January 4, 2016, from http://www.sued deutsche.de/wirtschaft/streit-um-griechenland-politik-twitter-gewitter -gegen-merkel-und-schaeuble-1.2563170.

22. Paul Krugman, "Killing the European Project," *New York Times*, July 12, 2015. Last accessed January 4, 2016, from http://krugman.blogs.nytimes .com/2015/07/12/killing-the-european-project/?_r=0.

23. Nikolaus Piper, "Warum ein Nobelpreisträger auf Deutschland losgeht," *Süddeutsche Zeitung*, July 13, 2015. Last accessed January 4, 2016, from http://www.sueddeutsche.de/wirtschaft/paul-krugman-deutschland-will -einen-regimewechsel-und-die-totale-demuetigung-1.2563504.

24. "Nicht so smart am Smartphone," *Focus Magazine* (June 13, 2015): 16. Last accessed January 4, 2016, from http://www.focus.de/magazin/archiv /griechenland-nicht-so-smart-am-smartphone_id_4745257.html.

25. Martin Wolf, "Mervyn King Has Lunch with the *FT*: Interview Transcript," *Financial Times*, July 5, 2013. Last accessed January 4, 2016, from http://www.ft.com/intl/cms/s/2/35844ddc-e57f-11e2-ad1a-00144feabdc0 .html.

26. Ambrose Evans-Pritchard, "The Euro Area Is in Bad Need of an Undertaker," *Daily Telegraph*, December 10, 2010. Last accessed January 4, 2016, from http://www.telegraph.co.uk/finance/comment/ambroseevans_pritchard /8197780/The-euro area-is-in-bad-need-of-an-undertaker.html.

27. Stephen Brown, "Merkel and Cameron Differ on Euro Crisis Weapons," *Reuters*, November 18, 2011. Last accessed January 4, 2016, from http:// uk.reuters.com/article/2011/11/18/uk-euro area-germany-britain-idukTRE7 AH00I20111118.

28. Alex Barker and George Parker, "False Assumptions Underpinned British Strategy," December 16, 2011. Last accessed January 4, 2016, from http://www.ft.com/intl/cms/s/0/6c5e100e-27ee-11e1-a4c4-00144feabdc0 .html#axzz3v4IOkBH2.

29. "The Ratings Game," *Economist*, December 3, 2011. Last accessed January 4, 2016, from http://www.economist.com/node/21541027.

30. Barker and Parker, "False Assumptions."

31. Ibid.

32. Ibid.

33. Philippe Ricard, "L'Europe à 27, c'est fini," *Le Monde*, December 9, 2011. http://www.lemonde.fr/a-la-une/article/2011/12/09/l-europe-a-27-c -est-fini_1616025_3208.html; Roland Nelles, "Bye Bye Britain," *Der Spiegel*, December 9, 2011. http://www.spiegel.de/international/europe/bye-bye -britain-the-european-union-s-new-face-a-802728.html.

34. Hugh Carnegy and George Parker, "French Frustration Boils Over against Britain," *Financial Times*, December 16, 2011. Last accessed January 4, 2016, from http://www.ft.com/intl/cms/s/0/28d0ab18-27ed-11e1-9433-00144 feabdc0.html#axzz2avMoFVxu.

35. George Parker and Jim Pickard, "PM Avoids Triumphalism in Commons," *Financial Times*, December 12, 2011. Last accessed January 4, 2016, from http://www.ft.com/intl/cms/s/0/de8173c8-24e8-11e1-8bf9-00144feabdc0 .html#axzz2avMoFVxu.

36. Tony Barber, "Euro Summit Was British Diplomatic Debacle," *Financial Times*, December 11, 2011. Last accessed January 4, 2016, from http://www.ft .com/intl/cms/s/0/86916a6a-25a1-11e1-9cb0-00144feabdc0.html#axzz2av MoFVxu.

37. James Kirkup, "David Cameron: I Can Imagine Britain Leaving EU," *Daily Telegraph*, December 17, 2012. Last accessed January 4, 2016, from http:// www.telegraph.co.uk/news/worldnews/europe/eu/9751026/David-Cameron -I-can-imagine-Britain-leaving-EU.html.

38. John Palmer, "Thatcher Sets Face Against United Europe," *Guardian*, September 21, 1988. http://www.theguardian.com/business/1988/sep/21 /emu.theeuro.

39. Nicholas Watt and Juliette Jowit, "Cameron Postpones Big Speech on Europe," *Guardian*, January 18, 2013. Last accessed January 4, 2016, from http://www.theguardian.com/politics/2013/jan/18/cameron-europe-speech -postponed.

40. George Osborne, speech at Shanghai Stock Exchange, September 22, 2015, at https://www.gov.uk/government/speeches/chancellor-lets-create -a-golden-decade-for-the-uk-china-relationship; Tom Phillips, "Britain Has Made 'Visionary' Choice to Become China's Best Friend, Says Xi," *Guardian*, October 18, 2015, at http://www.theguardian.com/uk-news/2015/oct/18 /britian-has-made-visionary-choice-to-become-chinas-best-friend-says-xi.

41. "EU Brexit and Migration Summit," *Politico*, February 18, 2016. http:// www.politico.eu/article/eu-brexit-migration-summit-live-david-cameron -angela-merkel-matteo-renzi-eu-reform/.

42. George Parker and Alex Barker, "How to Win Friends," *Financial Times*, January 23/24, 2016, 12.

43. Rowena Mason, Phillip Inman, Helena Smith, and Jennifer Rankin, "Greece Crisis: Osborne Seeks to Block Use of British-backed Fund in Bailout," *Guardian*, July 14, 2015. Last accessed January 4, 2016, from

http://www.theguardian.com/world/2015/jul/14/greece-crisis-osborne
-seeks-to-block-use-of-british-backed-fund-in-bailout.

44. Elena Moya, "'Positive' China Buys Spanish Bonds," *Guardian*, January 12, 2011. http://www.theguardian.com/business/2011/jan/12/supportive
-china-buys-european-bonds.

45. See for instance, Nicolas Sarkozy, "Address by Nicolas Sarkozy, President of the French Republic: Opening of the G20 Seminar on Reform of the International Monetary System," G20 Information Center, University of Toronto, March 31, 2011. Last accessed January 4, 2016, from http://www.g20
.utoronto.ca/2011/sarkozy-110331-en.html.

46. "Vladimir Putin and Francois Fillon Addressed Reporters on the Results of the 13th Head-of-government Meeting of the Russian-French Commission for Cooperation," Government of the Russian Federation, September 20, 2008. Last accessed January 4, 2016, from http://archive.government.ru/
eng/docs/1961.

47. "Putin and Berlusconi Seal 'South Stream' Pipeline Deal," *EurActiv*, May 18, 2009. http://www.euractiv.com/section/med-south/news/putin-and
-berlusconi-seal-south-stream-pipeline-deal/.

CHAPTER 14

1. *Paris Match*, 2540, January 29, 1998, 62.

2. Donald Moggridge, *The Collected Writings of John Maynard Keynes. Volume 25. Activities 1940–1944: Shaping the Post-War World: The Clearing Union* (Cambridge: Cambridge University Press, 1980), 1.

3. Armand Van Dormael, *Bretton Woods: Birth of a Monetary System* (New York: Homes and Meier, 1978), 6–7. Joseph Gold, *Legal and Institutional Aspects of the International Monetary System: Selected Essays II* (Washington DC: IMF, 1984), 19. Donald Moggridge, *Maynard Keynes: An Economist's Biography* (London: Routledge, 1992), 654.

4. Keith Horsefield, ed., *International Monetary Fund: 1945–1965: Twenty Years of International Monetary Cooperation*, vol. 3 (Washington DC: IMF, 1986), 31; see also Moggridge, *Maynard Keynes*, 673.

5. Rawi Abdelal, *Capital Rules: The Construction of Global Finance* (Cambridge, MA: Harvard University Press, 2009).

6. The Brady plan allowed lenders to convert their often delinquent illiquid outstanding bank loans into liquid tradable "Brady bonds," whose principal was usually collateralized by specially issued US Treasuries, held in an escrow account.

7. Milton Friedman, "Markets to the Rescue," *Wall Street Journal*, October 13, 1998. Last accessed January 4, 2016, from http://online.wsj.com/articles
/SB908229279775781500.

8. David Francis, "World Economy Hailed at Madrid Finance Meeting," *Christian Science Monitor*, October 4, 1994. Last accessed January 4, 2016, from http://www.csmonitor.com/1994/1004/04012.html.

9. Quoted in Harold James, *International Monetary Cooperation since Bretton Woods* (Washington DC: IMF; New York: Oxford University Press, 1996), 109.

10. Anne Krueger, "International Financial Architecture for 2002: A New Approach to Sovereign Debt Restructuring," address at the National Economists' Club Annual Members' Dinner, American Enterprise Institute, Washington DC, November 26, 2001. Last accessed January 4, 2016, from https://www.imf.org/external/np/speeches/2001/112601.htm.

11. IMF, "Cross-country Experience with Restructuring of Sovereign Debt and Restoring Debt Sustainability," August 29, 2006; Federico Sturzenegger and Jeromin Zettelmeyer, *Debt Defaults and Lessons from a Decade of Crises* (Cambridge, MA: MIT Press, 2007).

12. "IMF Urges Stimulus as Global Growth Marked Down Sharply," *IMF Survey Magazine*, November 6, 2008. Last accessed January 4, 2016, from https://www.imf.org/external/pubs/ft/survey/so/2008/NEW110608A.htm.

13. "Eurogroup's Juncker Says No Need for Greece IMF Aid," *Reuters*, January 14, 2010. http://www.reuters.com/article/eu-juncker-greece-idUSPA B00809520100114.

14. Ralph Atkins, "Tough Words and Hard Budgets for Euro Area," *Financial Times*, December 9, 2009. Last accessed January 4, 2016, from www.ft.com/intl /cms/s/0/0d5a6622-e4b4-11de-96a2-00144feab49a.html#axzz3GbmkmaX9.

15. Lesley Wroughton, Howard Schneider, and Dina Kyriakidou, "How the IMF's Greek Misadventure Is Changing the Fund," *Reuters*, August 28, 2015. Last accessed January 4, 2016, from http://www.reuters.com/investigates /special-report/imf-greece.

16. Charles Forelle, "Merkel Defends Role of IMF in Greek Deal," *Wall Street Journal*, March 27, 2010. Last accessed January 4, 2016, from http://online.wsj.com/articles/SB10001424052748704100604575145550516810926.

17. Ian Traynor, "Angela Merkel Agrees on Greece Rescue Package—But Wants New Euro Rules," *Guardian*, March 25, 2010. Last accessed January 4, 2016, from http://www.theguardian.com/business/2010/mar/25/angela -merkel-greece-package; Gerrit Wiesmann and Quentin Peel, "Berlin Shifts Stance on IMF Role in Greece," *Financial Times*, March 18, 2010. Last accessed January 4, 2016, from http://www.ft.com/intl/cms/s/0/3943e114-327f-11df -bf20-00144feabdc0.html#axzz3GbmkmaX9.

18. Forelle, "Merkel Defends Role of IMF."

19. "Une vidéo de Dominique Strauss-Kahn sur l'aide du FMI agace la Grèce," *20 Minutes*, May 4, 2011. Last accessed January 4, 2016, from http://www.20minutes.fr/economie/717974-20110504-economie-une-video-domi nique-strauss-kahn-aide-fmi-agace-grece.

20. Dominique Strauss-Kahn, "The Global Jobs Crisis—Sustaining the Recovery through Employment and Equitable Growth," text of speech given at the Brookings Institution, Washington DC, April 13, 2011. Last accessed January 4, 2016, from https://www.imf.org/external/np/speeches/2011/041311 .htm.

21. "IMF Document Excerpts: Disagreements Revealed," *Wall Street Journal*, October 7, 2013. Last accessed January 4, 2016, from http://blogs.wsj.com /economics/2013/10/07/imf-document-excerpts-disagreements-revealed.

22. Wroughton, Schneider, and Kyriakidou, "IMF's Greek Misadventure."

23. The staff proposed getting rid of the systemic exception in June 2014.

24. IMF, Greece: Ex Post Evaluation of Exceptional Access Under the 2010 Stand-By Arrangement, IMF Country Report 13/156, June 2013.

25. Paul Blustein, "Laid Low: The IMF, the Euro Area and First Rescue of Greece," CIGI Paper No. 61, April 2015, 7.

26. In her speech in Jackson Hole in August 2011, the new managing director, Christine Lagarde, called for "mandatory substantial recapitalization—seeking private resources first, but using public funds if necessary." Christine Lagarde, "'Global Risks Are Rising, but There Is a Path to Recovery': Remarks at Jackson Hole," text of speech at Jackson Hole, August 27, 2011. Last accessed January 4, 2016, from https://www.imf.org/external/np/speeches/2011/082711.htm.

27. Blustein, "Laid Low," 16.

28. International Monetary Fund, "Euro Area Policies: 2011 Article IV Consultation—Staff Report; Public Information Notice on the Executive Board Discussion; and Statement by the Executive Director for Member Countries," IMF Country Report No. 11/184, July 2011. Last accessed January 4, 2016, from http://www.imf.org/external/pubs/ft/scr/2011/cr11184.pdf.

29. Simon Carswell, "Scheme Designed to Protect Banks First and Then Ordinary Depositors," *Irish Times*, October 2, 2008, http://www.irishtimes.com/news/scheme-designed-to-protect-banks-first-and-then-ordinary-depositors-1.890174 .

30. Paul Williams, "Anglo Tapes: Give Me the Moolah, Warned Drumm," *Independent*, June 27 2013. Last accessed January 4, 2016, from www.independent.ie/business/irish/anglo/anglo-tapes-give-me-the-moolah-warned-drumm-29376066.html.

31. Jamie Smyth, "IMF Boosts Irish Debt Relief Case," *Financial Times*, September 10, 2012. Last accessed January 4, 2016, from http://www.ft.com/intl/cms/s/0/b08e0720-fb60-11e1-b5d0-00144feabdc0.html#axzz3GbmkmaX9.

32. Graeme Wearden and Phillip Inman, "Greece Faces New Debt Crisis Amid Fears of Default," *Guardian*, April 14, 2011. Last accessed January 4, 2016, from http://www.theguardian.com/business/2011/apr/14/greece-debt-crisis-euro area-george-papaconstantinou.

33. James Neuger, "Strauss-Kahn Saga Exposes Flaws in Euro Debt-Crisis Management," *Bloomberg*, July 10, 2011. Last accessed January 4, 2016, from http://www.bloomberg.com/news/2011-07-10/strauss-kahn-saga-exposes-flaws-in-europe-s-greek-debt-crisis-management.html.

34. See, for example, George Georgiopoulos and Ingrid Melander, "Greece Default Hangs in Balance," *Financial Post*, September 19, 2011. http://business.financialpost.com/news/economy/greece-told-shrink-state-to-avoid-default-2.

35. Wroughton, Schneider, and Kyriakidou, "IMF's Greek Misadventure."

36. Larry Elliott, Phillip Inman, and Helena Smith, "IMF Admits: We Failed to Realise the Damage Austerity Would Do to Greece," *Guardian*, June 5, 2013. Last accessed January 4, 2016, from http://www.theguardian.com/business/2013/jun/05/imf-underestimated-damage-austerity-would-do-to-greece; International Monetary Fund, "Greece: Ex Post Evaluation of Exceptional Access under the 2010 Stand-by Arrangement," IMF Country Report No. 13/156, July 2013. Last accessed January 4, 2016, from http://www.imf.org/external/pubs/ft/scr/2013/cr13156.pdf.

37. Paul Taylor, "Analysis: Euro Bailout Troika Nears End of Road with Patchy Record," *Reuters*, June 10, 2013. Last accessed January 4, 2016, from http://www.reuters.com/article/2013/06/10/us-euro area-troika-idU.S.BRE 95904420130610.

38. "Update 1—Bundesbank: C'bank Reserves Will Not Help Fund EFSF," *Reuters Africa*, November 5, 2011. Last accessed January 4, 2016, from http://af.reuters.com/article/metalsNews/idAFL6E7M50PH20111105.

39. Peter Spiegel, "How the Euro Was Saved," *Financial Times*, May 11, 2014. Last accessed January 4, 2016, from http://www.ft.com/intl/cms/s/0/f6f4d6b4-ca2e-11e3-ac05-00144feabdc0.html#axzz3mI04JHK8.

40. Olivier Blanchard and Daniel Leigh, "Growth Forecast Errors and Fiscal Multipliers," IMF Working Paper 13/1, January 2013; Ashoka Mody, "In Bad Faith," *Bruegel*, July 3, 2015. Last accessed January 10, 2015, from http://bruegel.org/2015/07/in-bad-faith.

41. Paul Taylor, "Exclusive: Europeans Tried to Block IMF Debt Report on Greece: Sources," *Reuters*, July 3, 2015. Last accessed January 4, 2016, from http://uk.reuters.com/article/2015/07/03/us-euro area-greece-imf-idukKCN 0PD20120150703; Mody, "In Bad Faith."

42. John B. Taylor, "The Lesson Greece's Lenders Forgot," *Wall Street Journal*, July 9, 2015. http://www.wsj.com/articles/the-lesson-greeces-lenders -forgot-1436482117.

43. IMF Press Release 16/31, January 29, 2016. Last accessed January 31, 2016, from http://www.imf.org/external/np/sec/pr/2016/pr1631.htm.

44. Ibid.

45. Ibid.

46. Liz Alderman, "After WikiLeaks Revelation, Greece Asks I.M.F. to Clarify Bailout Plan," *New York Times*, April 3, 2016, 4.

CHAPTER 15

1. European Central Bank, "Verbatim of the Remarks Made by Mario Draghi," speech at the Global Investment Conference in London, July 26, 2012. Last accessed January 4, 2016, from http://www.ecb.int/press/key/date /2012/html/sp120726.en.html.

2. Quoted in Robert L. Hetzel, *The Great Recession: Market Failure or Policy Failure?* (New York: Cambridge University Press, 2012), 282.

3. When Lithuania joined the Euro on January 1, 2015, a new system of rotating voting rights in the ECB governing council came into force. As a consequence of the rotation principle, there were inevitably decisions on which national central banks (including the Bundesbank) could not vote.

4. European Central Bank, "The Stability-oriented Monetary Policy Strategy of the Eurosystem," *ECB Monthly Bulletin*, January 1999.

5. Otmar Issing, ed., *Background Studies for the ECB's Evaluation of Its Monetary Policy Strategy* (Frankfurt am Main: European Central Bank, 2003); Otmar Issing, *The Birth of the Euro*, translated by Nigel Hulbert (New York: Cambridge University Press, 2008).

6. European Central Bank, *The Monetary Policy of the ECB*, 2nd edition (Frankfurt am Main: European Central Bank, 2004). Last accessed January 4, 2016, from https://www.ecb.europa.eu/pub/pdf/other/monetarypolicy2004 en.pdf.

7. Jürgen Stark, "The Role of Money," in *The Role of Money—Money and Monetary Policy in the Twenty-first Century*, edited by Andreas Beyer and Lucrezia Reichlin (Frankfurt am Main: European Central Bank, 2008).

8. See Jean-Claude Trichet, "Central Banking in Uncertain Times: Conviction and Responsibility," Jackson Hole speech, August 27, 2010, available at https://www.ecb.europa.eu/press/key/date/2010/html/sp100827.en.html.

9. See for instance Jörg Eigendorf, "Eklatante Schwächen der EZB bei der Geldschöpfung," *Welt*, January 6, 2013. Last accessed January 4, 2016, from http://www.welt.de/wirtschaft/article112434760/Eklatante-Schwaechen -der-EZB-bei-der-Geldschoepfung.html; and M. Brendel and Sebastien Jost, "Die europäische Notenpresse gerät außer Kontrolle," *Welt*, January 6, 2013. Last accessed January 4, 2016, from http://www.welt.de/finanzen/article11 2420942/Die-europaeische-Notenpresse-geraet-ausser-Kontrolle.html.

10. Hans-Werner Sinn, "Neue Abgründe," *Wirtschaftswoche*, No. 8, February 21, 2011, 35; Hans-Werner Sinn, "Tickende Zeitbombe," *Süddeutsche Zeitung*, No. 77, April 2, 2011, 24.

11. See Hans-Werner Sinn and Timo Wollmershäuser, "Target Loans, Current Account Balances and Capital Flows: The ECB's Rescue Facility," NBER Working Papers 17626, 2011. For a contrasting view, see Ulrich Bindseil, Philippine Cour-Thimann, and Philipp König, "Target 2 and Cross-border Interbank Payments during the Financial Crisis," *CESifo Forum*, vol. 13, 83–92.

12. This point has been made by Frank Westermann of the University of Osnabrück.

13. Jean-Claude Trichet, "Recovery, Reform and Renewal: Europe's Economic Challenge," speech at conference, "The ECB and Its Watchers" XII, Frankfurt am Main, July 9, 2010. Last accessed January 4, 2016, from http:// www.ecb.int/press/key/date/2010/html/sp100709.en.html.

14. Sewell Chan and Liz Alderman, "I.M.F. Help for Greece Is a Risky Prospect," *New York Times*, March 5, 2010. http://www.nytimes.com/2010/03/05 /business/global/05imf.htm.

15. "IMF Finance Role Embarrassing for ECB," *Financial Times*, March 26, 2010. https://next.ft.com/content/bab67356-3905-11df-8970-00144feabdc0.

16. Bastasin, *Saving Europe*, 225–26.

17. European Council, "Statement by the Heads of State or Government of the Euro Area and EU Institutions," Brussels, July 21, 2011. Last accessed January 4, 2016, from europa.eu/rapid/press-release_DOC-11-5_en.doc.

18. For more details see Jeromin Zettelmeyer, Christoph Trebesch, and Mitu Gulati, "The Greek Debt Restructuring: An Autopsy," *Economic Policy*, July 2013, 515–563.

19. Walter Bagehot, *Lombard Street: A Description of the Money Market* [1873], reprint New York: John Wiley, 1999, 52.

20. Ulrich Bindseil, "Theory of Monetary Policy Implementation," in *The Concrete Euro: Implementing Monetary Policy in the Euro Area*, edited by Paul

Mercier and Francesco Papadia (Oxford, UK: Oxford University Press, 2011), 5–114.

21. See Willem H. Buiter and Ebrahim Rahbari, "The ECB as Lender of Last Resort for Sovereigns in the Euro Area," CEPR Discussion Paper No. 8974, May 2012. Last accessed January 4, 2016, from http://willembuiter.com/lolr.pdf.

22. See for instance "Press Review Tuesday 12 July 2011," RNW Archive. Last accessed January 4, 2016, from https://www.rnw.org/archive/press -review-tuesday-12-july-2011.

23. Jan Schäfer, "Wer passt jetzt auf unseren EURO auf?" Bild, February 11, 2011. Last accessed January 4, 2016, from http://www.bild.de/politik /wirtschaft/banken-krise/wer-passt-jetzt-auf-euro-auf-15924766.bild.html.

24. John Hooper, "Berlusconi's Partners Grow Restive over ECB Prescription for Italy," Guardian, August 11, 2011. http://www.theguardian.com/business /2011/aug/11/berlusconis-partners-grow-restive-over-ecbs-prescription -for-italy.

25. Patrick Honohan, "Resolving Ireland's Banking Crisis," Economic and Social Review 40 (2009): 207–31.

26. Jörg Asmussen, "The Irish Case from an ECB Perspective," speech at the Institute of International and European Affairs, Dublin, April 12, 2012. Last accessed January 4, 2016, from http://www.ecb.europa.eu/press/key /date/2012/html/sp120412.en.html.

27. European Central Bank, "Irish Letters," November 6, 2014. Last accessed January 4, 2016, from http://www.ecb.europa.eu/press/html /irish-letters.en.html.

28. "'Very Difficult' Obstacles to Talks on Euro Debt Crisis," Irish Times, September 16, 2010. Last accessed January 4, 2016, from http://www.irishtimes .com/news/very-difficult-obstacles-to-talks-on-euro-debt-crisis-1.651363.

29. RTE Radio One interview with Patrick Honohan, November 18, 2010, reported in http://www.theguardian.com/business/ireland-business-blog -with-lisa-ocarroll/2010/nov/18/ireland-central-bank-governor-transcript.

30. Jean-Claude Trichet letter to Brian Lenihan, November 19, 2010. Last accessed January 4, 2016, from http://www.ecb.europa.eu/press/shared /pdf/2010-11-19_Letter_ECB_President_to%20IE_FinMin.pdf?83824135ba733 b6091e930d3a25314c9.

31. "Schäuble: Zypern ist selbst schuld," Welt, March 23, 2013. Last accessed January 4, 2016, from http://www.welt.de/print/wams/article114716938 /Schaeuble-Zypern-ist-selbst-schuld.html.

32. European Central Bank, "Governing Council Decision on Emergency Liquidity Assistance Requested by the Central Bank of Cyprus," Press Release, March 21, 2013. Last accessed January 4, 2016, from https://www.ecb.europa .eu/press/pr/date/2013/html/pr130321.en.html.

33. European Central Bank, "Decisions Taken by the Governing Council of the ECB (in Addition to Decisions Setting Interest Rates)," External Communication, February 2015. Last accessed January 4, 2016, from https://www .ecb.europa.eu/press/govcdec/otherdec/2015/html/gc150220.en.html.

34. Martin Hellwig, "Die EZB und die Deutschen in der Griechenlandkrise," Öekonomenstimme, July 7, 2015. Last accessed January 4, 2016, from

http://www.oekonomenstimme.org/artikel/2015/07/die-ezb-und-die
-deutschen-in-der-griechenlandkrise.

35. Martin Hellwig, "Zur Diskussion um die Notkredite der griechischen Zentralbank für griechische Banken," *Öekonomenstimme*, July 11, 2015. Last accessed January 4, 2016, from http://www.oekonomenstimme.org /artikel/2015/07/zur-diskussion-um-die-notkredite-der-griechischen -zentralbank-fuer-griechische-banken; Paul Krugman called the ECB "Germany's debt collector." Paul Krugman, "A Game of Chicken," *New York Times*, February 6, 2015. Last accessed January 4, 2016, from http://www.nytimes .com/2015/02/06/opinion/a-game-of-chicken.html?_r=0.

36. Purchasing government securities has never been considered as unconventional for the U.S. Federal Reserve Bank, the Bank of England, and the Bank of Japan, for whom this is the standard way of conducting monetary policy.

37. European Central Bank, "Decision of the European Central Bank of 14 May 2010 Establishing a Securities Markets Programme," ECB/2010/5. Last accessed January 4, 2016, from https://www.ecb.europa.eu/ecb/legal/pdf /en_dec_2010_5__f_sign.pdf?586b8d9fc867110a94788fe073d2b3a7.

38. Nicholas Comfort, "Draghi Raids Bankers in Rush to Hire 1,000 for Supervisor," *Bloomberg Business*, January 9, 2014. Last accessed January 4, 2016, from http://www.bloomberg.com/news/articles/2014-01-08/draghi-raids -bankers-in-rush-to-hire-1-000-for-supervisor.

39. Simone Meier and Christian Vits, "Weber Says ECB Bond Purchases Pose Significant Risks," *Bloomberg*, May 10, 2010. http://www.bloomberg .com/apps/news?pid=newsarchive&sid=a83PaKeT_tF0&pos=4. The interview originally appeared in the German newspaper *Börsenzeitung*.

40. "Irish Borrowing Costs 'Ridiculous,'" *Irish Times*, August 10, 2010. Last accessed January 16, 2016, from http://www.irishtimes.com/news/irish -borrowing-costs-ridiculous-1.862493.

41. *Spiegel* Interview, February 14, 2011. Last accessed January 4, 2016, from http://www.spiegel.de/international/germany/spiegel-interview-with -axel-weber-it-is-not-important-which-nation-puts-forward-the-ecb-president -a-745350.html.

42. Quoted in Johan Van Overtveldt, *The End of the Euro: The Uneasy Future of the European Union* (Chicago: B2 Books, 2011), 101.

43. Statement by the President of the ECB, August 7, 2011. Last accessed January 15, 2016, from https://www.ecb.europa.eu/press/pr/date/2011 /html/pr110807.en.html.

44. Paul De Grauwe, "The European Central Bank as a Lender of Last Resort," *VoxEU*, August 18, 2011. Last accessed January 16, 2016, from http:// www.voxeu.org/article/european-central-bank-lender-last-resort.

45. See Tom Fairless, "Bundesbank Maintains Opposition to ECB Bond Buying," *Wall Street Journal*, July 27, 2012. Last accessed January 16, 2016, from http://www.wsj.com/articles/SB1000087239639044334370457755242365 54 64012.

46. Brian Blackstone and Marcus Walker, "How ECB Chief Outflanked German Foe in Fight for Euro," *Wall Street Journal*, October 2, 2012. Last

accessed January 4, 2016, from http://www.wsj.com/articles/SB10000872396 39044350720457802023544183926.

47. Deutsche Bundesbank, Monthly Report 64/8, August 2012, 7.

48. Quentin Peel, "Merkel Reaffirms Backing for Draghi Plan," *Financial Times*, September 17, 2012. Last accessed January 4, 2016, from http://www.ft.com/intl/cms/s/0/585598cc-00e0-11e2-99d3-00144feabdc0.html#axzz 3vBTXBpxK.

49. Stefan Riecher, "ECB's Asmussen Says Bundesbank Isn't Isolated, Rundschau Reports," *Bloomberg Business*, August 20, 2012. Last accessed January 4, 2016, from http://www.bloomberg.com/news/articles/2012-08-20 /ecb-s-asmussen-says-bundesbank-isn-t-isolated-rundschau-reports; "Bundesbank President on ECB Bond Purchases: 'Too Close to State Financing Via the Money Press,'" *Spiegel Online*, August 29, 2012. Last accessed January 4, 2016, from http://www.spiegel.de/international/europe/spiegel-interview-with -bundesbank-president-jens-weidmann-a-852285.html.

50. Ibid.

51. European Central Bank, "Technical Features of Outright Monetary Transactions," Press Release, September 6, 2012. Last accessed January 4, 2016, from http://www.ecb.int/press/pr/date/2012/html/pr120906_1.en.html.

52. Bundesverfassungsgerichtes, "Principal Proceedings ESM/ECB: Pronouncement of the Judgment and Referral for a Preliminary Ruling to the Court of Justice of the European Union," Bundesverfassungsgericht, February 7, 2014. Last accessed January 4, 2016, from https://www.bundesverfassungsgericht .de/SharedDocs/Pressemitteilungen/EN/2014/bvg14-009.html.

53. Claire Jones and Stefan Wagstyl, "Mario Draghi Vindicated as Court Backs ECB Bond-buying Plan," *Financial Times*, June 16, 2005. Last accessed January 4, 2016, from http://www.ft.com/intl/cms/s/0/c200c62e-1402 -11e5-9bc5-00144feabdc0.html#axzz3wyBMTO6E; "Reaktionen auf EuGH-Gutachten: 'Das kommt einem Freibrief für die EZB gleich,'" *Spiegel Online*, January 14, 2015. Last accessed January 4, 2016, from http://www.spiegel.de /wirtschaft/soziales/eugh-und-ezb-staatsanleihen-afd-und-oekonomen -empoert-ueber-gutachten-a-1012967.html; and "Ifo-Chef Sinn kritisiert EuGH,"- *FAZ*, June 16, 2015. http://www.faz.net/aktuell/wirtschaft/eurokrise /ifo-chef-sinn-kritisiert-eugh-urteil-zu-ezb-anleihenkaeufe-13649888.html.

54. Mario Draghi, "Unemployment in the Euro Area," speech at annual central bank symposium in Jackson Hole, August 22, 2014. Last accessed January 4, 2016, from https://www.ecb.europa.eu/press/key/date/2014/html /sp140822.en.html.

55. See Robin Harding, "US Quantitative Measures Worked in Defiance of Theory," October 13, 2014, retrieved from: https://next.ft.com/content /3b164d2e-4f03-11e4-9c88-00144feab7de.

56. See for instance Hyun Shin, "The Second Phase of Global Liquidity and Its Impact on Emerging Economies," remarks at 2013 Federal Reserve Bank of San Francisco Asia Economic Policy Conference, 2013. Last accessed January 4, 2016, from http://www.princeton.edu/~hsshin/www/FRBSF_2013 .pdf.

57. Open Market Committee Transcripts, Nov 2–3 2010, 179. Last accessed January 15, 2016, from http://www.federalreserve.gov/monetarypolicy /fomchistorical2010.htm.

58. Admittedly, a low oil price can damage global growth as it makes investment in energy savings and alternative sources of energy uneconomical. It destroys capital by making some technology (say wind farms) uneconomic.

59. Henning Klodt and Anna Hartmann, "Deflation und Konsumstau: Mikroökonomische Evidenz," Kiel Working Papers No. 1935, July 2014. Last accessed January 4, 2016, from https://www.ifw-members.ifw-kiel.de /publications/deflation-und-konsumstau-mikrookonomische-evidenz /KAP_1935_Deflation.pdf.

60. Michael D. Bordo, John Landon Lane, and Angela Redish, "Good versus Bad Deflation: Lessons from the Gold Standard Era," NBER Working Paper 10329, 2004; Claudio Borio, Magdalena Erdem, Andrew Filardo, and Boris Hofmann, "The Costs of Deflations: A Historical Perspective," *BIS Quarterly Review*, March 2015. Last accessed January 4, 2016, from http://www.bis .org/publ/qtrpdf/r_qt1503e.htm.

61. Barry Eichengreen, "Secular Stagnation: The Long View," *American Economic Review Papers and Proceedings* (May 2015), 66–70.

62. Holger Steltzner, "Euro-Geistesverwirrung," *FAZ*, March 23, 2016. http://www.faz.net/aktuell/wirtschaft/wirtschaftspolitik/kommentar-zum -helikoptergeld-euro-geistesverwirrung-14142378.html.

63. Comfort, "Draghi Raids Bankers."

64. Harold James, *Making the European Monetary Union* (Cambridge MA: Harvard University Press, 2012), 313.

65. Ibid., 292.

66. Ibid.

67. Ibid., 316.

68. See Markus Brunnermeier, "Optimizing the Currency Area," in *The Great Financial Crisis: Lessons for Financial Stability and Monetary Policy* (Frankfurt am Main: European Central Bank, 2010), 14–22.

69. Marvin Goodfriend, "The Elusive Promise of Independent Central Banking," *Monetary and Economic Studies* 30 (2012): 39–54.

70. Jean-Claude Trichet, "Building Europe, Building Institutions," speech on receiving the Karlspreis 2011 in Aachen, June 2, 2011; Mario Draghi, "A European Strategy for Growth and Integration with Solidarity," a conference organized by the Directorate General of the Treasury, Ministry of Economy and Finance—Ministry for Foreign Trade, Paris, November 30, 2012.

Chapter 16

1. Dani Rodrik, *Economics Rules: The Rights and Wrongs of the Dismal Science* (New York: Norton, 2015), 84.

2. *The Five Presidents' Report: Completing Europe's Economic and Monetary Union*, June 22, 2015. https://ec.europa.eu/priorities/publications/five-presidents -report-completing-europes-economic-and-monetary-union_en.

3. Ibid., 7.

4. IMF, World Economic Outlook, April 2015, Table A8, 182.

5. Samantha Early, "Merkel, Hollande Call for 'More Europe' in Dealing with Refugees," *Deutsche Welle*, October 7, 2015. Last accessed January 4, 2016, from http://www.dw.com/en/merkel-hollande-call-for-more-europe-in-dealing -with-refugees/a-18766659.

6. Jean Monnet (transl. Richard Mayne), *Memoirs* (London: Collins, 1978), 417.

7. William Shakespeare, *Hamlet*, Act IV, Scene 5, lines 78–79.

8. John Ikenberry analyzes these ordering moments. John Ikenberry, *After Victory: Institutions, Strategic Restraint, and the Rebuilding of Order after Major Wars* (Princeton, NJ: Princeton University Press, 2000).

9. Sendhil Mullainathan and Eldar Shafir, *Scarcity: Why Having Too Little Means So Much* (New York: Time Books, 2013).

Index